IN HIS FATHER'S SHADOW

To Bob & Jan

with the hope that
this election, you'll
both press the right lever.

Stanley Renshon

ALSO BY STANLEY A. RENSHON:

AMERICA'S SECOND CIVIL WAR:
Dispatches from the Political Center

THE CLINTON PRESIDENCY:
Campaigning, Governing, and the Psychology of Leadership

GOOD JUDGMENT IN FOREIGN POLICY:
Theory and Application (with Deborah Larson)

HANDBOOK OF POLITICAL SOCIALIZATION:
Theory and Research

HIGH HOPES: The Clinton Presidency and the Politics of Ambition
Winner of the American Political Science Association's Richard E. Neustadt
award for the best book on the presidency, and the National Association for
the Advancement of Psychoanalysis' Gradiva Award for the best biography.

ONE AMERICA?:
Political Leadership, National Identity, and the Dilemmas of Diversity

POLITICAL PSYCHOLOGY:
Cultural and Crosscultural Foundations (with John Duckitt)

THE POLITICAL PSYCHOLOGY OF THE GULF WAR:
Leaders, Publics, and the Process of Conflict

THE PSYCHOLOGICAL ASSESSMENT
OF PRESIDENTIAL CANDIDATES

PSYCHOLOGICAL NEEDS AND POLITICAL BEHAVIOR

FORTHCOMING BY STANLEY A. RENSHON

THE 50% AMERICAN: National Identity in an Age of Terrorism

IN HIS FATHER'S
SHADOW

The Transformations of George W. Bush

STANLEY A. RENSHON

palgrave
macmillan

IN HIS FATHER'S SHADOW
Copyright © Stanley A. Renshon, 2004.
All rights reserved. No part of this book may be used or reproduced in any manner
whatsoever without written permission except in the case of brief quotations
embodied in critical articles or reviews.

First published 2004 by PALGRAVE MACMILLAN™
175 Fifth Avenue, New York, N.Y. 10010 and
Houndmills, Basingstoke, Hampshire, England RG21 6XS.
Companies and representatives throughout the world.

PALGRAVE MACMILLAN is the global academic imprint of the Palgrave
Macmillan division of St. Martin's Press, LLC and of Palgrave Macmillan Ltd.
Macmillan® is a registered trademark in the United States, United Kingdom and
other countries. Palgrave is a registered trademark in the European Union and other
countries.

ISBN 1–4039–6546–3 hardback

Library of Congress Cataloging-in-Publication Data
Renshon, Stanley Allen.
In his father's shadow : the transformations of George W. Bush / Stanley A.
Renshon.
    p.   cm.
  Includes bibliographical references and index
  ISBN 1–4039–6546–3
  1. Bush, George W. (George Walker, 1946—Psychology.   2. Presidents—
United States—Biography.   2. Children of presidents—United States—
Biography.   4. United States—Politics and government—2001.-   5. United
States—Politics and government—2001—Psychological aspects.   6. Political
leadership—United States—Psychological aspects.   7. Political leadership—
United States—Case studies.   I. Title

E903.3R46   2004
973.931'092—dc22
                                                                          2004
                                                                          047802
                                                                          [B]

A catalogue record for this book is available from the British Library.

Design by Letra Libre, Inc.

First edition: September, 2004
10   9   8   7   6   5   4   3   2   1

Printed in the United States of America.

For my son David,
smart, thoughtful, and caring.
With great love and affection.

Despite the mounds of ink expended
on the current president of the United
States, he's still in many ways a mystery. . . .
Who, after all, is the real Bush? The
jokester or the statesman? The bumbler
or the war leader? The cipher or the captain?

Andrew Sullivan,
Sunday Times of London (March 17, 2002)

CONTENTS

ACKNOWLEDGEMENTS

THIS IS MY SECOND BOOK ABOUT AN AMBITIOUS and controversial president. Both works lie at the intersection of individual psychology, presidential leadership, and public psychology. Yet the origins of the two studies differ.

My main interest in the first study, on Bill Clinton, began with his psychology. I was impressed with how well he recovered from self-induced disaster, but puzzled about why he had to do it so often. With George W. Bush, I began with more of an interest in the other side of the equation, his political leadership. It is that aspect that I think is, in a number of ways, the most important dimension of his presidency.

Mr. Bush's psychology, while complex, seems less mysterious than Bill Clinton's and certainly less at war with itself. This is not to say that George W.'s psychology is unimportant. On the contrary, it is critical to what he wishes to accomplish and his chances of doing so; for that reason, what Mr. Bush's psychology is, how it developed, and what role it plays in his leadership is at the center of my analysis.

This book, like the others before, owes much to the people who have helped bring it about. My work on the George W. Bush presidency began in 1999 as the 2000 presidential campaign was moving into high gear. My work on presidential leadership in the context of the 2000 election was aided by a fellowship from the Joan Shorenstein Center on the Press and Public Policy, The Kennedy School, Harvard University. I would like to thank the center's director, Thomas Patterson, for that opportunity. My work on presidential leadership both before and after 9/11 was facilitated by two grants from the City University Faculty Research Award Program. I would like to thank the anonymous external reviewers for their comments.

Finally, my work on the George W. Bush presidency was greatly assisted by an appointment as a Visiting Scholar at Harvard University's Center for Public Leadership during the 2003–2004 academic year. I would like to thank David Gergen, Barbara Kellerman, and Scott Webster for facilitating my stay and my work.

My research assistant, Rebecca Blanton, has been a tremendous help throughout this project, as has always been the case in our work together. Whether the task was tracking down papers, citations, or people, she did her job, as always, very competently.

My literary representative, Andrew Blauner, has been a strong advocate and supporter for many years now. He is also a supportive, intelligent, and thoughtful friend. Every author should be so lucky.

I would like to thank my editor at Palgrave Macmillan, David Pervin, for his many helpful suggestions and good questions. Thanks are also much due to the fine copyediting of the manuscript by Bruce Murphy. Alan Bradshaw skillfully guided this book through the production process.

John Fiscilini, my long-time friend and a senior analyst at the William Alanson White Institute, read the chapter on G. W. Bush's early development, and was always willing to listen and respond to my thoughts as I worked on my analysis. Richard Haass and Alexander L. George read earlier drafts of my work on judgment in the Bush administration and made many helpful comments.

No appreciation would be complete without acknowledging my family, who mean so much to me and whose presence and love allow me the freedom to undertake my work. My wife, Judith, has been a warm, smart, supportive, and loving partner for 27 years. I am a fortunate man indeed. My children, David and Jonathan, have been a continuing source of pleasure and pride over many years. For that I am truly blessed. I love them all.

This book is dedicated to my son David, whose mind and character are a father's pleasure. I have learned a great deal from him and very much appreciate the continuing opportunity to do so.

Stanley A. Renshon
New York City

GEORGE W. BUSH
CHRONOLOGY*

July 6, 1946—George W. Bush born, New Haven, Connecticut.

1948—Family moves to Midland, Texas. Father, George H. W. Bush, begins
work with International Derrick and Equipment Company, a Dresser
Oil subsidiary in Odessa, Texas, as a salesman.

1949—Bush family relocates to California as George H. W. Bush pursues sales
career with Dresser Oil.

1949—Sister, Robin, born.

1950—Bush family moves back to Texas (Midland-Odessa).

February 11, 1953—brother, John Ellis (Jeb) Bush, born.

Mid-February 1953—George W.'s sister, Robin, shows first signs of illness.

February 1953—George H. W. Bush founds Zapata Oil, with Hugh Liedtke, and
begins drilling for oil. Within a year they have drilled 71 wells and
struck oil on all of them.

March–October 1953. George and Barbara Bush are frequently in New York
City while their daughter Robin receives cancer treatments.

October 11, 1953—Robin dies.

1954—George H. W. Bush founds Zapata Off-Shore, an oil company worth $4.5
million.

January 22, 1955—Brother Neil Mallon Bush born.

October 22, 1956–Brother Marvin Pierce Bush born.

August 18, 1959—Sister Dorthy Walker Bush born.

September 1959–June 1961—George W. attends Kinkaid Preparatory School.
He is known for being popular and intense.

September 1961–June 1964—George W. attends Andover, which his father had
also attended. He is known for being prominent for no ostensible reason. He plays JV basketball and baseball and becomes head cheerleader and "high commissioner" of the intra-mural stickball league.

1964–1968—George W. attends Yale University. He becomes a member, then president, of Delta Kappa Epsilon (DEKE). He is initiated into Skull & Bones, a prestigious secret society, which his father had also joined.

November, 1964—George W. meets Yale Chaplain William Sloan Coffin, who tells George W. that his father lost the Senate race to "a better man."

January 19, 1968—George W. completes Air Force Qualifications tests.

May 27, 1968—George W.'s National Guard application approved. He is accepted for pilot training.

July 1969–1973—George W. on active duty in the Reserves.

September 18, 1973—George W. placed on inactive duty in the Reserve for six months to attend Harvard Business School.

1973–1975—George W. attends Harvard Business School.

Spring break, 1975—George W. visits Midland, Texas on his way to Arizona and decides it is the land of entrepreneurial opportunity.

Fall 1975—George W. moves to Midland, Texas to make his mark in the oil business, as had his father. He starts out as a "land man," searching court records for mineral rights and trying to put deals together.

Fall 1976—George W. founds Bush Oil, with a one-room office above a bank.

August, 1977—George W. meets Laura Welch at a mutual friend's backyard cookout.

November 5, 1977—George W. marries Laura Welch at age 31.

May 6, 1978—George W. wins the GOP nomination for Congress in the West Texas district.

November 7, 1978—George W. loses congressional race to Kent Hance.

November, 1978—George W. forms his own oil company named, prophetically, Arbusto.

November 25, 1981—Bush children, Barbara and Jenna, born.

December 1981—George W. acquires "working interests" on property owned by Pennzoil and lands big investor, Phillip Uzielli.

1983—Bush's oil company ranks 993rd, near the bottom, in terms of oil production in Texas.

February 29, 1984—Arbusto merges with the more successful Spectrum 7. Bush is paid $75,000 a year and given 1.1 million shares.

December, 1985–April 1986—World oil prices collapse. Spectrum 7 faces bankruptcy.

Summer 1985—George W. has long talk with the Reverend Billy Graham and begins studying the Bible.

May 1986—George W. begins negotiations to sell Spectrum 7 to Harken Oil.

July 1986—The Bushes and several friends travel to the Broadmoor Hotel to celebrate turning 40. George W. wakes up with a hangover, goes for a run, but can't shake it as he had in the past. He decides to quit drinking, cold turkey, and does.

September 30, 1986—Harkin deal to acquire Spectrum 7 signed. Harken offers one share of Harkin for every five shares of Spectrum 7. Bush's stock is worth $530,000.

Spring–Fall, 1988—George W. serves as senior advisor to his father's successful presidential campaign.

October 1988—Texas Rangers Baseball team put up for sale. George W. is asked if he is interested in trying to help put together a group to buy it.

December 1988—George W. moves back to Dallas, Texas from Washington.

March 17, 1989—George W. announces that the deal to buy the Texas Rangers has been completed. Bush is named "managing" general partner.

April 28, 1989—Barbara Bush publicly throws cold water on her son's possible interest in running for governor in 1990.

1994—George W. runs for the Texas governorship and defeats incumbent Ann Richards.

1998—George W. runs for reelection as Texas governor—wins in landslide.

2000—George W. wins GOP nomination for president of the United States.

2000—George W. wins office of the presidency, November 2000.

2004—George W. runs for reelection to the office of the presidency.

---

* See also page 246, note 86.

UNDERSTANDING THE GEORGE W. BUSH PRESIDENCY

AT A TALK I GAVE ON THE GEORGE W. BUSH PRESIDENCY, one of the audience members asked me if I thought George W. was an "as-if personality." She was referring to a term first developed by the psychoanalyst Helen Deutsch in the early 1930s to describe characters who present outward façades of normality that mask deep interior psychological disturbance. No, I answered. George W. seemed to me to be an "as-is" personality—what you saw was, in large part, what there was.

Explaining George W. Bush, the man and the president, is at once a difficult and an easy thing to do. He is in many ways a paradoxical president—a fact reflected as well in his psychology. It is true that "what you see is what you get." Yet it is also true that there is more to George W. Bush than meets the eye and that includes his psychology. What that psychology is, how it developed, and the role it plays in his surprising, historic, ambitious, and controversial presidency is the focus of this work.

Mr. Bush is a president who invites caricature. His critics see him as cipher, if not a dunce, a puppet rather than an actor. Yet, more than a moment's attention to his actual behavior shows him to be the rarest of politicians, one who actually acts on the principles that he expresses. In a profession in which pandering, opportunism, and masked agendas are the rule, George W. Bush has proved to be an exception.

George W. Bush's presidency is, in many ways, an unlikely and unexpected one. He had, after all, not devoted his life, as others had, to gaining the presidency. Nor had he shown much early promise in politics—or in adult life more generally for that matter.

Bush obviously comes from a family of wealth and achievement, not a log cabin or a small town called Hope. Yet, his advantages were a double-edged sword. Indeed, they are more accurately seen as a sword of Damocles ever-hanging over his head in the form of expectations he could never evade, or for most of his life, fulfill.

He grew up in the shadow of a family that treasured and expected success and a father who epitomized it. His achievements, though, for much of his life were limited, and his setbacks many. Rather than being the golden boy to whom things came easily, Bush sputtered, and his efforts to build a successful adulthood stalled. He appeared to relinquish to his younger brother Jeb his rightful place as first-born son to follow in his father's footsteps. In his father's shadow, George W. paled by comparison.

To some, the narrative of Bush's development is that of a spoiled child of a rich family, propped up by connections, with no legitimate claim to the money he made or the offices he held. His many failures, in this view, are proof of a lack of character, purpose, and skill. Yet this view raises difficult questions for its adherents. If he is so spoiled and self-centered, how has he managed to develop and maintain a close and loyal group of friends from every period of his life? If his youth and early adulthood were marked by half-hearted efforts and failures from which others bailed him out, what explains the drive and successes he has achieved since?

In fact, it is paradoxical yet true that Bush is, at his core, a self-made man. Bush's development is obviously no rags-to-riches story. Yet, it is an archetypical American story of failure and redemption, of second and even third chances, and of the eventual triumph of character over circumstances. Bush is a man who has overcome the burden of his advantages to recreate himself by drawing on inner strengths and capabilities that few saw in him and many still don't.

Understanding who Bush is, as a man and a president, requires an exploration of his development. This is not to suggest that an intensive investigation of his childhood, adolescence, and adulthood provide answers to every question about Bush, or anyone else for that matter.[1] But there is truth in the saying that the child is the father of the man. Bush's upbringing—the influence of his parents, key events, and what he did with it all—help explain who he is.

Freud believed we are formed, for better or worse, in childhood. We now know that is only part of the story. Psychological development continues into adulthood. George W. Bush, however, remained a work in process longer than many. Indeed, while Bush began his presidency farther along the path of adult maturity than many had thought possible, it wasn't until the transforming events of 9/11 that he truly escaped the dilemmas of his family psychology and found his life's purpose in a national trauma.

Understanding the George W. Bush Presidency / 3

In his early forties Bush faced, and overcame, a transforming personal crisis. It was not an ordinary "mid-life crisis." Those are stimulated by questions about whether what you thought you wanted and have are really proving satisfying. Bush's problem was more profound. He had not accomplished much in spite of his efforts. It wasn't a question of whether he should keep what he had built, but what to do with the fact that he hadn't built much.

How Bush overcame this crisis is crucial to understanding the man and his presidency. For Bush the personal became political, in the sense that the confidence that he gained from his own transformation underlies his conviction that 9/11 was a test for America, and to overcome it, to deal with a new world of immense danger, necessitated a transformation of America's domestic scene and interaction with the world.

It was more than that. Mr. Bush had personally experienced the power and the capacity of self-transformation. He had a successful model for achieving it: focus, will power, perseverance, and resilience. What he did for himself would become his model for dealing with his country and the world.

THE FOUR TRANSFORMATIONS
OF GEORGE W. BUSH

By circumstance and ambition, George W. Bush is poised to become either one of America's historic figures or an abject lesson of the dangers in trying to transform foreign and domestic policies in a divided electorate. How the Bush presidency came to occupy its precarious historical and political pinnacle is best understood through the framework of four transformations: of George W. from a young man trying (not always successfully) to find his place to a president who found his purpose; from a president whose administration was struggling in the year after he was elected to one that was profoundly transformed as a result of the terrorist attack on 9/11; from a president with policy views but no overarching vision to a president trying to transform American political culture; and finally, from a president with little knowledge of the world to a president trying to transform it.

The first transformation of George W. was from a relatively immature and somewhat privileged adolescent and young adult to a maturing man whose sense of purpose and political skills have been picking up speed in a steep trajectory. Mr. Bush is, in some psychological and political respects, a "work in progress." He did not come to the presidency after a long and distinguished career, as did Dwight Eisenhower. He was not a man who gained the presidency after a steady and ambitious rise through the ranks of early ambition as had Woodrow Wilson. Nor had he arrived in the presidency young, politically gifted, and ambitious, but with the basic parts of his psychology stuck in adolescence, as had Bill Clinton.

George W. Bush arrived at his ambitions later in life, and his successes even later. As a result, by the time he became president some elements of his psychology were consolidated, while others were in the process of becoming so. Mr. Bush is not a president like Bill Clinton whose personal appetites were at war with the public ambitions he professed or the skills with which he pursued them. Mr. Bush is a president in whom remnants of an immature adolescent psychology were on obvious display as he sought the office he now holds.

The presidency has become a personal testing ground of Mr. Bush's psychology. He is an impatient man who has, nonetheless, had to learn patience. He is a man who doesn't avoid conflict, but who has had to learn to hold his tongue— sometimes in the face of extreme provocation. He is a man with strong views, but has had to learn to encourage dissent. Sometimes the strain shows.

The second transformation is from a president struggling to find his footing and in some ways losing ground during his first year in office, to a president whose public purposes were profoundly reframed in the space of a few moments one September morning. Those moments changed the public's view of the Bush presidency, the president's view of his presidency, and crucially, the president himself. George W. Bush's character reached its developmental destination in the aftermath of 9/11.

His adept handling of the crisis surprised many people. Their image of the inexperienced, sheltered, unseasoned, and even rash Bush was inconsistent with how he handled the crisis and its aftermath. If nothing prepares a president for how to react to such a crisis, then Bush, according to this image of him, was more ill prepared than anyone would want. And yet he understood what was expected of him, as a man and as the president, and rose to the occasion. He could only do so in large part because he had successfully navigated the tests of an early personal crisis. Not surprisingly, the same character traits helped him in both circumstances.

Having found his place and his purpose, George W. was ready to turn to the major tasks of his presidency: to transform the political center of gravity of American domestic and foreign policy. This effort had gotten off to a mixed start when the terrorist attack of September 11 profoundly altered the domestic and international landscape. The 9/11 attack profoundly changed the calculus of international politics and Mr. Bush's view of it. As a result, Mr. Bush has turned his efforts toward transforming American's place in the world and the world in which America has its place.

September 11 not only changed Mr. Bush, it also profoundly changed the presidency. We used to talk of two presidencies, one domestic and the other focused on foreign affairs.[2] After 9/11 many of the distinctions between them collapsed. Homeland security and American national security policy became opposite sides of the same coin. Foreign policy is no longer just "over there." It is here. Traditionally domestic policies like immigration must now also be viewed through the lens of national security.

In both domestic and international politics, Mr. Bush's ambition is not only to alter policies, but paradigms. He wants to change how Americans think about and act on domestic and international problems. Domestically, Mr. Bush aspires to re-place a dominant but fading way of viewing public policy, interest-group liberal-ism, with a new, moderately conservative approach to solving public problems. In so doing, he seeks the largest change of all, of American political culture itself.

Internationally, Mr. Bush wants to reshape the prevailing emphasis on mul-tilateral commitments as the primary prism though which American policy is evaluated and replace it with a more direct consideration of American security interests shaped within traditional values and ideals. Given America's unprece-dented power and reach, this profound shift of perspective has enormous impli-cations for questions of war and peace and the myriad policies related to them.

The attempt to simultaneously transform American political culture and the world in which it operates are enormously ambitious goals for any president, es-pecially one who came into office under such controversial circumstances. Their full realization is unlikely, and perhaps impossible to accomplish. Nonetheless, they represent the aims that Mr. Bush has set for himself, his presidency, and the country.

Mr. Bush is undertaking these ambitious goals in a country that is *politically* divided, but not (as commonly asserted) polarized. That difference is fundamen-tal to Mr. Bush's prospects for accomplishing any transformation. Divisions sim-ply reflect the fact that people have different views on a policy matter. Being divided, even evenly divided, is not the same as being polarized, although pun-dits often use the terms as if they were equivalent. They are not. Polarization means people not only have different views, but that these views are diametri-cally opposed and strongly held.

Americans are uncertain about what kind of leadership they want. Ameri-cans used to crave heroic leaders, those who stood out for their vision and the force of their determination to bend history to their will. Now they also want leaders who connect in direct emotional ways with them, taking in their pain and reflecting back to them personal reassurance. Can Mr. Bush be both heroic and down to earth at the same time?

If he succeeds, even in part, George W. will have not only transformed a country and its culture, politics, foreign policy, and the world in which they op-erate. He will have also transformed himself once again—from an electoral cu-riosity, a president who gained office with the intervention of the Supreme Court while losing the popular vote, to a truly historical figure of the first rank.

A FRAMEWORK FOR ANALYSIS

CHAPTER 1

A HISTORIC AND CONTROVERSIAL PRESIDENT

THE ENGLISH HISTORIAN THOMAS CARLYLE wrote that "all of history is the biography of great men." In this he was surely mistaken. All leaders, even great ones, govern in a set of circumstances that precedes them. What's more, they must deal with circumstances as they develop, rather than as they wish them to be.

Biography and psychology are important because they reflect the experiences, motivations, and skills that a leader brings with them as they navigate an uncertain environment they cannot completely control. Personal psychology cannot dictate historical circumstances, but it can alter them. Moreover, the same circumstances may elicit different responses depending on the psychology of the leader. George W. Bush's response to 9/11, "This is war," was neither obvious nor necessary. Different people will react differently to the same event or situation. These different reactions have important implications for the president and the public he leads.

KEY ELEMENTS OF THE BUSH PRESIDENCY

The analysis of every presidency remains a story with four key parts. The first is the president himself. It is his ambitions, his judgments, and his skills that set his presidency in motion and guide it, for better or worse, as it unfolds.

Psychology and Leadership

Mr. Bush may have a transparent psychology, but it is at the same time an unusual one, especially compared to his predecessor. Mr. Clinton disliked and avoided conflict. Mr. Bush certainly does not avoid it. Many asked whether Mr. Clinton had any real principles; some ask of Mr. Bush whether his have sufficient flexibility.

Mr. Clinton was one of the smartest and most knowledgeable of the modern presidents. However, his intelligence was often trumped, to his disadvantage, by his psychology. Mr. Bush faces a different and almost opposite set of questions. Is he smart enough? Is he curious enough to ask difficult questions of his staff? Does he delegate too much decision-making? Are his decisions essentially those of his chief advisors, perhaps Karl Rove, Donald Rumsfeld, or Dick Cheney?

These questions and others about Mr. Bush's psychology and leadership are likely to be at the forefront of the 2004 presidential campaign. They are certainly at the center of his presidency. And they are a critical part of any assessment of Mr. Bush and his presidency for 2004 and beyond.

The Presidency's Circumstances

The second key element of any presidency is its particular historical and political context. Presidents may try to shape events, but they cannot escape them. *Whether* and *how* the president responds to his circumstances tells us a great deal about the man who occupies that office.

Consider the economic circumstances that faced the Bush presidency on taking office. The economy began to slow and subsequent data showed that it had slipped into a recession, formally defined as two successive quarters of negative growth. Mr. Bush touted his tax cuts as a remedy and passed three of them. Consumer spending, one strong element in an otherwise faltering economy, was apparently helped by the infusion of tax rebates, and by the second quarter of 2003 the economy had begun to pick up steam.

These tax cut bills were highly contentious and their effects questioned. However, it cannot be said that Mr. Bush awaited the upturns that the economic cycle *might* eventually bring. I don't know if Mr. Bush is familiar with Richard Neustadt's classic analysis of *Presidential Power* and the critical need for presidential self-help,[1] but he acts as if he is.

Consider another example. Mr. Bush was at an elementary school in Florida when he received news that a first, and then a second, plane had stuck the World Trade Towers. His first response, recorded by several of those present, was "This is war." There are many other possible responses Mr. Bush might have had, but didn't. As a result, his presidency and life in America profoundly changed. Later I will look more closely at this judgment, noting here only that Mr. Bush's response underlines the importance of focusing on *how* a president responds to circumstances and not just the fact that they need to do so.

The President's Office

The third key element is the institution of the presidency itself. The office of the presidency, and its powers, provide the instruments for leadership and the realization of the president's policy ambitions. Here, as in the case of the president's response to circumstances, *if* a president uses the powers of his office, and *how* he does so, tell us important things about a president, his skills, ambitions, and prospects.

Mr. Bush has not been shy about using the powers of his office. These powers go well beyond "setting the agenda" or the capacity to "go public" in an attempt to pressure Congress. Those powers include presidential orders, directives to his chief operational agencies, appointment powers, using the machinery of party majorities in the Congress, giving or shielding information, and the basis for congressional partnerships with the White House. Internationally, they include committing troops and resources, forging initiatives, redefining partnerships, reframing treaties, and reassessing priorities. Mr. Bush has used all of these, as well as others.

Mr. Bush entered a presidency whose power had contracted in recent years. He sought to reverse that trend even before 9/11 and provided a strong rationale and set of tools to do so. His action ignited charges that Mr. Bush had rekindled the "imperial presidency."[2] Whether and to what extent that is true is certainly relevant to any assessment of the Bush presidency.

Public Psychology

Finally, the fourth critical aspect of a presidency is the public's psychology—its views, attachments, and feelings. Just as a president comes into office with a particular party line up in Congress, and a particular set of nine people on the Supreme Court, so he begins by inheriting an already formed public psychology. This means that he starts out dealing with the public's expectations; their recent experiences as well as what they can recall of their historical ones; their hopes and fears; and their understandings of their circumstances.

Sometimes a president bends in the direction of public psychology, telling the public what it says it wants to hear, even if the president doesn't believe it or isn't doing it. "The era of the big government is over," said President Clinton in a

State of the Union message that listed copious numbers of new governmental initiatives. "Watch what we do, not what we say," said Nixon's chief of staff Bob Haldeman. Mr. Bush has proved to be very different.

A president must decide how he will respond to the public psychology he faces upon entering office. He can accept it as an immutable given and adapt his agenda to it. He can pretend to accept it, as he tries to finesse or work around it. Or, he can, like George W. Bush, try to change it by example and policy.

Yet, it is also true that the president also brings to his time in office his own psychology. Therefore, an important but rarely asked question is how good the fit is between the two psychologies. Given Mr. Bush's ambitions to transform American domestic policy culture—and after 9/11, America's stance in the world—this fit has become a pressing question.

Americans have traditionally been multilateralists when they have not championed isolationism. Mr. Bush entered office with a feeling of reservation, bordering on skepticism, that agreements themselves were the key to national security; 9/11 did nothing to change his view. But Americans are ambivalent about going it alone, even when necessary. In this area, as in others, the president's ambitions meet the public's psychology, and it is an open question as to whether the public will follow the president's lead or even be able to tolerate it.

A VERY CONTROVERSIAL PRESIDENCY—WHY?

George W. Bush is a controversial president and even if reelected is likely to remain so. It is worth asking why. His critics believe the reasons are obvious. Mr. Bush, they say, can never escape the taint of being put into office by the Supreme Court despite clearly losing the popular vote. Moreover, they say, he lied when he pledged he would be the "president of all Americans." Instead, he has disregarded any pretense of bipartisanship and governed as if he had earned a mandate.

In office, critics argue, he has proved to be a rigid ideologue masking his hard-right agenda behind the thin veneer of a meaningless term—"compassionate conservatism." Domestically, his critics say, he favors only the wealthy and is committed to "turning back the clock" on all the hard-won policy advances of minorities, workers, immigrants, environmentalists, and women. Internationally, they argue, he has turned his back on the world community and its commitment to the rule of law as evidenced by his negation of the Kyoto Treaty, the International Criminal Court, and the Anti-Ballistic Missile treaty. Worse, he has abandoned deterrence, the cornerstone of American security for 50 years, to pursue his unilateralist doctrine of preemption. In the process, he has turned world opinion and our traditional allies against us. Americans are less safe, and government policies are less fair as a result, say his critics.

The president is openly disparaged by many in the Democratic Party and self-described "progressive" policy circles. People with these views are routinely found in America's political institutions, media venues of all kinds, and in the myriad policy advocacy communities. Indeed, the rage about Mr. Bush has been an important emotional and strategic element in critics' mobilization against the administration for the 2004 presidential election.[3]

Critics, and this includes senior Democratic party politicians, openly express their harsh judgments of the president's integrity, competence, and intelligence. He has been called an "idiot,"[4] a "fraud,"[5] a danger to the republic,[6] and a "miserable failure."[7] Pundits have been even less restrained, comparing him to Hitler[8] and Joseph Goebbels,[9] calling him a "madman,"[10] a "war criminal,"[11] one of the worst presidents in American history,[12] and a president dedicated to the "intentional destruction of the United States of America."[13] Not surprisingly, some Democrats have introduced a resolution to impeach him.[14]

Mr. Bush may be one of the few presidents about whom symposiums[15] have been held and articles written on the hatred he has engendered. In one of these, entitled "The Case for Bush Hatred," Jonathan Chait, a senior editor at *The New Republic,* wrote:

> I hate President George W. Bush. . . . I hate the way he walks—shoulders flexed, elbows splayed out from his sides like a teenage boy feigning machismo. I hate the way he talks—blustery self-assurance masked by a pseudo-populist twang. I even hate the things that everybody seems to like about him. . . . And, while most people who meet Bush claim to like him, I suspect that, if I got to know him personally, I would hate him even more.[16]

If one were to summarize the critics' views, they would be that Mr. Bush is an arrogant dimwit who is in over his head in complex policy matters and thus dependent on a small group of right-wing domestic advisors and their neo-con counterparts in foreign policy. They see him as a president who has turned his back on the bipartisan domestic and international policy consensus of the last four decades, and in so doing has put this country at risk of losing its many benefits.

Obviously, my evaluation of the Bush presidency will have to assess these claims; however, it is not too early to underscore that the reality of the George W. Bush presidency is much more complex and interesting than the shallow caricature drawn by many of his critics. It is true that Mr. Bush has turned away from a number of domestic and international policy orthodoxies. Yet this is precisely what one would expect of a *transforming president.* Indeed, it is difficult to see that such a project could be accomplished without stepping away from "conventional wisdom."

The president's attempts to change the way Americans view the world has led him to take some controversial policy steps. Americans have always felt strongly that they are entitled to fight back when attacked. Yet, what should be done when fighting back *after* an attack may result in tens of thousands, or even hundreds of thousands, of American deaths in their homes and workplaces? Do you attack first? On what basis? These are questions that have only recently come into focus for Americans, and answers are by no means settled in the public's mind. They are, however, settled in Mr. Bush's. In this area, as in others where Mr. Bush has proposed significant policy changes, Americans are caught between new circumstances, old policy paradigms, unanswered questions, and a confident, determined president. This is a major, but by no means the only, reason that Mr. Bush is so controversial.

Americans: Divided not Polarized

Contemporary American politics seems to be the political equivalent of "the perfect storm." It is raked by a number of turbulent elements, each of which by itself would be challenge enough for a president with strong policy aspirations. Together, they have created the political equivalent of a nationwide typhoon. The question is: What kind of captain is Mr. Bush?

The primary fissures in American politics are variously described as cultural or political. In reality, they are both. Unlike America's first Civil War, the cultural wars that began in the mid-1960s did not pit commerce against agriculture, urban centers against rural traditions, or North against South. Rather, the culture wars are being waged in *every* section of the country.

Unlike the first Civil War, contemporary combatants cannot take refuge in the primary institutions in their part of the country—their families, or their religious, social, cultural, or political organizations. These are precisely the places where the second Civil War conflicts are being fought.

In reality, of course, there are many such wars. There are the abortion wars, school wars, military culture wars, gender wars, family wars, history wars, marriage wars, museum wars, and classics wars, and as well as wars over flags, statues, pledges (of allegiance at school, to our country during naturalization ceremonies), and traditional holidays like Mother's Day (which is said to exclude children with gay parents).[17] The consequences of these wars are not to be found in the number of killed or wounded. Rather, they are to be found primarily in the retreat from common ideals; basic cultural values abandoned, atrophied, or under siege; and institutions floundering in a stormy sea of shrill and conflicting demands.

Advocacy campaigns against every major American cultural and political institution are not the result of a groundswell of American public sentiment.

They are the result of groups of determined activists, and their allies, amplifying their positions through media strategies in an attempt to engineer what they see as necessary changes in American cultural institutions. The result is a series of institutions under siege and cultural foundations undermined.

At the same time, Americans have become more politically divided. Some of this has to do with the cultural battles that have made their way into politics—gay marriage rights would be one example. Others are plain old vanilla policy differences. Both, however, appear to have a growing geographical dimension.

This divide is most starkly framed by the famous "red and blue" map of the 2000 election vote. Looking at the blue states that Al Gore won and the red states that George W. Bush won, Terry Teachout argues, "Except for Alaska and New Hampshire, all 29 states won decisively by Bush are geographically contiguous, forming a vast L-shaped curve that sweeps down from the Rocky Mountains across the Great Plains, then through the Midwest and the South. By contrast, except for California and Washington, most of the states won decisively by Gore are bunched tightly around the urban and industrial centers of the Northeast and Great Lakes."[18]

However, Mr. Teachout clearly has more than geography on his mind. He writes further that

> they are very different places. On one side the of the fence is an urban-and sub-urban-based congeries of government employees, union members, blacks, and those highly educated comparatively affluent "knowledge workers" known to political scientists as the New Class. On the other side is the contemporary equivalent of what H. L. Mencken dubbed the Bible Belt . . . in which rural and small town America have joined forces with the fast growing group of Americans who live in "exurbia," the new middle-class communities that are springing up beyond the rim of the older suburbs.[19]

Some time ago, the distinguished historian Gertrude Himmelfarb[20] pointed out that America seemed to be separating into two distinctive cultures, each occupying the same nation. The two groups found themselves on different sides of many policy issues that have characterized America's cultural wars and swept thorough its major institutions. Mr. Bush must figure out a way to lead and govern both Americas.[21]

In considering Bush's dilemma, it is critical to keep in mind several key distinctions. Most Americans think it perfectly fine to celebrate Mother's Day. Most Americans want their children judged on their performance, not on their skin color or ethnicity. Most feel that faith is an important part of their lives. Most are comfortable with civil unions for same-sex couples, while most are opposed to same-sex marriage.

In talking about America's divisions, it's important to distinguish between the generally strong support for America's basic cultural traditions and the fights that activists instigate about them. Disagreements over policies are not the same as disagreements over basic cultural premises. Few people hold their policy views strongly at whatever the cost. Disagreements over cultural premises are more difficult to resolve. People tend to feel more strongly about them and feel they are more central to their country's definition.

Finally, it is also essential to distinguish between *divisions* and *polarization.* Divisions simply mean that people have different views on a matter. It implies nothing about how strongly they hold these views. I can be for or against a drug benefit for seniors, but it matters a great deal to questions of national division whether I, and my fellow citizens, hold such views strongly, or don't really care that much. Polarization means not only having different views, but that these views are diametrically opposed and strongly held.

Presidential Leadership for a Divided Society

Just as the electorate has divided in the last several decades, so too has the political leadership in our major state and national political institutions. From roughly 1998 to the election of 2002, a divided electorate produced what Michael Barone refers to conceptually as the 49 percent nation.[22] It is a country in which the public and their leaders are divided in a way that does not produce the clear majorities that are needed for public mandates and effective governing. These are *political* divisions.

The 9/11 attacks had an impact on these divisions, but only temporarily. Barone, writing in the authoritative *Almanac of American Politics,* notes, "September 11 changed everything. How often have we heard or thought that since that awful morning? Yet for 14 months, September 11 seemed to have changed very little in America's politics. The nation's electorate still seemed split evenly between the parties.[23]

Some figures underscore this. In the 2000 presidential race, Mr. Bush won 47.9 percent of the vote, while Mr. Gore won 48.4 percent of the vote. In the House, Republican candidates were getting 49.2 percent of the vote, while Democrats garnered 47.9 percent. In the 1996 presidential race, Mr. Clinton won with 49.2 percent of the vote. The Republican margin of victory in the House that year was 48.9 percent to 48.5 percent. In 1998, those figures were almost the same, 48.9 percent and 47.8 percent..

Moreover, those years also reflected several other trends that helped to heighten partisan divisions. In Congress, the number of truly contested political districts is shrinking. Or, to put it another way, more districts have become "safe," ensuring that the domination of candidates from one or the other political party is the rule, not the exception. The increasing number of safe districts enable more ideologically committed candidates to win office. As a result, there are fewer "moderates" (defined in relation to the dominant center of gravity of their party) elected to office. So, both parties have become more partisan and the political "center" of gravity for each has moved accordingly.

Not surprisingly, party-line voting in the House and Senate has risen dramatically in recent years. In both houses of Congress there are fewer moderates in either party willing to stand apart from their more ideological colleagues. Given the increasingly plain differences between the views of each party on a variety of policy issues, and the fact that senators and congressmen are individually and collectively more likely to reflect them, bipartisanship has withered. How can a president provide political leadership or govern in these circumstances? There are no obvious answers, yet answer them Mr. Bush must.

Party Identification Decreasing, Partisanship Increasing

One of the many paradoxes of contemporary American domestic politics is that while the significance of party identification has declined among the general public, it has heightened significantly among those who count—those in positions of political leadership and those who elect them. There are several reasons for this. First, the decline of party identification and the corresponding rise of "independent" voters masks the fact that many so-called independents lean toward one of the two major parties. Other potential voters labeled as independent are, in reality, more disconnected politically than equally poised between two parties. As a result, they are less likely to vote.

The long-term decline in voter participation has increased the importance of core constituencies, and they tend to be more ideological. The most ideologically engaged are also more likely to vote. In a general electorate in which fewer and fewer eligible voters actually do so, those who vote exert a disproportionate influence.

Surveying the pre-2004 election setting, Fineman and Lipper write "the electorate is back to where it was: Red versus Blue, deeply divided." They quote one GOP election operative as saying "We're looking at, in effect, two nations that, on some level, barely seem to know or understand each other."[24] This is an overstatement to be sure, but one with some real implications for Mr. Bush's attempt to transform the country's political culture.

Another reporter with access to both parties has written that "Because the country remains so polarized, Mr. Bush's strategists have concluded that their core task in 2004 is mobilizing the Republican base, not persuading a diminishing pool of swing voters. To win, any Democratic nominee will have to generate intense support within the party to match that Republican fervor."[25] What this reporter means of course is that because citizens who are strongly identified as Republicans support Mr. Bush, Democrats will have to be sure that even their conservative and moderate members support their party.

A Polarizing Figure?

Mr. Bush campaigned as a president who would unite, not divide, the country. At one of his final campaign rallies he said the nation needed "a president who can unite this nation, a president who puts aside the endless partisan bickering that seems to gridlock our nation's capital, a president who puts the people first, a president who lifts this nation's spirits. I'll be that president."[26] Not so, say his critics. Howard Dean said of Mr. Bush, "This president promised that he would be a uniter, not a divider, and that was a lie!"[27]

It almost seems quaint to recall that in his first weeks in office, some thought Mr. Bush uncontroversial.[28] How that has changed. Now it's said by his critics that he is a polarizing figure. But is he? He certainly seems to have polarized his critics. But that's not the same as being a polarizing figure more generally. It is worth asking why critics see Mr. Bush that way. Hunt explains that "He commands awesome support among Republicans and conservatives and *is reviled by many Democrats and liberals*."[29] The fact that liberals and many Democrats dislike Mr. Bush, however, does not make him a polarizing figure—especially if, as we shall see, Democrats are not all of one mind on Mr. Bush.

George W.'s support among Republicans is extremely strong and steady.[30] However, behind these numbers is a country that views Bush and his policies through very different lenses, depending on party affiliation. Democrats and Republicans see him very differently on economic and domestic issues, but also on issues of national security. On the day Baghdad fell in April 2003, when Bush's approval rating was at 77 percent, 95 percent of Republicans and 62 percent of Democrats said they approved of his handling of the presidency. In a later poll, GOP support was statistically unchanged, but Democrats turned sharply negative in their assessments, with 64 percent saying they disapproved.[31]

On the surface, these figures appear to support Hunt's view of the Bush presidency as "polarizing." Yet they are misleading. One reason is that traditional party identification has been declining.[32] So "polarization," as defined by Hunt, to the extent that it is happening, is happening among a smaller proportion of the electorate. That means that the number of voters who don't identify with either party, and are thus not available to be polarized by party, is increasing.

Moreover, as noted, polarization doesn't just mean that the parties differ, but that they are locked in extreme and diametrically opposed positions. They are not. Consider the relationship between President Bush's tax cuts and the question of how best to pay for defense and Social Security costs. A Pew survey found that, overall, 41 percent of its sample would solve the problem by postponing tax cuts and 23 percent thought that cutting domestic spending was the answer.[33] Yet there were substantial differences *within* each partisan group.[34] Neither Democrats nor Republicans thought in lockstep with the most partisan and polarized views.

In a *Washington Post* poll of self-identified Democrats, 25 percent thought that the current party leadership was taking the party in the wrong direction and another 9 percent were unsure.[35] However, the most telling split came in answer to the question: Has the leadership of the Democratic party been too willing or not willing enough to compromise with President George W. Bush? On the specific issue of tax cuts, 58 percent of Democrats said that their leaders had "not been willing enough." On the specific issue of the war in Iraq, 54 percent of Democrats said "not enough." These are not the results one expects of a "polarized" electorate. Clearly there is room within the Democratic Party to move closer to the views of the president.

Indeed, there is a fair amount of policy play between the two parties. Of the 41 percent that supported postponing the president's tax cuts, 28 percent were conservative Republicans, and 39 percent were moderate or liberal Republicans; 44 percent were conservative or moderate Democrats and 63 percent were liberal Democrats. On a policy issue on which you would expect Republicans and Democrats to present mirror percentages of agreements if they were polarized, they simply don't. These figures are important in understanding one way in which it might be possible for Mr. Bush to accomplish his domestic transformation.

President Bush as a Person and Leader

It is difficult to reconcile views of Mr. Bush as a polarizing figure with public views of him as a person and leader. A *New York Times* poll released on October 3, 2003, found that 67 percent thought President Bush had strong qualities of leadership.[36] Sixty-seven percent said they thought he cared about the needs of "people like me." This specifically extended to minority groups as well. Sixty-one percent thought he specifically cared about the needs of African Americans, and the same percentage of those polled thought that he cared about the needs of Hispanic communities.

In general, in the first three-and-one-half years of his administration, Mr. Bush has been given strong ratings by the public on a number of personal attributes. He is seen as honest, a person who keeps his promises and is trustworthy; a person who inspires confidence, is able to understand complex issues, and puts the country's interests ahead of his own; and as someone who provides good moral leadership, and is sincere. He was even admired by almost a majority of the country at the time these polls were taken.[37]

These figures suggest that "polarization" is an inadequate concept to describe the complexity of the public's response to the unfolding Bush presidency. It is clear that the public distinguishes between the president as a person and leader, and the president as proponent of particular policies or practices. This is not a novel distinction. Jimmy Carter, Gerald Ford, and George H. W. Bush were seen in a positive light on personal grounds, but failed to win a second term (in Ford's case, the first election after his ascension to office on President Nixon's resignation).

The same distinction was quite obvious during the Clinton presidency. After Congress took up his impeachment, his overall approval ratings remained high, but evaluations of him personally were quite negative.[38] Indeed, Mr. Clinton and Mr. Bush present in some ways mirror images of each other's relationship with the public. Mr. Clinton got high marks for his policies and low marks for his character, while Mr. Bush gets high marks for his character and lower marks for his policies. The latter makes some sense considering that it is Mr. Bush who is leading against the grain when it comes to domestic and international policy. That is one price that Mr. Bush pays because of his transformational agenda.

PRESIDENT BUSH'S LEGITIMACY AND THE MANDATE QUESTION

George W. Bush became president in a close and disputed election. That election has continued to galvanize the rage and sense of thwarted entitlement of his opponents. The Congressional Black Caucus tried to block certification of the election results.[39] Four years later, the Democratic Party and its presidential candidates are running partially, or in some cases substantially, on their accumulated anger.[40]

Mr. Bush's victory was extremely narrow in a number of important respects. He received fewer popular votes than his opponent. About 51.2 percent of the nation's 200 million eligible voters cast ballots in the 2000 presidential election. This was marginally greater than the rock-bottom level seen in 1996, but significantly lower than the 1992 level.[41] Out of more than 105 million votes cast, Mr. Gore received 50,996,064 votes, or 48.39 percent; George Bush received 50,456,167 votes (a difference of 539,947), or 47.88 percent.[42]

These voting margins resulted in an extremely close electoral vote that ultimately had to be decided, in what some saw as an unwarranted and controversial decision, by the U. S. Supreme Court. In the Electoral College, Mr. Bush won

271 votes, one more than necessary; Mr. Gore won 266, having received one less than he actually won because of a protest vote by a District of Columbia elector protesting the "colonial status" of the district.[43] The state whose vote count finally put Mr. Bush over the needed 270-vote requirement was Florida. That state's votes were only awarded after a long and bitter fight about recounts and irregularities that was settled in Mr. Gore's favor by the Florida Supreme Court, and finally in Mr. Bush's favor by the U.S. Supreme Court.

The election also produced a mixed and contentious result in the distribution of power in the Congress. In the Senate, Republicans lost ground and that institution was tied at 50–50. That meant that with Vice President Dick Cheney casting any deciding vote to break a tie, Republicans could prevail. On the other hand, that required unanimity among Republicans and didn't reflect the power of Democrats to hold legislation hostage to a 60-vote majority necessary to overcome minority-erected procedural hurdles. In the house, the GOP's five-vote majority was hardly the basis for actualizing strong presidential initiatives.

Anne L. Wexler, a veteran Washington lobbyist with good connections in both parties, suggested that Mr. Bush might treat the results almost like a parliamentary election, reaching out to the Democrats to form something approaching a coalition government, with Democrats in key posts.[44] Democratic Senate Leader Tom Daschle was even more blunt: "The bottom line has to be that we must and will be full partners in the legislative process. We're no longer in the minority. We're going to be co-partners."[45]

Lowered expectations for President Bush's agenda were fairly widespread within the GOP as well. Michael Beschloss reported that, "Since the moment President-elect Bush finished his acceptance speech in Austin on Wednesday night, his allies and advisers have spoken frankly about the limits that the close election and a divided Congress may impose on the new leader's compassionately conservative agenda."[46]

Mr. Bush, however, had other views. "It is a unique moment, and I intend to seize it," Mr. Bush told *Time*.[47] He went on in that interview to say he would not settle for a scaled-down version of his campaign agenda. He argued that having won the election he had certainly gained political capital and a mandate from the perspective of foreign leaders.[48] Asked in the interview, "So you think you truly have a mandate?," he replied, "I do."

Indeed, from the first, in spite of his narrow victory, George W. Bush pursued an expansive list of domestic and foreign policy initiatives. Critics complained that he governed as if he had received a mandate. But such criticisms missed an essential point: He was trying to build one.

Mr. Bush's choice here revealed something very important about his psychology, although it was not much noted. Much has been written about how Mr.

Bush in his political career has outperformed the low performance expectations that people have of him. Less well understood is that Mr. Bush is quite at ease in going against what is expected of him or what others think he should and ought to do. It is a trait strongly rooted in his character psychology and one that has the most important implications for his leadership both here and abroad.

Election and Post-Election Mandates

It is obvious that large electoral victories provide big political mandates. FDR's sweeping electoral victory was a mandate to fix America's reeling economic system. Ronald Reagan's 49-state victory over Walter Mondale in 1984 surely reflected the public's preference to move the government's center of political gravity rightward, not leftward.

Sometimes, however, the meaning of a "mandate" is not always clear. Lyndon Johnson's sweeping 1964 victory over Barry Goldwater was certainly a vote for the continuation of a Democratic administration in the aftermath of John F. Kennedy's tragic death. It was also clearly a vote for a candidate that was viewed as the more moderate of the two. Yet it surely was not a vote for Johnson's "Great Society" programs, since those weren't discussed during the campaign and were only put forward after he had been elected.

Winning elections by narrow margins presents issues of a wholly different kind. On what basis can a political leader claim a "mandate" if his or her margin of victory is razor thin? What if the candidate actually loses the popular vote, but wins the electoral vote? What if, like Bill Clinton or George W. Bush, you never gain a majority of the votes cast?

Mr. Clinton won both of his elections, in 1992 and 1996, by a plurality of the votes cast. In no case did he receive a majority of the votes cast. What was Mr. Clinton's solution? In 1992, he added the votes of his opponent, Ross Perot, to his and claimed that both groups "had voted for change," and he therefore had his mandate.

John F. Kennedy won the presidency with the smallest popular vote margin in history. He responded to his narrow victory with a sense that he could ill afford large policy ambitions. Secretary of State Dean Rusk recalled, "He did not feel that he had a strong overwhelming mandate from the American people, and so he would rather be careful about the issues on which he wanted to make a fight."[49] There was, however, another side to Kennedy's reticence. He was essentially bored with the details of the legislative process.[50] Moreover, a Kennedy aide, Ralph Dugan, said of him that "he was bored silly with day to day executive work. . . ."[51] As a result, his domestic programs, which included changes in Medicare, federal aid to education, and civil rights, were stalled in Congress at the time of his death.

Mr. Bush has been compared to President Kennedy,[52] but there is at least one important way in which the two differ. President Kennedy, for all the carefully cultivated aura of his mystique, youth, and vigor, was psychologically not a political risk-taker. His natural inclination toward caution in his political stands was very evident in many of his domestic programs. Speaking with reporters in the White House, he said "there's no sense raising hell and then not being successful. There is no sense putting the office of the presidency on the line on an issue, and then being defeated."[53]

This is the voice of caution, political prudence, and risk-averse psychology. Although gaining office by the slimmest of margins and very controversial circumstances, Mr. Bush's response was quite different than that of John F. Kennedy or Bill Clinton. He did not claim some overarching principle that united his opposition with his camp, as Clinton did. Nor did he adopt a strategy of scaled-back ambitions. On the contrary, he proceeded as if he had a mandate, or as one reporter put it, "in landslide fashion."[54]

Here, as elsewhere, a president's psychology is revealed in his choices. President Bush's choice was filled with risk. He would doubtlessly alienate, and did, those who thought his narrow and controversial win required acts of political contrition in the form of shared governing and a lessening of his policy ambitions. He also risked startling the public with a fast start toward what were new ways of thinking about government and policy. And he risked startling America's allies and competitors abroad. Yet this is precisely the path that President Bush chose.

Mr. Bush's Mandate?

Mr. Bush certainly received no popular mandate, if the size of the popular vote is the measure. Nor did his one electoral vote more than necessary provide a strong policy mandate. But Mr. Bush did receive a mandate—a mandate to govern and an audition.

We can distinguish between a *policy* mandate and a *legitimacy* mandate. A policy mandate occurs when a candidate puts forward a specific set of policies and is rewarded by a substantial victory in the election. In these circumstances, it is a reasonable inference that the voters have spoken in favor of what they have heard and decisively prefer that to the views of the losing candidate. In closer elections, like Bill Clinton's two pluralities or George W.'s win, the public vote does not reflect a decisive policy preference. But it has selected, however narrowly, someone to govern.

A *legitimacy* mandate accrues to a president by virtue of the fact that he did win a victory, however small, so long as it was a result of the rules and standards in place at the time of the election. Simply put, the mandate is this: If you have won your victory fairly in accordance with the rules, you are accorded legitimacy, and with that you have a right to try to govern in accordance with your principles.

The *policy* mandate differs from the legitimacy mandate in several key ways. A president who earns a policy mandate can argue that he deserves to have his programs put into place. A president with only a legitimacy mandate, like George W. Bush, can only argue that he should be given a chance.

A president with a policy mandate keeps his agreement with the public if he puts into place the policies for which they voted. A president with a legitimacy mandate has no such agreement with the public, and can only hope to forge one after assuming office.

Finally, the attempt to create a post-election policy mandate is much more politically risky. Not only may policies fail in their purpose or intent (a danger for policy mandates as well), but the public may not understand or like what the president desires to do.

Either type of mandate involves the responsibility of governing. This in turn requires defining problems and setting priorities. When a president publicly points to what he sees as a problem, he assumes the responsibility for addressing and trying to resolve it.

Some presidents propose specific policies; some prefer to articulate general philosophical views or general approaches to problems. Mr. Bush has made use of both strategies. In either case, the president with only a legitimacy mandate from his victory has also earned the right to *try* and put his vision and policies into effect. I emphasize the word *try,* not only because the outcome of any policy effort is in doubt; but also because the real mandate that accompanies gaining the presidency is the right to try to convince the public that a president's views and policies ought to be the ones that govern. This is the cornerstone of the relationship between the legitimacy mandate and presidential leadership, and it is the basis for Mr. Bush's steps into the risky policy arena of persuasion. His bold, blunt articulation of his views is one tool he has used, but it has its limits.

BUILDING A MANDATE FOR TRANSFORMATION

Americans have traditionally preferred their leaders to govern from the political center—whatever that term means. Its iconic status is equaled only by the esteem in which Americans hold bipartisanship, another term with often muddled meanings. Yet, what is very clear is that changes in the structure of congressional districts nationwide, as well as strong divisions within the electorate, make it difficult to establish bipartisanship or know where the political center lies.

Both parties have been seeking ways to break the deadlocks imposed by a "49 percent nation." Both Republicans and Democrats have sought the basis for forging a new governing majority. So far neither has succeeded.

Most voters are not strong liberals or strong conservatives. So the political territory from which a strong governing majority will be forged is still to be found somewhere in the political center. The question is, where exactly is that? That center may emerge as a moderate right-of-center or moderate left-of-center, but it will obviously not be found at the farthest regions of the ideological positions of either party.

Given the state of American politics, whether characterized as red and blue or the 49 percent nation, there are essentially four ways to occupy the political center. The first, and the major paradigm for the past two decades, has been bipartisan trench warfare. Partisans of both sides have waged increasingly aggressive warfare against each other, with one side or another getting more (or less) of what they want, and immediately going on to the next battle. In this case it is clear that "center" is not an arena of agreement, but of exhaustion and stalemate.

The second method of occupying the middle is through segmented coalitions. This is a George W. Bush specialty. In this mode, the "center" is floating, rather than a permanent place; the president builds one coalition for one program (for example, a tax cut), another for a second program (say, an education policy), and so on. The advantage of segmented coalitions is that they provide a method to accomplish some presidential purposes, given a deeply divided government and country. The major disadvantage of sequential coalitions is that they are not truly governing coalitions. They clearly don't bring a change in the overall policy equation or political understanding that Mr. Bush aims to develop. Segmented coalitions can pass policies, but not accomplish transformations.

And make no mistake, it is transformation that George W. Bush is after. He wants to transform the Republican party and make it a governing political majority. And most ambitiously, he wants to transform America's domestic policy and political culture.

A third way of finding the political center is some form of "split the difference" or blended ideology. This has many versions, but it essentially entails combining, at least rhetorically, elements of left and right philosophy. This is a tempting strategy and many modern presidents have used it, but it has its limitations. A primary one is that it doesn't provide the basis for changing a political and policy culture as Mr. Bush feels needs to be done.

There is only one way that Mr. Bush's policy ambitions can be realized: He must succeed in changing the conceptual center of gravity in the vast and amorphous political center. This is the real thrust of the Bush presidency and its ambitions. The outlines of these ambitions were clear from the early moments of his presidency, but they were accelerated by the 9/11 terrorist attack, especially in foreign policy.

The 9/11 Transformation
of American National Psychology

When highjacked planes demolished the World Trade Towers and part of the Pentagon, they did more than destroy buildings. They assaulted core beliefs of American national psychology. Among the most primary of these were the country's sense of exceptionalism and exuberant, some might say, naïve optimism. Americans came face to face with a hard emotional fact: It can happen here.

After a time, on the surface many things appeared to become "normal" again. Religious attendance that had risen dramatically after 9/11 returned to pre-attack levels. Overt manifestations of patriotism, like displaying flags, did the same. Domestic political issues began to draw increasing concern in the period before the 2002 congressional and state elections. Life went on, as it must.

But in other respects America was profoundly changed. Before 9/11 the news reports were worried more about shark attacks than national and domestic security. After 9/11, it took some suspension of disbelief to believe the country was truly safe.

The events of 9/11 brought America face to face not just with terrorism, but *catastrophic terrorism.* I use this term to reflect the rise of terrorist groups with the will, the desire, and, if they can acquire the means, the intention to unleash chemical, biological, or nuclear weapons against their sworn enemies—primarily the United States, but more generally the Western democracies.

With this attack, those terrorists declared war on America. Mr. Bush in turn declared war on them, with consequences that will continue to ripple through the world's domestic and international communities. Deterrence, the cornerstone of American national security in a bipolar and even multipolar world, seemed ill-equipped to deal with groups whose purpose was to kill as many of their enemies as possible or inflict the most damage without regard to territorial or strategic political aspirations.

President Bush added wars of preemption and prevention to the mix of possible American responses in a dangerous world. Preemption reserved the right to strike immediately if an attack was imminent. In fact, this was hardly a new policy for the United States. President Eisenhower had considered it a viable response should it become clear that the Soviet Union was about to attack the United States.[55]

What was more controversial was the president's willingness to consider and undertake wars of prevention, as he did in Iraq, when the United States and its allies had not been attacked. The Bush doctrine reflected the view that in an age of catastrophic terrorism the country could no longer afford to wait until it was under attack. Given the lethality of weapons of mass destruction, waiting until the United States was attacked could cost tens of thousands of lives and irreparable economic, political, and psychological damage to the country. However, putting those concepts into operation involved fearsome questions of assessing intent and capability—and as the United States learned in Iraq, it could also carry with it substantial domestic and international political consequences.

The 9/11 attacks changed a basic tenet of American national psychology. Americans could no longer afford the luxury of indifference to governmental performance, especially in national security matters. Foreign policy was no longer "out there." It had the most direct and dire domestic consequences. Concern with whether the president "cares about people like me" became secondary to whether the president exhibited strong, perhaps even heroic, leadership.

Mr. Bush, by virtue of his psychology, was well positioned given this turn of American public psychology. A man of strong principles and even stronger views, he did not mince words or actions. Compassion took a back seat to strength. And it is in the context of that transition in American public psychology and its fit with Mr. Bush's psychology that a principal lever was established for political transformation.

THE BUSH TRANSFORMATION

President Bush's transformation of American politics will depend less on specific policy issues than on the new ways of thinking about issues that his presidency represents. The Bush presidency is antithetical to domestic policy liberalism, unimpressed with its conventional wisdom, and decidedly "outside the box" of much of its policy thinking. Think about it: he wants portions of Social Security accounts owned by individuals; he wants real attempts at accountability in schools; he wants to try faith-based government partnerships; and he wants to try new market-based approaches to energy sufficiency and the environment, new approaches to regulation, a new approach to foreign aid and poverty alleviation, new approaches to our strategic and national defense, and new partnerships with previously unfriendly or ambivalent countries (China, Mexico, Russia, Pakistan, India, and the Eastern European countries).

The point here is *not* that each of these policies is flawless. It is that together they represent more new thinking about a wider range of policy areas—many with significant consequences—than this country has seen since the last great consolidation of new ideas, FDR's New Deal and Lyndon Johnson's Great Society. It is not only that Mr. Bush is a transforming leader, but that his ideas are as well.

But just because they represent new ways of thinking, which Mr. Bush believes are better and more effective, it does not follow that they will be readily accepted. On the contrary, they are and will remain controversial and unsettling for some time precisely for those reasons, even if Mr. Bush realizes his ambitions. And there are many, domestically and abroad, who are working to ensure he does not succeed.

A Critical Presidency—But No Clear View of It

It is George W. Bush's fate to be president of the United States at a critical historical juncture for both the United States and the world. He leads a country whose power is equaled only by its vulnerability. He governs a citizenry in whom realistic appraisal has been long overtaken by extravagant expectations. And he operates in the paradoxical world of globalization in which countries, cultures, and religions are increasingly interconnected, but not necessarily interrelated. Clearly, a good part of the controversy surrounding the Bush presidency can be laid directly at the feet of his responses to these circumstances. He has not only taken the proverbial bull by the horns, but is attempting to ride and direct it.

The stakes for the United States in successfully addressing these issues are enormous. The possible answers are fraught with risk and uncertainty. The consequences of mistakes are potentially devastating. The prospects for success are daunting.

In these circumstances, never has a clear view of the president been more necessary. And yet, for a variety of reasons, never has it been more difficult to ascertain. With this Bush presidency, there are the usual problems of a protective and enamored staff presenting the president as they would prefer him to be seen. This is a particular issue given this White House's insistence on discipline, its premium on loyalty, and its attempts (not always successful) to enforce message consistency. Yet there is also the fact that Mr. Bush is a president most often observed through the haze of strong emotion. Books that purport to analyze him either caricature[56] or idealize him.[57] The first outnumber the second by a large margin. There are very few that try to understand him.[58]

As President Bush runs for a second four-year term, it would be helpful to have an appraisal of this man and his presidency that doesn't mistake either caricature or idealization for fact.

SECTION II

SEARCHING FOR HIS PLACE

CHAPTER 2

IN HIS FATHER'S SHADOW

IN MANY WAYS, THE DEVELOPMENT OF GEORGE W. BUSH comfounds expectations drawn from general developmental theory. Unlike the typical first-born son, George W. showed little conventional ambition and arguably even less success through his own efforts. His younger brothers, Jeb in particular, outshone him. By the time George W. turned 30, a time when he should have settled down, made significant inroads professionally, and been married—according to conventional dictates of development—he had achieved none of these milestones. Instead, he "viewed portions of his life as something of a wastrel's guidebook," time he spent, as he subsequently put it, "'drinking and carousing and fumbling around.'"[1]

Arguably worse than failing to meet conventional expectations of development was George W.'s apparent failure to meet those of his prestigious family. Success was not only expected, it was assumed to come naturally to the Bush family. Grandfather Prescott had been a successful businessman, a U. S. senator, and a pillar of the eastern Republican establishment. Father George Herbert Walker Bush was himself a highly successful businessman, diplomat, politician, and president. George W. surely was expected to follow in their footsteps and continue the family traditions of making money and public service.

Whether or not there was a sense of entitlement, there clearly were a set of standards and expectations. And these, for the first part of his life, George W.

met more with form than with substance. Like his father, he had gone to the highly prestigious prep school Andover, and then on to Yale University. He was a "legacy," but did not create his own. His path seemed paved rather than blazed. While not exactly a failure, neither was George W. an obvious success.

Having confounded the expectations of his family, George W. further confounded the expectations of developmental theory at age 40 by having a reverse midlife crisis, marked by increased and growing success. Whereas the quintessential midlife crisis is a rejection of responsibility, Bush's led to an embrace of responsibility and sustained success that would have been little expected from his performance until then.

This reversal is often seen (including at times by George W. himself) as having been sudden. This is doubtful, for many of the characteristics he was to display after his transformation had been somewhat evident before it. The psychology of George W. Bush has changed less than the purpose to which it has been put and that required finding a place where his talents fit.

Mr. Bush started out with great promise and many assets. However, these advantages all carried with them demands for performance that he had trouble meeting, and that led to a profound psychological impasse. Every family message as well as his personal ambition pushed him to reach success. Yet, every time he undertook to gain a foothold, he found little solid ground.

The result was an erratic commitment to conventional success, from adolescence to early adulthood and finally into middle adulthood. Bush became the family rebel and in school the campus cut-up. In his early adulthood he combined spurts of hard work with equally hard living, including too much drinking. Self-medication with alcohol and acting out in late adolescence and middle-early adulthood became a partial substitute for the success he wanted, but which remained out of reach.

The story of how Mr. Bush forged a stable and successful adulthood is a story of perseverance, resilience, and determination. Not surprisingly, these characteristics have been on display in his presidency. It is a story often presented by Mr. Bush as an example of the transforming power of faith, as he went from someone who rejected a personal God to someone who accepted Him. Yet in reality, it is far more than a story of inner faith; it is a story of inner psychology.

GEORGE W. BUSH:
A DEVELOPMENTAL NARRATIVE

George W. Bush was born into a wealthy and extremely accomplished family. His father, whose name he carried, had been an outstanding scholar, athlete, war hero, successful businessman, congressman, ambassador to China, head of the CIA, vice president, and finally president. Measured against these august accomplishments, George W. Bush paled. That is one reason why his educational program "No Child Left Behind" has a special resonance for this president. So too does his pleasure now in repeatedly confounding the low expectations that his critics and pundits have of him. As he has said, "I like being misunderestimated." One can easily understand why. Now low expectations are a critic's trap, instead of being a family rebuke.

George W. was not an outstanding student, nor an accomplished athlete. Nor did he seem to have a special talent that would help set him apart in any other way, unless it was his capacity to be a key member of the group for no obvious reason except that people liked and were drawn to him. The earliest known manifestation of this occurred when he ran for class president in junior high school and won.[2]

George W. attended Andover, where he again stood out for being at the center of things for no apparent reason. He went on to Yale where he had an adequate, but in no way outstanding, record. When he graduated from college, he recalled, "I didn't have much of a life plan."[3] Many years later he said of himself, "I had dabbled in many things. . . ."[4]

After graduating from Harvard Business School in 1975, George W. set out for Texas, as his father had before him, to make his fortune. But again, where his father succeeded, George W. didn't. He tried his hand at politics, running for Congress, as had his father. Again, where his father had succeeded, he didn't. His unfocused adolescence and undistinguished early adulthood were threatening to turn into a failed adulthood.

By the age of 40, his oil business and political prospects had reached a dead end. In the fall of 1975 George W. had moved to Midland, Texas to make his mark in the oil business. He started out as a "land man," searching court records for mineral rights and trying to put deals together. A year later, in the fall of 1976, George W. founded a company with a one-room office above a bank. Prophetically, he named it Arbusto. The company drilled ten wells a year and had limited success (expenditures outweighed revenues), but investors were helped by tax write-offs. In December 1981 Mr. Bush acquired "working interests" on property owned by Pennzoil. He also landed a big investor, Phillip Uzielli, who pumped $1 million in capital into the company in return for a 10 percent share. George W. tried to raise more capital by going public with the company's stock, but bank failures related to oil company overextensions shadowed the effort.

By 1983, Bush's oil company ranked 993rd, near the bottom, in terms of oil production in Texas. On February 29, 1984, Bush merged his floundering company with the more successful Spectrum 7. Bush was paid $75,000 a year and given 1.1 million shares. Unfortunately, the next year world oil prices collapsed and Spectrum 7 faced bankruptcy. Mr. Bush began the search for a savior and found it in the larger, more successful Harkin Oil Company. It is a small wonder that Bush lamented in a 1986 interview "I'm all name and no money."[5] He had tried hard, but never found what he called "the liberator"—a major oil find that would cement his future and justify his promise.[6]

That term, "liberator," is suffused with psychological significance. It meant, of course, to be liberated from financial worries, but it also carried deeper meaning as well. It meant to be liberated from the inability to measure up to family expectations. It meant to stand on an equal footing with his father's successful history. And it meant to have engineered his own first major adult success.

Sometime during this period Mr. Bush began to have a real issue with drinking. George W. has both alluded to its seriousness and downplayed it. But David Frum quotes George W. as telling a group of religious leaders, "You know I had a drinking problem. Right now I should be in a bar in Texas, not the Oval Office. There is only one reason why I am in the Oval Office and not in a bar. I found faith, I found God. I am here because of the power of prayer."[7]

Duly respecting the power of prayer, I think the origin of his transformation lies elsewhere. It is true that George W. quit drinking suddenly and totally. This was in itself an act of determination, of courage—to face his life as it was—and optimism that he could and would find a way out of his deep developmental impasse.

How did this happen? He credits the Reverend Billy Graham, the evangelist, and his wife, Laura. I credit his psychology.

Just one year after he stopped drinking he was offered an opportunity to develop a partnership in a local baseball team—the Texas Rangers. Yet this time, unlike so many others, George W. leveraged this opportunity into something more important than a job: a foothold in the adult world and an opportunity to earn, due to his own skills and developing capacities, a larger place in it. Having accomplished this, he could turn his attention to politics, an area to which he had been drawn at least since adolescence.

THE BUSH FAMILY

Family businesses are notoriously hard on the psychology of the family children, as they raise issues of measuring up to success. They raise also issues of forging a separate identity in an area already successfully staked out by others. And they raise stormy emotional currents connected with competition among and between all concerned. Else Walker, a Bush family cousin, has said that "this is not an easy family to grow up in. All of us had to come to grips with the fact that there are enormously successful people in it and a lot of pressure to be a big deal. All of us have had various successes in coming to grips with those pressures."[8] George W. was buffeted by all these elements.

The Bush family business can be characterized in two words: money and service. George W.'s grandfather, Prescott Bush, had provided the family model by first making millions on Wall Street and then establishing a long career of public service. He served first as a moderator of town meetings and next as a United States senator from Connecticut. Tall and imposing, Prescott served as a senator for over a decade, and was the acknowledged leader of the Bush extended family. His son, George H. W. Bush, suffered from the same set of issues that would later afflict his son. He too grew up in his father's shadow. And like his son after him, he also left the family's well-endowed nest to go west to try out his independence in the oil business. Unlike his son, he succeeded.

In spite of going off to Texas to seek his fortune, George H. W. was hardly a rebel. He never cut his ties to the Eastern Establishment that viewed success and service as natural, and even as an entitlement. In fact, he followed in *his* father's footsteps by first making money and then going on to a long career in public service.[9,] In these steps too, George W. followed his father.

His Father's Son

Both George W. and his brother Jeb referred to their father as a "beacon." That is an enlightening term, for it means a source of guidance and inspiration, something to be followed, even emulated.[10] In family life, imitation is the most sincere and deepest form of identification. That is precisely what George W. had done, from Andover to the presidency. One can see to this day George W.'s strong identification with his father in a number of instances before and after he became president.

Of his decision to become a pilot George W. writes in his autobiography, "I'm sure the fact that my father had been a fighter pilot influenced my thinking."[11] Of his loss in his first run for political office he writes, "I was following in some *very big footsteps* when I lost my first political campaign for Congress in 1978. My dad lost his first political race for Senate in 1964."[12] In the first moments of the 9/11 attack George W. reached back to his father's famous vow in response to Saddam Hussein's invasion of Kuwait, "This will not stand," to give his own version, "Terrorism against our nation will not stand."[13] Even the phrase "compassionate conservative" made its first appearance in his father's campaign.[14]

George W. grew up with and has a strong emotional connection to his father. In his autobiography, George W. singles out for special mention the cufflinks his father gave him on the day of his inauguration as governor and an accompanying letter signed "devotedly yours"; the recollection "still brings a lump to my throat."[15] During George W.'s campaign for president, reporters noted that "he cried on about half the occasions when he talked about how supportive his father had been."[16] Asked about his father by eighth graders at a middle school campaign stop in 2000, George W. said, "I didn't like it when people criticized my dad. That's because I love him, I love him more than anything."[17] Asked 100 days into his presidency whether his father had been helpful to him, George W. replied, "He's been helpful to me by telling me he loves me, and that he's proud of me. There's nothing like a dad giving a son the kind of words that only a dad can give."[18]

Another reflection of that strong attachment was George W.'s fierce loyalty and protectiveness of his father. His father didn't like conflict and avoided confrontations. Richard Nixon had viewed him as "too nice" with "no killer instinct."[19] Interestingly, given his importance in George W.'s administration, so did Donald Rumsfeld.[20]

But George W. was more than determined to stand up for his father whenever necessary. He admitted to being the "Roman candle of the Bush family, quick to spark and that's true when it comes to defending my dad."[21] He would "run through a brick wall for my dad,"[22] he said, and "I'm a fierce warrior when it comes to my father. I'm in it for love, not for power."[23] More than a few reporters have felt the wrath of the son in defense of his father.

George W. not only loved his father, but also idealized him. Idealization is the fusion of strong positive feelings toward a person with an emphasis on the person's admirable characteristics; it is a psychological recipe for strong personal attachments.

And there was much for this son to idealize. His father was successful, kind, thoughtful with others, had an easy-going style, and loved his children.[24] When one day Barbara Bush called George H. W., who was on the road, to complain that their son had just hit a baseball through one of their neighbor's windows, he replied, "My gosh, what a great hit."[25]

Surely part of George W.'s idealization of his father was due to George H. W. having been on the road quite often when George W. was growing up. George W. doubtlessly missed his father, and this longing helped to fuel his strong attachment. Given this strong attachment and idealization, it is not surprising that George W. tried to follow in his father's footsteps.

Both went to Andover and Yale, and then became pilots. Both sought their independence from their fathers by looking for their fortunes in the Texas oil business. And both turned to politics as a mid-adult career choice.[26] But of course the actual results differed. Whereas for George H. W. success followed success, for his son detour followed detour. George's father was a good student, excellent athlete, war hero, millionaire oil-man, and successful politician. George W. was an average student, no athlete, a pilot in the reserves, an unsuccessful businessman, and until he won the governorship of Texas, had failed to win the one political race he had run.

They also shared certain family experiences and traits. Both had fathers who were awe-inspiring figures. Both had powerful tart-tongued mothers. Both had fathers who were often absent because of business or political ambitions. And both grew up in families that valued competition and expected high performance. Neither was an intellectual,[27] both had trouble with words,[28] and both had a personality that drew others to them.[29]

If one of the most important steps in any person's development is separating and distinguishing him- or herself from his or her parents, George W. clearly was in trouble. How does one distinguish oneself from a highly successful father? Perhaps by appearing not to be driven by success. The result was a profound mismatch between a father whom his son admired but had little hope of emulating, and a son whose father was the North Star of his idealization and the curse of his unrealized ambitions. As a result of this unresolved dilemma, George W.'s adolescence and early adulthood were unfocused, wholly ordinary, and, by family measures, undistinguished. For George W. this role—as the self-described "black sheep" of the family—can be seen as a way of embracing his difficulty in finding a way to measure up. Whatever Freudian dreams he might have harbored of surpassing his father were buried deep in his own failures to find much conventional success.

Throughout his life his father's shadow loomed over him. He was from very early in his life viewed by others primarily through the frame of his father.[30] Growing up in Midland, Texas, he was known as "little George."[31] Running for Congress in Texas at the age of 32, he was repeatedly forced to remind people that he would be "campaigning as me," not his father.[32] However, long before that the questions were so persistent and so troubling to George W. that he "began pulling out his birth certificate at speeches to prove that his middle name was different from his father's."[33] Apparently without effect: On the day before his official announcement as a candidate for governor, a newspaper ran a picture of his father instead of him.[34] When officials of Air National Guard coordinated efforts to clean up the F-102 that Bush had piloted and put it on display, they painted on the wrong name, Lieutenant George Bush, Jr.[35] Even when he ran for governor of Texas, the *Houston Chronicle* used a picture of his father to illustrate a story about George W. speaking at a Republican woman's group.[36]

Being mistaken for your father is no joke, especially when you are trying to establish your own identity. The repeated name and identity confusion must have rankled George W., and it is likely that he often cursed his fate, and perhaps even his father occasionally. George W. was not only *in* his father's shadow, he also seemed to be stuck there.

Visiting in the White House, Frank Bruni noticed a painting hanging above the fireplace of George W. and his father fishing. George W. had commissioned it, and the placement of the figures drew Bruni's attention; "His father was in the foreground . . . reeling in a big catch. . . . The son was behind him in profile, less easily noticed, with no fish on the line."[37]

Mother and Son

Because George W.'s father was so often away, it is not surprising that his mother, Barbara, had most of the family-raising responsibilities and had a major influence on his personality. Told by a supporter that he had "your daddy's eyes and your momma's mouth," George W. found it "a pretty accurate assessment. My mother and I are the quippers of the family, sharp-tongued and irreverent. I love her dearly and she and I delight in provoking each other, a clash of quick wits and ready comebacks. Occasionally, our comebacks are too quick, too ready."[38]

Barbara Bush has a direct, no-nonsense approach, and a not-infrequently critical (some have said sarcastic) approach to people and life. Her mother, Pauline Pierce, had encouraged her to say what she thought,[39] and she spent a lifetime as a mother and central figure in the Bushes' political careers doing just that. She was known for speaking her mind in an era when most political wives said and did little to rock their husbands' political boats. Among many tart public comments, she is famously recalled for having characterized Democratic vice-presidential candidate Geraldine Ferraro with a word that rhymes with "rich."[40]

Nor was her pointed directness limited to others. Her children called her "the enforcer," though not in front of her; interestingly, it is a term she used to describe herself as well. Jeb Bush called his mother "our drill sergeant." Barbara Bush herself said, "I would scream and carry on." George W. put it more bluntly: "I've been reprimanded by Barbara Bush as a child and I've been reprimanded as an adult. And in both circumstances, it's not very much fun."[41] She nurtured her children through the ups and downs of childhood and adolescence, but her style was strong, not warm.

Moreover, she was charged with almost the sole responsibility of raising the children. It was a time "of long days and short years; of diapers, runny noses, earaches, more Little League games than you could believe possible, tonsils, and those unscheduled races to the hospital emergency room, Sunday school, and church, of hours of urging homework, short chubby arms around your neck, and sticky kisses."[42] Combined with the joys of motherhood, there were times, she later recalled, of "experiencing bumpy moments—not many, but a few—of feeling that I'd never, ever be able to have fun again; and coping with the feeling that George [H. W.] Bush, in his excitement of starting a small company and traveling around the world, was having a lot of fun."[43]

Whatever resentment she might have felt was likely aggravated by her husband's very different approach to discipline and boundary setting. He was easy-going, and when he did come home wanted to nurture, not discipline. It is not unusual when the father is away while the mother has primary responsibility for rearing the children that the latter is more likely to seek to set strict boundaries and feel comfortable with enforcing discipline while the former may, in an effort to offset his absence, be more tolerant and even coddling.

Reporters who have covered the family attest that "their loyalty to, and support of, one another was unquestionable . . . love and admiration . . . transcended the competitive instincts they all had."[44] That might well be very true, but there were family undercurrents. Throughout George W.'s life his mother has spoken her mind, and he has not always liked the result. In 1994, George W. recalled, "My mother told me that I couldn't beat Ann Richards."[45] He made it into a standing joke, but the lack of confidence must have been telling.

Four years before, in 1990, just after he had taken up his position with the Texas Rangers, George W. began considering a run for governor. His mother first told him privately not to, and then was quoted publicly as saying that, "When you make a major commitment like that [to baseball], I think maybe you won't be running for governor."[46] George W. responded in a fury: "Mother's worried about my Daddy's campaign affecting my race. Thank you very much. You've been giving me advice for forty-two years, most of which I haven't taken."[47] He later softened his stance, but the damage had already been done. How could he mount a campaign after his mother, the first lady, had told him not to? In August 1990, he publicly decided against making the race at that time.

One reason for the conflict between Geoge W. and his mother, beyond what is normal between parent and child, is that they have similar psychologies. They both have rebellious streaks in their makeup that often became a test of wills. Her sarcasm indicated a certain questioning of convention and it encouraged a similar tendency in George W.; she surely didn't realize that it is difficult to both enforce and subvert convention at the same time.

George W. had once remarked in an interview that he realized when he was growing up that his mother "put her relationship with her husband above her relationship with us."[48] That hard knowledge contributed to the strain between George W. and his mother. Their relationship may be close, but it isn't tranquil.

A Death in the Family

When George W. was six years old, his younger sister Robin became ill with leukemia. Short of the death of a parent, that of a sibling can be particularly devastating, and it was in George W.'s case. Both the responses of the family at the time *and* the memories of the trauma provide important insights into Bush's psychology.

After Robin became ill, her parents tried to save her by taking her to New York's Memorial Sloan-Kettering Cancer Center for treatment. For seven months, George Sr. commuted to New York, and his wife understandably stayed in New York with her ill daughter. Notwithstanding the sacrifices of George H. W. and Barbara, Robin's life could not be saved.

The death of a child is the most devastating loss that a family can suffer, and its effects rippled through the family for years. George W. recalled being "sad and stunned. . . . Minutes before I had had a little sister, and now I didn't. Forty-six years later, those moments remain the starkest memory of my childhood, a sharp pain in the midst of an otherwise happy blur."[49]

One moment George W. was a typical kid, riding his bike through the streets of Midland with his group of friends on the way to play baseball or share adventures. The next moment he was learning a hard early lesson about loss and the fragility of what seems solid in life. It would obviously be a mistake to reduce anyone's psychology to one event, even a major one. Nonetheless it is difficult to ignore the enormity of that tragedy, or the period in his life when it occurred. John Kidde, a high school classmate, recalls George W. telling his classmates, "You think your life is so good and everything is perfect; then something like this happens and nothing is the same."[50]

George's brother Marvin has suggested that the experience made George W. live fully in the present, "seizing opportunities as they came without fretting about what tomorrow would bring."[51] George W. had his own take on the lessons of that tragedy: "I learned in a harsh way, at a very early age never to take life for granted."[52]

What is striking about the death from George W.'s standpoint is clearly its unexpectedness. While his parents had told him that Robin was sick, they had not told him of the real possibility of her death. At that age it is unlikely that he would have fully grasped the implications of death's finality. Through the years, the decision not to tell George W. just how sick his little sister was has weighed on Mrs. Bush: "I don't know if that was right or wrong. I mean, I really don't, but I know he [George W.] said to me several times, 'You know, why didn't you tell me?' I said, 'Well, it wouldn't have made a difference.'"[53]

George W.'s specific words of remembrance about that time are worth noting as well. One minute he had a sister, the next minute he didn't. His comment could just have easily applied to his parents. They had left George W. and his baby brother, Jeb, with friends in Midland, Texas.[54]

Some have suggested that Robin's death created a strong mother-son bond.[55] As evidence they point to the fact that George W. tried to console his grieving mother, something Barbara Bush remembers him doing as well.[56] Young George was attempting to compensate for his mother's loss by being two children, himself and "the good child," hoping to repair the loss. However, Mrs. Bush wisely realized that his attempt to cheer her up "was too much of a burden for any child to bear."[57]

Others have suggested that this was the start of George W.'s impish, devil-may-care attitude toward life. The suggestion is tempting, but it is inconsistent with the facts. In elementary school, before his sister's death, George W. was sent to the principal's office for disrupting a music class by painting a moustache on his face. Rather than being contrite or scared, George W. swaggered into the principal's office, "as if he had done the most wonderful thing in the world." Fearing that George W. was on his way to becoming the "class clown," the principal took a board to his behind to make his point. Mrs. Bush went to the principal to complain but upon hearing the story wound up agreeing with him.[58] This was the first but, as already noted, not the only instance of Mrs. Bush not backing her son.

One of the antidotes to unexpected and traumatic events is routine. George W. is famous for his daily routine, from his limited and repeated favorite foods (peanut butter and jelly on the campaign trail), to his exercise regime, to his famous demand for punctuality, and even to taking his own pillow with him as he travels. One reporter following George W. on the campaign trail noted the behavior and realized its deeper implications: "his almost obsessive adherence to the daily campaign schedule that had been laid out and his famous punctuality were not only about politeness, they reflected a desire to make his world as predictable—and manageable—as possible."[59]

Yet his behavior as president raises the question of how someone who likes routine became a president willing to take so many large policy risks. The answer is that while routine is a not unusual antidote to the unexpected, the deeper lesson George W. seems to have learned was: Make the most of every moment, because you never know.

Discipline and Will

Beneath the surface image of George W.'s persona as scamp and imp lies a strong will and capacity for substantial discipline and focus. You just have to know where to look. We can start with baseball.

Mr. Bush had a childhood love of baseball. He wanted to be like his childhood baseball idol, Willie Mays,[60] perhaps influenced by his father's success in the sport. But he wasn't talented like his father, and so his interest was displaced into a fascination with baseball statistics.[61]

That "skill" carried over to Bush's ability to remember people's names, an important component in making them feel comfortable. At Andover Academy he was always remembering people's names, birthdays, habits, parents, brothers, and sisters. . . . At Yale he memorized everyone's name the instant he met them and it pleased them that he did. It was something he did even better than his father and grandfather. *Ten, twenty, hundreds of names,* he could recite them all, total recall, minutes after meeting them.[62]

The discipline of recalling statistics is one thing; that of learning successfully how to fly a jet quite another.[63] While a member of the Texas Air National Guard George W. qualified to fly the F-102 fighter solo. George W. excelled at it and loved it. In George W.'s otherwise dutiful campaign autobiography, his excitement at being a pilot is the only part that literally leaps off the pages.[64]

Learning to fly a jet is complex and demanding, both physically and mentally. It involves considerable mastery of written material and the application of theory to practice; flight itself requires rapid-fire decisions and there is little margin for error. As Bush notes, "cockpits of jets are tiny and close, and they force you to learn economy of motion. They also force you to master yourself, mentally, physically, and emotionally. You have to stay calm and think logically. One mistake and you could end up in a very expensive metal coffin."[65]

In his autobiography, George W. recalls flying and executing a turn that the flight manual said should be a 20-degree bank, followed by a level 90-degree turn. However, "I banked at 18 . . . not level and the degree of my turn was closer to 100 rather than 90. I'll never forget the instructor's harsh admonishment: 'In the Air Force when we say twenty, we don't mean eighteen. And level is level, and anything else is sloppy.'"[66]

George W.'s military service also revealed another trait that was central to his psychological development and to his later success as governor and president. Those who worked with him at the time saw him as a natural leader. Military records released in response to Democratic allegations that Mr. Bush was AWOL from his guard service included his personal evaluations. His commanding officer at the time, Texas Air National Guard Lt. Col. Jerry B. Killian wrote, in his 1970 evaluation of Mr. Bush, then 24, that "He is a natural leader whom his contemporaries look to for leadership. Lt. Bush is also a good follower with outstanding disciplinary traits and an impeccable military bearing."[67]

George W's discipline was also evident in 1977, at the age 31, when Bush announced that he was a candidate for Congress. He worked hard to win. Bush "campaigned harder than anyone expected, impressing even Reese [his opponent] with his tirelessness."[68] He "knocked on more than 60 doors a day in the windswept district, flat and treeless as far as the eye could see. He would often start his week in Midland, drive the 20 miles to Odessa, and then hit the 115-

mile stretch north to the farms of Lubbock, rolling into every strip mall along the way. The way he focused on what he had to do was 'Extraordinary,' Reese recalled. 'He didn't relax. He worked all the time.'"[69]

Finally, there is George W.'s discipline and dedication to running. He is not a jogger who runs to get a little exercise; rather, he is a *runner* who sets a fast pace, keeps track of time, and tries to extend his endurance and capacity. He has been doing this for decades. He ran with hangovers. He ran when things were going well, and he was especially likely to run when things weren't.[70] That pattern of increasing his training during times of stress continued in the White House. Reflecting on his running times during the Iraq war, he said, "*It's interesting that my times have become faster right after the war began.* They were pretty fast all along, but since the war began, *I have been running with a little more intensity.*"[71]

As Bush put it in an interview in *Runner's World,* "Running does a lot of important things for me . . . it keeps me disciplined. . . . For me, the psychological benefit is enormous. You tend to forget everything's that going on in your mind and just concentrate on the time, distance or the sweat. . . . It helps me to clear my mind. . . ."[72]

Barbara Bush adds one more illustration of her son's growing discipline— Harvard Business School. She has said, "Harvard was a great turning point for him. I don't think he'd say that as much as I would, I think he learned, what is that word? Structure."[73] Harvard was a rigorous discipline for its students.[74] So it does say something about George W.'s capacity for discipline and focus that he did make the grade there. Harvard also revealed something else about George W.—a growing streak of independence.

HIS OWN DECISIONS

Andover Prep School, Yale, becoming a pilot, and then going to Texas to seek his fortune and independence. In each case George W. followed in the footsteps of his father, and ended up in his shadow. But George W. was to make two decisions that showed his increasing independence and would be crucial to his subsequent development. The first was to choose to go to Harvard Business School; the second was to marry Laura Welch.

Harvard Business School

George W. had applied to the University of Texas Law School in 1970 at the age of 24 but had been rejected, notwithstanding his family connections. He then applied to Harvard two years later, on his own "without telling anyone in his family."[75] He also didn't tell his parents he had been accepted, at first. When his brother Jeb revealed this fact and added that George W. didn't know if he would go, "the family was stunned." When George W.'s father said he should really think seriously about the opportunity, his son replied, "Oh, I'm going. I just wanted to let you know I could get into it."[76]

His comment to his parents is revealing. It suggests some sense on his part that he still had to prove himself to his parents as well as to himself. It was, after all, his younger brother Jeb who was supposed to be the political star. George W. said so himself: "He was the brother who was supposed to have won in 1994, the Bush brother given the better shot at defeating Florida governor Lawton Childs than I had to upset popular incumbent Ann Richards. But it had not worked out that way."[77]

The decision to apply to Harvard on his own suggested that George W. was beginning to set his own course and wanted to be judged on his own merits or potential, rather than in connection to his father. Perhaps he did not tell his parents of his application because he did not want to risk another public setback. Yet even if such were the case, he showed perseverance, in addition to independence, by applying. His ambition, channeled in more conventional paths, seemed to be asserting itself.

Laura Welch—An Anchoring Partner

George W.'s marriage to Laura Welch was a key emotional and structural development for him. They married three months after they met, on November 5, 1977. George W. was 31 years old. Interestingly, as was the case with his Harvard Business School application, George W. surprised his family with news that he had asked Laura to marry him. Barbara Bush later said, "We didn't even know he wanted to get married until he showed up at the door with this beautiful creature, Laura, and announced that she was going to be his wife."[78] It is unclear whether his mother is observing or complaining, or perhaps both. What is clear is that George W. was very close to his family, but he was also learning to stand apart from them.

One could not think of two more complementary psychologies than George W. Bush and Laura Welch. She was quiet; he was not. He loved to talk; she didn't. He had restless, unfocused energy that had yet to find its place; she had channeled hers into a life's pursuit. She preferred quiet things; he had trouble being quiet.

This young man full of energy and quirks must have also been very attractive to someone who led a conventional and somewhat staid life and had chosen a profession, teacher and librarian, that reflected those traits. In one interview she said, understatedly, "He's brought a lot of excitement to my life."[79] In an-

other interview, she called him "incorrigible," referring to his irrepressible impish nature, a characterization she made in an affectionate tone.[80]

Her husband's view of each of their psychologies is worth spending a moment on for what it reveals about them both:

> Laura is calm. I am energetic. She is restful; I am restless. She is patient; I am
> impatient. . . . Laura is naturally reserved, I am outgoing. . . . she is totally at
> ease, comfortable and natural, just calm . . . I, on the other hand, am in perpet-
> ual motion. I provoke people, confront them in a teasing way. I pick at a prob-
> lem, drawing it to the surface. She is kinder, much more measured, arriving at a
> conclusion carefully, yet certainly.[81]

Mr. Bush's comments, before the 2000 presidential campaign, reflect an interesting and fairly accurate assessment of himself. It suggests the ability to see
himself clearly, and for that matter at least one other person as well. Beneath the
differences between the two, however, lay an important foundation of comple-
mentarity. George W. needed someone to help him focus and channel his kinetic
energy. Her calm and calming presence provided that. She was instrumental
emotionally for Mr. Bush as he went through 9/11 and its aftermath,[82] and she
remains a fulcrum of his emotional life.

George W. frequently repeats in his many speeches that marrying Laura was
the best decision of his life. Inevitably, he follows that up by saying that he was not
sure the same could be said of hers. It invariably brings a laugh from his audience.
But there was something very serious here. His choice showed trust in his judgment of others, in himself and his choices. Certainly, considering his psychology,
he chose well. It seems clear that he chose to marry a woman whose psychology
and traits resembled those of his father, not his mother. Laura Bush has said that,
"In general, I don't give George advice."[83] Of course, his mother did.

As Bruni put it, his choice, "illustrated a key ingredient of George W.
Bush's luck, good instincts or talent: he chose people to accompany him through
life and career who invariably made him better and set him straight."[84] One need
only add to this observation that he was the kind of person who attracted them.

A First Political Run

Frank Bruni writes of George W. that "Few had entered the White House with
such a brief career in public service, such a late blooming interest in the position,
such a spotty body of knowledge, and such hurried preparation, in as much as
there could ever be any."[85] If by public service one means elected or appointed
positions, that point is correct. Yet, in reality, George W. has spent an adult lifetime immersed in politics.[86]

The long history of his involvement with politics began around the family dinner table throughout his childhood and young adulthood. Politics was like oxygen at the Bush family compound, a part of the environment, and there can be little doubt that George W., having grown up with a distant but idealized father, saw it as his future too.

George W.'s formal introduction to politics came early, in the summer of 1964 between high school graduation and Yale, when he accompanied his father on campaign trips in Texas.[87] Later, at 25, George W. considered but decided against a run for the Texas state legislature.[88] At the age of 32, he announced for Congress. Between that time and when he decided to run for governor of Texas, he repeatedly was involved in political campaigns, whether for his father or other politicians, in Texas or in other states. He clearly watched closely and drew lessons, not least from his own defeat and those of his father.

Father and son spanned more than generations. Their political careers overlapped with profound changes in the nature of American politics. The traditional Bush political ethos was service. One served not because one could, but because one should. Yet America was changing. The era of gentlemanly campaigning, if it ever existed, was passing. Television, negative advertising, and opposition research all made campaigns increasingly about image rather than issues and the traditional virtues of character.

As Hugh Heclo points out, for George W. there was a tension between "the new professional smash mouth version of [politics] that he had learned the hard way in the last half of the twentieth century and the patrician responsibility version that he had inherited more naturally from the older legacy of his family."[89] His father's defeat in 1992 drove the message home, for George H. W. Bush was a man of considerable achievement, substantial service, and irreproachable personal character. But he lost to Bill Clinton, an impressive politician to be sure, but one with limited experience who appeared driven more by personal ambition than public commitment, and whose character was tarnished at best.

That it took George W. some time to become fully ready for the political big time was evident after his 1977 run for Congress, in which he lost to Kent Hance. Consistent with George W.'s partying reputation, during the campaign a Bush staffer placed an add in a Texas Tech University newspaper offering free beer at a "Bush Bash." As Bush's biographer writes, "Hance's people picked up on the possibilities right away; it was no secret in Midland that Bush enjoyed drinking. He had once gotten up on stage with Willie Nelson."[90] Five days before the election, a Hance supporter sent out a letter to 4,000 members of the Church of Christ denouncing Bush for having a "free beer" event for college students.[91] Bush lost the campaign handily. It is hard to believe that the use of his drinking against him could not have failed to make an impression as

Bush considered his future, both personal and political, in the decade between age 30 and 40.

DRINKING AND SELF-REDEMPTION: THE FIRST TRANSFORMATION

If discipline and will is one side of George W.'s psychology, so too has been a lack of control. Perhaps nowhere was this more apparent than in his drinking problem and his behavior while under the influence. That Bush had a drinking problem is clear from his own testimony. Talking to recovering addicts in the 2000 presidential campaign, he said, "I'm just like you" and that "I used to drink too much."[92]

In September 2002, he also told a reporter on one of the campaign flights "You should have seen me twenty years ago, I would have been betting and drinking all at the same time." He recalled "drinking too much at Yale" and said that alcohol "competes with your affections, with your family," an indication that his drinking did both.[93] From a politician running for the highest office in the land, where any public doubts as to his capabilities could result in losing the election, such openness is rather surprising. It likely indicated an unusual level of self-confidence and self-acceptance, both hard won.

When George W. had a "few too many," to use his phrase, he became somewhat loud and occasionally belligerent. The *New York Times* reported that Mr. Bush once approached an older, well-dressed friend of his parents when he had had "one too many" and asked, "So, what's sex like after fifty, anyway?"[94] There is the famous story of his chance encounter with Al Hunt of the *Wall Street Journal,* who had just written that George W.'s father would most likely not get the GOP presidential nomination he sought. He approached Hunt, who was sitting with his family at a restaurant, and yelled at him, "you f*cking son of a bitch . . . I won't forget what you said and you're going to pay a f*cking price for it." Mr. Hunt was seated with his wife and four-year-old child.[95] Such instances are classic indications of an alcohol problem, combining a loss of inhibitions and poor judgment.

In his autobiography, Bush said that, "Drinking also magnified elements of my personality that probably don't need to be any larger than they already are—made me more funny, more charming (I thought)."[96] This is, of course, another classic formulation of those with an alcohol problem. Not surprisingly, what Mr. Bush took to be an outsized extension of his charm was "according to my wife somewhat boring and repetitive."[97]

Clearly, drinking too much released some repressed anger. This raises the question: What was Mr. Bush angry about? My view is he felt thwarted. He was a man who had begun life with many advantages that he had failed to capitalize on, often through no particular fault of his own. He had followed in his father's footsteps, though hardly filling them. His drinking and boisterousness were a method of self-medication. His antics were a continuation of what had been in his adolescence and very young adulthood a successful basis for finding his place in the world. The problem was that at this stage they were not wholly suitable for the adult world.

If George W.'s problem drinking draws attention to some of the more negative aspects of his personality, his overcoming the problem demonstrates some of the more positive aspects. For defeating the bottle was one of the most important transformations in George W.'s life.

The turning point came, in George W.'s telling,[98] in 1986 on his fortieth birthday, when he, Laura, and a group of friends went to the Broadmoor Hotel in Colorado to celebrate. He awoke the next morning, as he did often back then, with a substantial hangover. He got out of bed and went for his usual run, as he had almost every day for the last 14 years. However, "This run was different. I felt worse than usual and about halfway through I decided that I would drink no more. I came back to the hotel room and told Laura I was through. I've quit drinking."[99]

A number of reasons have been put forward for Mr. Bush's decision to stop drinking. Some attribute his decision to his father's launching of his presidential campaign and his son's worry that it might cause his father problems.[100] While this is touching, it is unlikely given that George W.'s problem drinking had begun at Yale and was not unknown, yet had not damaged his father's professional or political career. By that time his father had been vice president for six years, had served as head of the CIA, and had been ambassador to China and the United Nations. If George W. was worried about embarrassing his father, he had already spent many years running such a risk. Moreover, family friends report that George W.'s father had in the past asked him directly to stop drinking and spend more time taking care of his future.[101] It did not have the desired effect.

Laura Bush also is credited by some with helping her husband stop drinking, and she did try, several times.[102] Yet by her own admission, she was unsuccessful.[103] She has recalled that

> he had been working toward it for a long time. I think for a year at least he'd been thinking, "I really need to slow down or quit." Most people who try to quit drinking first think, "Well, I'm just going to only have one drink." And I think in his mind he thought, "Well, that's what I'll do." And then, of course, it didn't really work. Like for everybody, just about, who tries, it doesn't really work.[104]

Mr. Bush has given major credit for his turn away from drinking to his personal religious salvation helped in part by conversations with the Reverend Billy Graham the year before he decided to quit.[105]

What is clear is that Bush recognized that he had a problem, that it was adversely affecting his life and his relationships, including those with his father and, perhaps of greater importance, his wife. Drinking was a form of self-medication, dulling the senses and the pain he felt at not living up to the example of his father. Alcohol proved a poor substitute for the success he wanted and needed.

Whatever help others may have provided him and however long George W. may have been considering giving up drink, that he apparently came to a quasi-spontaneous decision and then stuck with it says a number of things. One is that he showed the capability to recognize his condition and the decisiveness to do something about it. The decision came at what might otherwise be considered a nadir in his life, as Spectrum 7, his scrappy but hard-pressed entry in the oil sweepstakes, was a short distance from being foreclosed on by the banks—only to be rescued by a merger with Harken Oil. Bush had been active and instrumental in finding a larger company to save his, and perhaps this is the basis for his bragging (with little reason) that the Harken deal showed his business prowess. The reality was that it was just one more lack of success.[106]

Bush had worked hard to make Spectrum 7 a success, but the oil market was collapsing. His search for a "liberator" had again come up dry; he could have hit rock bottom. But he confounded expectations. A weaker man, facing another defeat, might have thrown in the towel and drowned in the bottle. Instead he went dry, cold turkey. Put simply, given the circumstances this indicates enormous self-discipline and will.

Of all the explanations that have been put forward to account for George W.'s turn away from drinking, one is conspicuously absent. That is, George W. Bush, himself. Whatever role God,[107] or at least Bush's faith in God, may have played in his decision to stop drinking and his ability to stick to that decision, what is important is that Bush found faith in himself and in his own inner strength. Or, to put it another way, God provided an explanation; George W. provided the motivation. In the end, George W. Bush decided to stop drinking.

If there ever was a "mid-life crisis" this was surely it. The common conception of this overused term is of a middle-aged man wearing an earring, buying a sports car, and chasing young women. While this image is somewhat overdrawn and much overused, the phenomenon of reaching a point in life where the conventional becomes tiresome and change necessary is real, and when it occurs it reflects something psychologically profound and potentially transforming. For George W. the change in course was the opposite of the pony-tailed, middle-aged hipster who rebels against the straightjacket of success, for he had little success to rebel against. Rather, his rebellion was against failure.

Dorothy Bush Koch, George W.'s younger sister, provides a profound insight into what he had achieved: "It was a transformation . . . not an overnight transformation, but it was when he found happiness in his life and himself—we knew it right away. You could see a confidence. He's always had that bravado, but [this was] real confidence."[108] This is an important distinction.

In a very real sense, then, on his fortieth birthday, and in spite of another business setback, George W. had made important strides toward becoming an adult. The psychologist Daniel Levinson[109] says that one of the chief tasks of adulthood is to build a life structure that reflects and satisfies a person's needs. Freud thought the two pillars of a well-realized life were love and work. The first reflects emotional relationships that allow intimacy and partnership. With a loving, supportive, patient and level-headed wife, George W. had achieved one important adult success. The second, work, can be understood as a place in which one's ambitions and skills can be realized and validated by others who matter. Here he had a problem. And, if we add a third element, a life structure in which a person can realize their basic ideals and values, it is clear that George W. still had work to do.

George W. had always wanted to succeed on his own and on his own terms. In trying to do so, he was both blessed and in some ways cursed by the Bush family name, especially his father's. It opened doors and several times helped rescue him, but it did so at a price. As long as he relied on it, he would not be able to "find himself." At forty he had very little that he could point to that was truly his, of his own making.

THE FIRST TRANSFORMATION
OF GEORGE W. BUSH

We often think of the term "transformation" as reflecting a dramatic difference, a before-after sequence in which observable consequences are clear even if the causes of the change are not. Such transformations do, of course, occur, but they don't really describe George W.'s transformation. Bush's transformation entailed a reordering of various elements. The same elements that were present during Bush's years of difficulty, when rearranged or changed in emphasis and added to a new and better fitting set of circumstances, contributed to his subsequent successes. Bush's behavior changed, but his success could only have been achieved by his drawing on personal strengths that had long existed, even if they were not always apparent or in the forefront.

His transformation developed over a long period with many detours. He had worked hard, but unsuccessfully. From his days at Andover forward he was at the center of things and popular, without having excelled at any particular activity. The irreverent, wisecracking adolescent in turn became the president of the

DEKE fraternity and had a social life at Yale that, according to friends, rivaled the John Belushi character in the movie *Animal House*.[110] He arrived and went through Harvard Business School wearing his flight jacket and rumpled shirts, an iconoclast and clear dissenter from the conventional attire of his classmates. George W. was a part of the institutions he attended, yet in many ways he stood apart. That persona reflected well Bush's basic stance toward people and things; engaging but selectively engaged.

That stance provided another benefit as well. It provided George W. with a role, that of the cool insider/outsider, while he was engaged in the process of trying to figure just where he fit in the world. He was not an athlete. He was not an intellectual. He liked taking risks and flying planes, but that did not seem to immediately translate into anything career-specific. He was smart and hardworking when he was interested in something, but the very large question remained: What was he good at that would provide a life's work?

Figuring out where one fits in the world is one of the most important steps in successful adulthood; it is the turning point in one's maturation process. Up until his early forties, Mr. Bush had not found the answer to that question and time was passing. It was one thing to be an ambitious and promising member of a distinguished family in early adulthood. It was quite another at forty.

But his development had provided him with elements for success once he had gained inner confidence through finding himself, whether or not through God. He was good with people. He mastered what he set his mind to master, but he still hadn't found an occupational match. That focus could only come when he learned how to master himself. Bush discovered within himself a capacity for self-discipline that often stood at odds with his lack of discipline elsewhere. Laura Bush had an interesting insight when she said that she believed her husband always had discipline—he just didn't know it until he quit drinking.[111] His running regime, whatever his physical circumstances, his pavement-pounding work for a congressional seat, his mastery of flying jet planes, his Harvard experience, and finally overcoming his own drinking problem were all steps along the way to finding his own inner strength and his realization that it was his to use.

CONSOLIDATING A TRANSFORMATION

Mr. Bush had learned that he could rely on himself to overcome his most self-destructive tendencies. He had not become a new man, but rather a different one. He was able to be self-reliant because he had found he had qualities he could rely on. His strengths became more evident even if they had not yet found a focus and a match. That missing piece of the Bush life puzzle soon presented itself.

Baseball

Just one year after he stopped drinking, Bush was offered an opportunity to help develop a partnership in a baseball team—the Texas Rangers.[112] This time, unlike so many others, George W. successfully leveraged this opportunity into something more important than a job—a foothold in the adult world and an opportunity to earn, due to his own skills and developing capacities, a larger place in it. It provided an opportunity to match his talents and interests to a set of occupational ambitions and responsibilities that had been eluding him his whole adult life. He had found a place.

When George W. is asked to cite the career accomplishments of which he is most proud, they begin at the age of 42, when he played a lead role in developing an investment group that bought the Texas Rangers.[113] This was a complicated financial and personal transaction that required all the focus and persistence that George W. could muster. Partners—*Texas* partners—had to be found for the venture. Owners of the major league teams had to approve, and the commissioner of baseball had to make several important rulings.

While there is debate as to whether Bush is due all the credit he has claimed for putting the deal together, what is clear from the record is that George W. was in the thick of those fast-changing, strategic calculations and negotiations, and that he helped to pull it off.[114] He has himself said, "I pursued the purchase like a pit bull on the pant leg of opportunity."[115] He pursued that deal with the same tenacity and determination that he used to master jet planes, run for Congress, and pursue the oil liberator. Only this time was different—he succeeded. Bush's dogged determination to keep trying even after repeated setbacks finally paid off.

Bush's ownership role gave him a recognized venue, one that he had loved since childhood, and a place where his skills could be successfully engaged. George W. loved baseball, and it showed. He attended every home game, sitting in the box seats and not the owner's box, trading repartee with the players and with the fans from behind the plate, handing out autographed baseball cards with his picture on it, and thoroughly enjoying himself. He quickly became the public face of the Texas Rangers. Behind the scenes, George W. became involved in league politics, formulating plans for the public financing of a new stadium and helping to manage the Texas Rangers organization.[116] He broadened the team's appeal by initiating Spanish-language broadcasts, an early harbinger of his political outreach to this important group.

Ronald Betts, longtime friend and son of a man who had befriended young George W. as a child, said, "Before the Rangers, I told him he needed to do something to step out of his father's shadow. . . . Baseball was it."[117] George W.

was finally starting to achieve at 42 what had escaped him for so long. He was on the road to becoming his own man.

His success at the Texas Rangers also had another life-altering effect. When Bush was considering whether or not to run for governor in 1970, he sent a veteran Texas political operator around the state to see what people thought of his running. She reported back that "everyone likes you, but you haven't done anything. You need to go out in the world and do something, the way your father did when he left Connecticut and the protection of his family. You just haven't done shit. You're a Bush and that's all."[118] As Bush himself later noted, his involvement with the Rangers was a springboard to political involvement, for "it solved my biggest political problem in Texas. There's no question about it and I knew it all along. My problem was 'What's the boy ever done?'"[119]

Eventually, on selling his Texas Rangers shares, George W. became a millionaire, a status that had escaped him in decades of hard work in the Midland, Texas, oil fields. This was critical. Mr. Bush had found and, more importantly, earned, his liberator. It came not in an oil gusher, but in a childhood passion. And, critically, it also provided a springboard for a long-sought political career.

When his father lost his bid for reelection in 1992, George W. experienced a second liberation. Laura Bush has said that after their father's defeat, "George and Jeb were freed, for the first time in their lives, to say what they thought about issues."[120] George W. himself later recalled, "I knew that any political future I might have would be very difficult as long as my father was president."[121] But it was more than that. George H. W. Bush had reached the pinnacle, to be sure, but he then had been *rejected* by the American people and *beaten* by a man the Bushes felt unworthy, psychologically and morally, of the office of president of the United States. More than that: his father was no longer on the playing field. George H. W. Bush had experienced defeats in the past, but there was always the possibility of his achieving more. Now his father was an elder statesman with a limited place on the public stage. With his father no longer the standard bearer, the "beacon," George W. no longer had to directly compete. He could, finally, enter into politics as his own man.

Governor Bush

George W.'s first play for the political big leagues was to campaign in 1994 for the governorship of Texas. Yes, he had the Bush name. But Ann Richards was a popular and savvy incumbent. She was, in the words of one observer, "the most famous governor in America, an organic force with high steely Republican-style hair, a Texas-to-the-highest-power sense of what was truly droll, and a huge approval rating."[122] The Bush name may have helped George W. get on the playing field, but he was strickly on his own, against a very formidable opponent.

That election showcased George W.'s substantial political talents and strategies, although some of it wasn't evident until he became president. In a preview of the strategy that got him the presidential nomination, George W. first orchestrated the removal of all his potential Republican opponents. He did it quickly with a series of rapid behind-the-scenes maneuvers. It all happened so fast that local politicos said admiringly, it was "the only one-day gubernatorial primary in Texas history."[123] It was over before most people realized it was happening.

His campaign style emphasized a tight-knit advisory group and, above all, message consistency and discipline. He also applied the lessons of his father's mistakes, remarking, "My father let Bill Clinton decide what issues the two of them were going to talk about, and I wasn't going to let that happen to me."[124] He didn't.

Ann Richards relied on her popularity, her incumbency, and George W.'s famous temper. All three failed her. She called him an elitist and a "shrub." She seemed to believe that she was better than her opponent, and seemed to consider it an insult that she had to campaign against him. At a rally in Texarkana, she told a group of teachers, "You just work like a dog, you do well . . . *and all of a sudden you've got some jerk who's running for public office* telling everybody it's all a sham."[125] George W. didn't take the bait.

Bush's solid win over the popular incumbent Ann Richards fueled his reputation in some watchful circles as a "giant killer." He proved to be a successful and popular governor and his landslide reelection confirmed that he really did have substantial political skills and talents. His political success was no fluke.

Finally, in late mid-adulthood, Mr. Bush had established himself as his own man—and it might be added, a man to be reckoned with. In both business and politics he had leveraged the lessons of his self-transformation. His success in both places relied on the qualities that had been the basis of his salvation and personal transformation: focus, will power, perseverance, and resilience.

What he did for himself would become his model for dealing with his country and the world.

SECTION III

GEORGE W. BUSH: CHARACTER AND PSYCHOLOGY

CHAPTER 3

THE PRESIDENT'S CHARACTER

CHARACTER COUNTS. We know that in our everyday dealings with people—evaluating them, making judgments, choosing to trust some more than others. And it counts enormously in the evaluation of those who seek to be president.

"Character issues," the term that is ordinarily used to describe this debate, occupies a twilight zone between psychology and partisan politics. To the public, character is generally equated with the perception of honesty and integrity in a leader. It reflects the view that the president ought to be, to a great degree, who he presents himself to be.

Presidents and their critics generally subscribe to this view, with one major difference. A president wishes to display his character. Critics want to denounce it. Presidents and their allies therefore are often engaged in a full-scale effort to make sure a leader is presented in ways consistent with how he would like to be seen, and no doubt thinks that he is. Critics, on the other hand, have strong incentives to question not only the president's policies, but also the person behind them.

Most reporters are often ill-equipped to help the public sort through competing portrayals, on the one side harsh accusations and on the other fulsome praises. Worse, the amount of independent-minded reporting is rather small. Many reporters follow the prevailing news story lines, lemming-like, and are often vulnerable to and dependent on their sources. This fact is an obvious occupational hazard, but one that is rarely acknowledged or, more important, offset by true balance, objectivity, and a sense of inquiry. This being the case, the public is left to shift through the confusing welter of charges, countercharges, and pundit spin with little to guide them but their own good sense. Like other qualities in life, this one too is not evenly distributed.

CHARACTER IN THE WHITE HOUSE: WHY IT MATTERS, WHAT IT IS

Any discussion of presidential character has to start with the recognition that presidents are limited by law, precedent, public sentiment, and competing institutional centers of public authority. Furthermore, no president fully controls his own, or our, destiny. Yet, between constraint and fate lies the vast arena of presidential discretion.

The president's discretion lies in what he chooses to do or not do, in how he pursues his public and political ambitions, and the values and views that shape his policy decisions. The president's discretionary choices are enlarged by the office's immense authority. This authority is in turn amplified by the world's most powerful, sophisticated, and far-reaching instruments for implementing the president's will. All that power is set into motion by one force and one force only—the president himself; his ambitions, his degree of commitment to the values he espouses, his patterns of dealing with people, and his judgment. It is true that "the president is not the presidency." [1] However, the presidency is clearly an office in which its occupant's psychology counts.

Character can best be thought of as an individual's core psychology: It is the set of values, behaviors, and perspectives that show continuity over time and across situations. It is the patterns of choice and response across time and circumstances. This does not mean robotic consistency. Presidents have gotten to where they are by showing some degree of adaptation to the changing circumstances they encounter. A president's character reflects his basic psychological core, the bedrock of his motives, the ultimate source of the values he lives by (if he does), and, in the recesses of his mind, how he really feels about others—those who support or oppose him, those who can help or hurt him, and above all those who, like the American people, depend on him.

CHARACTER'S CORE

Character has three fundamental domains: ambition; character integrity; and relatedness, or a person's basic stance toward other people.[2]

Ambition defines what you want, whether you pursue it, and how you go about it. Simply put, it points to a president's level of desire to achieve his purposes, and the skills that he brings to bear on accomplishing them. While ambition has acquired an unsavory reputation, in and out of politics, it is absolutely necessary for consolidating an adequately functioning character structure. As the prominent psychoanalyst Heinz Kohut reminds us, ambition is the brother of what he calls "healthy narcissism."[3] Self-regard and self-interest are crucial, along with ideals and talent, to achieving an individual's goals. And achieving goals is one foundation of a well-realized life. Without ambition there is no achievement and without achievement there is little basis for consolidated self-regard.

Ambition does not develop in a vacuum. Its origins lie in family experience, while its realization is developed in life experience. Ambition alone is like an engine without a car. It can rev up dramatically, but rarely gets anywhere by itself. Ambition needs skills to reach fruition, and this is no less true for presidents than it is for ordinary people.

Character integrity reflects a person's fidelity to their ideals as they pursue their ambitions and forge an identity. Politically, it is reflected not so much in where a president stands on a particular policy, but rather what he ultimately stands for. It is not only about his stated political goals, but *how* he chooses to accomplish them. Character integrity does not guarantee that a president will not make costly political and policy mistakes, but its absence almost certainly guarantees that he will, especially in a political climate of public skepticism about government and leaders.

Ultimately, character integrity reflects a president's ability to maintain boundaries, the lines he draws and maintains regarding his ethics, his treatment of others, and the political positions he favors. Whether a president has a commitment to his ideals and values is an important psychological and political characteristic. Someone without integrity is likely to tack with the political wind—in everyday life, they are the feckless and the fair-weather friends. In political life, too, they are untrustworthy. Those with integrity believe that their values are important, worth fighting for, and worth enduring loss to maintain.

Relatedness refers to a person's basic stance toward others. The president's relationships with others can be seen as a series of external concentric circles. At the center is the president, in the first outer ring are his most intimate and trusted advisors, and so on.

Events, experiences, and especially people who have special emotional valence for the president are part of his internal psychological world. In clinical theory, the study of these internal images, how they got there, and what they mean is the study of "object relations." Among the important dimensions of this internal world of objects is whether a particular internal object is "good"—that is, whether it provides available memories, images, and feelings of warmth, support, firm and loving care, and so forth—or "bad." A person can rigidly categorize particular objects on either basis or see the object as having qualities of both.

In looking at the interior relational psychology of a president, we are dealing with a series of concentric circles measured by a proximity-distance radius, with the important difference that they are *internal* rather than *external* and organized according to their psychological meaning and significance to the president. In George W.'s inner psychological world, it is quite clear his father, for example, looms large as an idealized object (person). Others also have their place in the president's interior world. Some are "good objects," like his wife. Others are hated "bad objects," like Saddam Hussein or Osama bin Laden. Still others occupy an internal emotional space in between.

The nature and function of a president's internal world of "object relations" shape the external world of presidential relationships. The president is immersed in a sea of interpersonal relationships with his advisors, allies, opponents, and others. The presidency is as much a matter of dealing with people as of policy.

Each of these three character elements—ambition, character integrity, and relatedness—influences the twin pillars of presidential performance: leadership and judgment. Presidential leadership involves the president's attempts to *mobilize, orchestrate,* and *consolidate* activity in the pursuit of presidential goals. The quality and effectiveness of presidential leadership has as much or more to do with a president's candor and trustworthiness with others, and above all the public, as it does with actual policies.

Presidential judgment is, at its core, a president's ability to match solutions to circumstances. First, judgment requires that he see a problem clearly for what it is and then devise a fitting solution. Good judgment doesn't guarantee policy success, but it certainly raises the odds.

GEORGE W. BUSH'S AMBITION

Some people begin their presidential dreams in their youth. Others come to them later in life. There is an important distinction between personal and political ambition: the two are not necessarily synonymous, but they can become intertwined and even fused in some cases. It is also useful to further distinguish broad political ambitions from specific policy ambitions.

Ambitions can take a number of developmental paths. Strong ambitions can develop early and successfully focus a person's whole life. Ambitions can begin large and falter. Or, they can start small and develop. Or, they can be sidetracked and slow to reach fruition. This last path seems to have been George W. Bush's.

Generally, the earlier presidential ambition burns the more intensely it develops. The more intensely it develops, the more difficult it is to separate the fused nature of personal and political ambition. The two become inseparable with the result that for some it is political success, and that only, that provides the validation for self-regard and feelings of personal satisfaction. In those circumstances, public interest runs the danger of being in the service of personal interests.

Some presidents begin their assent, motivationally, in their teens. Lyndon Johnson, Woodrow Wilson, and Bill Clinton illustrate this path. Ambition burned furiously and early in all those cases. Some presidents, exposed early to the "family business" of politics, are expected eventually to make their contribution. John F. Kennedy, after the death of his brother Joe, and George Herbert Walker Bush come readily to mind. Some in the family business, like Al Gore, have a highly charged ambition ingrained by their parents since childhood. Others like George Herbert Walker Bush have ambition aplenty, but fused with an ethic that emphasizes service. And others, like Dwight Eisenhower and Harry Truman, come to their presidential interests later in life.

George W.'s presidential ambitions developed late in life. He himself has said of them, "I didn't wake up when I was 15 years old saying, 'I really want to be president.' I didn't feel that way at 21, 31, 41. I didn't run for governor to position myself to be president. I ran for governor to be the governor of the state I love."[4]

Yet it is also true that politics and service are part of the Bush family ethos. In that family, politics was like the air we breathe; it simply was taken for granted. George W. was introduced to politics at an early age and considered it as a profession. Recall that he considered a run for the Texas legislature when he was 25.

George W.'s political ambitions were part "family business" and part identification with his father. But he was not consumed with political ambition. Had he been burning with political ambition, he could have easily landed a high-level spot in his father's administration. For a son searching for ways to become his own man, this was not an attractive choice. So he returned to Midland, Texas, to seek his fortune. If he was consumed with anything, it was finding his place in the business world and adult life more generally. George W.'s chief ambition was to make good.

Understanding President Bush's Ambitions

It's hard to measure the scope of any president's ambitions by the number of laws or executive orders he signs. Every president can now assemble a long list of such items given the activist nature of modern government.[5] Those interested in presidential ambition must look elsewhere.

One place to look is whether presidential initiatives are incremental or transformational. The first builds in small steps on the policy frameworks bequeathed to a president. The second seeks to transform those very frameworks. George W. Bush's policy initiatives definitely mark him as a transforming president.

Sometimes strong ambitions are mismatched with incremental times. Bill Clinton had burning ambitions for large transformation projects, such as an attempt to federalize the American health care system, but that failed. Thereafter, he was forced to pursue more modest policy ambitions. Similar questions arise regarding the readiness of the American public for the transformations that Mr. Bush proposes.

George W.'s transformational aspirations do not appear to stem from an oversized personal ambition for glory or power. Rather, they seem to be tied to a profound personal and political dislike of the prevailing policy paradigms in both domestic and foreign policy. Bush is firmly convinced that the liberal paradigm has reached an impasse if not a dead end, a view doubtless fueled by his experience with the arrogance and presumption of some of those who champion it.

This view dates back at least as far as his famous college encounter with William Sloane Coffin, Jr., then Chaplin at Yale. They met just after young George W.'s father had lost a race for the Senate to liberal Democrat Ralph Yarborough. Coffin informed a young Mr. Bush that the "better man won." This was an insensitive, rude, and arrogant remark and George W. never forgot or forgave it. It was a gratuitous slight against his beloved father, but it also came to represent for George W. the presumptuousness of the liberal elite. Decades later he would recall with undiminished resentment, "What angered me was the way such people at Yale felt so intellectually superior and so righteous. They thought they had all the answers."[6] It is ironic that someone so often accused of arrogance should have his interest in transforming the liberal policy paradigm fueled in part by a real-life example of arrogance and presumption.

Bush's desire to transform the liberal paradigm was based on more than sour personal experience. It also stemmed from his conviction that the liberal paradigm of American foreign policy was inappropriate in a newly dangerous world. September 11 cemented his conviction that over reliance on multilateral agreements with no enforcement mechanisms, always accommodating allies with their own self-interest, and a reluctance to use force unless it was legitimized by the "world community" might prove suicidal.

In both domestic and foreign policy, George W. has stepped away from his father's legacy, and, in doing so, his shadow. George H. W. Bush was a moderate who lacked strong convictions about most of the domestic policies he encountered. Internationally, he subscribed to many of the tenets that his son now clearly rejects or wants to modify. In policy, leadership style, and in policy views, like father, *not* like son.

Foreign? Domestic? Both?

Most presidents have, by interest or circumstance, specialized in either domestic or foreign affairs. Of course, every president must pay some attention to both. Yet it is easy to discern where a president's focus lies. Eisenhower, Nixon, and George H. W. Bush specialized in foreign policy, and presidents Ford, Carter, and Clinton specialized in domestic policy.

Sometimes presidents are forced to spend significant time in areas in which they are, by either inclination or experience, less suited. Lyndon Johnson, master of the Senate and of domestic policy, was nonetheless forced to spend considerable time on foreign policy, at which he did not excel. George H. W. Bush preferred foreign to domestic policy at a time when the public wanted presidential attention focused on the home front.

What happens when presidents are forced to deal at length with matters they neither favor nor are well prepared for? The answer seems to be: Trouble. Lyndon Johnson spent his long Senate career mastering horse-trading, cajoling, and when all else failed, bullying people to get his political way. Given that background he could just not understand why Ho Chi Minh would not jump at the chance to compromise if given a dam for the Mekong Delta.

George H. W. Bush was masterful in mobilizing allies and the world against Saddam Hussein's 1991 invasion of Kuwait. He was much less masterful in domestic policy leadership and it cost him the presidency. Jimmy Carter gained the White House on the basis of his probity and honesty in the wake of the Watergate scandal. Yet he proved inept in both domestic and foreign policy and was not reelected.

Only two modern presidents have been able to maintain a successful dual focus on domestic and foreign policy—Franklin D. Roosevelt and Ronald Reagan. FDR did them in sequence. First, he addressed America's severe economic crisis and then he was forced to confront the gathering storm of Nazi ambitions. Ronald Reagan, on the other hand, focused on both domestic and foreign policy throughout his two terms in office. Yet he didn't face the domestic catastrophe of an economic meltdown as had FDR, nor did he have to fight a world war.

George W. Bush is a rare modern president. He seems at home both in domestic and foreign policy. In that way, his presidency is in the tradition of FDR and Ronald Reagan. Like FDR, he faces foreign policy circumstances that demand his attention. Yet unlike FDR, he faces no catastrophic domestic crisis.

What marks President Bush as truly unique among modern presidents is his desire to transform the frameworks of both American domestic *and* international policy. Only FDR transformed American domestic policy and then forced Americans to rethink their foreign policy isolation in response to Nazi ambitions. Ronald Reagan, to whom George W. is sometimes compared, also seemed equally at home in domestic and foreign policy. But while his rhetoric was transformational, his actual policies weren't. He railed against the welfare state, but didn't make it his mission to radically modify it. He did face down the Soviet Union and hasten its demise. Yet, while Reagan emphasized strength, resolve, and American self-interest, George W.'s specific policies in areas ranging from preventive war to foreign aid and efforts to change despotisms to democracy are substantially more transformational.

The Governor as President: Mistaken Parallels

One measure of a president's policy ambition is the extent and nature of his agenda. Observers looking to predict Mr. Bush's presidential ambitions naturally looked to his governorship. Did he initiate many laws? Did he build on other's accomplishments or set out in new directions? Did he fight hard for his agenda?

They saw a president "who would focus on articulating a few policies, pursuing them relentlessly."[7] After all, Mr. Bush's campaign for governor had featured four prominent themes: education, tort reform, strengthening anti-crime efforts, and welfare reform.[8] Extrapolating, they were certain that Mr. Bush would have limited presidential ambitions, work for consensus, and take few big policy risks.[9] They were dead wrong. And why they were is instructive.

Pundits forgot what should be the first two laws of punditry: Know the circumstances and know the person. The circumstances looked similar. Both the governorship and the presidency are executive positions with a legislature to deal with. But they could not be more different in practice.

The Texas governorship is a weak executive office with few of the muscular powers associated with its more powerful counterparts in other states. Moreover, the Texas legislature meets only 140 days every other year. More to the point, the powers of the Texas governorship pale in comparison to those of the presidency. Because of the enormous differences between the two positions, the governorship gave very little reliable information about a very key question. What would Mr. Bush do with these enormous presidential powers?

The second large pundit error was a familiar one when dealing with George W.—they underestimated him. They underestimated his ambition; they underestimated his focus and resolve; and they underestimated the seriousness with which he took his policy prescriptions. Far from avoiding conflict as predicted, his "right back at you" attitude embraced it.

Still, old thoughts die hard. *New York Times* reporter Adam Clymer[10] thought Bush's first address to the nation was narrow and limited. *Washington Post* columnist David Broder[11] did see a bold Bush agenda, but only because Mr. Bush proposed tax cuts while also calling for increased government spending in a range of areas like education, the military, and the environment. What they missed was that Mr. Bush's boldness was found not so much in the fact that he wanted to spend money, although this was somewhat of an innovation for a Republican president. Rather, the boldness was to be found in *what* he proposed.

President Bush announced on September 1, 2001, that his four priorities for the fall were the economy; education; his "faith-based" legislation; and security, including defense, Medicare, and Social Security.[12] In reality, this list did not add up to four. Two of these, the president's education bill and his faith-based bill, were embodied in a single bill. The other policy initiatives could only be accomplished in several other major bills. Mr. Bush's major tax cut, for example, was viewed as the first in a series of such steps. The fourth area, security, contained a number of important programmatic initiatives—among them defense strategy and reorientation. These in turn involved a number of new programs such as the missile-defense system.

Additionally, Mr. Bush wanted to revamp Social Security and Medicare, two politically sensitive and difficult undertakings. Small wonder that David Broder[13] revised his earlier assessment of the nature of the president's ambitions and asked whether Mr. Bush wasn't trying to do too much with too little (political capital). He noted the president had actually added to his "to do" list a comprehensive energy plan (itself made up of a number of far-reaching and controversial parts), an HMO reform bill, and a trade bill to give the president "fast-track" authority.[14] To this robust list he could have added many others.[15]

While many misunderstood, and some disparaged,[16] Mr. Bush's agenda, of this there could be little doubt: Far from presiding over an administration of limited policy ambitions, Mr. Bush's policy agenda was enormous, expansive, and geared toward providing examples of his new domestic policy paradigm for the public to consider. Observant reporters noted, "Any one of Bush's major campaign planks could keep a president occupied for most of his first year in office; Bush seems determined to try to do them all at once." [17] Indeed, it was precisely this fact that led his critics to complain that Bush led as if he had a mandate.

Critics expected, and then demanded, a scaled-back agenda or one that was consistent with *their* views. Mr. Bush did neither, and that decision reflected another important element of his psychology. Mr. Bush is a president who is comfortable taking controversial stands and sticking with them.

Yet there is more to this aspect of his psychology than taking a position and sticking to it. He is able to do so through sometimes severe storms of public anxiety and critics' cries to change course. Despite mounting American casualities in Iraq, a devastating abuse scandal with prison guards, and demands for the resignation of his Secretary of Defense, Mr. Bush sails ahead neither deflected nor deterred. Odysseus lashed himself to his ship's mast to keep from being lured and destroyed by the sirens' call. Mr. Bush's focus and resolve are his psychological tools to keep from being blown off course by the storms through which he must sail the ship of state.

THE PRESIDENT AND CHARACTER INTEGRITY

Character integrity lies at the core of presidential performance. A critical leadership tool, character integrity is built on the foundation of ideals and values. Yet it is not enough for a president to have convictions; he must also have the courage to follow them. To do so, he must be able to endure loss. Following your convictions can prove costly to your ambitions. You must be able to endure conflict and a degree of separateness from others. This is especially critical because presidential decisions always make some groups unhappy. It is easy to please those you agree with and so it is especially telling when a president is willing to make his own allies upset. It is even more telling when the president doesn't do so once, symbolically, but every time he feels it is necessary. Character integrity, then, is best found when sticking to conviction entails the possibility of real loss, political and otherwise.

Character integrity and ambition are closely linked. An absolutely critical question is this: Is the president's ambition primarily *personal* or *public?* A president driven mainly by personal ambition is likely to have low character integrity—after all, he's willing to do whatever is necessary to succeed, and sticking to principle can be controversial. Presidents who are motivated mainly by their visions of the public good are less likely to be self-serving and more willing to risk their political capital. Put differently, it makes a difference whether the president's ambitions are in the service of his ideals or visa versa.

Character integrity anchors personal ambitions. Without it, ambition is dangerous. Knowing whether a president's ambitions are mostly weighted in the direction of being self-serving is not easy. Most presidents, from the most to the least self-serving, profess laudable intentions. Moreover, even when a president follows through on laudable but difficult principles, we cannot escape the question of what political benefits he derives from them. A better answer to the question of ambition's purpose may be found in three elements of leadership style: a president's policy commitments, the extent to which he is willing to frustrate his friends, and his willingness to talk directly about his views or thinking. The first two reflect a president's willingness to put himself on the line for the purposes in which he says he believes. The third refers to the degree of "straight talk" a president is able and willing to allow.

Presidents willing to put themselves on the line and to risk the losses by doing so suggest by their actions that they have the courage of their convictions. The larger the personal and political risk a president is willing to take for his policies, the more he demonstrates his convictions. This is *not* an argument in favor of the content of any such policies. Nor is it an endorsement of recklessness in pursuit of a president's ideals and values. It is simply a measure of the president's willingness to put his convictions to the most extreme test: the test of loss.

Incremental initiatives are the easier path for most presidents since they are politically safe and don't risk large losses. A president does not show character integrity by proposing heartwarming social policies with which everyone agrees. Presidents who favor incremental policies as either a strategy or style force us to look elsewhere for evidence of their policy convictions and their willingness to put themselves on the line for what they believe.

George W. is certainly a president who has taken large political risks for what he believes. But where did George W.'s character integrity come from? One answer is that he was able psychologically to be engaged with others, yet also able to stand apart. He wasn't dependent on others for his basic sense of worth and confidence. He had had years of that kind of love in his family. And he had a long history of standing apart, against family expectations in general and his mother's in particular. It proved to be good practice.

As president, Bush has initiated an unusual number of policy initiatives that go against the public grain. They begin with different premises and propose different solutions than the prevailing conventional wisdom. As a result, the public is being asked to rethink many policy areas. This asks a great deal of the public and it is not surprising that they have doubts and anxieties. The president's critics know this and seek to fan the flames of public worry and doubt. Mr. Bush, if he is to succeed, therefore must not only confront and master a high level of public concern with the changes he proposes, but do so against the strong headwind of partisanship.

The president's tax cuts have drawn the united criticism of Democrats and have been received tepidly by the public. His vow to overhaul the Social Security system, allowing citizens to control and invest part of that income, is a major policy departure. So is the president's policy to tie educational policy to testing in order to gauge whether students are learning what is expected of them. And, of course, there are a number of new approaches to the environment, including forest thinning and management, using market mechanisms to cap pollution, and the refusal to enter the Kyoto agreements so long as developing countries are exempt from its provisions.

In foreign policy, the Bush administration has refused to sign the accords setting up an international tribunal for crimes against humanity. His administration has promulgated the strongest formulation in American history of this country's right to defend itself. He has specifically said that this policy envisions the possibility of going to war or attacking those who have not yet attacked this country. And this administration has taken on the responsibility for rebuilding Iraq while an insurgency rages, even as Democrats criticize the president and the public registers severe doubts and anxiety about the enterprise. In each case, President Bush has been criticized at home and abroad. Yet his focus, resolve, and commitment to his policies appear undiminished.

These represent only a partial list of policy initiatives put forward by the Bush White House. In matters large and small, domestic and international, this president has challenged convention assumptions and business-as-usual. This president's many policy initiatives are not a matter of a little more of the usual. They are designed to change the direction and understanding of policy debate. Mr. Bush's policy ambitions truly are transformational.

But they are more than that. They represent a commitment to the policy ideals and values that President Bush has developed and a willingness to fight for them. Whether the policy is tax cuts, reformulating forest policy, developing a new defense strategy, going to war in Iraq in the face of strong opposition and insisting that the United States will stay the course in the aftermath of that war, Mr. Bush is a president who has demonstrated repeatedly that he is willing to put himself, and his administration, on the line for his policies.

He is not by nature a supporter of triangulation, the nuanced strategy of incremental maneuver, playing one side off against another. He is not by nature, style, or skill a purveyor of smooth talk. Nor is he a president who is averse to risking his political fortunes. One may not agree with George W. Bush's convictions, but it is very hard to argue that he does not have any.

Mr. Bush is often accused by his critics of "pandering" to his "right-wing base." "Right-wing" of course is a polemical, not an analytical, term. Mr. Bush is a conservative, which is quite different. Still this criticism seems odd given the number of initiatives he has taken on policy issues that have resulted in clear unease, and even opposition, from various parts of the conservative side of the spectrum. He warned Republicans in Congress "not to balance the budget on the backs of the poor." He said point-blank that he would not abolish the Department of Education as Republicans had previously tried to do.[18] Instead, he has focused on improving educational results. And he has warned that "Too often, my party has focused on the national economy, to the exclusion of all else—speaking a sterile language of rates and numbers, of CBO this and GNP that. Government should be limited, but not to the point that Americans get hurt."[19] For some conservatives, the expansion of federal government expenditures, increases in deficits, and the potential threats to civil liberties entailed in the measures related to Homeland Security have been cause for concern.

Bush's willingness to bluntly state views unpopular with his party did not begin once he was in power. Rather, he was blunt during the campaign as well. Nicholas Kristof, then a reporter and now a columnist for the *New York Times,* observed that in Bush's speeches on the campaign trail "it is striking how little he panders to audiences." Rather than tailor his speech to garner support, he seemed to almost relish speaking home truths, as

> speaking to workers who worry about imports, he warmly recounts the benefits of free trade. Addressing wealthy Republicans decked out in pearls, he speaks sympathetically about Mexican immigrants and asserts that a single mother has "the hardest job in America." Before lily-white audiences that might favor English as the nation's official language, Mr. Bush occasionally drops a phrase in Spanish. The audiences stare back in puzzled silence.[20]

Bush emphasized the importance of education and the "strides that he said Hispanic and black students in Texas had made," and he refused to denounce illegal immigration, "reminding voters that many Mexicans streamed into the United States simply to seek a better life for their children."[21]

However unpopular such positions may have been to those audiences, Bush was willing to put them forward because he believed in them. The much-maligned phrase "compassionate conservatism" clearly echoes in these quotes, as do two other Bush principles: opportunity and responsibility. It is important, in Bush's view, to provide opportunities for people to improve their lives, and that apparently includes illegal immigrants—a position that angers his base.

Equally striking is Bush's conviction that it is the responsibility of the more fortunate to provide opportunity. When asked by a reporter whether this might create opposition among his natural supporters, Bush barked back, "I don't care if they do. People have a responsibility to give back, affluent people especially. And that's what I tell them."[22]

Telling your friends what they don't want to hear is difficult.[23] Telling them they won't get what they want on policy matters is a more difficult matter still. As president, the list of major policies on which Mr. Bush has decided against his conservative base is a long one, and not widely acknowledged.[24] Donald Lambro, writing in the conservative *Washington Times,* wrote:

> Mr. Bush has made several decisions in recent weeks that have infuriated conservative leaders here and out in the grass roots. He is pushing for amnesty to illegal

immigrants in the border-security bill in an attempt to appeal to Hispanic voters. He imposed higher tariffs on imported steel sought by the industry in West Virginia and Pennsylvania. He said he would sign the campaign finance reform bill that he opposed in his campaign. And he wants a 50 percent increase in foreign aid, a program that conservatives have been fighting for decades.[25]

There are examples of this tendency while he was governor as well. Nicholas Kristof reports that in 1998 when Governor Bush was considering whether to commute the sentence of convicted murderer Karla Faye Tucker, "there was tremendous pressure" from conservatives who were impressed by her stated turn toward God. Mr. Bush's liaison to the Christian Right wrote him a memo that stated in categorical terms, "You are losing the Robertson crowd over this. . . . [It will] Impact Iowa. You must have evangelicals to win the Republican nomination. . . . You don't look tough, you look insensitive. Grant the thirty-day reprieve. Gauge the reaction. Move on from there." Governor Bush didn't.[26]

True, Mr. Bush did not castigate the no-interracial-dating polices of Bob Jones University when he spoke there during the 2000 primaries. It is likely that Mr. Bush was aware of their policy, but chose to give his standard stump speech and not confront it. However, this raises a larger issue that can be simply framed: Is this behavior the exception or the rule?

Similarly, consider the president's imposition of steel tariffs that were obviously inconsistent with his free trade principles. Was the policy motivated by politics, helping industry and workers in key election states? Certainly. Yet a report to the International Trade Commission said that the three-year tariffs had indeed helped the domestic steel industry to reorganize and become more competitive. Was this a deviation from Bush's principles? Clearly. Was it politically advantageous to the president? Yes. Was it helpful policy? Apparently. Was it an exception to the rule, or one of many violations of it? A fair look at the president's record would indicate that it was an exception.

If saying no to your allies on policy issues is one measure of presidential character integrity, Mr. Bush has given clear and repeated evidence of it. Indeed, on all three possible measurements of character integrity—fighting for your policy principles and risking real loss, not saying what your allies want to hear, and not supporting the policy they want—the evidence suggests a persuasive case can be made for the president's character integrity.

PRESIDENT BUSH AND OTHERS

The third basic character domain concerns one's basic stance toward relationships with others. There are few political positions in which a leader's stance toward others is more important than in the presidency. The presidency is a highly personal and personalized institution, singular in its "one person at the top" status. However, while the president is *the* single person in charge, he is rarely alone. Everywhere the president turns, there are people: people whose sole responsibility is to ensure that he is taken care of, protected, informed, appraised, advised, bolstered, kept on track, reminded of deadlines; people to speak for him; people to find out for him; people to do what he can't do and, sometimes, what he shouldn't. The president's world is filled as much with people as it is with policy.

His relationships with Congress, with the press, with the public, with his own party, with the opposition, and with those who support and oppose him abroad all reflect the profoundly intense relational nature of the presidency. The American presidency is an enormous fulcrum of power for this country and for the world, so a president's ways of dealing with all these relationships are central to his prospects and theirs. It is a fact so obvious that its significance has not been fully appreciated.

President Bush is a man who likes others and gravitates toward them. They, in turn, gravitate toward him. After watching him over time on the campaign trail, one *New York Times* reporter wrote, "Mr. Bush is a natural politician—far more so than the vice president—with a down-home, one-of-the-guys charm that puts people at ease. He loves the crowds, relishes the limelight and invariably comes across to audiences as likable, funny, sincere and decent."[27] It was a trait of his that was evident at Andover Academy,[28] Yale,[29] in his position as part owner of the Texas Rangers baseball team, and of course, in the rise of his political fortunes. He is, in the view of many political pros, a "natural,"[30] and can work a room with the best of them.

Yet while Mr. Bush likes others and is drawn to them, he is not a man who needs to be liked. Some political leaders are drawn toward others in response to a dislike of conflict. They seek to minimize conflict not only as a political, but also as a personal strategy. Even a cursory examination of Mr. Bush's record as president shows that is not true of him. Mr. Bush not only doesn't avoid conflict, he is simply not afraid of it. Such a psychological stance is, of course, consistent with a capacity for character integrity. You can't stand on your own if you are unable or unwilling to stand apart.

George W. Bush: A Nice Guy, to a Point

George W. Bush is a likable guy. He is funny, irreverent, witty, and charming. He is a man with tender, thoughtful feelings toward others, and above all his country. Yet he is also a tough, impatient person full of strong opinions, and he is more than willing to back them up when he feels it is necessary. Mr. Bush captured himself perfectly in the aftermath of 9/11 when a reporter observed that the president appeared to have been a target of the terrorists and asked, "What kinds of prayers are you thinking and where your heart is, for yourself, as you . . ." Mr. Bush interrupted the question and responded, "I'm a loving guy but I have a job to do. And I intend to do it."[31]

Reporters covering Mr. Bush during the 2000 presidential campaign were surprised to find a candidate who seemed part Peter Pan, part adult, and only partially serious about the rituals that candidates are forced to endure. *New York Times* reporter Frank Bruni wrote of this time: "so much of what Bush said and did came with a little thought balloon over his head: 'Do we have to take all this so seriously?' . . . his antics were in part an acknowledgement or assertion that a well adjusted person could not approach all of the obligatory appearances, grandiose pageantry and forced gallantry toward the news media with a totally straight face. It made him likable. It made him real."[32]

Mr. Bush can be very playful. It is a trait that comes out often with the press. Asked about whether his State of the Union Address "would be shorter than the ones we're used to in the last eight years," he replied, "I don't know [laughter]. It depends on how loud you clap."[33]

Mr. Bush long ago perfected the role of a charming imp and has deployed it to good use. At a Washington lunch with Queen Elizabeth, Barbara Bush told the queen that she had seated her Texas son at the far end of the table away from her. Why, the queen asked. Mrs. Bush answered that her son had a habit of saying what he felt and also wearing cowboy boots that said TEXAS or GOD BLESS AMERICA. Later, when the Queen asked George W. whether he would be wearing those boots that evening at the formal reception, he replied, "Neither, tonight's pair will say GOD SAVE THE QUEEN."[34]

Bruni writes that the Bush he came to know on the campaign trail was "part scamp and part bumbler, a timeless fraternity boy and a heedless cutup, a weekend gym-rat and weekend napster, an adult with an inner child that often brimmed to the surface or burst through."[35] He characterizes W.'s humor as "tilting toward the Austin Powers school," broadly funny and by no means subtle.[36] Yet he could, in a flash, disprove the view that he was not very quick.

A month after the *New York Times* had published a story by Mr. Bruni suggesting that George W. was no great reader, Mr. Bush saw the reporter in a parking lot very early one morning. He rolled down his car window and shouted out, "How are you?" Bruni replied, "Tired," to which Mr. Bush responded that he had been up very early "because he was in the middle of a very good book," paused momentarily, and shouted "Touché!" before driving off. As Bruni notes, it was "clever and pointed and had just the right touch."[37]

Not all of Bush's antics were deft, "and the line between effervescence and inanity sometimes escaped him." Indeed, Bruni writes "there were times, early in the campaign, when Bush could be seen doing physical and emotional battle with his riskier impulses."[38] Yet many who covered him found Bush "a blast of bracing fresh air."[39]

Bush's connections with others go beyond verbal sparring. One of the reporters who accompanied the Bush campaign was Alexandra Pelosi, daughter of now House Minority Leader Nancy Pelosi, and, like her mother, a liberal. She was along to make a documentary about Mr. Bush and he developed a teasing relationship with her as he did with many covering him.[40] Toward the end of the campaign she ran into trouble with her fellow reporters because she revealed the existence of a straw poll among them as to whether Mr. Bush would win. Most said he wouldn't.

Because they were afraid of having their views revealed they began to ostracize Ms. Pelosi, until Mr. Bush caught on and came to her rescue. He made a show of specially summoning her for a one-on-one interview, and while the camera was rolling he is heard to confide to her in a low voice that he called her up to increase her status among those now giving her trouble. And then, in what must be the most revealing moment of the film, he says to her that although the reporters might laugh and be friendly with her, "they are not your friends." Further, it was important in life "to really know who your friends are."

One might add, that it is equally important to be able to be a friend. In the immediate aftermath of 9/11, the president came to New York. Many have commented on his rousing visit to the site. Less remarked upon is his visit to the families of those whose loved ones had gone off to work, never to return, and those who had tried to rescue them.

The scene is well recalled in Woodward's book.[41] Two hundred and fifty people awaited Mr. Bush in a large tent, many weeping and holding pictures of those they feared were lost. They applauded his arrival, but then the room fell deathly silent. In that silence Mr. Bush began to approach each person or family there, beginning a difficult conversation by asking each to tell him something about themselves and then offering what words of encouragement he could. Scheduled for only a short time, he stayed several hours until he had spoken personally with everyone there. Not every person could have been able to persist in the face of so much raw anxiety and grief.

This is not a new trait. Recall his attempt to console his mother when his sister Robin died. Or consider what he did when his oil company Spectrum 7 was failing because of changes in market conditions. Bush found a safe harbor in selling Spectrum to the larger and more-established Harken Energy. Yet a number of people had worked hard for Bush at Spectrum. What he did with and for them is instructive. According to Bush biographer Bill Minutaglio, *"Bush pushed hard* for some guarantees for Spectrum employees. Six of them landed work with Harken."[42] He found jobs for all the rest.[43]

It is instructive to compare Mr. Bush's behavior in these circumstances with Mr. Clinton's. When Mr. Clinton lost his 1980 reelection to Frank White, he "invited several aides to lunch . . . and launched into a melodramatic soliloquy on what he should do next. Should he practice law in Little Rock? Should he compete for the chairmanship of the National Democratic Committee, which would entail a move to Washington and a six-figure salary? Would he take another high-visibility public-interest job being dangled in front of him?[44] No one else at the table had any plans or job offers because they had not expected to be out of work so soon. One of his aides, Randy White, yelled at Clinton, "You son-ofabitch! You've got every offer. You can do all those things. What are we going to do?"[45] Clinton hadn't thought of that.

Knowing who your friends are and being capable of being a friend is the foundation of Mr. Bush's famous emphasis on loyalty. This emphasis comes up primarily with those who have come to occupy a position of trust in Mr. Bush's world. Part of it is political, but part of it is very personal.

A Tougher Side

When looking at the psychology of a president's interpersonal relations, it is important to distinguish between a tough man, and a man who can be tough. Mr. Bush falls into the latter category. He is engaging with people. Yet, in keeping with his tendency to stand apart, he is not naïvely optimistic regarding them. Ordinarily, he is reserved in giving his trust.

Ronald Reagan famously cautioned, "trust, but verify." Mr. Bush's version of that aphorism would be: Observe, then trust. Asked whether Yasser Arafat forfeited his trust, Mr. Bush tartly responded, "He certainly hasn't earned it."[46]

While Mr. Bush can clearly connect with people, banter with and befriend them, he can also be curt. Immediately after the successful conclusion of the fighting in Afghanistan a reporter asked Mr. Bush "whether the war on terrorism hadn't reached a stalemate," and he replied incredulously, "Is that a serious question?"[47]

Asked in August 2001 about his month-long vacation at his home in Texas, Mr. Bush replied, "I love Texas, it's my home. It's where I rest. It's where I do my work. It's where I see my friends. And that's just me *and people are going to have to get used to it.*"[48]

Sometimes he can be very tough, even harsh. In a pre-campaign interview Mr. Bush mocked a condemned prisoner's plea for commuting her sentence and her turn to religion that had become a Hollywood cause celebre.[49]

The Bush presidency began with a "charm offensive toward Congress in general and Democrats in Congress in particular. However, the Bush White House was equally capable of playing very tough to get its legislative way."[50] When a classified document that Mr. Bush had given to Congress was leaked, Mr. Bush was enraged and had an executive order prepared limiting review of such documents to senior congressional leaders only.

In a meeting with some members of Congress who supported a provision to make Iraqi development funds a loan, which Bush vehemently opposed, he pounded on the table in anger and insisted the provision be removed. He was reported to have said, "I'm here to tell you this is what we have to do and this is how we have to do it," and "It's not negotiable, and I don't want to debate it."[51] Mr. Bush got his way.

One report noted that "Although all administrations use political muscle on the opposition, GOP lawmakers and lobbyists say the tactics the Bush administration uses on friends and allies have been uniquely fierce and vindictive."[52] Perhaps, but they also report that the technique of playing tough, "has served the Bush White House well by maintaining the lockstep support among Republicans needed to pass Bush policies in a closely divided Congress."[53] Presidential scholar Richard Neustadt argued that those political players in Washington who surround the president watch carefully for hints of the strength of his views and resolve.[54] In Mr. Bush they appear to have found someone who is serious sbout his policy views.

Standing Apart

Some time ago, the psychoanalyst Karen Horney[55] suggested that people can be characterized as moving toward, away, or against people. People who move toward others generally show a willingness to take a chance on such relationships and are able to make solid, stable connections with them. People who move away from others generally are less inclined to take chances with people and hesitate to develop solid, stable connections. People who move against others are, in their basic psychologies, the most suspicious of other's motives and more likely to protect themselves from what they feel are the likely results of other's insular self-interest. Obviously, these persons will have the most trouble establishing stable, mutual relationships.

Over time, I have found it useful to add a fourth relational style to Horney's original three. These are people who can stand apart from people, still maintaining a real connection to them.[56] These people can develop warm, close, stable relationships with others, but they can when necessary stand apart. George W. Bush clearly has developed this relational character style.

A president's ability to stand apart from the influences that seek to shape him is one element of character integrity. Holding onto principles requires a president not only to frustrate his opponents, but his allies. It requires him to be able to hold fast and keep his focus when the doubt of others is pervasive. And it presents a presidential leadership question of the first magnitude: In a country where standing apart runs increasingly counter to basic American psychology and where fewer people feel comfortable in doing so, how will Mr. Bush fare?

Standing Apart and Unilateral Leadership

Mr. Bush is repeatedly and roundly criticized for being a "unilateralist."[57] The Kyoto treaty, the biological weapons convention, the International Criminal Court, the ABM treaty and, of course, Iraq, are all cited as evidence of Mr. Bush's unilateral "cowboy politics." The reality is much more complex.

If Mr. Bush is a unilateralist, he is an unusual one. He places tremendous stock in his relationships with numerous foreign leaders. He has genuinely embraced Vincente Fox of Mexico as a friend and policy partner. And, early on, he embraced Russia's resident Vladimir Putin. His relationships with British Prime Minister Tony Blair and John Howard of Australia are extremely close.

Paradoxically, a real problem is not that Mr. Bush doesn't invest enough in international relationships, but that he stands in danger of investing too much. Mr. Bush takes considerable pride in his ability to judge people. But this can sometimes be a pitfall.

Mr. Bush famously looked into the soul of Vladimir Putin and found a man he could work with, a man he trusted, and a man he liked.[58] His first foreign trip as president was to visit Mexico and his "old friend" Mr. Fox.[59] Asked about his relationship with the Crown Prince of Saudi Arabia, Mr. Bush replied, "I'm convinced that the stronger our personal bond is, the more likely it is that relations between the two countries will be strong."[60]

Yet, friendship and interests sometimes run in different directions. Perhaps carried away by friendship and the wish to make a dramatic gesture for his first foreign visit to Mexico, "President Bush, well before he had even the rudiments of an immigration team on board, allowed himself to be drawn pretty far down the road, at least rhetorically, towards an amnesty for Mexicans in the United States, or at least a guest worker program that would provide a temporary legal sanction for their staying and working."[61] What the administration found as it added staff to the immigration agency was that there were a number of highly complex issues that such a proposal raised. For example, should any amnesty be only for Mexicans? If not, that would raise the numbers involved dramatically. Who should be legalized and under what circumstances?

On the many occasions when Mr. Bush and Mr. Putin have met, their respective views of their relationship have been instructive. Of Mr. Putin, Mr. Bush said, "Vladimir and I had some very frank discussions about Iraq. I understand his position. He understands mine. Because we've got a trustworthy relationship, we're able to move beyond disagreement over a single issue. *Plus, I like him. He's a good fellow to spend quality time with.*"

Of Mr. Bush, Mr. Putin said, "There are two reasons why such problems between our states and between us, personally, have not emerged. We had differences over Iraq . . . but we had an understanding of the essence of this problem. And the second, and the *most important point, fundamental interests of our countries are much more solid, and much stronger than the developments you have just mentioned* [disagreements over Iraq]."[62]

For Mr. Bush, the capacity to engage in frank discussions leads to trust. And personal feelings of liking clearly enter into Mr. Bush's judgments. President Putin, on the other hand, puts his chief emphasis on mutual national interests."[63] The same problem arises with the Saudis. Mr. Bush may like the crown prince, and that relationship might be a useful lever. Yet the Saudi government contains many elements, some of whom are clearly hostile to American values and interests.

Criticisms that Mr. Bush is a unilateralist and has alienated "traditional allies" never really confront the questions that the president must answer. How much of America's security should he be willing to put into the hands of the French or Germans, whose national interests are not synonymous with those of the United States? How much of America's national security should be placed in the hands of the United Nations, given its track record on a number of international security matters? Until critics are willing to answer these questions, their critiques cannot be taken seriously.

The criticism that Mr. Bush goes his own way regardless of what allies suggest implies their policies are superior to his. Yet often there is little concrete discussion of the relative national interests involved. The fact that Mr. Bush followed his own assessment is not in itself evidence of the superiority of his critics' positions.

Mr. Bush's willingness to reject some allies' advice upsets critics. Should we sacrifice our interests to please others who have their own best interests in mind? Critics never ask or address this question. International collegiality, or the lack thereof, is not synonymous with good judgment. Indeed, going along for the sake of group harmony is a key element of groupthink.[64]

The reality is that the United States and the world have entered a new period of alliances. There are real and traditional allies like England, Australia, Japan, and Israel. There are new allies like Thailand and Poland. There are strategic partners like Egypt, Pakistan, and Russia. There are partial allies whose friendship cannot be counted upon, like France. There are strategic competitors like China, with whom, to quote George W., relationships are based on being able "to find common ground in certain areas."[65] They are neither allies nor enemies. There are neutral allies like Germany and Canada, which are generally aligned with the United States in theory but not often in practice. There are enemies like North Korea and, until recently, Libya, Afghanistan, and Iraq.

It is not that the United States is alone in the world and so be it.[66] Rather it is that with the rise of the United States as the major world power, others now calculate their interests accordingly. This sometimes means being an ally in theory rather than in fact.

Increasingly, Mr. Bush has had to repeat abroad what he has done in Congress: building coalitions of the willing for specific undertakings. This is exactly what the United States did in Iraq.[67] It is exactly what was done with the Proliferation Security Initiative developed by the United States with 11 other countries, who in turn have now been joined by 55 other countries. Interestingly, given the criticism of the Bush administration for failing to work with its "traditional allies" (e.g., France and Germany), both are part of this working group.[68] It was this group that intercepted missiles bound for Syria and Libya on the high seas.

Far from being like the sheriff played by Gary Cooper in *High Noon,* standing alone against the bad guys, Mr. Bush is a man who invests a great deal in the judgments he reaches about others, and is eager to work with them. The fact that he is able to stand apart from others when he sees the necessity does not make him a social or international isolate. Personally, Mr. Bush is clearly drawn toward people, but only after he has had a chance to gauge them. Once he has, he invests a lot—sometimes running the danger of investing too much—in their relationship. The popular misconception of Mr. Bush as some kind of Lone Ranger neglects the reality of his psychology.

CHAPTER 4

CHARACTER'S TOOLS

THE PRESIDENT'S PSYCHOLOGY

IN EARLY SEPTEMBER 2002, THE WAR CLOUDS WERE GATHERING. The president had made clear his determination to confront Saddam Hussein. Congress had voted to support the president's stance. Still, Americans were uneasy. To support a war against a country that had not attacked us, or our allies, was difficult. Worse, some in Congress and many among those we considered allies were demanding that the United States seek international authorization for the coming confrontation.

United Nations resolution No. 1441 had warned of "serious consequences" if Iraq did not comply with its responsibility to detail its weapons program as a prelude to destroying them. Now some at home, and abroad, were insisting on another UN resolution spelling out specifically just what the serious consequences would be. Clearly the pressure was on President Bush.

The president wanted to confront Saddam Hussein but needed, it was said, to gain the "unique legitimacy" that another UN vote would give him. Such a vote would reassure critics in Congress, address the concerns of the American public, and respond to world public opinion. Clearly the speech needed to be substantive, stressing the history and dangers of Saddam's regime. Above all, the president had to do everything possible to mollify reluctant Security Council members to bring about the desired and critical favorable vote. At least that is how the president's critics saw it.

What did President Bush do? Did he present a substantive case outlining Saddam's history of deception and violence? He did. Did he make every effort to enlist skeptical members and reluctant allies? Yes, he did. Did he do so by addressing and responding favorably to all their concerns? No, he didn't. Instead, he startled the United Nations by calling on it to "show some backbone" and "show its relevance."[1] Bush further made bluntly clear his intentions if they didn't. "The purposes of the United States should not be doubted." "Past resolutions would be enforced." "The just demands of peace will be met, or action will be unavoidable."[2]

Or consider another example. In May 2001, President Bush sent to Congress the nomination of Charles Pickering, Jr. for the Fifth U.S. Circuit Court of Appeals. His nomination was killed in the Senate Judiciary Committee, which was then controlled by the Democrats. The charge leveled at Judge Pickering was "racial insensitivity."[3] He joined a growing list of Bush nominees running into trouble either in the committee when the Democrats had control or on the Senate floor where Democrats could use a filibuster to essentially require a 60-vote majority to consent.[4]

The Democrats gave many reasons for their actions, but the most frequent complaint was President Bush's nominees were "outside the mainstream." They invited the president to discuss his nominations with them before he made them. He refused. They offered to let some of his nominations through if they could put in their own nominees for some new positions. The White House refused. Finally, they demanded that the president send them more "mainstream" candidates. And what did Mr. Bush do? He renominated Judge Pickering.

Then Mr. Bush nominated Brett M. Kavanaugh and Janice R. Brown. The *Washington Post* headline spoke volumes: "Bush Selects 2 for Bench, Adding Fuel to Senate Fire."[5] A *Washington Post* editorial entitled "Fueling the Fight" remarked, "We had hoped Mr. Bush would seek consensus nominees above partisan rancor—people about whom all sides could be enthusiastic. To put it mildly, Justice Brown is not what we had in mind. Justice Brown is one of the most unapologetically ideological nominees of either party in many years."[6]

Both the above illustrations, one in foreign policy and the other in domestic policy, mirror each other psychologically. In both cases, Mr. Bush wanted to accomplish something and ran up against strong opposition—in one instance a reluctant United Nations, in another a Democratic Senate intent on insisting that its views be given symmetrical weight to his. In both, Mr. Bush was strongly advised to compromise, to give his opponents some of what they wanted. And in both cases, Mr. Bush not only didn't compromise, but came right back at them with a bold reassertion of his position.

He reminded the United Nations of its founding mission and challenged it to live up to its professed ideals. The barely unstated implication, of course, was that it had not done so. In the second case, he not only turned aside suggestions that he involve Democrats in selecting his judicial nominees; he nominated more judges who were exactly like the ones that were being stalled, and, if possible, more so.

I have labeled this pattern *right back at you.*[7] It is at once defiant, but also affirmative of one's policy principles or convictions. It embraces conflict if it is not unavoidable. It is, importantly, one strong element in the pattern of this president's psychology.

A PRESIDENT'S PSYCHOLOGY

Patterns of behavior are built in part on the foundation of character and reflect the package of qualities that help define a person's psychological resources and limitations. One way to think about this is to view a president's character as the foundation of his psychology, and the patterns that arise from it as the publicly visible superstructure of his psychology. Psychology uses different terms for this superstructure, among them trait or personality. I prefer the term *character trait* because it makes clear the important relationship that exists between the content of a person's basic character structure, where he or she actually stands in the areas of ambition, character integrity, and relatedness, and the patterns that develop from that foundation.

For example, it's easy to link the character trait of competitiveness with the character element of ambition. George W.'s family was a loving, but very competitive, one. In the Bush family, competitiveness honed ambition and was practice for the rigors of expectation and achievement in real life.

It is easy to link the character element of standing apart with George W.'s tendency to come "right back at you." A person like George W., who can stand apart from others, has much less of a problem with conflict, which, after all, is one element that separates people from each other. A person like George W. is also much less susceptible to pressure that he respond to opposition demands, international views, or even, in several cases, public sentiments.

However, it is not my purpose here to develop lists of all George W.'s character traits. I only wish to call attention to the psychological patterns that help us to understand Mr. Bush as a president and leader. The analysis that follows therefore is selective for a purpose.

Ambition's Skills

Ambition cannot fulfill itself without the means of realization. These skills may take many forms. The person may be particularly smart, energetic, or both. A person may be a riveting speaker or have great organizational skills. A person may be extremely competitive or get along well with others.

The skills a person brings to realizing their ambitions are obviously varied. What matters is that the level of skill matches the level of one's ambitions. One's ambition can outstrip one's skills. It is possible not to make use of all the skills you possess, in which case ambition also falters. And it is possible to fail to find a match between your skills and your ambitions. This third possibility most clearly describes Mr. Bush during most of his adult life.

Mr. Bush is a not a good natural speaker although he can, occasionally, rise to eloquence as he did in speeches to the public and Congress after 9/11. Nor is he a compelling presence in televised venues. He does not have Ronald Reagan's easy relationship with the medium. In an age in which most people get their glimpses of a president through televised events, Mr. Bush's skills do not easily translate into an asset. Nor is George W. a man of extraordinary intelligence, although I will argue shortly that he is smart and clearly has an unusual type of intelligence for a political leader.

Mr. Bush's skills are primarily a set of inner psychological capacities that he has developed, rather than any external skills he has practiced and acquired. Their consequences are to be found in many areas of his presidential leadership, but their development is primarily a matter of having mastered himself and his experience.

Self-Control

George W. was buffeted by expectations he couldn't meet, ambitions he couldn't realize, and skills that had yet to find a niche. As a result, aspects of psychology that brought him acceptance in the outside world, such as his appealing quirkiness and his sometimes less appealing brashness, developed and grew. At the time, they did so at the expense of other character traits now much more in evidence.

The transition from mischievous imp to president required George W. to learn how to acquire mastery over his own inner psychology and impulses. He has *gradually* done that, although elements of his former self are still visibly on display. When George W. dared Saddam loyalists with the challenge "Bring 'em on," he was displaying in pristine form remnants of the brashness that has been substantially modified by his accomplishments of recent years.

Many who knew Mr. Bush well remarked that he needed to learn how to "channel his energy." Yet it was not his energy that had to be focused, but rather aspects of his interior psychology. Of these, three interrelated elements stand out in particular: his self-control, his focus, and his resolve.

Each of the three makes a distinctive contribution to Bush's psychology and presidency. Self-control is perhaps the pivotal element of the three, and the foundation upon which the others are built. Psychologically, self-control is built upon either prior restraint or redirection. Prior restraint is the equivalent of an internal stop sign for impulses before they are acted on. George W.'s cold-turkey cessation of both drinking and smoking fits this model.[8]

George W. acknowledged he had difficulty knowing when a few became too many. When he drank, he became more like himself, he said, with no implication from his perspective that more wasn't better. In such cases, just saying no is a simple and effective solution, if you can do it.

Stifling an impulse requires self-control. This is true whether the source of the impulse is triggered primarily by one's own feelings about oneself, as it was with George W.'s drinking, or outside provocations. When he first ran against Ann Richards for the Texas governorship in 1990, it was widely viewed in some quarters as a grudge match. After all, she had quipped at his father's expense on national television during the 1988 presidential campaign that "Poor George couldn't help it if he was born with a silver spoon in his mouth."

George W.'s reputation as a bit of an emotional loose cannon was well known and Richards sought to capitalize on it.[9] She told one crowd that you can't just wake up one morning, look in the mirror, and congratulate yourself on how good-looking you are and decide that you ought to be governor. Elsewhere she referred to George W. as "some jerk," and began referring to him derisively as "Shrub."

George W. refused to take the bait. He responded by saying he would not call the governor names and instead would keep the level of the debate where Texans wanted it. This was a sound strategy. By the time that Richards had banked on provoking George W., he had learned to keep his impulse to fight in kind under control.

Restraint does not come easily to George W. While he is a devoted born-again Christian, he has not mastered turning the other cheek, as his "right back at you" psychology makes clear. It is a trait that is consistently tested in his presidency.

When Mr. Bush secretly, and at some danger to himself, flew to Baghdad to show his support for the American effort there, President Clinton's former press secretary, Joe Lockhart, remarked, "This is a president who has been unwilling to provide his presence to the families who have suffered but thinks nothing of flying to Baghdad to use the troops there as a prop."[10] Presidential candidate Wesley Clark accused the president of having been responsible for 9/11 since it happened on his watch.[11] Hillary Clinton[12] wondered out loud in a Senate speech whether President Bush had advance knowledge of the 9/11 tragedy but did nothing about it. In an interview on *Face the Nation,* Democratic presidential candidate Bob Graham of Florida accused the president of a cover-up about 9/11 and the danger facing Americans.[13] This, he suggested, was an offense worthy of impeaching President Bush.[14] Senior *New York Times* reporter R. W. Apple thought these accusations and what he called politics as usual were "worth a cheer."[15]

These would be very strong accusations against any president. They are particularly personal for a president like George W. Bush whose deep love of country is a driving motivation in his post 9/11 transformation. Yet Mr. Bush responded calmly, noting that it was "the political season," that "second-guessing had become second nature," and saying dispassionately, "The American people know this about me and my national security team and my administration: had I known that the enemy was going to use airplanes to kill on that fateful morning, I would have done everything in my power to protect the American people."[16] Other times he has called such remarks "pure politics" and let it go at that.[17]

Good politics? Again, yes, but these accusations represent only a small number of an avalanche of harsh partisan criticism—some tempered, more not. Mr. Bush has obviously been getting a lot of practice in self-control.

Self-Control, Redirection, and External Constraints

Impatience is often politically unwise. It also interferes with effective judgment. Psychologically, impatience is related to impetuousness, a key element in Mr. Bush's adolescent psychology and the key to his former family role.[18] Given Mr. Bush's self-acknowledged impatience, an important question arises: How does he deal with it, if he does?

Stopping one's impulses before they are acted on is one method of self-control. It is, however, not the only one. Another useful method is redirection. Here the original impulse is allowed enactment, but is rerouted to more useful purposes.

Some may recognize here a parallel to the psychological defense mechanism of sublimation, but the two are not the same. In sublimation an unconscious and unacceptable impulse is redirected toward a socially useful outcome. In redirection, however, the process is consciously put in the service of something beneficial. Interests in other people's interior lives, for example, can be refashioned into socially acceptable roles like psychoanalyst or news reporter.

A third mechanism is to rely in part on external constraints. Here a president may depend on trusted aides to redirect, absorb, or harmlessly dissipate his impulses. Many a president has had angry outbursts at one or another source of irritation and then issued angry orders that their aides know need not be acted upon.

Mr. Bush has acknowledged that he is an impatient man.[19] It often shows. During the first months of his administration, a Chinese pilot buzzed an American plane and forced it to land on Chinese territory. A visibly tense and angry Mr. Bush made a brief appearance outside the Oval Office and said that the Chinese "must promptly" return the plane and crew, "and I expect them to heed that message."[20] Several days later, he had recovered, and stressed that he was "working all diplomatic channels," a process that is inconsistent with impatience.[21]

After the 9/11 attack, airlines were grounded and there was a White House discussion about when it would be safe to resume flights. The president declared that he would announce more security measures, but "would not be held hostage . . . we'll fly at noon tomorrow."[22] That impulsive statement, based in part on a right-back-at-you attitude toward opponents, would have to wait three more days until the necessary security procedures were put in place.

Speaking of his impatience, his wife, Laura, has said in an interview that "it is one of the characteristics that he says he has to work on the most."[23] Indications are he has. Probably at no time during the president's first term was this temptation more pressing than after the 9/11 attack. The American air strikes against the Taliban began October 7, almost a month after the United States had been attacked.

That period was a tense time for the nation, obviously, and for the president. The country he was honored to serve, and for which he had so often publicly expressed love and admiration, had been struck on his watch. When Mr. Bush visited the Pentagon after the 9/11 attack he said it made him "sad . . . [but] it also makes me mad."[24] Mr. Bush wanted revenge. In an October 2003 interview with Peggy Noonan he said, "What hasn't changed is the feeling I had on the first day of the attack: America is under attack and they will pay. I still feel the same way."[25]

Not only was Mr. Bush impatient, he understood that the country was as well. He told King Abdullah of Jordan, "We're ready, clear-eyed and patient, but pretty soon we'll have to start displaying scalps."[26]

The impulse to strike back was very pressing for all these reasons. Yet, Mr. Bush suppressed his impatience, avoiding a quick and satisfying response, in the service of a longer-term and more effective one. Revenge no doubt played a role in suppressing his impatience. Yet, he didn't get rid of his impatience, he only tempered and redirected it.

It was however, a severe strain on him.[27] Mr. Bush was anxious to begin the Afghanistan action. He told his national security advisor, Condoleezza Rice, that the country had been through an ordeal and needed "to hear from us" and "I have to know when something's going to get started."[28] Later he admitted that "I was becoming frustrated. . . . It was just not coming together as quickly as we had hoped . . . my body, my clock is just ticking. . . . I am pushing."[29]

The reasons were many. There were no useful invasion plans on the shelf, itself an indication of the country's lack of preparedness before 9/11.[30] The army was cautious.[31] "The president and the war council had to be decisive, but not hasty."[32]

To negotiate between the tremendous desire to strike back and the necessity to do so in a way that would further his and the country's objectives, Bush took on a role that had long been his in other contexts: provocateur. Here is Bush in his familiar role applied in new settings: "One of my jobs is to be provocative, seriously, to provoke people into—to force decisions, to make sure it's clear in everybody's mind where we're headed."[33]

Finally, aware of the impulsive elements in his psychology, Mr. Bush has enlisted external constraints to help overcome them. The president explained to Bob Woodward that, "One way you're not impulsive is to make sure you listen to an experienced group of national security advisors."[34] Debates not only serve to flesh out the issues for the president and deepen his understanding, they also clearly act as an external constraint on his psychology.

Mr. Bush used his advisors to constrain his impatience in another more direct way. He told Bob Woodward of an incident when he was pushing for the start of action against the Taliban but was being frustrated by the lack of a target list. Mr. Bush lost his patience several times, yelling at Condoleezza Rice "That's not acceptable." Bush admitted to Woodward that, "I was growing a little impatient." He then added this insight into his psychology and Ms. Rice's relationship to it: "Sometimes, that's the way I am—fiery. On the other hand [Rice's] job is to bear the brunt of some of the fire so that—it takes the edge off a little bit. And she's good at that."[35]

Mr. Bush is a man who can be patient in some circumstances only with the greatest difficulty. Realizing this about himself, he has taken steps. And those steps rely on the help of others—one more reason why the "Lone Ranger" image of Mr. Bush is at odds with reality.

Impatience is certainly part of his psychology, but it is also part of his leadership strategy. One of Mr. Bush's principles of leadership is that a leader must be provocative. Pushing others is one method of doing so. It's a useful strategy when dealing with bureaucracies whose standard operating procedure is to take time, sometimes in the service of thoroughness, and other times in the service of avoidance. When plans for the invasion of Afghanistan were being delayed by the time needed to develop a combat search-and-rescue operation for any downed pilots, Mr. Bush gave the general in charge two days to come up with a plan.[36]

The danger, of course, is that haste can be the enemy of success. Yet it is also true that delay can be an enemy as well. Bush summed up the dilemma well in weighing what to do when he said, "We can't wait forever, but we also can't rush."[37]

Focus

In the expansive world of personal and presidential choice, focus helps to conserve energy and direct motivation. It is an emotional sibling to self-control. But they are not twins. Self-control reflects an adaptive mechanism for controlling impulse. Focus is a mechanism for directing it once that has been accomplished.

The primary benefit of focus is that it allows the leader to concentrate on what he feels is important. This in turn requires that the leader accept some limits on his ambitions. Not all do.

Mr. Bush has repeatedly underlined the importance of leaders setting priorities.[38] Comparing George W. and his predecessor shows in sharp relief the ways in which ambition and focus are related. Both President Bush and President Clinton promised to focus like a laser on the economy, but only one of them did.

When Mr. Bush announced his agenda for fall 2001 he included six areas: tax relief, education reform, faith-based legislation, national security, Medicare, and Social Security.[39] His then–press secretary, Ari Fleischer, promised that the president "is going to focus like a laser beam" on his agenda, recalling a remark that Mr. Clinton had made about the economy after his election in 1992.[40]

In fact, the administration and Mr. Bush did focus on each of these areas. Yet he did so by using the principle of first things first. Richard Neustadt had warned presidents about how immediate claims on their attention often interfered with matters they wanted to accomplish.[41] Mr. Bush has proved no exception to this rule.[42] Given this fact, a president's ability to attend to his agenda in the face of competing, sometimes compelling external circumstances is one measure of focus.

Mr. Bush has accomplished his agenda items, one at a time. First came the first tax cut, then the education bill. As these were making their way through Congress, the groundwork was being laid for his other initiatives. Only hours after Mr. Bush won his major legislative victory on Medicare, Bush announced he was "moving his plan for limiting medical malpractice lawsuits to the front burner of his domestic agenda."[43] Even before the Medicare win and the announcement of the malpractice initiative, administration officials had already disclosed plans to resurrect the president's Social Security reform initiative.

Herein lies a strategic insight into the president's use of focus. *It is a focus on one thing at a time* in a longer list, not just one thing period. In many respects, Bush's legislative strategy parallels the "just-in-time" manufacturing strategy that many industries now use, in which parts that are needed are not warehoused but delivered just in time for their use in product assembly. It takes an intense investment of time and patience to make a just-in-time policy a success. Consider President Bush's successful initiative for a Medicare reform bill that included a drug benefit for seniors. That legislative victory was brought about in part by an alliance with the AARP (American Association of Retired Persons), which had historically allied itself with the Democratic party. When that group officially backed the Bush proposal, it gave it not only a stamp of legitimacy but legislative momentum. Little appreciated was the fact that the Bush administration and Mr. Bush personally had cultivated that relationship for three years before it came to fruition.[44] Thus, the policy apparatus in Mr. Bush's White House is like a series of parallel conveyer belts fed by Mr. Bush's stated policy ambitions and those developed by the long-term policy planning groups in the White House.[45]

Focused policy ambitions aren't necessarily limited ones. Consider Mr. Bush and his predecessor Mr. Clinton.[46] Both presidents had much they wanted to accomplish, but Mr. Clinton lacked Mr. Bush's focus. Mr. Clinton was deeply involved, often at a level of extraordinary detail, but not for long: "He was soon on to new subjects, and he only sporadically argued his budget case."[47] One of his cabinet members compared him to a kid who "wants to do everything at once."[48] Another said the problem was that Clinton would say his scheduling was the issue "*because he never thinks he has taken on too much.*"[49] Whatever the cause, the result was clear. His first term was not memorable for getting results.[50]

Mr. Bush's capacity for focus has delivered undeniable policy results in his presidency. His first-things-first rule has allowed him to set priorities from among the myriad things he *could* do. During the lead-up to the Afghanistan War, some of his advisors pressed for a consideration of Iraq as well. Mr. Bush cut it off with a curt statement: "That's out of the question at this point."[51] Those kinds of decisions allowed him to channel his energies, attention, and judgment.

A capacity for focus is not an unalloyed benefit. Too narrow a focus on results, whether legislative or otherwise, can result in the neglect of other larger and important issues. A president must have vision to see the big picture, but he also must have perspective. Focus also can lead to single-mindedness. That in turn can lead to stubbornness that prevents needed flexibility. Mr. Bush has been accused of both, and it is an issue to which I will turn in the chapters that follow.

Resolve

Many skills associated with the tasks of political leadership can be improved with practice. A president can improve his debating skills, or at least become more substantively prepared. He can learn how the political system operates and thus improve his chances of success in it. Or he can hire advisors who will help navigate treacherous political currents. But some aspects of the presidency are beyond the reach of practice or astute hiring, and these are especially critical to presidential success in a highly partisan political context.

The most critical skills are more often a matter of internal psychology than external aptitude. One that is of particular importance is resolve. Resolve reflects an inner determination to succeed. It consists of equal parts of emotional stamina, balance, and resilience. It is reflected in the ability to keep on going through difficult circumstances without losing sight of your destination or being thrown off course by the many roadblocks in your path.

Psychologically, resolve is a sibling of character integrity. In the case of character integrity, a president begins with ideals and values. In the case of resolve, he begins with ambition's goals. Both require something further. For a president's character integrity, it is the capacity to have the courage of his convictions, and for ambition's goals, he requires the psychological strength to get there. Both become evident in tests of adversity.

Character integrity is not tested when the person risks no loss by being true to his ideals. Resolve is tested by reaching beyond present agreements, and especially by going against the political grain. In both types of circumstances George W. Bush has surely put himself, and the country, to a test.

In the 2000 presidential campaign, George W. Bush made it very clear that part of his economic policy involved substantial tax cuts. Polls showed that many Americans were indifferent to tax cuts. Yet, Mr. Bush did not back off.[52] One can see here a candidate with strong views who is not willing to be turned away from them on the basis of public sentiment. This worries some and is applauded by others. Yet there is little doubt that it reflects Mr. Bush's capacity for resolve.

The proof of resolve, however, is not only in the capacity for it, but also in a demonstrated ability to follow through on it. The tax cuts in Mr. Bush's first two years in office provide one domestic example of follow-through. On February 8, 2001, Mr. Bush proposed a ten-year, $1.6 trillion tax cut, the size of which surprised both supporters and critics. Republican moderates and the Democratic opposition tried to first block and then reduce its size. Liberal and business advocacy groups were mobilized, talking heads analyzed, experts opined, Democratic party presidential candidates called for the postponement or roll back of tax cuts, moderate Republicans blanched, and the public registered its preferences. Mr. Bush then settled for a figure of $1.3 trillion and declared victory.

One former Clinton official said Bush got his victory "on sheer force of perseverance."[53] Yet Mr. Bush did not gain his victory only because of the abstract concept of "resolve." He did so also because he was able to translate his determination into successful leadership. It began with recognizing he had a continuing economic problem and a desire to do something about it. It continued with asking his advisors for ideas to help a sluggish economy. Mr. Bush had put himself in a stronger political position by having successfully campaigned in the fall 2002 elections, adding seats to GOP margins in the House and regaining control of the Senate. He met with, and leaned on, Senate and House leaders. He logged many thousands of miles campaigning across the country and paying particular attention to the districts or states of wavering lawmakers. And he succeeded.

The first lesson of this case is that it is clear that resolve is the internal psychological counterpart of what presidential scholar Richard Neustadt referred to as "self-help," the activities that a president undertakes on his own behalf. You can't help yourself if you don't have the internal determination to do so. Resolve is also most clearly evident when a president faces formidable obstacles, and it requires more than the rhetoric of determination—it requires specific demonstrations of it. In a politically divided country with highly partisan governing institutions, resolve is a critical psychological resource for presidential leadership.

Yet resolve by itself is insufficient for political success. Real political skills are needed. Those skills must be versatile. They must certainly reflect a good sense of political timing. Mr. Bush, for example, chose not to present his full plans until after the congressional elections of 2002.[54] Skills must be enlisted to find effective ways to neutralize opponents, win over uncertain allies, and maintain commitments—and to do so in a Congress in which the parties are deeply divided and your own political party has fissures. The president must recognize when hardball is best and a soft touch better. He must be sensitive to when it is important to hold the line and when to compromise. In demonstrating both the resolve and the accompanying skills, Mr. Bush has proved himself to be a most politically adroit president and leader.

Finally, like most outstanding elements in a president's psychology, resolve has important leadership implications. A president who is seen as a "strong leader," as Bush is, does more than display a trait that the public approves of or admires. A president's courage in pursuing his convictions can also strengthen public resolve as well. Perhaps this is most clearly on display in the difficult situation in Iraq. After a very difficult three-week period that included incendiary accusations by former national security advisor Richard Clarke, mounting battles and American casualties in Iraq, the loss of American allies (Spain, the Dominican Republic, and Honduras), the continuing failure to find weapons of mass destruction in Iraq, and a disheartening prison abuse scandal in Iraq, Mr. Bush's support declined, but did not go into free fall. More to the point, the public did not abandon the effort to develop a new, more stable Iraq. A May 12, 2004, Pew poll found that after all these disturbing events a majority of Americans (53%) were still committed to the president's plans to stabilize Iraq. That number broke down to 72 percent of Republicans and 54 percent of swing voters. Forty percent of Democrats favored this position.[55] One way to read this data is that Mr. Bush's resolve has steeled the public for the difficult times it faces in Iraq. This is not merely a matter of presidential rhetoric. It is not just the words themselves, but what the words, coupled with actions, reflect. Having a leader who shows courage and fortitude not only models that behavior, it makes it available for public emulation.

CONFIDENCE

George W. Bush is a confident man. Stuart Stevens, who worked on the media team that helped elect Mr. Bush in 2000, says that "George W. Bush was a fundamentally confident person . . ."—indeed, "one of the most confident men he had ever known."[56] Others are not so sure. At the very same time that some were describing the most confident man they had ever known, Frank Bruni was describing a candidate who was "Cautious to the point of timidity, and disciplined to the point of paralysis."[57] Bruni wondered whether George W.'s "preference for prefabricated locutions could be read as . . . a phobia of risk."[58] Yet this was the same man who risked his presidency on an epic effort to rid the world of Saddam Hussein and rebuild and democratize Iraq, all the while incurring the ire or concern of allies, world opinion, congressional Democrats, and an increasingly worried American public. Mr. Bush's presidency cannot be characterized as risk-averse. Mr. Bush has clearly shown himself to be much more inclined toward policy than personal risk, a reversal of the psychology of his predecessor whose presidency faltered because of a risky and unnecessary sexual affair.

"Arrogance" is seen by some as the hallmark of the Bush administration.[59] And of course, the "arrogance of American power" is a staple of foreign criticism of American foreign policy in general and Mr. Bush in particular.[60] Still others agree that Mr. Bush seeks large results, but note that the danger of such ambitions is "arrogance. If you think you're right and the world says 'no' and you win more initial successes than expected, you can get cocky."[61]

Others see the "arrogance" as more personal, essentially Mr. Bush's. Arrogance, of course, is the excessive sibling of confidence, and many believe Mr. Bush has long since crossed that line. During the 2000 campaign there was much commentary on George W.'s "small half-smile, which some critics have called a smirk and interpret as a sign of arrogance."[62] New York Times columnist Frank Rich characterized Mr. Bush as a "narcissist" with an "arrogant world view."[63] Maureen Dowd agreed.[64] In the view of Dowd and Rich, George W.'s privileged upbringing led him to be spoiled and thus arrogant.

Others have offered different explanations, but not particularly positive ones. Thomas Mann argues, "There's something about born-again adults who screwed around for much of their lives and then had a religious experience, who then gain great confidence in what they're doing, a righteousness. It makes them better citizens, but it's not clear it makes them more thoughtful, deliberative, or wise."[65]

Which is the real George W. Bush? Is he the unpretentious president who is satisfied with his favorite food, peanut butter and jelly sandwiches? Or, to quote the title of a critical editorial, are we now at war because a "Smug President Has Painted U.S. into a Corner"?[66] Is he merely confident, and if so, on what basis? Or does his love of habit reflect a lack of real confidence?

The answers to these questions are critically important. They go to the heart of the president's psychology. And they have the most direct and obvious implications for almost every aspect of the Bush presidency, from his leadership to his policies.

The Psychology of Confidence

Confidence can be understood as the degree of sureness that one has regarding one's choices and one's ability to accomplish one's goals. These in turn rest on a sense of optimism and the belief that the skills one has are up to the demands that will be placed upon them.

Basically, confidence is the result of successful experience. Yet that relationship is more complex that it sounds. Confidence has two major dimensions: Who I am and what I do. The first reflects assessments of the kind of person you are. The second reflects assessment of how good you are at what you try to accomplish. We can, for ease, think of these two as involving skills related to *personal confidence* and task or *occupational confidence,* respectively. In good circumstances the two overlap. Yet each has its own developmental path. If they don't develop in tandem, difficulties can easily result. This is clearly what happened with George W. Bush.

The development of *personal* confidence begins in the family with their love and acceptance. That confidence then begins to branch out as the person tests the waters of interpersonal relationships and performance outside the home. Whether the person can find ways to effectively make and sustain emotional connections with others helps to consolidate the sense of personal confidence.

At almost the same time, the building blocks of task confidence are being laid down. Every child is faced with the need to learn how to do things early on. Often this early experience takes place around "play." However, from the standpoint of learning about one's self and one's skills, play is a serious matter indeed. In play, as in life more generally, one learns what one can do and also importantly what one can't do. As a child, Mr. Bush aspired to be a major-league baseball player until he realized he couldn't hit. He then looked elsewhere for his life's work.

All successful work experience requires the development of skills that are appropriate to the tasks at hand. A mismatch of skills to task depletes rather than builds confidence. More discouraging to confidence is that fact that even a good match between skills and task doesn't guarantee success. George W. worked hard at both the oil and the political business as a young man, but with limited success.

If confidence comes from successful experience and George W. didn't have that much, how do we account for his confidence? There are two possible answers to this question. One is that he somehow earned it, in spite of not having any obvious success. The other is to see it as the product of the spoiled indulgence of a rich kid who grew up with a sense of entitlement. That entitlement would be the basis of having an unearned confidence, one that comes from privilege rather than performance.

This is the view many Bush critics hold. It is embedded in characterizations of Mr. Bush's "smirk," which suggests he feels superior; his "swagger," suggesting a pumped-up and artificial confidence; and "cowboy politics" that suggest a lack of concern with others. It is that possibility to which I turn first.

Confidence, Narcissism, and Arrogance

Psychoanalysts are familiar with these characteristics, but know them by another name: pathological narcissism. That term basically describes a person who is almost wholly self-absorbed, indifferent to others and their concerns, and who feels smugly superior to others, most often as a rationale for exploiting them. It is not hard to see how such a person might be seen as arrogant.

Among true narcissists, overvaluation of oneself and one's accomplishments is common. Indeed, it is so common that it has spawned its own term: grandiosity. Psychologically, grandiosity reflects a *substantial* mismatch between one's view of one's capacities and one's performance. Small mismatches don't measure up to that term.

Grandiosity leads people to try more than they can possibly accomplish, to claim more than they have done, and to be dismissive of others' contributions while extolling their own. It can easily be seen why narcissism and grandiosity would be closely allied with arrogance.

The family circumstances that give rise to true narcissism are also of interest. Generally, true narcissism takes root among children whom a family or parent have singled out as both special and entitled. Being seen as special is not enough. Most children are so considered by their parents. Rather, the breeding ground of narcissism and grandiosity is conveying to the child the sense that he or she is so special, so entitled, that they are therefore beyond the rules that govern ordinary people.

The contrast to "normal" children is obvious. Hopefully, they too are brought up feeling that they are special, but they are nonetheless expected to conform to rules and expectations. Raising children with the understanding that they must earn what they desire is very different than the expectation that you ought to have what you want because you are you.

Indulged children grow up feeling highly confident in their own self-worth and importance, but that view is not tempered by much understanding of others' worth. If such children have or develop talents, they only serve to reinforce the narcissism. Their confidence easily develops into arrogance, because their skills only serve to reinforce the view that they are special and entitled.

The general description of the family circumstances associated with true narcissism and its psychological siblings, entitlement and arrogance, do not much resemble the Bush family. George W.'s father was raised to avoid self-promotion and his grandmother, Dorothy Walker Bush, enforced that rule with a vengeance. One day when George W.'s father said that he had lost a tennis match because his game had been off, his mother replied, "You don't have a game."[67] "We," not "I," was the chief pronoun in the Bush household. Service, not self-aggrandizement, was a primary Bush family value. And, of course, an ethos of service is inconsistent with a psychology of narcissism and entitlement.

George W. grew up in a Bush family household with all that history and the sense of decorum it entailed. And it is clear that George W. did internalize the family ethos. George W. remarked that he had learned that "money and material things were not the measure of a life in the long run . . . and if you had them, they came with a price tag: the obligation to serve."[68]

George W.'s father was often away and the day-to-day household was his mother's responsibility. There is ample evidence that she loved her children; there is no evidence that she required less deportment from any one of them. Recall that both George W. and his brother Jeb referred to her as "the enforcer." This was a role conferred on her by circumstance and consistent with her psychology. Clearly, she didn't act as if her children were beyond rules.

She was, as noted, a tart critic of George W. on occasion throughout his adolescence, young adulthood, and beyond. When George W. ran in his first marathon in 1994, his parents, who were watching, had very different reactions as he passed by. His father cheered and his mother yelled out to alert him, "There are some elderly women ahead of you,"[69] a dig at his efforts.

When, as president, he visited his family in Kennebunkport and put his feet up on a table, his mother yelled at him to get his feet down. His father said that she should not talk that way to the president of the United States, to which she replied, "I don't care who he is, he can't put his feet all over my table." As these anecdotes, and there are others, make clear, George W. was hardly singled out for a sense of entitlement. Indeed, his mother's stern attempts to enforce the rules suggest exactly the opposite. The Bush household was an infertile breeding ground for narcissism, grandiosity, and entitlement.

George W.'s Arrogance: A First Look

Still, it is possible that George W. became arrogant (if he did) without any help from his parents. If this were the case we would expect to see evidence of his arrogance elsewhere in his developmental history or as a pattern of behavior. It certainly was not evident in his childhood, but perhaps a form of it did develop in his adolescence and early adulthood.

During those years, George W. assumed the role of a wisecracking rebel whose tongue outpaced his judgment. These were his so-called wild years, but in reality they were not so wild. He finished college, learned how to fly jets, went to Texas, and worked hard to make a living. He was, however, stymied since his occupational skills never fully helped him realize the success he sought.

During this period George W. perfected his rebel role, but it must be kept in mind that he did so while pursuing very conventional ideas of success. Part of that role contained a certain degree of bravado, perhaps even cockiness. The hard-living, hard-drinking entrepreneurial Bush family rebel was part pose, part reality.

Growing up, George W. faced the trials that come from being born into a family that had excelled for generations. The family name was both a benefit and a curse; it opened doors, but that made it hard to settle the question of exactly what George W. had accomplished on his own.

A young man who wanted so much to become his own man, especially while following in the footsteps and shadow of a famous father, would have an especially difficult time. He would certainly want to see his own efforts as instrumental in any success, but would always remain unsure about just how to measure his actual contribution. Sometimes, in his eagerness to garner evidence of his own contributions to success, he downplayed the helpful role of others.[70]

Of course, his family connections helped. His Uncle Jonathan helped in raising capital for George W.'s oil business. Philip Uzielli, a friend of James Baker, also helped raise capital. But these men were making business, not charity, decisions, and they expected results. George W. worked hard to get them.

Did George W. play an important role in putting together the Texas Rangers deal? Serious biographers agree he did.[71] Were others important too? Yes, clearly.

What a person does with credit is deeply revealing of their psychology. Ambitious narcissistic presidents, like Bill Clinton, begin with the view that the world revolves around them and there is little room to acknowledge others, except briefly and perfunctorily. George W. has evidenced little, if any, of these tendencies.

Mr. Bush was, I'm sure, conflicted and unsure in his own mind at points about exactly what *he* had accomplished. It was sometimes hard to tell. But no more. One benefit of success is that it shifts the internal psychological balance between promise and accomplishment. When Mr. Bush's promise was more prevalent than his accomplishments, any evidence of success was precious. Now that the balance has decidedly shifted, that need is not quite so pressing. Here is Mr. Bush discussing his role in the GOP's successful 2002 midterm elections in a Q & A:

Q: Thank you, Mr. President. You were very gracious earlier, giving credit in this last election to the individual candidates. But a lot of those candidates say they have you to thank . . .

THE PRESIDENT: And I was pleased with the results. I was more particularly
pleased for the candidates, who worked so hard, and their families and their
workers. . . . But if you're really interested in what I think, I think the fact
that Norm Coleman ran a very difficult race in difficult circumstances and
won speaks volumes about Norm Coleman. . . . I know what it's like to run
for office. I know the strains it puts on families. I know the tired—the endless hours you spend campaigning, and all the wonderful questions you
have to answer as part of a campaign. I know all that. . . . *And these candidates deserve all the credit.*"[72]

Looking back, it is possible to see a callow young man taking credit for
the work of others, too full of himself, and brash to the point of arrogance.
There would be *some* truth in that view. Yet it is also possible to see a young
man passing through a developmental phase, desperate to make good and having a tough time forging a successful adulthood. The rebel role and the
bravado that came with it were a continuation into adulthood of the successful
role that he developed in high school and college. It was his vehicle for personal confidence and it had to bear all the weight of his adulthood until he
could develop a real and substantial basis of work confidence and success.
This was a major reason why Mr. Bush had an extended adolescence and a delayed adulthood.

I want to be very clear here. It is *not* that Mr. Bush was an adolescent in his
adulthood, but rather that he had one foot in both periods. Recall that his rebel
role did not keep him from learning to master and fly jet planes. It did not keep
him from applying to, gaining entry to, and graduating from Harvard Business
School. It did not keep him from working very hard to make a success of his oil
business. Nor did his privileged background keep him from pounding the pave-
ment from sunup to sundown as he worked to win a congressional seat. And his
brashness did not keep him from making sure all of his employees found jobs
after he merged his company, Spectrum 7, with Harken Oil.

In short, Mr. Bush may have been privileged, but he was not spoiled. He
may have been brash, but he was not uncaring. And he may have claimed too
much, but there were some legitimate claims to be made.

It is obvious that the Bush family name both paved the way and clouded
George W's path. George W. only gradually, and at some places along the road
grudgingly, accepted this two-sided fact. His palpable desire to become his own
man ran headlong into the fact that in so many ways he was his father's son.

These tendencies faded as George W. was able to point to a list of his own
real accomplishments. That word, "faded," is a very important one in considering George W.'s psychological development. When patterns fade, they don't always disappear completely. Sometimes vestiges remain.

Consider two of them in the first years of Mr. Bush's presidency. His comment that he wanted Osama bin Laden "dead or alive" no doubt reflected the president's essential feeling. Yet it is also the language of adolescent macho, and Mr. Bush recognized "it was a little bit of bravado."[73] When after the fall of Baghdad, Mr. Bush challenged Saddam Hussein loyalists with the phrase "Bring 'em on," it had the sound of a schoolyard taunt, but of course the stakes and the sentiment were deadly serious. Mr. Bush's feelings may be understandable, but their expression was a partial residue of earlier times.

Arrogance in the White House?

If arrogance is a cornerstone of George W.'s White House, we would expect to see evidence of it. There are many places one could look. We could look to Mr. Bush's own view of himself as president and in the presidency. We could examine Mr. Bush's personal behavior as president. Does he exhibit signs of substantial or excessive self-reference? Does everything revolve around him personally in his presidency as they did around Bill Clinton in his? We could examine his relationships with others. Is there evidence that his needs and views come first, with others as an afterthought? And finally, we could examine his role as leader and policymaker, which is where the largest numbers of such charges have been lodged.

To gain some perspective on the first question, consider this: When Bill Clinton took his very long goodbye from the White House on the day of George W. Bush's inauguration, he gave a thousand-word goodbye speech at Andrews Air Force Base in which he used the pronoun "I" or "me" 56 times.[74] It is certainly possible to view Clinton's presidency, with some legitimacy, as an eight-year political and personal psychodrama with Mr. Clinton as its central star.

Mr. Bush's approach to the presidency has been quite different. He has tried to downsize the pomp of the presidency to keep more in line with his own dislike of pretense. During his first months in office, he banned the Marine band from playing "Hail to the Chief" when he appeared in public.[75] That rousing introduction, one reporter noted, "was like oxygen to Clinton."[76] When the crew of a downed aircraft returned from their brief captivity in China, he wasn't there to meet them because he thought it would take away from *their* homecoming. David Broder said it was a "welcome change not to have a president who seizes every situation as a stage for dramatizing his care for those in distress, aggressively taking the spotlight for himself."[77]

The one clear exception to this general rule has been Mr. Bush's public role as commander-in-chief. Here, Mr. Bush has been front and center, both publicly and behind the scenes. There are many examples and they reflect on important characteristics of the president's leadership. One incident reported by Bob Woodward underscores the point.

As part of the worldwide war on terrorism, the president and his war cabinet determined that the terrorist money flow had to be stopped. Accordingly, a presidential order was drawn up freezing the financial assets of terrorists and their suspected allies worldwide. At first, Bush's chief aide, Karen Hughes, drafted a press release for the secretary of the treasury when announcing the freeze. This brought an annoyed call from the president who informed her this was no routine announcement, but the very first public shot in a global war; "I should be making the announcement," he said,[78] and he did.

Arrogance might be reflected in a president's expansive view of his own importance and centrality. Is this the case with Mr. Bush? It appears not. Asked "how it felt to be the most powerful man in the world," the president replied, "Humbling."[79]

What of George W.'s relationships with others? Does he put himself first and think of others as an afterthought? Some would argue that this is precisely what he does when dealing with American allies. However, that is a different issue and deserves its own analysis (see chapters 3 and 8). If Mr. Bush is putting anyone first in these matters it is *this country,* not Mr. Bush personally.

Is Mr. Bush's presidency a "me first" one? There have been several telling interviews in which the subject of George Bush and his relationship with and concern for others has come up in very personal ways. Asked repeatedly early in his presidency about the missing intern Chandra Levy and whether he had watched, as millions had, an interview with Gary Condit, with whom she had had an affair, he said: "No." He then added, "I hope that the Levys' prayers are answered. That's my hope. This isn't about a congressman or a network. This is about a family who lost a daughter, and that's what I'm concerned about."[80]

Immediately after the devastating 9/11 terrorist attack Mr. Bush was asked, "Could you give us a sense . . . as to where your heart is, for yourself, as you— . . ." Mr. Bush interrupted the question and responded, "I don't think about myself right now. I think about the families and children."[81] Waiting for the results of the 2000 election, Mr. Bush was asked by *New York Times* reporter Frank Bruni how a person got through a night like this when his whole future was on the line. George W. responded that he didn't think his whole future was on the line, and then added, "'I'm not worried about *me* getting through it,' with his head motioning toward his parents."[82]

This pattern of thinking about others started early. Interviewed about the death of his sister Robin when he was six, Bush didn't recall many details but said, "I do remember the sadness, yeah. I do, I do, a lot. I remember being sad. *I remember being sad for my parents.* They were sad."[83] The charges that Bush is an arrogant narcissist simply don't survive scrutiny.

Confidence, Conviction, and Doubt

Mr. Bush is a man of strong convictions. Having those convictions and keeping to them has been an invaluable asset to Mr. Bush personally and to his presidency. It has fueled the public view of him as a strong leader, itself an asset in building political capital. And it provides a psychological cushion for Mr. Bush personally in coping with the emotional rigors of being a controversial and determined leader.

Yet, conviction can shade off into rigidity. Has this happened to Mr. Bush? Consider the last-minute decision to go after Saddam Hussein, thus delaying the official onset of the battle plan at the start of the war, or the many changes that have accompanied the effort to rebuild Iraq, or an array of domestic policy initiatives. In all these areas, Mr. Bush has provided ample evidence that his focus on what works (or what doesn't) trumps any need for black-or-white consistency.

Doubt is one psychological mechanism that can keep this from happening. A president with doubts is more likely to be prudent than one without them. Yet doubts are a double-edged sword for presidents and their advisors. Too much doubt inhibits action that may be risky, but necessary. Too little doubt may lead to ill-advised action.

This issue arose publicly when Mr. Bush was quoted in a *Newsweek* article as saying he had no regrets about the decisions he had made.[84] But was that true? Apparently not, by Mr. Bush's own admission.

In a nationally televised interview with Barbara Walters, the subject came up again. She asked the president about the *Newsweek* quote and asked skeptically, "You never have doubts?," to which Mr. Bush replied, "If I do I'm not going to air them on national TV."[85]

Woodward reports that during the lead-up to the Afghanistan War, when things on the ground did not seem to be moving in the right direction, his national security advisor, Dr. Rice, asked Mr. Bush if he was concerned. He replied, "Of course, I'm concerned about the fact that things are not moving!"[86] Here Mr. Bush is clearly worried, and worries are the handmaiden of doubt.

Mr. Bush has apparently given the role of doubt in reaching decisions some thought, as he has the nature of leadership more generally, and here is what he has concluded: "a president has got to be the calcium in the backbone. If I weaken, the whole team weakens. If I'm doubtful, I can assure you there will be a lot of doubt . . . it's essential that we be confident, determined and united. I don't need people around me who are not steady . . . and if there's a kind of hand-ringing attitude going on when times are tough, I don't like it."[87]

Mr. Bush is correct about the impact of a leader's confidence and resolve on his team of advisors and the public more generally. If he doesn't have confidence, why should others? As for the possibility of his advisors having a "hand-ringing attitude," Bush attributes some of it to concerns generated by the media and the instant analysis "of every expert and former colonel" with an opinion. He goes on to note "we've got these very strong people on the National Security Council who do get affected by what people say about them."[88]

Mr. Bush clearly prefers that doubts be expressed *before* a decision is made, not afterward. The evidence is that the various plans for Afghanistan and Iraq were the subject of vigorous debate within the administration. Yet Woodward reports that a few days into the war in Afghanistan there seemed to be no progress, and members of the press were starting to raise pointed questions about the war's tactics and strategy.

Worse, Dr. Rice told the president that all of his advisors had some doubts, and no one was sanguine about what they were achieving and might achieve.[89] Mr. Bush told Mr. Woodward that "if people were having second thoughts about their judgment, I need to know what they were, and they needed to lay them on the table."[90] And indeed at the next National Security Council meeting, the president did ask whether anybody had any reservations, or any new ideas to put on the table. No one did. He then gave a pep talk.

Woodward observes that the president did not really open the door to discussion more than a crack.[91] Perhaps most of the doubt among his advisors was the worry and nervousness that attend this most consequential of presidential decisions. Perhaps some were afraid for their reputations if their plans should falter. Yet, clearly, no one had a better idea and the plan that had been developed had been repeatedly refined and was the best that could be devised given the constraints.

In the Afghanistan case, the situation took a turn for the better. But as this episode makes clear, Mr. Bush might well add one more responsibility to his role as team leader—he needs to help his advisors explore doubts. Are they a natural byproduct of anxiety? Are they related to specific aspects of the plan under construction? Are there aspects of the plan that could be readjusted to reduce doubt? Mr. Bush would benefit by considering doubts, whether they occur before or after a decision is made.

How Did George W. Get His Confidence?

So how did George W. Bush get the confidence he so clearly seems to have? And how did he gain it with such a lackluster record of conventional success stretching back so many years? The answer in brief is: by degrees, with his *personal* confidence helping him through long rough periods without the other—professional experience and success.

Recall that confidence is both personal and occupational. The first is about who you are, the second is about what you do. My theory is that George W. early on excelled at the first, and that this helped to carry him through a long tough period until he developed and consolidated the second.

George W. started out life in a loving family. Mr. Bush elaborated on the specific impact of that early family experience in an interview with *Time*. Asked "What is the most important thing about your family legacy?" he replied: "The unconditional love I got from my family liberated me. It gave me a sense of security. . . . It helped Jeb and me not be afraid of defeat."[92]

The death of his younger sister, Robin, when he was six drew George W. and his mother closer together. He had always, of course, felt close to his father. He had many friends in Midland, Texas, as he would throughout his life. He played a lot of baseball. George W. was not a good hitter, but he was scrappy. What's more, he played catcher and that ensured he would be in every game and play. In some ways the choice of playing catcher was prophetic. It was a position at the center of things, without necessarily requiring him to excel at any of the conventional indicators of baseball success.

Locals who knew George W. as a boy in Midland have commented on his "quick wit" and "little remarks."[93] Later, when the Bush family moved to Houston, George W. was remembered for playing baseball, "being popular," "intense," "a joiner," and, interestingly, being able to "work a room" at many of his father's business parties.[94]

Young George was developing a feel for people and so being a part, and sometimes center, of a group naturally carried over into his high school years at Andover. There, George was a BMOC (big man on campus), but his claim to that status did not rest on any conventional avenues of achievement. One Andover student, reflecting back, put the matter succinctly: "He rose to a certain prominence for no ostensible visible reason."[95] He became a cheerleader, then head cheerleader, and self-appointed "commissioner of a popular intramural stickball league." He and his group of cheerleaders began to do skits as part of their school spirit, which became very popular and led to worries that they were taking too prominent a place at the school.[96]

At Yale, George W. also excelled at interpersonal relations. He was well known for knowing "everyone." He remembered their names and little details about them. In his Junior year he pledged DEKE fraternity, where he drank, smoked, and generally carried on. He was no scholar, but he was definitely one of the boys. As had his father before, George W. was invited to join the small, select, secret club called Skull and Bones.

George W.'s early developmental history clearly shows that he had specialized in one of the two foundations of confidence, *personal* confidence. While others were finding the skills that would anchor the beginnings of their own vocational moorings, George W. did not. This imbalance persisted into his early adulthood.

Along the way, he found skills that he could and did master, but they didn't
build on each other in any coherent way. He learned to fly a jet, but it was unclear how that would help him find grounding in the adult world. He was admitted to Harvard Business School, but those skills didn't translate to success in the
oil business.

Into his late twenties, thirties, and even into his early forties, George W.'s
sense of confidence was literally forced to stand on one leg, his skill at relationships. And, as his drinking suggests, even that leg was wobbling. In fact, George
W. did not begin to put the disparate pieces of his competence together until he
became the part owner and the public face of the Texas Rangers. There, for the
first time, at 42 years of age, George W. had found a place in the adult world in
which he could make use of his interpersonal and occupational skills together.

That role saved his life, psychologically. His childhood love of the game
and his knowledge of it, his hard work when he was interested, his capacity to
make decisions, his ability to relate to a variety for people, his enjoyment of the
position, and his natural optimism combined to make George W. the ideal point
man for the team.

THE FOUNDATION OF POLITICAL CONFIDENCE: GEORGE W. AS GOVERNOR

That foundation became the basis for the next, more political step in George W.'s
adulthood, his election as governor of Texas. Developmentally, winning the governorship was a needed success in a life in which they had not been abundant.
Yet it was much more than psychological. Winning against long odds and
against the advice of doubters like his mother was only the second time in his
adult life that he had made his interpersonal and occupation skills come together
successfully. What's more, once in office he seemed to be good at leading and
governing and he enjoyed it.[97]

George W. began his governorship by calling on the powerful Democratic
Lt. Governor Bob Bullock, a crusty and legendary veteran of Texas politics. He
developed such a close relationship with Bullock that Bush invited him to sit in
on all his legislative strategy sessions. Contrary to the Lone Ranger theory of the
Bush administration, George W. reached out to cement relationships with powerful allies. He met one-on-one with 29 of the 31 Texas state senators. Bullock, of
course, had unparalleled knowledge and mastery of Texas politics and the levers
of power in the state legislature. Bush had a strong vision of where he wanted to
lead the state.

The new governor ran on four major themes: educational reform, reforming
the juvenile justice system, welfare reform, and tort reform. The state already

had in place a testing program on academic accomplishment. What Bush did was actually use that information to halt the widespread use of social promotion, passing failing students onto the next grade. More than that, in 1996 he instituted a reading initiative that required all students to be able to read by the third grade. This was clearly the template for his "No Child Left Behind" act in the first year of his presidency.

On his other platform issues Bush had moderate success, but made some rookie mistakes. Crime did go down in Texas during this period, as it did nationally, but this seemed to have more to do with an expanding economy than with any of the Bush proposals, like the bill he signed allowing Texans to carry concealed weapons. He did increase the penalties for serious juvenile crime, but his campaign pledge to end parole for child molesters and murderers ran afoul of the court's interpretation of the Texas constitution.

On welfare and tort reform, the governor made progress as well. During his first term, through his welfare-to-work program Bush decreased the welfare rolls by half.[98] Here again, a strong economy helped, but it seems clear that the continued success of a similar federal program even during the recent time of economic downturn suggests the program's basic premises are correct. On tort reform, he instituted a limit to the amount that courts could order in punitive damages.

One exception to Bush's general record of getting what he wanted from the legislature came in the area of taxes. Texas operated under a system whereby property taxes funded education, which meant in effect that the richer property owners subsidized poorer school districts. Bush had campaigned on the promise to make it more equitable and, once in office, he proposed a $3 billion a year cut in the taxes to be offset by a small increase in the sales tax and a new fee for professional partnerships. Although the governor campaigned for his initiative it was defeated in the legislature, and instead a $1 billion a year property tax cut was passed. Putting the best face on his defeat, Bush claimed victory.

Looking back on Governor Bush's first term, several points emerge. Bush not only made campaign promises regarding his policies, he followed through on all of them. "Meaning it" was clearly important early on. He also emerged as an astute politician and leader. Knowing how the Texas legislature worked, he worked with it. He forged key relationships with powerful allies and didn't neglect to try to get to know and involve legislative members.

George W. was clearly proud of the *team* that he had put together. When asked whether he could carry his success to Washington, Bush replied, "It's not just me. . . . It's an administration."[99] Whatever reluctance he had had in giving others due credit seemed to be fading, as he had clearly earned his own success.

Bush also anticipated his presidential style in Texas by being famous for on-time meetings and a blunt style. When a group of Texas university chancellors

came to ask him for $1 billion more from the state budget, the governor asked
them if they would settle for $500 million, to which they immediately agreed.
Bush then told them he that he was only kidding and that, since they had agreed
to a fifty percent cut in the request without quarrel, they would have to come
back to him with a detailed justification for any new money.[100]

George W. was no one's fool. Texas citizens thought so, too, and liked him
personally as well as his policies. They re-elected him by an overwhelming margin. George W. had found a life's vocation.

There were other confidence-building occupational experiences on the road
to his success as governor. George W.'s role as a trusted troubleshooter for his father's 1988 presidential campaign marked an important step. Others, including
his wife, Laura, saw it as a turning point because for the first time he was on
equal footing with his father, that is, in an adult-to-adult relationship.[101] There is
something to her observation. In selecting him for this important role, George
W.'s father had indicated his trust and faith in his son's skills. More important, he
was giving his son a most profound personal and political assignment—his own
political career. The fate of the father was now, to some degree at least, in the
hands of his son.

It was certainly a major step, but because George W. still had an uncertain
professional future in front of him after the campaign, it was not a turning point.
That would only come with his role as head of the Texas Rangers. Even then, it
is more accurate to speak of consolidation than a turning point. And consolidation is not synonymous with instantaneous transformation.

The Texas Rangers experience and his political success as governor cata-
pulted George W. to a presidential nomination. Yet, as Bruni's portrait of candidate Bush makes clear, the consolidation of his adulthood was by no means
uniform. He had resisted some of the hard work, long hours, and endless campaign stops that are the lot of any non-incumbent. He had sometimes preferred
charm to hard work.

Yet, over time, he found that he could not take anything for granted, least of
all his own success as a candidate. When John McCain beat him handily in New
Hampshire, Bush buckled down, motivated in part by an embarrassment to his
pride, and found a rekindled sense of determination to do something about it. He
and his staff retooled their campaign and went on to win the nomination.

Even before he faced Al Gore in the general election, George W.'s commitment had intensified and become less episodic. Early in the campaign,
when Stuart Stevens suggested four mock debates with five people playing the
other candidates and then critique meetings afterward, Karl Rove and Mark
McKinnon summed up their view of Bush's likely response: "Never gonna
happen."[102] It didn't. Yet Frank Bruni reports that, three months before the Re-

publican national convention, Bush began to work hard with advisors Mike Gerson and Karen Hughes on his speech.[103] He did the same for his debates with Al Gore.[104]

By the end of the presidential campaign, Mr. Bush had been through the political version of hell, but the point was that he had gone through it. Slowly at first, but with gathering momentum, Mr. Bush committed himself to do what was necessary for him to win. If that meant long days and weeks away from the comforts of home that he held so dear, so be it. If it meant endless hours of preparation and endless venues of wholesale politics, he would do it.

Mr. Bush has not yet, and probably never will, fully rid himself of the quirky elements of his psychology. He had many strengths and some important weakness as a candidate. The same is true as well for him as president. Still, if he has not strived for or reached perfection, he has at least fully entered his adulthood.

PRESIDENT BUSH:
JUDGMENT AND LEADERSHIP

CHAPTER 5

GEORGE W. BUSH

GOOD JUDGMENT OR COWBOY POLITICS?

ON SEPTEMBER 11, 2001, SEPARATE TEAMS of Middle-Eastern terrorists hijacked four American commercial airliners. Loaded with fuel for their transcontinental trips, at 8:46 A.M. American Airlines flight 11 crashed into the World Trade Center North Tower; at 9:03 A.M. United Airlines flight 175 crashed into the World Trade Center South Tower; and at 9:40 A.M. American Airlines flight 77 crashed into the western section of the Pentagon. The fourth and last hijacked plane, United Airlines flight 93, never reached its intended target because of the actions of several of its passengers, who gave their lives in a successful attempt to prevent a fourth suicide plane crash. The two planes that flew into the World Trade Center caused their total destruction. There were close to 3,000 deaths as a result of these attacks. Economics losses, direct and indirect, were in the billions.

To be sure, planes had been hijacked in the past, but the normal pattern was for them to be diverted to some destination other than intended, or for there to be a hostage crisis ending either in the storming of the plane or the safe release of the passengers and the bringing of the culprits to justice. On 9/11, the usual script was not played out, and the inconceivable had become reality. The result was an unparalleled, unforeseen attack on American soil, at symbols of American power—economic for the World Trade centers, military for the Pentagon.

On the morning of September 11, 2001, President Bush was at the Emma Booker Elementary School in Sarasota, Florida as part of his efforts to showcase his educational initiatives. "I was sitting outside the classroom waiting to go in, and I saw an airplane hit the tower; the TV was obviously on. And I used to fly, myself, and I said, 'Well there's one terrible pilot.' I said, 'it must have been a horrible accident.' But I was whisked off there. I didn't have much time to think."[1]

He was listening to a presentation about the school's reading program and listening to individual students read. Shortly after 9:05 A.M., Andrew Card, the president's chief of staff, entered the room and whispered in Mr. Bush's ear, "A second plane has hit the tower. America is under attack."[2]

That moment is indelibly etched and caught by photos and video. Mr. Bush's head is cocked to one side. His eyes and expression reflect shock and dismay. He is clearly struggling to grasp what he has just been told. Given the savagery of the attacks, it is hardly surprising that George W. Bush's initial response was shock.

Mr. Bush stayed listening to the students for a few more moments before getting up and leaving to talk with his advisors. What was the president thinking in those moments? He has said, "*I wasn't sure what to think at first.* You know, I grew up in a period of time when America coming under attack never entered my mind . . . and *I started thinking hard about what it meant to be under attack. . . .*"[3] As he later recalled, "*I made up my mind that if America was under attack, we'd get them.*"[4]

As Bush told two reporters some time later, "I made up my mind at that moment that we were going to war. They had declared war on us, and I made up my mind at that moment that we were going to war."[5] This resolution was conveyed to Karl Rove, the president's chief political advisor, who recalls that "there was a lot of fog, confusion. The President came walking into the room, took one look at the television set and said, '*We're at war.* Get me the Vice President and get me the Director of the FBI.'"[6]

JUDGMENT

Presidents are powerful because they combine enormous resources with substantial decision-making discretion. What they choose and how they choose it matters enormously. If, as Alexander Hamilton believed, presidential leadership is the engine of political progress, then surely presidential judgment is its compass.

We can understand judgment as the quality of analysis, reflection, and ultimately insight that informs the making of consequential decisions. Decisions that pose significant risks and therefore have significant consequences for presidential areas of responsibility raise issues of good or flawed judgment. These major forks in the decision road are *framing decisions.*[7] Framing decisions are crucial because they represent key, and sometimes (but not always) starkly contrasting alternatives, each of which will point to different paths, open up some options, close others, and result in starkly different consequences. Framing involves a judgment about what is at stake, what principles will guide action, and what actions must be taken. It is a way of seeing the world.

For the president, judgment is a joint function of the match between his analytical and reflective abilities on the one hand, and the nature of the problem to be faced on the other. Judgment is a consequence of analysis, framing, and reflection. Appreciating the nature of a problem is crucial to deciding what is at issue and is a critical first step. *Analysis* is required to discern the essential nature of problem, the potential avenues of response and their implications, and a sense of the methods by which these might be accomplished. Disparate pieces of information must be connected with each other, and with other frames of reference such as past experience, values, and interests. *Reflection* requires a capacity to consider and evaluate information from a series of perspectives. Good judgment also requires the ability to place information in a framework that makes intellectual, experiential, and emotional sense, not only to the president but also to those whom the decisions affect. Reflection, therefore, rests on the capacity to anchor analysis in frameworks of understanding, evaluation, and feeling. In the end, judgments must point to action. Reaching a good judgment is important, but it will lie fallow or fail if it is not well acted upon. That means a president must find and utilize the appropriate means to bring his judgments to realization.

Let us look back at Bush's judgments in the period immediately after learning of the attack. Bush's initial confusion was soon replaced by a recognition that however unique *this* specific form of attack may have been, it clearly was an attack. The by-whom and the why may not have yet been clear, but incontrovertibly it was an attack. And an attack warranted, required, a response. "We'd get them" has the ring of Texas frontier justice; "We're going to war" that of a commander-in-chief; "Get me the Vice President and get me the Director of the FBI" that of a president fully understanding his constitutional obligations to ensure continuity of government and the internal security of the country.

Good judgment provides a *fitting* solution to a set of circumstances. The word "fitting" is used purposefully: each set of circumstances must be met on its own ground. The attacks of 9/11 presented a new set of circumstances. Bush's judgment of what was at stake and what had to be done fit the circumstances. What Bush quickly realized was that whoever had launched the attacks had imagination, skill, cunning, incredible resolve, and profound hatred for America. Bush prides himself on being a good judge of people, and in this instance he was certainly right on target.

The act revealed a great deal about the psychology of those who did it. They were full of rage, wished for blood vengeance, saw their targets as objects not persons, and would sacrifice their lives to take ours. Whoever was behind the attack had declared war. War is not a skirmish. It is not just a conflict, since that presupposes that there are differences that might or can be reconciled. A war is a battle between adversaries, each using the full measure of their resources, to vanquish or mortally wound the other. A limited response—whether legal, military, or diplomatic, as had been the case in the past—would no longer suffice for this new set of circumstances. A new response was therefore called for that applied the full resources of the United States in all three areas over an extended period of time, and in the many locations that would be necessary.

There is a distinction to be made between the quality of the judgment at this framing stage and its actual implementation, just as there is a difference between strategy and tactics. Put another way, taking one fork in the road may be the right decision, although a flat tire or rough ride along the road may lead to criticism and second thoughts. The crucial question then becomes: "If we had taken another route, would we be any closer to reaching our goal?" And we must keep in mind that even if we had taken the other route, we may nonetheless still have had a flat tire, and experienced substantial problems.

The fact that there are ups and downs after a good judgment is made does not mean that judgment wasn't fitting. No decision, even a good judgment, results in perfect outcomes. Nor can a good judgment guarantee success. That can only be determined by what the president does after he has reached a good judgment.[8] Ordinarily a good judgment is a critical first step in a long and difficult process. Or to put it another way, realizing correctly you're at war doesn't win it.

Even critics of the administration who question the subsequent implementation of the war on terrorism recognize that the fundamental framing decision, which took the United States down one path rather than another, was basically correct. Ivo H. Daalder and James M. Lindsay of the Brookings Institution, two severe critics of the Bush administration's foreign policy, write "The Bush administration is right to see the trinity of terrorists, tyrants, and technology as the principle threat to national security."[9] The question is what to do about it.

Critics of the Bush administration like Daalder and Lindsay focus on the rough road and the unforeseen problems. What they do not do is provide convincing arguments that alternative frames of understanding and action would have been more effective or fitting—that is, evinced better judgment. If Bush had framed the circumstances as just an "attack" and responded accordingly with, say, bombing the country giving haven to the culprits, would that have been commensurate with the attack America suffered? Would it have been militarily, politically, or emotionally fitting? Would it have been strategically fitting, in the sense of deterring future attacks? Obviously a limited bombing would not have been emotionally fitting: retribution had to be made. And deterrence was unlikely to be fully effective. These were obviously people willing to kill themselves, and thus could not be deterred, and in any case past experience of limited attacks on countries providing haven to terrorists had clearly been ineffective in deterring new attacks, as 9/11 made clear.

Mr. Bush could have framed it as a legal issue. Again, this would have been emotionally incommensurate with the nature and scope of the attack. It was not a crime. It was an attack. Nor was there any reason to believe such a frame would be effective: after all, the FBI caught the culprits responsible for the first World Trade Center bombing in 1993, and they were brought to justice. In the case of 9/11, the culprits could not be caught and brought to justice because they were dead. A supporter of such a framing would have to develop convincing evidence that such an approach would address the widespread and worldwide nature of the terrorist threat, as well as demonstrate that this approach would be successful in preventing further terrorist acts like the one that took place on 9/11. Critics obviously can't.

Bush could have responded by framing the issue as a diplomatic one. Such a strategy might have entailed a demand that the United Nations pass a resolution condemning this act of aggression. But, aggression by *whom?* The United Nations, and indeed diplomacy itself, is set up for interactions among *states.* It is not set up for terrorists who do not follow the rules, indeed whose entire reason for being is in conflict with these rules and norms. And if we assume for the moment that it was a *state* that planned and carried out the attack, surely its leadership would have recognized that a direct attack on the sovereign territory of another state is the very definition of war, one that justifies and legitimates a military response. Any state leadership that would have conceived of an attack on the United States would have had to assume that the United States would respond with the full might at its disposal, which would end in their defeat and elimination.

All three frames clearly would have been at the least inadequate given the nature of the attack. They would not have been fitting emotionally, psychologically, or strategically. Recalling those moments sitting there in the classroom, Bush said, "I wasn't interested in lawyers; I wasn't interested in a bunch of debate. I was interested in finding out who did it and bringing them to justice. I also knew they would try to hide, and anybody who provided haven, help, food, would be held accountable by the United States of America."[10]

GOOD JUDGMENT: INSTINCT OR SKILL?

Mr. Bush has said of his own decision-making, "I think it's just instinctive. I'm not a textbook player. I'm a gut player."[11] What he calls "instinct" is really judgment. His assessment of the nature of the attack and its meaning, as well as a consideration of what it revealed about the persons who did it, were instrumental in making the judgment. The fact that Mr. Bush came to his judgment with a flash of profound insight does not make it instinctual.

Facing a situation not in any textbook, Bush thought outside the box. This was not "business as usual," calling for a conventional response. Indeed, insight itself simply reflects reaching a central understanding about the circumstances you face and how they do and do not fit into the understandings you have available to process them. Central to being able to arrive at good judgment is having a clear-eyed view of what you see.

Cleared-Eyed Judgment

The best judgments are made with clear eyes. It is difficult, if not impossible, to reach a good (fitting) judgment without seeing clearly what the circumstances are. Yet seeing things for what they are is no small matter, either psychologically or cognitively. There are many ways to be thrown off track.

A president may not, for a variety of reasons, wish to see things as they are. Wishful thinking is one common reason why that happens but it is not the only one. Conventional wisdom, preconceived categories, or preferred assumptions may all operate to keep people from seeing things as they are. Obviously, any or all of these can keep a president from making a good judgment, which is to say to correctly match the circumstances that he sees with the categories appropriate to them.

One of Mr. Bush's underappreciated decision-making skills is the capacity for clear-eyed views and an equally important capacity to act on them. I put both together for the obvious reason that, from the standpoint of making a good judgment, it does little good to see things clearly but be unable or unwilling to act on what you see. Acting on what you see, especially if following through brings with it the possibility of real risk or loss, is of course one aspect of character integrity. Generally, that term refers to a president's values and ideals. However, it also seems clear that this can be applied to what a president sees in his circumstances and is prepared to act upon. It is another manifestation of having the courage of your convictions—in this case not of your ideals and values, but what you see.

In some ways, writing about clear-eyed views in the case of George W. Bush seems paradoxical. This is after all the man who had trouble owning up to how much he drank, preferring the ambiguous "one too many" to the reality of his circumstances, which were that he drank too much. On the other hand, when Mr. Bush went out for his hung-over run the morning after his fortieth birthday celebration, it was him, and him on his own, who saw his drinking for what it was and determined that day to stop.

He is also the man who had trouble owning up to how much his family name and friends helped him at a time he was desperately trying to establish his own successful adulthood. Perhaps he saw, but had trouble saying it, for the obvious reason that if he did, his own contributions would shrink as a result, and at the time he needed all the evidence of success that he could get. Certainly, his lament at the height of his difficulties in finding the "liberator"—"I'm all name and no money"—was a lightning bolt of self revelation.

Some seeds of clear-eyed thinking can be found in his childhood. George W. told students at Sam Houston Elementary School that when he was young he "wanted to be a baseball player like Willie Mays, *Then I realized I wasn't going to be a very good hitter,* so I wasn't going to be like Willie Mays."[12]

Over the years, the family and especially his father came to depend on him as the person who could look circumstances in the eye—and not blink. And this trait showed up as well in dealings with the league owners and management when he helped run the Texas Rangers.

Mr. Bush became involved in league politics when his longtime friend Fay Vincent fought for his job as commissioner of baseball. Owners were angry at a series of decisions Vincent had made. George W. urged Vincent to fight for his job, but he ultimately decided not to. One of Bush's biographers, writing about that experience, said, "When discussing Vincent, an unhappy *George W. gave this clear eyed assessment:* 'He made a lot of tough decisions and because of that he was not popular.'"[13] He has applied that same clear-eyed assessment to his father's and his own presidency.

George W. could be clear-eyed about the mistakes of his father, even though that relationship could not be deeper and more psychologically important to him. If there ever was a relationship in which a son's view of his father might be clouded by his psychological attachments, this would be it. Noting that George H. W. had not used his success and high public support after the 1991 Persian Gulf War adroitly, thus not winning reelection, George W. said that "It doesn't matter whether you won by one point, two points, even 10 points, it's important to move as quickly as you can in order to spend whatever capital you have as quickly as possible."[14] The observation obviously carries a criticism, and suggests that George W.'s love for his father did not keep him from seeing clearly one reason for his father's fate.

It seems clear, in retrospect, that George W. had trouble seeming himself clearly on occasion because the sight was so painful. His drinking was clearly one such illustration, his lack of independent personal successes another. Yet, in both cases he had flashes of painful self-insight. In one case it led him to stop drinking cold, in the other it led him to keep on trying to dull the pain of failing to measure up by working harder toward success.

A Clear-Eyed Presidency

It is, however, in the presidency that Mr. Bush's ability to see things clearly and say what he sees is most evident. There are many examples of the link between Mr. Bush's blunt talk and his clear-eyed views of matters. After 9/11 Mr. Bush was asked about public concerns with the economy rather than the war on terror. He responded that while economic statistics or conditions are likely to change, the threat of terrorism to the security of the United States and the life of its citizens was now a constant. Making reference to a badge of a police officer killed on 9/11 that he had received from the officer's mother, he said, "the American people have to understand that when I held up that badge I meant it: This war on terrorism is my primary focus."[15] Losing a job is an awful experience; however, it cannot be compared to losing a life. Bush had a clear-eyed view of the impact on individuals of the threat of terrorism.

Bush has also been clear-eyed in recognizing that bad leadership and bad government are fundamental impediments to peace and security—as evidenced by his goals in Afghanistan and in Iraq. Another instance involves Yasser Arafat, leader of the Palestinian Authority (PA). While Bush has come out in favor of a Palestinian state, he has directly tied that outcome to the performance of the PA and especially that of Arafat, both of which have been found wanting.

President Clinton had invested a great deal of political capital on the success of his Middle East peace efforts with Yasser Arafat, and wound up being severely disappointed. Bush drew a lesson from that. But even if he hadn't, his psychology would have led him to the same stance. Bush generally looks, assesses, and then acts.

So, typically, he came into office with a "watch and see" attitude toward Mr. Arafat's role. Bush started out with a skeptical but open mind, and then set clear tests. He called upon Arafat a number of times to lead and show evidence of doing something concrete to stop the terrorism against Israel.

Bush was blunt in pointing to what he saw as Mr. Arafat's inconsistent behavior: "He can't close the front door of his prisons and let prisoners out the back. . . . Arafat criticized us. He urged us to put more pressure on Israel. Who is he kidding?"[16] How could Arafat expect the United States to place pressure on Israel when Arafat himself was either doing little to help his own case or actively doing things to harm it?

One of the central indictments of Arafat came during the second week of January 2002, when Israeli commandos seized a ship carrying 58 tons of weapons bound for Palestinian-controlled territory. The captain of the vessel revealed that he was to deliver the weapons to Fatah, a part of Mr. Arafat's organization.[17] In response, Mr. Arafat ordered an "investigation." By April, Bush said that Arafat had not earned his trust because "Here's a man who said he has signed on to Oslo, that he was going to fight off terrorism. . . . We thought a couple of month[s] ago that we thought we had an agreement. The next thing we know, he's ordering a shipment of arms from Iran."[18]

By June 24 of that year, Mr. Bush had come fully to the position that marked a startling departure from recent American policy based on attempts to broker a peace agreement with Yasser Arafat. In a Rose Garden address, he called on "the Palestinian people to elect new leaders not compromised by terror." Asked almost two years later about Mr. Arafat, the president said, "I took an assessment of what was possible and realized that it was impossible to achieve peace with Chairman Arafat."[19] That decision placed Mr. Bush in opposition to the State department and several traditional American allies in Europe.

Straight talk? Yes. Blunt talk? Certainly. Yet it was more than that. Mr. Bush could not reconcile and thus abandoned the irreconcilable position of having a leader involved in an ongoing and major terror campaign against the very people with whom he was supposed to be reaching a peace agreement. In one more way, Mr. Bush signaled this was not business as usual.

A Watchful Man

Mr. Bush is a watchful man. That is related to but not the same as being clear-eyed. Being watchful involves carefully looking; being clear-eyed involves what and how well you see when you do. Being watchful is a form of curiosity and information seeking. Watching carefully what people do, what they say, and how they respond to different circumstances can be very revealing. Being watchful is a trait that is very consistent with Mr. Bush's character psychology as well as his capacity to both engage and to stand apart from others.

I said above that George W. adopted a "watch and see" stance toward Mr. Arafat. It was not a figure of speech. Rather, it was descriptive of a little-known aspect of how Mr. Bush reaches his judgments about people, their views, and their trustworthiness. In the documentary made by Alexandra Pelosi, George W. is heard on camera saying, "I spend a lot of time watching people watch me."[20] He is of course watching them. In his autobiography, he says of himself, "I'm an observer, a listener and a learner."[21] The first and third certainly seem true. As I will detail shortly, he has a mixed record on the second.

In an interview during the 2000 presidential campaign, Bush described what he does while giving a stump speech: "*I'm looking, I'm watching.* I can tell you who hasn't made up their mind yet when I go through that business about 'If you're for me, thanks, and if you're not for me, thanks for listening.' When I said that in Anderson [South Carolina], I was talking to two women who had come to see what this guy is all about. And I knew they hadn't made up their minds yet.'"[22]

You won't catch Mr. Bush up late at night in a long discussion of the meaning of life, or a policy for that matter. Yet it would be a large mistake to conclude that Mr. Bush is not interested, especially in the things he might observe while looking carefully. In Jordan, he summoned Israeli Prime Minister Ariel Sharon and Palestinian Prime Minister Mahmoud Abbas away from the conference table to chat outside on the lawn for 30 minutes. Why? "What I wanted to do is to observe the interplay between the two; did they have the capacity to relax in each other's presence, for starters? And I felt they did. In other words . . . the body language was positive. There wasn't a lot of hostility or suspicion."[23]

According to Woodward, "Bush insisted that General Franks, in charge of the planning for the Iraq War, come to Texas to brief him personally for the same reasons. Bush recalled that he was interested in 'reading Franks.' During the presentation, 'I'm watching his body language very carefully,' the eyes, the demeanor. It was more important than some of the substance.[24]

Mr. Bush uses the same technique to make judgments about his advisers. During the 2000 campaign several reporters examined Mr. Bush's decision style.[25] That style was quite clear. Mr. Bush carefully selected his advisors, worked with them to develop confidence in their loyalty and judgment, and then relied on them.

When Bush violated his own rule, he ran into trouble. A major example was the appointment of Treasury Secretary Paul O'Neill, a man Bush didn't know and whose appointment proved to be a disastrous mismatch on psychological and policy grounds. The mismatch between them seemed to be between a man who liked to be in charge and thought, as president, he ought to be, and the man he hired, who also liked to be in charge and thought, as the brilliant accomplished person he was, *he* deserved to be in charge.[26]

Mr. Bush's watchful approach to judging people and circumstances is an important form of curiosity. What will persons do in response to their circumstances? How will they act with others? Mr. Bush is not incurious.

Assessing Risks and Taking Them

In the area of risk, Mr. Bush is the exact reverse of his predecessor. Mr. Clinton gambled needlessly in his personal life, putting his presidency at risk. In this respect, he was reckless. Yet politically, he was willing to risk little. He masked his real commitments with rhetoric that suggested he believed other than he acted. Only in his support of NAFTA and his wife's failed universal health care initiative can one see a willingness to put his convictions on the line. The rest was triangulation.

Mr. Bush is the direct opposite. He is, as the campaign demonstrated and the number of hours he spends on the Washington social circle attest, a homebody. He loves his wife and family and one can easily and safely predict there will be no Monicas to distract Mr. Bush from his public responsibilities and aspirations.

It is in his presidency that it is easier to see the president's risk-taking proclivities. The largest and most obvious gamble was the war in Iraq. In a front-page *Washington Post* cover story aptly titled "Bush Bets Future on Success in Iraq," the reporter observed, "By accident or design, President Bush has allowed Iraq to become the gamble of a lifetime."[27] William Schneider wrote of this war and Mr. Bush, "He has staked his entire presidency on it."[28]

The risks are large and numerous. The initial invasion could have gone badly in many ways. There could have been high civilian or military casualties. The advance on Baghdad could have gotten bogged down. There could have been humanitarian disasters, ecological disasters, or political disasters such as the splitting apart of the country.

The war rearranged alliances in ways that will not be clear for years. We have gained new allies, lost older ones, or at least reevaluated them. It put the United States' military, diplomatic, and national rebuilding skills in the spotlight. It is now clear that the United States has no equal in winning wars, but it is also evident that the risks don't end there.

The war unsettled and inflamed the Middle East and set in motion processes whose results may or may not remake the region in ways the president hoped for. A democratic, progressive Iraq would be an unparalleled accomplishment, but a failure to accomplish it would set back Mr. Bush's vision for the Middle East for decades, if not permanently. It has and will have a profound effect on the war against terror, but again, whether these results will be salutary overall cannot now be truly assessed. The war may give terrorists pause, enrage them further, or both. The war certainly has emboldened critics, both domestically and internationally.

This has consequences for American standing abroad and for Mr. Bush's standing at home. And it has certainly set in motion the rearrangement of international politics in ways whose consequences will surely be felt for many decades.

Added to this large list were the risks for Mr. Bush politically. Any of the above items could have, and still could, cause a meltdown in his political standing. The risks to him personally (that is politically) were magnified because of the divided electorate. Even on a good day, Mr. Bush can count on no more than a support level in the low to mid-50 percent range on many policies. Adding up all these circumstances, it seems clear that Mr. Bush put his political convictions before his reelection chances.

Mr. Bush's approach to risk is a direct outgrowth of two major elements of his character: having the courage of his convictions and being able to stand apart from and withstand those who don't. Mr. Bush appears to operate by the general rule that if, after consideration, you think something is good policy and the right thing to do, find a way to do it. Mr. Bush is willing to take more risks because he is more willing to put his judgments on the line. He is also more willing to stand apart from those unwilling or unable to do so.

This is a rule because its applications far outweigh its exceptions. Iraq is clearly the largest example of risk-taking by this administration, but it is surely not the only one. Almost all the president's policies, domestic and international, are suffused with risk. When Mr. Bush chose to push ahead with his own agenda after the close and contested 2000 presidential election, that was a risk. When he chose to champion three successive tax cuts in the face of intense Democratic opposition and public indifference, that was a risk. When he chose to withdraw from the ABM treaty and unsign the Kyoto treaty, that was a risk. The administration's promise "to spread democracy and free markets to the Middle East, promising to move beyond the recent focus on Iraq and the Israeli-Palestinian conflict in an ambitious but vaguely defined project to transform a troubled region," represented another risk-filled undertaking.[29]

It is one thing to take risks, another to manage them. How Mr. Bush does so is indicated in Bob Woodward's interviews: "I'm the kind of person that wants to make sure that all risk is assessed. But a president is constantly analyzing making decisions based on risk, particularly in war—risk taken relative to what can be achieved."[30]

Although reassuring, Mr. Bush's answer still doesn't give much of a specific understanding of what factors go into the mix and how they are weighed. There is as yet no good data available on which to base any conclusions on these matters. Still, there are some clues.

One indication of how the president operated in the run-up to the war in Afghanistan can be seen in two facts. First, there were no readily available contingency plans for a military response against Afghanistan.[31] Second, when presented with three options—a cruise missile attack, a missile and bomber attack, and both with some limited combat troops[32]—Mr. Bush rejected them all and at least several other more robust plans. As he later told Mr. Woodward, he had not yet seen what looked like a successful plan, and "a president likes to have a military plan that will be successful."[33] All of this took time and patience.

Another element in how Mr. Bush calculates risk is found in a press conference Q & A:[34] Mr. Bush was asked about a CIA analysis that suggested that Saddam Hussein would be less constrained if the United States attacked him. Mr. Bush replied,

> it's like some people say, "Oh, we must leave Saddam alone. Otherwise, if we did something against him, he might attack us." Well, if we don't do something, he might attack us, and he might attack us with a more serious weapon. The man is a threat, Hutch, I'm telling you. He's a threat not only with what he has; he's a threat with what he's done. He's a threat because he's dealing with Al Qaeda. . . . a true threat facing our country is that an Al Qaeda-type network trained and armed by Saddam could attack America and not leave one fingerprint. It is a threat. And we're going to deal with it.[35]

I am aware of the controversial nature of the extent and nature of the links between Mr. Hussein and Al Qaeda. A number, however, have been documented. Colin Powell said the following about these linkages in his February 5, 2003 presentation to the United Nations Security Council:

> Going back to the early and mid-1990s, when bin Laden was based in Sudan, an al Qaeda source tells us that Saddam and bin Laden reached an understanding that al Qaeda would no longer support activities against Baghdad. Early al Qaeda ties were forged by secret, high-level [Iraqi] intelligence service contacts with al Qaeda. . . . We know members of both organizations met repeatedly and have met at least eight times at very senior levels since the early 1990s. In 1996, a foreign security service tells us that bin Laden met with a senior Iraqi intelligence official in Khartoum and later met the director of the Iraqi intelligence service. . . . Iraqis continued to visit bin Laden in his new home in Afghanistan. A senior defector, one of Saddam's former intelligence chiefs in Europe, says Saddam sent his agents to Afghanistan sometime in the mid-1990s, to provide training to al Qaeda members on document forgery. From the late 1990s until 2001, the Iraqi embassy in Pakistan played the role of liaison to the al Qaeda organization.[36]

His description was drawn from intelligence data and assessments of the FBI, the Defense Intelligence Agency, the CIA, and the National Security Agency.

The fact is that Mr. Bush must not only calculate the risks of action, but of inaction. As Robert Jervis points out, "actors are prone to accept great risks, when they believe they will suffer unless they act boldly."[37] This is how Bush saw it, too. Asked whether a war wouldn't incite more anger and hatred of the United States, Mr. Bush replied, "listen, *there's risk in all action we take. But the risk of inaction is not a choice, as far as I'm concerned.* The inaction creates more risk than doing our duty to make the world more peaceful. And obviously, I weighed all the consequences about all the differences."[38]

The problem is, how do you calculate these risks? Jervis notes that, after 9/11, "worst case analysis is now hard to dismiss."[39] That is especially so for a president, and moreover one who was caught flatfooted by 9/11.

There is obviously the danger that the risk of disaster can be overestimated. There is also the danger that risk can be underestimated relative to outcome. This is not the kind of risk that can be easily managed by making an initial prudent, limited, and restrictive decision, as Mr. Bush did with stem-cell research[40] or dredging the Hudson to remove toxic chemicals.[41] In those cases, an initial judgment was made precisely with the idea of managing risk by seeing how the processes unfolded—an example of the president's look, see, and judge approach.

That is not possible in the case of catastrophic terrorism. A wrong judgment on either calculation could prove disastrous. How to navigate and manage that risk is one of the true security dilemmas of the twenty-first century.

Domestic Risk and Political Capital

The term capital, as in political capital, suggests a surplus—something that you have beyond sufficiency, which enables you to do something else of value. A president can accumulate political capital in many ways. He may gain by a resounding election victory. This Mr. Bush clearly did not do. He can gain increased capital by trying to increase his political clout and position during off-year elections. This Mr. Bush did in 2002. He can gain it by showing that he makes skillful use of the political cards that he is dealt and winning respect, if not grudging approval. This Mr. Bush has succeeded in doing through his adroit use of his House majority, his flexibility in the Senate, and his use of the House-Senate reconciliation process to press his agenda.

He can also do it by winning victories in areas that he promised to address as a candidate. Mr. Bush has done this domestically with the passage of his Education bill and the Medicare Reform bill. And, a president can gain political capital by responding in an exceptional manner to events as Mr. Bush did after 9/11. Finally, a president can gain political capital by taking audacious policy steps and succeeding, as Mr. Bush did in Afghanistan and in the war against Saddam Hussein.

This listing of how a president can accumulate political capital suggests an important point about the Bush presidency. Starting from a position of having little political capital after the contested election of 2000, Mr. Bush has managed, through various means, to accumulate a fair amount of it. This is a point worth noting when considering the political skills of this president and others.

But as important as the question of how a president can earn political capital is, an equally compelling question is what he does with it. One can marshal one's capital to expend on large undertakings; one could fail to spend it; or one can use it as one accumulates it.

George W. clearly subscribes to a "use it or lose it" psychology. That psychological and political maxim can be directly traced back to his ambitions. Mr. Bush wants to accomplish what he considers large and important things. Many presidents do. But Mr. Bush not only wants to, he intends to. It is matter of being serious about his ambitions, of meaning it, and of fidelity to the ideals and judgments that led to his policies. That commits Mr. Bush to a certain level of political risk. A president who is always looking for ways to invest and leverage his political capital is a president who will obviously be an activist, but also one who is ready to take risks. In Mr. Bush's case these have been large ones.

GEORGE W. BUSH'S DECISION STYLE

A president's decision style grows out of his character. If he is ambitious and wants to be successful, he has to hone those skills that will help him realize his ambitions. If he is a president who likes people and wants to be liked by them, he will surround himself with friends. If, like George W. Bush, he prefers accomplishment and respect to being liked, he will surround himself with strong-minded people, and watch and listen carefully as problems are hashed out. If he has convictions and the courage of them, he will view the decision process from a different starting frame than a president with either or neither.

Some things about Mr. Bush's decision style are fairly clear and well established. Both as governor and president, Mr. Bush has disliked long meetings, long presentations, and long policy papers.[42] As he says of himself, "I like to get to the point."[43] He was well known to interrupt long-winded presentations to say, "Why don't you just close the book and tell me what you think is most important."[44]

One question that arises about Mr. Bush's style in reaching a decision is whether he listens and to whom he listens. Critics say Bush is close-minded and rigid. As a result, they say, he makes bad judgments and avoidable mistakes. These traits are not attractive attributes in a president. However, the question is: Have Bush's critics confused conviction with certainty, and rigidity with resolve?

And finally, the most basic question raised about Bush is whether he's smart enough to be a good president. Many critics think he is simply in over his head. In their minds, his success long ago outstripped his capacity. But if this is true, how did he become a two-term governor and then president?

Incurious?

"Is he curious?" is a question often raised about Mr. Bush. Its origins are the view among his critics that he is a dim bulb, made so by his lack of interest. It's a fatal flaw in a president, but is it true?

A good question is one of the most powerful information tools that a president has at his disposal. A president asks questions if he doesn't know and wishes to find out. A lack of interest in asking questions would reflect either that the president thinks he knows everything that matters, or it might reflect disinterest.

Mr. Bush has never been accused of thinking he knows everything worth knowing. Rather, he has been accused of being incurious and intellectually lazy. A *New York Times* editorial called Mr. Bush "one of the most incurious men ever to occupy the White House."[45] Richard Gephardt, Democratic presidential candidate said of Mr. Bush, "he is uninformed, he is inexperienced and *he has no curiosity.*"[46]

Mr. Bush has even been accused, indirectly, of being responsible for 9/11 because he was incurious. This incendiary, and unsupported, charge was made in a *New York Times* editorial about the 9/11 commission hearings entitled "The Price of Incuriosity."[47] No evidence was presented that Mr. Bush was incurious or even that he should have been doing a particular thing when warnings about a possible terrorist attack came in over the summer of 2001. The *Times* editorial reported that CIA director George Tenet briefed the president in person two times that month and suggested by implication that more briefings might have avoided 9/11. The *Times* did not report the fact that Mr. Bush was frequently briefed on these matters during the period involved. The number of briefings was not the issue in preventing 9/11, what was understood about the specific plans of the attack was.

Alternatively, the *New York Times* implied that if Mr. Bush had been more curious 9/11 might have been avoided. What should Mr. Bush have been curious about? That is the subject of David Broder's pundit piece.[48] He criticized the president for not having spent his time reaching down into the various national security bureaucracies to personally "shake loose" information that might have or could have been relevant to preventing the attack. Left unanswered is how the president, who is not trained in intelligence analysis, would have had any better success getting the facts and assembling them in time and in such a way so as to prevent 9/11 than his own national security professionals. It is an exceedingly harsh and unfair charge.

Still, the question of Mr. Bush's level of interest in and curiosity about policy matters is a long-standing issue among his critics. Moreover, even if they raise it in inappropriate and unfair ways, it is an appropriate question to ask about a president. So, is Mr. Bush incurious? The answer seems to be that he is not curious about everything, but that does not make him incurious.

Howard Gardner has said that Mr. Bush has great "people intelligence." However, when it comes to "existential intelligence," meaning the capacity to ask and consider big questions—such as "Who are we?" "What are good and evil?" "Will we survive or falter?" Or "What should we want from our lives?"— "Mr. Bush," Gardner says, "seems to be clueless."[49]

Gardner's remarks raise the question of whether we should prefer a president who is a good judge of people and circumstances, or a president who can have an interesting discussion about the meaning of life. Mr. Bush does not have the kind of curiosity that inquires deeply into questions of motivation, including his own: "You know I don't spend a lot of time thinking about myself, about why I do things."[50] Mr. Bush prefers the world of action to that of self-contemplation. And it is in the real world of action that the president must govern and decide.

It isn't that Mr. Bush can't reflect. He's on record as having done so repeatedly. Speaking in a post-election interview Mr. Bush had this to say about the experience, "Once I'd gotten over the frustration of the campaign not ending and had accepted the reality that it was going to take a while and become used to the fact that lawyers were going to [be] everywhere, *I had time to reflect.* And I gave it my best shot. I worked as hard as I possibly could."[51]

Bush told Woodward that he thought "long and hard" about a number of things after the terrorist attack. He thought about the importance of humanitarian aid, he thought about who would run the country in the aftermath of the invasion. He also took time out to reflect on his decisions after he gave the final go-ahead for the Iraqi operation:

I was in the Situation Room, and it was a dramatic moment. It was a heavy moment for me, and *I wanted to come outside and reflect,* so I came out and got the dogs and we walked around the South Lawn a couple of times. And it was—for me it's like going to walk in a forest. I came and walked a couple of times and . . . *gathered my thoughts and thought very seriously, a serious reflection about what I had just done,* and said a prayer or two.[52]

Considering whether to discuss the issue of the link between terrorists and weapons of mass destruction in his major speech to Congress, Bush says, "I left it out. It could overwhelm the whole speech. At some point we have to brief the nation. But I took it out. It's going to stay out. *I thought long and hard about it.*"[53] Asked about the possible infusion of large numbers of American troops into Afghanistan, Bush said, "I've thought long and hard about the use of troops, I think about it all the time."[54] Speaking to Bob Woodward about the National Terror Alerts, Bush said, "National alerts are very interesting issues, if you think about it," which implies, of course, that he has.[55] He then went on to raise a series of concerns he had thought about among them, "how many national alerts does it take to numb the American psyche."[56]

The fact that Bush thinks "long and hard" about things doesn't guarantee that his thoughts have depth, accuracy, insight, or subtlety. Yet given that Mr. Bush is clearly capable of clear-eyed observation, it's fair to say he's much more thoughtful than he is given credit for being.

Pragmatic Curiosity

Mr. Bush has a definite political and policy philosophy, but he is not a theoretician. Nor is he a policy-detail man. He won't be able to quote you Medicaid reimbursement rate trends in Michigan.

Mr. Bush *is* a president who is intensely interested in what works and in getting results. We tend to think of curiosity as theoretical, but it can also be very pragmatic. Bush's focus on results reflects his preference for immersion in the real rather than the theoretical world. "What works?" is an antidote to theory, which Bush dislikes if it leads nowhere. As Mr. Bush says of himself, "I like clarity,"[57] and the focus on results is certainly one way to achieve it. A focus on results also leads to questions. George Tenant said of Bush, "When you took a problem to him he always asked, 'Well, what's a solution? How do you fix it? How do you take the next step? How do you get around this?'"[58]

Pragmatic curiosity has many virtues. In a world of full of ambiguity and risk, it allows action to take place. If you are intensely interested in what can work and get that information, you will be more likely to be able to choose a course of action. Action itself can beget further action. To the extent that an interest in what works leads to action, it also provides another benefit. People and nations know where you stand. They don't have to guess. In a world in which subtle signals critical to deterrence can be lost or ignored, decisive action can provide benefits.

Pragmatic curiosity is no cure-all. Nor is it a substitute for understanding why action might work. When a policy no longer works, you want to know why, and that requires some knowledge of how it works.

Sometimes asking "why" questions can be answered with a policy principle, and that policy principle can be based on a deep insight. Mr. Bush's
policy that America must be strong is predicated on his view that there are
countries and groups that would like to destroy us. It is not an intellectually
complicated analysis of why terrorists hate us, but in the wake of 9/11 it reflects a profound fact.

In the early months of the 2000 campaign, Bush was described as hesitant
and tentative, a man who clung to the script. Yet in the early moments of the
Iraqi War, Mr. Bush threw out the opening script and went after Saddam when
intelligence pinpointed his possible location. Bush is willing to move quickly on
unexpected opportunity to get results.

He also moves fast when decisions bring poor results. When it became clear
that the administration had erred in believing Iraqis would easily shake off
decades of terror and help coalition troops, the administration moved quickly.
Lieutenant General Jay M. Garner, the chief administrator of Baghdad, was reas-
signed after less than three weeks in Iraq and was replaced by Paul Bremer.[59]
The Pentagon then abandoned its long-standing reluctance to develop peacekeeping forces as part of its mission,[60] and the United States sped up the
timetable for transition to an Iraqi government.[61] Finally, a decision to disband
the Iraqi army was reversed when it became clear they were needed.

Bush and his administration don't let strong views or commitments to action trump strategic and tactical flexibility, and, above all, results. This is hardly
consistent with the "my way or the highway" views attributed to him. While it is
reasonable to ask why these issues were not better foreseen and prepared for,
Bush does not appear wedded psychologically to policies that aren't working.
That is a key marker of rigid thinking, and there's no evidence that President
Bush is like that. Mr. Bush has convictions and a determination to follow the
judgments derived from them. But he does not do so blindly; when it comes to
follow-through, he is no robot.

Questions?

Mr. Bush's classic question is, "Have you told me everything I need to know?"
"If he doesn't know, he'll say, 'Hold it.' If somebody uses an acronym he doesn't
know, he'll stop him or her and say, 'What does that mean?' Sometimes he says,
'Use plain English.'"[62] In getting information, Bush prefers "discussions to in-
depth reading, although he has been known to needle his advisors when something they say diverges from something they wrote."[63] He also likes to hear
different views on the same policy problems. During his 1990 campaign for governor, "George W. took great glee in assembling the most diverse group he could

find and then let the discussion fly for several hours. He would ask hundreds of specific questions, demonstrating the same intense curiosity he displayed on the back roads of Texas."[64]

You could see that curiosity and personal concern on display when China downed an American aircraft early in his term. Bush "was constantly peppering his closest aides, particularly Ms. Rice and her deputy, Stephen J. Hadley, with questions about the state of the crew, the strategy to get them home, their interpretation of what was going on within the Chinese leadership."[65] When the Chinese agreed to release the crew, his questions didn't stop; "How long would it take to refuel the pickup plane in China? What would be the flight path? How long would the plane be on the ground?"[66]

Among the most important times for a president to ask questions is when he is deciding on peace or war. At one meeting, Colin Powell asked whether the United States should help pay for Soviet weapons for the northern alliance. Mr. Bush answered by asking a question, "Does it help advance the mission?"[67] He was told it did and gave the go-ahead. Later, Mr. Bush raised the question of the Uzbecks allowing the United States to use their airspace and landing fields for search-and-rescue missions for downed pilots, and asked, "If the Uzbeks say 'no,' what's the plan?"[68] Bombing in the north could not take place without that search-and-rescue structure in place. Mr. Bush then asked, "You could start in the south and do the north later? Are we ready to go in the south?" He was then given a figure for the total number of targets, 700, and asked, "How many of those are in the south?"[69] They had not been broken down by north and south. At another point, Vice President Cheney and Secretary Rumsfeld were having a heated debate about whether to strike Afghanistan first and then go after other terrorist targets, or begin by hitting other targets as well as Afghanistan. Mr. Bush brought the discussion back to Afghanistan by noting, "I'm thinking a lot about endgames, and if we're stalled by the weather are we where we want to be?"[70] Mr. Bush not only asks questions about the here and now, he also has his eyes on the horizon.

Rebuilding Iraq was also discussed before the war. At one point, Deputy Secretary of Defense Paul Wolfowitz and Dr. Rice talked about getting other countries to put up the money that would be necessary for rebuilding. Mr. Bush interrupted with a question: "Who will run the country?" Rice later recalled that she felt awful. *"Her most awful moments were when the president thought of something the principals, particularly she, should have anticipated.* No one had a real answer, but Rice was beginning to understand that it *was the crucial question.* Where were they headed."[71]

Bob Woodward reports that in the run-up to the Iraq war Bush was heavily involved in the planning and asked numerous questions of those who briefed him. When, at the onset of the war, a chance arose to kill Saddam Hussein and his sons based on in-time intelligence information. Bush closely questioned his CIA director on their reliability and the implications of civilian causalities.[72] When Mr. Tenant presented the president with the CIA's conclusion that Mr. Hussein did indeed have weapons of mass destruction, a skeptical Mr. Bush questioned him closely.[73]

More quotes could be added, but the point is fairly clear. Mr. Bush is not a boob, nor is he a rube. The view of Mr. Bush as passive and incurious as a generalization is simply wrong. Not only is it wrong as a matter of fact, it is untrue to Mr. Bush's psychology. Here is a man who has struggled from adolescence to find his place, to succeed on his own skills. He has wanted to be in charge of his own life and its successes his whole adulthood, and has strived to do just that. Critics would have us believe that, having now finally attained the pinnacle of his life's dream of a place for himself by dint of his focus and perseverance, he is too lazy to care what happens to him, his country, and his presidency.

Simple Questions?

One indication of intellectual courage is not being afraid to say publicly that you don't know something or want to understand better. Bush asked many such questions of his advisors, "Just what is the Social Security debt, who is it owed to and how does it get repaid? What would happen if the United States were attacked by chemical or biological weapons and how could we defend ourselves? Why does the United States have a military?"[74]

Some, like the questions on debt and chemical and biological questions, are clearly informational. Others, like why do we have a military, do seem basic— yet sometimes "simple" questions lead to startling consequences. In his initial exposure to the grim details of how much destructive power he would have at his fingertips, Bush posed a deceptively workaday question: Why do we need so many nuclear weapons now that the Soviet Union has disappeared? That question led Mr. Bush to propose taking the unilateral step of making deep cuts in American nuclear-missile strength.[75]

"Naïve" questions can also be revealing in another way. At the principal's meeting on September 23, 2001, Mr. Bush said, "I want a humanitarian aid drop in the north and the south. I want it coordinated with the military. Can we have the first bombs we drop be food?"[76] This couldn't be done because the slow-moving cargo planes would make easy targets. Yet that idea, which had not been much discussed by the principals, their deputies, and sub-deputies before Mr. Bush moved it front and center, was integrated into the war plan and enacted after ground fire had been suppressed. Looking back, Mr. Bush saw it as a strategic and moral decision. It was strategic because he wanted the United States to be seen as a liberator, not a conqueror. And it was moral because "we've got to deal with suffering."[77]

Sometimes, though, simple questions can cut to the heart of a matter. When intelligence information indicated that terrorists would try to highjack a plane during the New Year's holiday period in a reprise of 9/11, a number of at-risk flights were canceled. Yet although specific routes and airlines were possible targets, the intelligence information, as is often the case, was not fool-proof. Faced with a decision, Mr. Bush asked his homeland security advisor Tom Ridge, "Would you let your son or daughter fly on that plane?," according to a senior administration official privy to the conversation. "Absolutely not," the secretary responded. "Well," Mr. Bush said, "neither would I."[78]

Listening?

Asking questions is one thing; listening to the answers is another. When a president has strong views, as Mr. Bush does, it is important to listen. A major criticism of Mr. Bush is that he simply doesn't listen, especially when it's not something he wants to hear.[79]

Mr. Bush himself can be harsh and dismissive with people he doesn't respect. When told of Al Gore's pander to a Hispanic group by saying he hoped his next granddaughter was born on Cinco de Mayo, Mr. Bush responded by calling that "pathetic." He also had little but contempt and "palpable disgust "for Mr. Clinton's cruise missile strategy as a response to terrorism.[80] What Mr. Bush has seemed to learn from these individuals is a renewed determination not to be like them.

Mr. Bush tends to be impatient with criticism, and he sometimes has reason to be. After the Allied forces entered Baghdad, there was a period of looting and general disorder. When a reporter raised the issue of Iraqis being frustrated and asked whether he cared about the disorder and looting going on in Baghdad, Mr. Bush responded dismissively, "*You know, it's amazing, the statue comes down on Wednesday and the headline starts to read: Oh, there's disorder. Well, no kidding.* It's a condition that's chaotic because Saddam Hussein created the conditions for chaos. He created the conditions of fear and chaos. It's going to take a while to stabilize the country."[81]

Mr. Bush is right about the reporters' impatience for immediate results, but Bush's own impatience didn't address an obvious fact: There were not enough troops to stem the chaos.[82] A similar pattern emerged in a December 2003 interview with Diane Sawyer. She kept pressing the president about not having found weapons of mass destruction in Iraq so far. After being asked the same question four or five times Mr. Bush said, "Well, you can keep asking the question and my answer's gonna be the same. Saddam was a danger and the world is better off that we got rid of him." Ms. Sawyer then asked the same question again, "But stated as a hard fact, that there were weapons of mass destruction as opposed to the possibility that he could move to acquire those weapons." Mr. Bush then replied,

> *So what's the difference?:* The possibility that he could acquire weapons. *If he were to acquire weapons, he would be the danger.* That's, that's what I'm trying to explain to you. A gathering threat, after 9/11, is a threat that needed to be—dealt with, and it was done after 12 long years of the world saying the man's a danger. And so we got rid of him and there's no doubt the world is a safer, freer place as a result of Saddam being gone.[83]

This much-commented-on interchange suggests that in the president's mind, from the standpoint of potential risk, a Saddam who had weapons of mass destruction was equally as dangerous as a Saddam who wanted and was trying to get them. Recall that Saddam had used biological weapons against the Kurds, so there was no doubt that he had had such weapons and had used them. From the perspective of a president trying to assess the risk to the United States *at that time,* the fact that Saddam Hussein had had and used such weapons had to weigh heavily in any such assessment.

Yet more could have been added. In response to Ms. Sawyer, for example, he could have discussed the ambiguities of intelligence in relation to risk. He could have mentioned the fact that Saddam Hussein had developed and used biological weapon against the Kurds, and had sought WMDs for decades. He could have said this was the view of all of the American security agencies involved, with some caveats on one or another matter. He could have mentioned this was also the view of the intelligence agencies of American's traditional European allies.

Indeed, any or all of these would have served the president and the public better than his attempt to argue that there was no difference between Saddam's wanting and having the weapons. Obviously, finding what happened to Saddam Hussein's weapons program has important implications for Mr. Bush's theory of preventive war. If Americans and others in the world cannot have substantial confidence that a gathering danger, made more lethal by WMDs, is in fact necessary to face by making difficult choices about war and peace, it is not likely to provide the support necessary to make preventive strike or war a viable option.

Mr. Bush might be understandably annoyed at being asked the same question repeatedly. He might well bristle at the stated implication that he was not precise at best and deceptive at worst, especially the latter. Deception, misleading, and lying are things that Mr. Bush has constantly been accused of by his critics. But what is really startling in reading through the transcripts of Mr. Bush's press conferences and interviews is how often the premises of the questions challenge either his integrity or competence. Some who question are simply hostile to the policies of the administration. Others seek to strike controversy, believing it to be, perhaps, a superior form of information.

A similar pattern of aggressive, even hostile, questioning occurred at the president's televised news conference on April 13, 2004. After a statement by the president, fifteen different reporters asked the president questions, only six of which were intended to elicit information. Most of the rest were attempts to trap Mr. Bush in an inconsistency that would reflect badly on him, accusations of error regarding his Iraq plans, or demands that he personally assume culpability for 9/11.

A good example of the tone and premises of the questioning is *New York Times* reporter Elisabeth Bumiller's query about a statement by Bush to *Washington Post* reporter Bob Woodward, in which he said he didn't feel "that sense of urgency" about terrorism before September 11,[84] which she used as a springboard for a question about whether, "two and a half years later, do you feel any sense of personal responsibility for September 11th?"[85]

The subtext of that question was whether or not Mr. Bush would "own up" to a personal failure on his part for not having prevented the attacks, and apologize. The raw premise of that question was that he could have stopped the attack, should have done so, but didn't. That harsh premise was inconsistent with the vast majority of testimony up to that point in the 9/11 commission hearings that detailed the difficulties of predicting the 9/11 attack and the many structural reasons, often decades in the making, for why it wasn't possible to head it off.

Mr. Bush likes to talk. Although he is seen as a man of few words, even a cursory examination of the *Weekly Compilation of Presidential Documents,* which records all of the president's talks, exchanges, and remarks, shows this is far from the case. In reality, this president speaks often and at length.

Mr. Bush can also sometimes talk on in meetings. At a meeting of his principal public affairs advisors, Karen Hughes, Dan Bartlett, and Ari Fleischer, also attended by Condoleezza Rice, they discussed what the president expected from his communication team in the upcoming war against terrorism. Woodward reports, "His advisors remember the conversation as mostly one way."[86]

At the National Security Council meeting of October 26, 2001, Mr. Bush went around the room and asked each person present whether they agreed with the plan. They did. He then asked if anyone had a better alternative to suggest. They didn't. Bush then took the floor. "In fact, the president had not really opened the door a crack for anyone to raise concerns or deal with any second thoughts. He was not really listening. He wanted to talk. He knew that he talked too much at times, just blowing off steam. It was not a good habit, he knew."[87]

Some of the criticisms about listening are Monday-morning quarterbacking of controversial policies. For example, critics say that if the administration had listened to its own army chief of staff, it would have put more troops into Baghdad.[88] But more troops meant a heavier occupation. Another criticism from the same pundit was of the United States' decision to disband the Iraqi army.[89] These did prove to be decisions that brought trouble, but they were not over-looked or ignored. They were chosen from among alternatives for good reasons. The deployment decision had to do with available troops and other American commitments worldwide. It also reflected the type of troops that might be avail-able. Artillery units are not much good in rooting out an insurgency. The United States has a manpower-missions mismatch, and so a decision was made to make use of Iraqi police and newly trained military to make up the gap. This proved problematic.

What of the decision to disband the Iraqi army? Many knowledgeable offi-cers believed it riddled with Saddam's loyalists who might aide him on the in-side. It had a brutal reputation—hardly a building block of civic trust in a new democracy. Were these policies errors? Judged in retrospect they were, but policy in real life must be made at the time. These were tradeoffs that many thoughtful people concluded were worth making. Many voices are raised in a policy debate and a president can't listen and act on them all.

Many people confuse not listening with not agreeing. It's perfectly possible to both hear and disagree. Nor is choosing a policy option that requires correc-tion evidence of a failure to listen. Uncertainty is a basic reality of most impor-tant political and policy decisions.

For every example of the president having trouble listening there are others of him encouraging discussion and dissent. Asked about George W.'s decision style, Colin Powell said, "What's very pleasing to me with respect to working with the president is that he listens to all the options. He allows us to debate the pros and cons of all the options, and . . . then he makes his decision."[90]

In the lead-up to the wars in Afghanistan and Iraq there were a large number of intense debates. As Woodward notes, Bush became concerned that:

> the war cabinet had not had sufficient time to really debate and evaluate their course of action, consider the options and plans. The NSC meetings were too rushed and short, lasting 60 to 90 minutes, sometimes much less. His time was being chopped into small pieces to accommodate the demands of both his pub-lic and private roles. *They had not had time to chew on the issues the way he wanted, so he asked his advisors to come to Camp David. . . .* [91]

Early in his administration, Mr. Bush decided that, "I wanted a flat organiza-tion chart rather than the traditional chief-of-staff approach; I wanted the senior managers of different divisions in my office to report directly to me, instead of working through a chief of staff."[92] In watching his father's presidency, George

W. saw first hand the poor results of having a powerful gatekeeper keeping the president from learning what he needed to know. He did not repeat his father's mistake. President Clinton needed and got a strong chief of staff to impose some order on his administration.[93] This is much less of an issue for Bush given his "tendency to surround himself with people he's taken the measure of."[94] As a result, Bush has forged relationships with a number of people whose judgment he has learned he can rely upon. It would therefore make no sense for Bush to deprive himself of the helpful advice of those he's invested so much time in gauging, and he doesn't.

Bush says, "I like to get information from lots of different people."[95] In fact, Mr. Bush sits at the hub of a quadrangle, a position that is quite congenial to the president's psychology and experience.[96] He had, after all, been at the center of the groups to which he belonged (although he was not *the* center) since grade school.

Mr. Bush's cabinet was diverse in the usual ways, but different in an important respect. Both domestically and in foreign affairs, Mr. Bush's advisors have a center of political gravity that ranges from the moderate to conservative right-of-center.[97] George W. chose people not only on the basis of their resumes, but on their ideas.[98] Most have long been associated with center-right policy debates and were therefore supportive of the transformations that Mr. Bush envisioned in social welfare, the economy, the environment, and foreign policy.

Some considered Bush's major cabinet appointments "retreads."[99] Yet in selecting men with outstanding records like secretaries Rumsfeld and Powell, Mr. Bush showed no fear that he would be eclipsed, or that he needed lesser lights so that he might shine. He also had another purpose in making these selections.

Asked about his choice of two very senior and established figures for his foreign policy team, Mr. Bush said, "I expect there to be some pretty darn interesting discussions in our national security team. *I hope there is. I put it together with that in mind, of being able to have some strong-willed folks hash things through.* And there are going to be some strong-willed folks in that room. But *a president needs the benefit of strong-willed people.*"[100]

As noted, Mr. Bush is not an avid reader of policy papers or enthusiastic about sitting through long policy briefings. Frank Bruni was told by one Bush confidant that he had participated in meetings that were to last 20 minutes, but that ended in 10. That was supposed to illustrate Bush's famous preference to getting to the heart of the matter, but the reporter found himself dwelling on the following: "It was only going to consume twenty minutes in the first place? Was it an example of impatience with even the kinds of details that might matter?"[101]

We don't know exactly what policy matter Bruni is referring to, yet as a general rule it often it takes time to get to the heart of the matter. Moreover, what constitutes the heart of the matter is not always immediately clear except through discussion. The same is true for facts. You have to master a certain number of them to know what the heart of the matter is. Yet when it came to important issues like war and peace, Bush made sure there was time.

So how does Bush master his facts? He appears to make good use of debates. And he ensures having robust debates by appointing senior people in areas of critical importance, who have the standing and the stature to have and express strong and well-developed views, and letting them go at it.

In foreign policy, he certainly got what he wanted. The debates between Rumsfeld and Powell,[102] between Cheney and Powell, and between Cheney and Rumsfeld leading up to the Afghanistan and Iraq wars were intense. How much of the war on terror should focus on the military aspect and how much on the diplomatic aspect, how much deference should we show our traditional allies who disagreed with us, and so on. To some extent they were disagreements about degree. Yet underneath there were more fundamental divides. There was an intense debate about whether to bypass or approach the United Nations while attempting to build a war coalition. Powell took the position that an attempt to get a United Nations mandate was a necessity and good strategy as well. Cheney, and to some degree Rumsfeld, worried that going the United Nations route was bound to lead to delay, political compromises, and ultimately frustration.

At that point Powell, who had never asked for time alone with the president, did so, and presented his case for two hours. Bush listened, and as a result agreed to give the United Nations a chance.[103] Yet his September 12, 2001, speech was a "right back at you" one, challenging the United Nations to show some backbone. Bush had listened to Powell and followed through on what he had heard and agreed with, but did it in his own way.

Asked how as president he would weigh conflicting advice from economic advisers, Bush replied: "It's just a matter of judgment. It's a matter of a person in my position sorting out, amongst all the voices, who's got the best judgment, who's got the best common sense."[104]

His Own Man

A major misconception about George W. is that he is a front for other's intelligence or skills. For example, Senator Joe Lieberman said that Bush didn't make the decisions about the downed aircraft in China, "*it did appear that at different times that others in the administration were playing a more active role.*"[105] Some critics believe Mr. Bush isn't smart. Others believe he is essentially a spoiled and lazy man who has traded on his family name and connections to get where he is. Maureen Dowd saw both Dick Cheney and Donald Rumsfeld on permanent assignment as babysitter for the infantile president.[106] Richard Cohen put forward

Dick Cheney as the man behind the curtain pulling the levers, noting, "Cheney, in fact, is sometimes referred to as George W. Bush's brain or, to be even more mocking, his ventriloquist."[107]

The most recent candidate for the position is Bush advisor Karl Rove. Two recent books make the point clear in their titles. One title is, *Bush's Brain: How Karl Rove Made George W. Bush Presidential.*[108] The other is entitled *Boy Genius* and subtitled *Karl Rove, the Brains Behind the Remarkable Political Triumph of George W. Bush.*[109] Even the conservative *Weekly Standard* had earlier picked up the same theme. Its August 27, 2001 cover featured a large drawing of Mr. Rove carrying presidential briefing papers in his hands and a small puppet-like figure of George W. Bush, smiling, in the breast pocket of his suit.

But if Mr. Rove's chief aim in public life is to keep Mr. Bush, and thus himself, in power, how did he allow the president to invade Iraq? That was an extremely risky decision. The initial attack, as noted, could have resulted in many casualties, urban warfare in Baghdad, and interethnic war.

Mr. Bush says of himself, "I love to make decisions."[110] Asked by an elementary student whether it was hard to make the decisions as president, Bush replied: "Not really. If you know what you believe, decisions come pretty easily. . . . I know who I am. I know what I believe in, and I know where I want to lead the country. And most of the decisions come pretty easily to me, to be frank."[111]

On the morning of September 12, 2001, Vice President Cheney asked the president whether someone should chair a war cabinet and make reports back directly to Mr. Bush as it might streamline decision-making. According to Woodward, Mr. Bush replied, "'No, I'm going to do that, run the meetings.' This was a commander in chief function—it could not be delegated. He also wanted to send a signal that it was he who was calling the shots."[112]

There are numerous other instances in the discussions leading up to the Afghanistan and Iraq wars of Mr. Bush taking charge. In the debate over whether to deal simultaneously with Iraq Woodward notes, "Bush made it clear that it was not time to resolve the [Iraq] issue."[113] The discussion moved on.

When working on a draft of his speech to the country following the attack, Bush and his speechwriter clarified what came to be known as the Bush Doctrine. This essentially said the United States would make no distinctions between terrorists and those who aid them. This was a bold assertion of American and presidential prerogative that committed the country to a profound change in foreign policy. As Woodward notes, "the decision was made without consulting Cheney, Powell or Rumsfeld."[114]

At one point, when Mr. Bush thought that the decision process was not moving along crisply enough, he decided he would be somewhat provocative at the next meeting of his war council. Mr. Woodward asked him in the interview if he alerted his national security adviser, Dr. Rice, about his plan, to which the president replied, "Of course not. I'm the commander in chief—see . . . I don't need to explain why I say things. That's the interesting thing about being president. Maybe somebody needs to explain to me why they say something, but I don't feel like I owe anyone an explanation."[115]

Asked after the 2002 mid-term elections whether the results would allow him to govern more from the center and take fewer cues from conservatives, he bristled, "*I don't take cues from anybody,* I just do what I think is right. That's just the way I lead. And I ran on a political philosophy; I'm not changing my political philosophy. *I am who I am prior—the same guy after the election that I was prior to the election. That's just who I am and how I intend to lead this country.*"[116]

These quotes don't sound like a president who is shy about asserting himself. Purveyors of the Bush-as-puppet line have never explained how a president who has demonstrated that he won't be pushed by pundits, public opinion polls, mass demonstrations against his policies, traditional allies who oppose him, and opponents who would like to wound him would be pliant putty in the hands of strong-minded advisors. They have never explained how Mr. Bush can at one and the same time be called unilateralist and yet not in charge of his own administration. They have never explained the psychological inconsistency of saying that Mr. Bush is at once arrogant but also passive and compliant. And they have never explained, because they can't, why a man who had spent his whole adult life struggling to become his own man would, on having achieved this lifelong goal, abruptly abandon it.

A Smart Man

Smart is an imprecise word, especially when used by Bush's critics. They prefer ridicule to fact. A *New Republic* cover had a picture of George Bush wearing a dunce cap with his hands up, palms out in an Alfred E. Neuman "I don't know" pose, alongside the title of the cover story, "Why America Loves Stupid Candidates."[117] They prefer to assume that because he wasn't an outstanding scholar in high school and college, he's dim. Yet his grades were no worse than Al Gore's for most of Gore's four years at Harvard, and better than John McCain's. His 566 score on the verbal portion of the SATs before they were "restandardized" beat out Bill Bradley, who got below 500 but went to Princeton.[118]

Critics nodded in agreement when Mr. Bush failed to correctly name four foriegn leaders in a pop quiz. Yet, John McCain failed a pop quiz, too, and never could get the difference straight between Medicare and Medicaid in spite of having been a senator since 1986.

Did Mr. Bush mangle more syntax? Critics assume if he's not a fluid talker, he can't think.[119] Yet Dwight Eisenhower mangled public speaking, but was an incisive thinker.[120] Mr. Bush is also an extremely able and smart man. He is no intellectual, but he is possessed of a singular intelligence, one that is well-suited to his presidential tasks.

Mr. Bush has a quick mind. He is surprisingly dexterous with off-the-cuff humor and verbal jousting. Consider the following:

> Q: What do you think about a third presidential term in the United States?
> THE PRESIDENT: Against it [laughter]. I'm only supportive of a second term these days [laughter].[121]
> * * * * * * * * * * * * * * *
> Q: According to the latest polls, you are the most popular foreign leader in Poland.
> THE PRESIDENT: Really? I usually say I don't believe in polls, but I may have to change my mind. [Laughter][122]

Or consider this round of jousting with reporters on his campaign plane:

> MR. BUSH: I don't read half of what you write.
> REPORTER: We don't listen to half of what you say.
> MR. BUSH: That's apparent in the other half of what I read.[123]

Banter, and especially verbal dueling and repartee, takes a fast mind and a quick wit. You must be able to almost instantaneously grasp the point and be able to turn it back toward the speaker in a way that reflects both appropriateness and wit. It is not a skill of the dim-witted or slow-minded.

Nor is it the case that, because George W. prefers short briefing memos to long detailed position papers, he's intellectually incapable to gasping too much substance. On the contrary, Bush biographer Mitchell notes that as governor he would "virtually commit policy memos to memory and pick them apart in meetings searching for the weak spot that the author was trying to hide. His approach as governor sounded remarkably similar to his manner at meetings back at Arbusto when he would effortlessly dissect a salesman's half baked pitch."[124]

Skepticism is a natural expression of his psychology and a reflection of one aspect of his leadership intelligence. When the president was first informed of the spiking of operations against Iraq as part of the war plan, he chuckled; "Shock and Awe" was a catchy notion but he wondered, "is it a gimmick?" .When George Tenet's assistant John McLaughlin made a presentation on the evidence of Saddam Hussein's WMDs before the war, Bush responded, "Nice try, but I don't think this is something that Joe Public would understand or gain a lot of confidence from. . . . is this the best we've got?"[125]

Mr. Bush not only has a sharp mind, but an inventive one as well. At a campaign gathering of GOP presidential contenders, all were asked, "Which two things would you put in a time capsule to best represent America as it begins the twenty-first century?" Merida notes that most of his rivals felt compelled to include the Constitution or the Declaration of Independence. Bush's answer: "Martin Luther King Jr.'s 'I Have a Dream' speech and the microchip—something to show the heart of America and something to show the entrepreneurial spirit of the country. He had the most interesting answer of all."[126]

It's not enough for a president to be intellectually smart if he is not emotionally wise—capable of emotional balance and perspective. Many intellectually smart presidents have been thoroughly undone by their psychologies. Bill Clinton and Richard Nixon come readily to mind.

Being smart in the presidency requires an ability to learn and a capacity to clearly see and understand the circumstances before you for what they are and to devise a solution. Presidents not only need to be smart about circumstances, but about people. They must figure out whom to trust and when to do it. They must be public as well as personal psychologists, able to take the emotional pulse of the varied persons and groups with which they must deal.

No president is perfect and Mr. Bush is no exception to that rule. Yet he was smart enough to see 9/11 clearly for what it represented. He was smart enough to see through the irreconcilable contradictions in Yasser Arafat's duplicity. And he was smart enough to see his father's limitations and learn from them.

WHY GEORGE W. RARELY ADMITS ERROR

Critics and supporters agree: the president rarely admits error publicly. Left-leaning *Washington Post* columnist Jackson Diehl characterizes Mr. Bush as a president "who never admits error."[127] Jonah Goldberg, an editor at the conservative *National Review,* says of Bush: "Unfortunately, the administration seems to think that admitting any fault, even institutional fault, will cause confidence in Bush's leadership to evaporate."[128] *USA TODAY* columnist Walter Shapiro has written, "It is not in Bush's nature, and certainly not the style of the administration, to admit error."[129]

The President's Press Conference

This view seemed to get resounding confirmation during the president's televised news conference on April 14, 2004.[130] The president was asked in the most direct and pointed way to admit numerous errors of policy and judgment, take personal responsibility for them, and apologize to the nation for them. David Gregory of NBC News asked the president, "One of the biggest criticisms of you is that whether it's WMD in Iraq, postwar planning in Iraq, or even the question of whether this administration did enough to ward off 9/11, you never admit a mistake. Is that a fair criticism, and do you believe that there were any errors in judgment that you made related to any of those topics I brought up?" ABC's Terry Moran asked about WMDs, Iraq oil money being available for reconstruction, and Vice President's Cheney's prediction that the United States would be greeted as liberators: "How do you explain to Americans how you got that so wrong?" Elisabeth Bumiller asked the president, "Two-and-a-half-years later, do you feel any sense of personal responsibility for September 11th?" This question led to a more direct question along the same lines by CBS's John Roberts, who. after taking note of Richard Clarke's public apology on behalf of the government, asked "Do you believe the American people deserve a similar apology from you?"

Mr. Bush's generally strong defense of his decisions predictably led many who supported him to praise his resoluteness, and many who dislike him to criticize his stubborn unwillingness to admit error on all the matters brought up to him or apologize for his many lapses. In fact, the president's answers to the many pointed questions asked were revealing, but not in a way that was much discussed. Asked what his biggest mistakes were before and after 9/11, the president began to review the major decisions that he had made and said, "I would have gone into Afghanistan [before 9/11] the way we went into Afghanistan [after 9/11]. Even knowing what I know today about the stockpiles of weapons, I still would've called upon the world to deal with Saddam Hussein. . . ."

Mr. Bush seemed clearly to be running through the *major* framing decisions that he had made—invading Afghanistan after 9/11, but not before, and going after Saddam Hussein even though weapons of mass destruction have not yet been found, and held to the conclusion that his framing judgments were correct. Then he added, "I'm sure historians will look back and say, gosh, he could've done it better this way or that way . . ." and further on in his reply he said, "I don't want to sound like I've made no mistakes. I'm confident I have." On these and other matters, there are obviously different and deeply held views, but the president's view that these were sound decisions are not rebutted by the fact that everything did not go as hoped or planned once the decisions were made.

In answer to the question of whether he felt personal responsibility for 9/11, a question premised on the assumption that the president might have done things to anticipate and avoid the 9/11 attack, the president replied, "There are some things I wish we had done, when I look back. I mean hindsight is easy. It's easy for a president to stand up and say now that I know what happened it would have been nice if there were certain things in place." He then went on to mention the lack of information-sharing between various intelligence agencies and the fact that the country, and by extension the White House, was not on a war footing. This is vintage Bush. He admits regret that some things weren't done before 9/11, a reflection of an obvious wish to undo the damage to his beloved country, but then switches right over to the other side of that regret, that the things that might have avoided 9/11 could most likely only have been done in the as-if world of counterfactuals, things that might have happened in some alternative, but implausible, universe.

The Alternative Universe of What-If

What if Mr. Bush had demanded before 9/11 that the America be put on a war footing? Would he have been able to develop the support of the American public? What if he had tried to break down the barriers between domestic and foreign intelligence? Would civil liberty interest groups and their supporters have gone along? What if he had sent troops into Afghanistan? Would the Democrats have joined him in this bold move to protect the country from an undocumented and future harm based on a possible, but undocumented, threat in the future? A fair answer to all these questions would seem to be: Absolutely not.

But haven't mistakes been made both before 9/11 and in the planning and carrying out of the invasion of Iraq and it's aftermath? The answer to these questions is: Absolutely yes.[131] The only problem is that some of these mistakes only became evident in retrospect. Judgments about the questions of more troops and disbanding the Iraqi army, were, as noted, issues on which smart, thoughtful people disagreed because the balance of correct judgment did not flow unambiguously in one direction. Critics now claim these and other decisions are examples of major errors. Yet every option had its negative consequences and there is no reason to think that the options preferred by critics would have been immune to them.

Most people have no idea of the complexities and uncertainties of war and critics act as if every setback could have and should have been anticipated and prevented. What they are essentially arguing for is a near-perfect unfolding of an unbelievably technologically, politically, and psychologically complex war. Even if situations are anticipated, there is no guarantee they can be controlled. Some critics act as if anticipation of an issue will guarantee a successful, difficulty-free outcome.

It now seems clear, for example, that when Saddam Hussein's armies melted away as allied forces took Baghdad it was part of a plan already put in motion to fight an urban insurgency against the American forces.[132] Could this have been anticipated? Perhaps, but it was one of a large number of possible things that could have happened. It is literally impossible to prepare in advance for every eventuality of war.

Consider Cheney's comment that allied soldiers would be greeted as liberators. According to surveys taken in Iraq, a majority did. Didn't the administration underestimate the effects of decades of brutal rule on the psychology of Iraqis and their tolerance for a long occupation? Yes. It would be surprising, and an error of the first magnitude, if the one or more government agencies charged with planning the war didn't make some assessment of the impact of those decades in relationship to an American intervention, or the impact of a long-term American presence, or the hopes and expectations that would be freed up for expression after Saddam's regime was gone. Were such studies done? We don't know one way or the other. However, it can't be assumed that Cheney's remark captures the only or complete understanding of what the administration understood about what might unfold. Yet it has.

Mistakes?

Mr. Bush dislikes hand-ringing, secondguessing, and the Washington blame game. He is more likely to look ahead than behind. Critics would have a major point in their favor if Mr. Bush failed to act in correcting unfavorable developments, but he hasn't. On the contrary, the Bush record of flexibility in Iraq is clear. One need only look at his flexibility and willingness to try new avenues in the development of a legitimate interim authority in Iraq. In fact, his changing responses to circumstances in Iraq as they develop have resulted in a criticism that he "has no plan." But the truth of the matter is that that even the best plans do not guarantee that they will be accepted by others, or proceed through implementation without problem, especially in Iraq's volatile mix of psychological, political, and military circumstances. Moreover, when the administration does specifically admit a mistake and moves to correct it, as was the case with rehiring some former Iraqi military personnel, few take note.[133]

Presidential Strategy in a Time of War

What of Mr. Bush's refusal to acknowledge the failure to find weapons of mass destruction in Iraq? Former U.S. weapons inspector David Kay came to the conclusion that a "serious burden of evidence" suggests that Saddam Hussein did not have caches of chemical, biological, and nuclear weapons at the beginning of the Iraq war, and added "you are better off if you acknowledge error."[134] Mr.

Bush's view was that we haven't found them yet, "they could still be there," and, more specifically, that Saddam "had the capacity to make them."[135]

Before dismissing Bush's position too quickly, it is useful to recall David Kay's answer to a question put to him by PBS's Jim Lehrer, "What did you expect to find?" Kay answered, "Going in we expected to find large stocks of chemical and biological agents, weaponized, ready for use on the battlefield, as well as a fairly substantial nuclear program. We did not find that. We have found a lot. *We have found program activities in those areas. We found a resurgent missile program.* But, the large stockpile of actual weapons, chemical and biological weapons simply have not *yet* been found."[136]

While there are elements in Mr. Bush's make-up that do not lend themselves to the easy expression of error or doubt, it would be a mistake to reduce the whole issue to his psychology. Mr. Bush is the leader of a country that is at war. Resolve and conviction are not only matters of personal inclination, they are serious elements of leadership strategy in these circumstances. In some cases, as, for example, the question of whether Saddam Hussein was a gathering danger and had to be dealt with, Mr. Bush continues to believe he was right. It is hard to think that it could be seriously argued that he wasn't. In some cases, the WMDs for example, Mr. Bush simply does not believe all the evidence is in, and so admitting error would be premature. In a majority of the cases, the errors alleged are really matters of selecting from a range of alternatives that each have advantages and disadvantages. The choice is not, as it is often portrayed, between a policy that will easily lead to a rosy conclusion and a mistaken one that will lead to hardship. It is between two or more options that will be difficult and costly, even if they succeed. Underestimation is not synonymous with a failure to consider.

One question that is rarely raised is just what admissions of error or expressions of regret and apology are meant to provide. Why was the press so insistent that Bush own up to all the errors he's accused of? One answer comes from George Stephanopoulos, who said "They want to see some responsibility of concession by the president—'Listen, I'm not perfect.'" [137] Yet, Bush agreed that the Iraq war and its aftermath were not error free, several times. Critics clearly wanted something more.

Another possible reason comes from Samantha Power, the Pulitzer Prize–winning author who asked in response to 9/11-preparedness questions, "How do you fix a system when you aren't willing to say something is wrong?" Yet it is clear in the many thousands of ways that Mr. Bush set the country on a new course of preparedness that he is rectifying mistaken pre-9/11 policy. His initiatives have ranged from heightened scrutiny of domestic and foreign airline passengers to stationing customs agents abroad to check cargoes before they are loaded. Clearly the president has moved very forcefully to address the many deficiencies that the 9/11 attack uncovered.

Ms. Power finds that what is "astounding is not simply the absence of an apology but the absence of any acceptance of responsibility or even acknowledgement of a mistake."[138] However, Mr. Bush has expressed regret more than once, including, in the press conference she was commenting upon, a wish that certain things had been done before 9/11. Regret is different of course than remorse, which is more closely allied with personal fault. The expression of regret does not carry with it an implication of personal responsibility. I can regret that you suffered a financial setback, for example, without at the same time taking personal responsibility for it.

As to accepting personal responsibility for 9/11, what exactly does that mean? What, specifically, is Mr. Bush's personal responsibility for 9/11 and in what way does he owe an apology, as opposed to expressions of regret that it happened? An apology is for something you have done, or didn't do and could have and should have done, that caused harm. Asking Mr. Bush to take personal responsibility implies that there are things he could have done to prevent 9/11 but didn't, so that 9/11 is in some direct way his fault. Yet, the hearings of the 9/11 commission to date make very clear that the many structural problems at all government levels in threat assessment and prevention were long-standing and could only have been overcome in that alternative or parallel universe of "as-if." Here again, critics seem to want something more than what seems warranted by the facts of the circumstances.

CHAPTER 6

THE SECOND TRANSFORMATION

GEORGE W. BUSH
AND THE 9/11 PRESIDENCY

IN THE SPRING OF 2001, THE BUSH PRESIDENCY was floundering. Five months into his presidency, George W. Bush's approval ratings had fallen to a tepid 50 percent. These were the lowest presidential approval ratings measured in the past five years.[1] At the same time, on almost all the major domestic policy issues with the exception of taxation, the public preferred Democratic party policy positions to those of Mr. Bush.

The president had enjoyed only a relatively weak seven-week honeymoon.[2] Thereafter, public views began to crystallize and Mr. Bush's ratings fell to between 50 and 60 percent. They continued to fall through July and August.[3] The president's problems were many, and accumulating.

He had lost the popular vote and been put into office by a controversial Supreme Court ruling. Yet he had decided to govern as if that had not happened. His power ranking on entering office, as measured by political and legislative standing, was "second to last of all postwar presidents; dead last behind Richard M. Nixon in political standing upon first entering office."[4]

His policy initiatives also met a mixed and increasingly difficult fate. His faith- based initiative ran into a brick wall of opposition and had to be started by executive order. His energy bill was passed in the House but was killed in the Senate, and not supported by the public. And his party lost control of the Senate when Jim Jeffords of Vermont became an independent but aligned himself with the Democrats.

He had won some victories: a major tax cut right before Senator Jeffords switched parties, free-trade negotiating power, and an education bill that was a mixed success, given his original positions. However, he did benefit from low expectations in some quarters about his competence and capacity. As a result, even his mixed success projected a larger aura than might otherwise have been the case. Yet overall, the prospects for the Bush presidency were not bright, especially for someone who wanted to introduce the public to new ways of thinking about policy problems. Worse, unemployment rates began to rise and the country's economic circumstances began to deteriorate. In the words of one of his former speechwriters, David Frum, "on September 10, 2001, George Bush was on his way to a not very successful presidency."[5]

Among the reasons Frum gives, one stands out as particularly important. The administration lacked "a big organizing idea."[6] Bush's "compassionate conservatism" was more of a concept than an organizing principle for a new administration. And it was hardly a match for the entrenched welfare-state philosophy that had begun with the New Deal and continued its ascendance even through the administrations of popular Republican presidents like Ronald Reagan.

In his criticism, Frum was both right on target and way off base. It was and remains true that the Bush administration has not developed an easily understandable way of framing its alternative to the liberal policy paradigm. Recently he has experimented with the phrase "ownership society."[7] It remains to be seen whether this term can carry all the rhetorical weight of what Mr. Bush would like to accomplish.

It is important, though, to distinguish between having a paradigm alternative and naming it. Mr. Bush is still searching for the second, but there is little doubt regarding the first. In every area in which the Bush administration has put forward its alternatives, they were foreshadowed either by Bush's policies as Texas governor, or his discussions as candidate. The one exception was the doctrine of preemption or prevention, which can be directly attributable to 9/11. The events of 9/11 transformed Bush's opportunities and constraints for realization of his transforming policies but did not bring them into existence. September 11 was, however, ground zero for two remarkable transformations, of the Bush presidency and of the president himself. And it forced on the United States a profound fact, the reality of catastrophic terrorism[8] and American vulnerability.

THE BUSH PRESIDENCY TRANSFORMED

On the morning of September 11, 2001, George W. Bush was transformed from a struggling to a wartime president. It was immediately clear to observers from across the political spectrum that this was a defining moment for both Mr. Bush and his presidency.[9] The crucial issue, given the questions that had been raised about Mr. Bush's readiness for the presidency, was quite simple and profound: Would he measure up?

The public thought he had. After a difficult beginning, many but not all observers praised Mr. Bush for his forceful, steady response. Before 9/11, Mr. Bush's irreverent, sometimes impish humor was frequently on display. After 9/11, it receded to the periphery and was replaced by a deadly seriousness of purpose.[10] It has since reasserted itself somewhat.

Gravitas is a sense of presence, standing, and authority necessary for leaders wishing to command attention and stimulate agreement. It is a byproduct of presidential psychology, but it is also a critical tool in mobilizing the public behind the president's agenda. Before 9/11 questions had arisen regarding Mr. Bush's level of and even capacity for *gravitas*. In the hours following 9/11 a number of commentators, many critics, saw Mr. Bush as barely filling his role.[11]

A short time later, Mr. Bush appeared before a national audience in a prime-time live news conference. In an editorial entitled "Mr. Bush's New Gravitas," the *New York Times* said:

> [T]he George W. Bush who addressed the nation at a prime-time news conference yesterday appeared to be a different man from the one who was just barely elected president last year, or even the man who led the country a month ago. He seemed more confident, determined, and sure of his purpose and was in full command of the complex array of political and military challenges that he faces in the wake of the terrible terrorist attacks of Sept. 11. It was for the most part a reassuring performance that gave comfort to an uneasy nation. . . . [12]

Why the jump in gravitas? In some respects the answer is simple. Gravitas reflects a seriousness of purpose and a corresponding commitment that must be taken seriously by others. It is hard to think of a more serious issue for a country than its survival.

But there was more to it than that. For Mr. Bush the attack was personal in the most direct and profound way. His deep patriotism, specifically expressed as love of country, is one explanation both for his new mission and his measurable rise in gravitas. The stakes could not be higher, and Mr. Bush recognized them for what they were: matters of life and death for this country. And he was profoundly and personally affected by that knowledge.

From a solid, steady, but hardly robust public approval level in the low to mid-50s, President Bush surged to unprecedented heights of public approval. They remained there for a record period before descending back down to the range they had inhabited before 9/11.

Yet, if the overall approval ratings looked the same, the public's views of President Bush had dramatically altered as a result of the crisis and subsequent war in Afghanistan. Terrorism became the frame through which the public assessed their approval of the president. He was seen to have handled the 9/11 crisis with strength and conviction. Mr. Bush's ratings on the particular policy issues would return to pre-9/11 levels, but the view of his leadership and character did not.

President Bush said that his administration was now wholly refocused on the worldwide fight against terrorism. The work of almost all the White House aides was reoriented away from the president's previous agenda toward responding to the terrorist attack.[13] These include a range of domestic and foreign policy initiatives including, but not limited to, mobilizing internationally and domestically to eradicate terrorist organizations and sponsors, implementing various anti-terrorism legal and economic initiatives, and rebuilding the sense of domestic confidence and security that was damaged by the attack. For a man who had often been portrayed before 9/11 as working at his job on a relaxed schedule, Mr. Bush has become very busy indeed.

GEORGE W. BUSH:
THE SECOND TRANSFORMATION

Reports that the Bush presidency was transformed by 9/11 were clearly right. Mr. Bush said so, his advisors have said so, his critics said so, and the administration has acted consistently with that view. Whether Mr. Bush himself had been transformed, however, remained a matter of debate.

Some reported that Mr. Bush had dramatically changed.[14] Others, especially in the administration, perhaps not wanting to admit that Mr. Bush was ever anything other than stellar, seemed to subscribe to the view captured by one *Newsweek* headline, "Same As He Ever Was."[15] Asked whether he was the same or had changed, Mr. Bush responded characteristically, "I don't know. I don't spend a lot of time looking in the mirror except when I comb my hair."[16]

Certainly, a president's response to dramatic and extremely critical events gives us a measure of the man and his leadership. Yet it is also true that responses to even momentous events must begin with the basic building blocks and raw materials of a president's psychology, character, and leadership skills. Yet even if Mr. Bush's basic character and psychology were already in place, it is not inconsistent to say that traumatic events can be transforming. Mr. Bush was not reborn as a new person after that second plane hit the World Trade Center, but I would argue that he was a transformed one, for the second time in his life.

George W. Transformed? The Evidence

Before 9/11 Mr. Bush had many domestic policy ambitions and several major foreign ones. After 9/11 all those competing priorities were reframed through a policy lens of singular focus; ridding the world, but more specifically the United States, of the scourge of catastrophic terrorism. As Mr. Bush put it, the war "is now the focus of my administration."[17] Asked whether 9/11 had "changed everything," Mr. Bush replied, *"Absolutely."*[18] Aaron Wildavsky's theory of two presidencies, one focused on domestic politics and the other on foreign affairs had, for Mr. Bush, become one.[19]

It is hard to underestimate the importance of this two-into-one presidency for both the institution and Mr. Bush. Before 9/11 Mr. Bush's presidency was struggling with an almost united and hostile opposition party in Congress and a public increasingly unmoved by his efforts; 9/11 changed at least the second of those two. The American public was hit very hard psychologically by 9/11. It could happen here, and it had.

Later public opinion polls would show the public returning to what seemed to be normal, but it was a new normality. Immediate concerns with the domestic economy eclipsed the war against terrorism, but it was difficult to completely forget the lessons of 9/11. It could happen here again, and next time could be worse.

For the president personally, the attack was a grievous injury. Of course, any president would consider an attack on this country a grave and awful event. However, my point here is that for Mr. Bush it was very personal, unusually so. Mr. Bush is very much a traditional patriot. He is unabashedly proud of the United States, clearly feels that its virtues easily outweigh its failures, respects its traditions and institutions, and takes seriously and personally his oath to protect and preserve.

Mr. Bush is not the only president to have many of these feelings, but it is rare to have a president display them so openly and often. Mr. Bush's campaign theme stressing the need to bring honor back to the White House obviously had a strategic dimension. It underscored his difference from Mr. Clinton. Yet it was much more than just that, and to miss that fact would be to miss something very important about Mr. Bush and his presidency.

Mr. Bush's love for this country is palpable, and, like some other of his emotions, it is easily discernable. Elisabeth Bumiller called attention to the fact that "students of the presidency have noticed that he says 'fabulous' an awful lot."[20] However, she and they missed the real tip-off to the president's most important words—"proud" and "honored." Before 9/11 you could read through transcripts of his talks and interviews and repeatedly come upon his expression of how proud he was to serve the country and represent it.[21] This wasn't just rhetoric; he truly loves and admires this country.

Given the depth of these feelings and the large role they play in shaping Mr. Bush's approach to the presidency, the terrorist attack of 9/11 could not have failed to cause him great personal anguish. But it also had the effect of providing strong emotional fuel to an already high level of resolve, framed by an intense focus on bringing those responsible, and their allies, to justice. After 9/11 Mr. Bush said that the war on terrorism was *the* focus of his presidency. These were not just the words of a leader whose country had been attacked. They were the words of a man, who was also the president, forced to experience the vicious, unprovoked, and successful assault of a venerated object of his affections. There was no statute of limitations on his wish to get even.[22]

Part of the blunt language Mr. Bush used to describe the attackers—"barbarians," "evil," "dead or alive"—were reflections of his own raw trauma and rage. He said of September 11, "I will not forget as long as I am on this earth."[23] He told Bob Woodward that the attack had made his blood boil.[24] The list that Mr. Bush keeps of Taliban and Al Qaeda operatives in his desk drawer, crossing out the names when they are killed or captured, is certainly characteristic of his well-known penchant for measuring results.[25] But it is also about revenge.

September 11 also changed Mr. Bush's perspective in a profound way. It wasn't only that his administration became reoriented and refocused. Mr. Bush did, too. Looking back on 9/11 later he said that, *"My vision shifted dramatically after September the 11th because I now realize the stakes.* I realize the world has changed. My most important obligation is to protect the American people from further harm."[26] Mr. Bush had found his mission. Indeed, he had found his life's purpose, and this laid the foundation for his second transformation.

The president's use of the word "now" points to another element in Mr. Bush's 9/11 transformation—guilt. Mr. Bush had taken an oath to protect and defend a country he loved. The attack, however long in planning and motivation, had happened on his watch. Mr. Bush felt enormous regret and personal responsibility. I am not referring here to the ugly suggestion that he could have and should have known the exact nature of the attack and did nothing beforehand, but something more deeply personal.

Mr. Bush acknowledged that he felt differently regarding Osama bin Laden before and after 9/11. "There was a significance difference in my attitude after September 11. *I was not on point,* but I knew he was a menace, and I knew he was a problem. . . . I was prepared to look at a plan . . . to bring him to justice, and would have given an order to do that. I have no hesitancy about going after him . . . but *I didn't feel that sense of urgency. . . ."*[27]

This is a remarkable statement for any president, but especially for one so personally and emotionally attached to the country. It was an admission of deep regret. Embedded in it no doubt was the wish to undo it. But since that was impossible, the next best stance was to do everything possible to make sure it never happened again.

In gaining the presidency, Mr. Bush had reached the pinnacle of his chosen profession. In that role he showed that he had purpose. Now, however, he had purpose to the nth degree. He had a mission.[28]

This was not, as some have implied, a religiously preordained mission. When someone told Bush his leadership at this time was part of God's plan, Bush responded, "I accept the responsibility."[29] This was not, however, a belief that he had been endowed with divine purpose. Bush was specifically asked in a nationally televised interview with Barbara Walters whether "there is a reason why you were president at this time." He replied, "No, I don't think so . . . I don't think so. Somebody said, 'Well you know, gosh, God put you here.' I don't believe God picked who was going to be the president. I do believe that in God we can find great strength and great solace and great comfort."[30]

There is a great deal of misunderstanding about George W.'s religious faith. In his personal religious world there is a divine presence and purpose, but it is *not* revealed to individuals, even those who have found faith and established a personal relationship with the Savior as Bush says he has done. Nor is the preference of divine purpose preordained. We all have free will, even though we are at the same time constrained by our circumstances. Since an individual can never know or guess divine purpose, and since a person must still confront the necessity to make choices, a person can only hope that his choices are in accord with divine preferences.

When George W. was asked about the role of his faith and winning or losing the 2000 presidential election, he replied, "I want to win and I'm a tough competitor, but I also understand that winning this election may not be in the larger plan of things. I think it will be, but it may not be. Prayer helps me keep perspective."[31]

That perspective has an element of equanimity, and perhaps even fatalism, embodied within it. There is a divine plan but we can't know it. On the other hand, we have free will and must exercise it wisely and to the fullest. Yet, in the end, we must know that there is only so much we can do. It is a curious anomaly in such a competitive man.

Another anomaly is found in how George W. personally makes use of his faith in the presidency. Asked by Diana Sawyer whether he prayed to God for the capture of Saddam Hussein, he replied, "No. I prayed to God for wisdom and strength and guidance. It's like saying, do you pray to God that you get a vote? No."[32]

Nor does Mr. Bush frame his work as president through the lens of his personal faith. During the 2000 presidential campaign Al Gore, attempting to buttress his credentials as a religious person, let it be known that he too had been "born again" and then told the *Washington Post* that when faced with important problems he often asks himself, "What would Jesus do?[33] Bush, asked by Tom Brokaw how he reconciled his national security obligations and his spiritual obligations, replied:

> I don't bring God into my life to be a political person; I ask God for strength and guidance; I ask God to help me be a better decision[maker]. The decision about war and peace is a decision I made based upon what I thought were the best interests of the American people. I was able to step back from religion, because I have a job to do. And I, on bended knee to the good Lord, asked Him to help me to do my job in a way that's wise.[34]

Here Bush reveals himself as both a humble supplicant and determined activist. He asks for help in making better decisions, but not what decisions to make. He is "on bended knee," while at the same time, in real life, we know he has embraced his new life's mission in the presidency with a commitment and tenacity that reflects a determination to engage the country's new circumstances, and his, head on. Mr. Bush's religious beliefs provide him with a source of personal and psychological support, not a rationale for his presidency or his decisions.

A Life's Crossroad

Mr. Bush had arrived, a second time, at a crossroads of his life. His sense of anger, regret, and purpose fueled his resolve. Equally important, they gave Mr. Bush a single primary mission whose importance dwarfed anything he had ever done. A close friend of the president reported that "Bush had come to believe that his actions from September 11 onward would define not only his presidency, *but, really his time on earth.*" This friend said that Bush felt "he had begun a new life that is inextricably bound to September 11 and all that implied."[35]

That mission galvanized Mr. Bush in another way as well. Mr. Bush's confidence had developed in an unusual, episodic way. The development of his personal confidence had far outpaced the development of his occupational confidence. The latter had been picking up steam intermittently during his early adulthood, and really started to develop in his mid-forties. Mr. Bush was only seven months into his presidency when terror struck. He had hardly had time to get a feel for the office or establish himself firmly in it. Dealing with Congress was one test of a young president; dealing with the major and successful terrorist strike of 9/11 was quite another.

No president can foresee how they will respond to such circumstances. Mr. Bush's reaction was instructive. Knocked off stride by this cataclysmic event, he quickly recovered his balance. There followed a rapid-fire series of National Security Council meetings designed to respond to the attack and a number of public events to console and rally a shocked nation. On September 20, 2001, he gave a nationally televised speech to the joint houses of Congress watched by 80 million Americans. At one point before the speech, his guest, Prime Minister Tony Blair, asked if the president wanted some time alone before the speech to gather himself. Bush replied, "I know exactly what I need to say, and how to say it, and what to do." After the speech, the president called his speechwriter, Mike Gerson, and told him, "I have never felt more comfortable in my life."[36]

After several false starts, occupational cul-de-sacs, and personal lapses, Mr. Bush seemed finally to have arrived at his life's destination. He had won the highest political office in the land, and now had an urgent mission to accomplish. His comment about never feeling more comfortable in his life suggests the views of a man who knows what he must do and is confident he can do it. Mr. Bush's entry into adulthood was, for all intents and purposes, complete.

Mr. Bush had found his voice as he moved from struggling to enact his political vision in a divided and contentious society to a leader pursuing the larger purpose of a national mission. Karl Rove argued that the times don't make the man. Yet the evidence in George W.'s case is that circumstances can have profound effects. Mr. Bush did not become a new man after 9/11, but he certainly became a transformed one. It crystallized his life's purpose. He had, in gaining the governorship and presidency, achieved substantial success in his chosen work. There was no longer any question about whether he was his own man.

His new personal and presidential mission provided something else as well: a focus and set of questions that were independent of his father's accomplishments. No other president, including his father, had faced the question of catastrophic terrorism so directly. Whether future 9/11-type attacks could be prevented, and how, become new and urgent questions that only he and the presidents who followed him could answer. He was now not only his own man, but one with a new and unique set of problems on which to be judged. How well he succeeded would depend on many things, but certainly his judgment and leadership would be central to any conclusions.

GEORGE W. BUSH IN THE 9/11 PRESIDENCY

As a wartime president, Mr. Bush was now faced with the possibility of needing to make devastating life-and-death decisions. He might have to order the destruction of a civilian airliner highjacked and on its way to a suicide mission. He might have to quarantine an American city hit by biologically produced plague. But, most importantly, he not only had to respond to the attack, but ensure it didn't happen again.

Mr. Bush also faced an abrupt switch in public expectations. In the 1992 and 1996 presidential elections the public said they wanted a president they could relate to, who would feel their pain. Now, understandably, they were less interested in someone who felt their pain and more focused on someone who would protect them from having to feel it again. The circumstances called for strong steps, and Mr. Bush took them, but not without public criticism by some for "going too far." He was accused of creating an "imperial presidency" and sacrificing American civil liberties for his mission. These were among the many strong denunciations of the steps he took, but he took them.

September 11 and the Dilemmas of Heroic Leadership

September 11 not only transformed important elements of American psychology, it gave rise to the demand for a new kind of leadership. Bill Clinton had been successful in two elections in part because he represented a new kind of *reflective* presidential leadership. He promised to "put people first," and seemed to care about and connect with many Americans. They, in turn, connected with him. His was a very personal candidacy and presidency.

Yet traditionally Americans have preferred strong, heroic leadership. Its archetype is Franklin D. Roosevelt, its metaphor the hierarchy, and its motto, decide and command. The task of the heroic leader is to convince the public of what it is that he already thinks they *must* do. It envisions the leader as struggling against, and overcoming through determination, courage, or otherwise heroic efforts, the circumstances he must surmount. It envisions leaders as "titans—. . . Mao and Gandhi, Churchill and Roosevelt, Stalin and Hitler and Mussolini. . . . These giants strode across our cultural and intellectual and political horizons."[37]

Freud believed that when crowds (publics) were beset by anxiety they turned to leaders, but that, in the process, group members became disconnected from each other.[38] In these circumstances, Freud argued, group members were only indirectly allied to each other—and then only through their joint connection to the leader. This is one drawback of heroic leadership.

Reflective leadership, unlike heroic leadership, seeks to develop common, horizontal ties, not direct and hierarchical ones. Its prototype, but not its archetype, is Bill Clinton. Its metaphor is the prism, and its motto is select and reflect. It is not reflective in the sense of being introspective. Rather, it is reflective in the sense of gathering the disparate elements of frayed or fractured political and cultural consensus and mirroring them so that publics can see the basis for their common purposes. The reflective leader tries to diffuse conflict, not sharpen it. It is leadership whose purpose is not to choose and impose, but to engage and connect. The reflective leader does not bend the public to his will, but rather leads by serving as an expression of a more common one. He does not so much command as explain. He does not so much tell as discuss. And he is not so much the author of the public's common interests as its reflection.

Countries in which there are no great mobilizing crises, but which are nonetheless deeply divided, are ripe for reflective leadership. This was America's psychological state before 9/11. Many Americans felt separated from their major institutions and each other, and this, too, favored reflective leadership.

Technology and the increasing segmentation of political and other markets also have decreased the necessity to be connected, but increased the desire for it. Americans can shop online, rent videos instead of going to movies, and may soon be able to vote online at home. The result is a political culture and system in which the issues that divide the country have been less responsive to traditional heroic leadership.

September 11 helped Americans realize that heroic leadership has its virtues. Strong, decisive leadership is necessary in time of mortal threat. The question then arose: Was George W. a heroic or reflective leader?

Mr. Bush campaigned as a reflective leader, not a heroic one. He would set "a new tone in Washington." He would bring people together around common ground, not a political master plan.

But within a brief time of his arrival, it was clear that Mr. Bush had a psychology that didn't quite fit with being a reflective leader. For a start, he had strong views on what was right and followed through on them. He governed as if he had won a mandate to try out his policies, not abandon them. His belief that he had a mandate brought forth a litany of complaints. A reflective leader might have reached out further to decrease conflict at the expense of his own programs. Mr. Bush did not. A reflective leader with heroic aspirations like Bill Clinton might have tried to mask his true intentions with reflective rhetoric, while pursuing his view of heroic leadership. Mr. Bush didn't do that either.

On the contrary, in a striking illustration of his "right back at you" psychology, he went right after his signature tax cuts, and he did so repeatedly. Mr. Bush could work well with opposition leaders, but they turned out to be momentary allies and not longer-term political friends. Mr. Bush proved to be a tough bargainer and a very strategic political thinker. Yet he was less interested in reducing conflict for its own sake than in doing so in the service of what he wanted to accomplish.

Yet for all his policy toughness, Mr. Bush was a person who genuinely seemed to care about people. He certainly did not see himself, as Mr. Gore did, as the smartest person in the room, and act accordingly. His style with the public was one of reducing the distance between them, not heightening it. When Mr. Bush said of himself that he was a loving guy but he had a job to do, he not only captured well two aspects of his psychology, but two aspects of his leadership style, both *heroic* and *reflective.*

The attacks of 9/11 had the effect of accentuating the heroic aspect of Mr. Bush's leadership style. His blunt rhetoric did as well. "Dead or alive" or "as long as it takes" are *heroic* assertions. Such talk was well-suited to his new heroic mission.

Yet domestically, given the sharp partisanship that still permeates Washington even during a war, he is being called upon by the public, and loudly by his opposition, to develop and reflect common ground. One large paradox of the Bush presidency is that he is called upon by circumstances to provide *heroic* leadership, principled, strong, and purposeful, while at the same time his opponents, and some members of the public as well, also demand a *reflective* consensus be built. These are Mr. Bush's two presidencies, and his ability to successfully engage both of these somewhat disparate demands will shape his political and historical fate.

The President as New World Prophet

President Bush has made clear he is a man who favors blunt talk. His blunt phrases, like "Axis of Evil," "Dead or Alive," "show some backbone" (to the United Nations), and others reflect a president unusually willing to say what's on his mind. David Brooks has called it "A Fetish for Candor."[39]

That approach was evident in the first months of his administration. In matters large and small Mr. Bush has often, though by no means always, said what was on his mind. Asked about the difficult, and in many people's minds, unsuccessful, WTO trade meetings, Mr. Bush said, "The meetings in Cancun did not go well, but I wouldn't condemn the WTO round to failure yet."[40] Asked about the violent protests that accompanied the G–8 meetings held in Genoa in July 2001 to discuss international trade, Mr. Bush talked about the "right" of leaders from rich and poor countries to gather and discuss their plans, and "those who protest free trade are no friends of the poor. Those who protest free trade seek to deny them their best hope for escaping poverty."[41] Asked about the capture of a boat laden with tons of weapons for Mr. Arafat's Fatah organization, Mr. Bush said, "Obviously, we were first surprised and then extremely disappointed when the *Karina A* showed up loaded with weapons, weapons that could have been used for only one thing, which was to terrorize."[42]

Straight talk[43] and its sibling, blunt talk,[44] are a byproduct of meaning what you say. Both are rooted in Mr. Bush's psychology. Yet they carry with them critical implications for his presidential leadership.

Mr. Bush has used such talk to directly challenge and rebut the presumption of business as usual. Recall that one aspiration of this administration is to change the framing of politics as it is currently understood and practiced. Forcefully calling direct attention to the inconsistencies, dead-ends, hypocrisies, and faulty logic of existing ways of thinking about and doing things is one important, indeed necessary tool, in realizing that goal. If Mr. Bush were a trendy postmodern theorist giving a jargon-filled paper at the Modern Language Association meeting, an apt title for his enterprise would be: Subvert the paradigm!

Mr. Bush's blunt assertions stand in sharp contrast to his predecessors in the office. They used ambiguity as a vehicle for leadership. Mr. Bush says of himself, "I like clarity."[45] Asked about the shades of gray that often characterize political circumstances, Mr. Bush replied, "look, my job isn't to nuance. My job is to tell people what I think . . . and people can make all kinds of excuses, but there are some truths involved . . . and one of the truths is, they're sending suicide killers in—because they hate Israel. That's a truth and you can justify it anyway you want, nonetheless it is the role of the President, as far as I'm concerned, to stand up and tell the truth and I did today."[46]

Mr. Bush's blunt talk makes some nervous. Early in his administration when asked what he would do if China attacked Taiwan, he said "the U.S. would do whatever it took to help Taiwan defend itself."[47] That comment caused widespread concern. Some were critical because they feared it might upset China. Others were concerned that the president seemed to be abandoning the ambiguity that had been a cornerstone of U.S. policy regarding this question.

Winston Lord, ambassador to China during the Reagan administration, came to the president's defense but in a somewhat double-edged way: "It's pretty clear to me that this was inadvertent. The language on Taiwan is very arcane, very nuanced, and people are apt to make mistakes with it. It seems to me, if this was going to be purposeful, it would be done in a different way, such as in a speech."[48]

Yet Mr. Bush's remarks had nothing to do with a failure to understand the nuance associated with traditional ambiguity about U.S. intentions. The fact was quite the opposite. Mr. Bush understood that American policy was to keep the Chinese guessing about our intentions to defend Taiwan. Mr. Bush didn't want the Chinese to guess and perhaps miscalculate.

Two years, later Mr. Bush bluntly told the Taiwanese not to hold a referendum calling on China to withdraw ballistic missiles aimed at that country.[49] Mr. Bush expressed the worry that such a move would incite China and those in Taiwan who were working for status as an independent state. Such a move would surely trigger a strong response, perhaps a military one, from China.

Are these two blunt strong assertions inconsistent? Not really. It seems perfectly possible to entertain a policy that warns China against attacking Taiwan, a position Mr. Bush strongly reiterated to Chinese premier Wen Jiabao, and also to warn Taiwan against provoking an attack. Ambiguity leaves room for error and misjudgment. Clarity lets both parties know where they stand, and coupled with a reputation for meaning what you say, adds weight to the president's views.

Mr. Bush is well aware that his tendency toward blunt talk rattles many. Speaking of his blunt assessments of the new war on terror he said:

> I know there's a lot of angst about my statements about these nations, but I have a responsibility to speak as clearly as I possibly can about how I view the nature of these regimes. . . . I know some in the world don't particularly want to hear that. It's much easier not to be confronted with the truth, because it means that there's going to be sacrifice, and worry and concern. . . . [50]

Blunt talk and clarion calls are ordinarily the tools of heroic leaders. Yet Mr. Bush is not by nature a heroic leader. As governor and as president before 9/11, he issued no rousing calls to convince the public of what it was that *he* had already decided they *must* do. He had no single, organizing mission that fueled his psychology and agenda.

Mr. Bush's heroic role is strictly an outcome of 9/11, one more element of his second transformation. Mr. Bush's new presidential mission, to save his beloved country, has become a heroic undertaking. And Mr. Bush therefore, like the Old Testament prophets, must rally his people while getting them to change their habits and adjust their understanding of a new, more dangerous world. However, unlike Isaiah, he must also deal with a world united in ambivalence, envy, and anxiety toward America and its foreign policy.

After 9/11, Mr. Bush reached what he felt was an essential insight about the new nature of the world. What he saw, he vowed never to forget. Yet his task was larger than himself, carried with it an enormous public responsibility and burden, and had the most profound consequences—almost the exact definition of a heroic quest.

In an interview with Barbara Walters on the subject of Americans forgetting the lessons of 9/11 as it receded in the historical distance, Mr. Bush said, "The human psyche is such that they'll want to forget the terror and the tragedy, they'll want to move on. But I'm not moving on, because I understand that we're in a fight for civilization itself."[51] America might move on. Mr. Bush cannot. It is his fate to have been transformed and transfixed by 9/11.

Mr. Bush doesn't always use straight talk and is perfectly capable of deflecting questions he doesn't wish to answer. Moreover, every president knows more than he can or should tell. After 9/11 the president was stunned to learn that the FBI had 331 suspected terrorists on their watch list for entry into the United States, but had no real idea whether they were here. Mr. Bush kept that number from the American people, because they had just been through a national trauma.[52]

Mr. Bush has also made a number of remarks that stress *his* view of things, when there are clearly other views and ways to understand them. The economic statistics associated with the benefits of his tax cuts come immediately to mind in that regard. So do his prewar remarks on the status of weapons of mass destruction in Iraq. Those will be matters of ferocious political debate in the 2004 presidential campaign.

But his stark, bold rhetoric placed his critics in a dilemma. He argued that to ignore the evidence of Saddam Hussein's history and motivations was "a reckless gamble with the lives of millions." This forced his critics to say why it wasn't a gamble or worse from their standpoint, to agree that it was a gamble and then specify the level of risk they were asking Americans to take.

The view that the president was "in over his head," both rhetorically and substantively, in this new phase of the war blinded critics to the strategic motive behind the assertiveness. It was not so much a case of cowboy politics as of coercive diplomacy, deterrence characterized by blunt threats and the willingness to back them up. Paradoxically, therefore, the best road to peace may well have been a vote for war. Yet, the test of that option was lost in the UN failure to agree on a resolution defining the consequences of which it had so often warned.

Mr. Bush's bold rhetoric does not always lead to equally blunt action. Mr. Bush told Bob Woodward "I loathe Kim Jong Il," leader of North Korea, and he meant it.[53] But there has been no precipitous rush toward confrontation.[54] Quite the opposite. Mr. Bush has engaged in a long slow dance with North Korea in an attempt to get them to renounce their nuclear ambitions.

In the wake of 9/11 Mr. Bush lashed out and struck relatively swiftly, but not indiscriminately. The land war in Afghanistan did not begin with the massive infusion of American troops, but rather by relying on local allies. And both the wars in Afghanistan and Iraq were carefully calibrated to avoid, insofar as possible, civilian deaths and to maintain the infrastructure. Blunt words do not, to repeat, equal blunt actions.[55]

Mr. Bush's blunt talk is unusual in the modern presidency, and given the dangers revealed by the 9/11 attack, some of it is doubtlessly warranted. Yet it carries with it dangers as well. One is that it can be heard as hectoring. Another is that it can be heard as arrogant. Mr. Bush loudly complained at one point in preparing a speech on the Middle East that he was being "nuanced to death."[56] But sometimes circumstances truly are complex and ambiguous. And of course, bluntness sometimes leads people not to listen. This gets to the heart of the dilemma of blunt talk. It may be true, but it is not necessarily educational. The best purpose to which a president's view of truth can be put is to educate people. Some people respond to blunt truth, but many do not. Bluntness and tact are difficult to reconcile.

Mr. Bush has proved far better at asserting than explaining. Yet ultimately public education on the critical security issues facing the United States needs some measure of both. It is surprising, yet true, that a president who has been so versatile and flexible in his legislative and leadership strategies has been so narrow in his rhetorical ones.

Mr. Bush sometimes speaks as if his asserting his views is synonymous with explaining them. The president sometimes makes the mistake of thinking that because the virtues of his policies are evident to him, they are equally evident to others. This is obviously not the case. Thus, a question arises as to how Mr. Bush can better defend his policies by explaining rather than asserting. It is a critical task if Mr. Bush is to accomplish the domestic and international transformations to which he aspires.

After 9/11: An Imperial Presidency?

One of the most serious charges made against President Bush is that he is establishing an "imperial presidency."[57] That charge, made by Arthur Schlesinger, who coined the term to describe presidents who had slipped the bonds of formal and informal constitutional and psychological constraints, raises an important question about a possible second Bush term. Is Mr. Bush really an "imperial president," and should the public worry that if he gains a second term they will lose their freedom and their constitution?

It is true that presidents like George W. Bush, with the courage of their convictions, strong policy ambitions, and powerful psychologies, tend to see the world through their own point of view. They are not afraid to act accordingly. In times of crisis, these tendencies are magnified, but they remain a powerful current throughout such presidencies.

In the past such presidents have taken strong, even drastic steps. Abraham Lincoln suspended *habeas corpus* during the Civil War and Franklin D. Roosevelt authorized the internment of Japanese Americans in camps. Both presidents felt these acts were necessary for the good of the country.

Strong presidents sometimes test constitutional and political limits even when there aren't dire national emergencies. Mr. Roosevelt felt so frustrated about the fate of his domestic initiatives before the Supreme Court that in a surge of power and pique he tried to pack it with more of his supporters. Harry Truman tried unsuccessfully to temporarily nationalize the steel mills during the Korean War.

With Republicans in control of both the House and Senate and likely to remain so after the 2004 election, and with a strong president like George W. Bush reelected, is the republic in danger? Some think it already is. Critics argue Mr. Bush has already done the equivalent of suspending civil liberties with his "roundup of Muslims" after 9/11 and his holding of several American citizens as "enemy combatants." The use of the term "roundup" is meant to conjure up visions of police sweeps, detention centers, and, of course, the internment of the Japanese during World War II.

The question is how true are these incendiary charges and how likely are they to characterize a second Bush term? When Mr. Schlesinger characterized the Nixon and Johnson administrations as imperial, his list of particulars was a mélange of disparate elements. For President Johnson, the list included: not fully consulting with Congress after getting the Gulf of Tonkin Resolution to pursue war in South East Asia,[58] a failure to encourage dissent among his advisors about the course of the war,[59] becoming caught up in the mystique of the commander-in-chief role,[60] and conducting military operations against Cambodia when there was no imminent threat.[61]

Nixon's list of particulars included that he appointed a mediocre cabinet,[62] had a tendency to centralize power in the Executive Office,[63] enlarged the White House staff, [64] didn't like presidential press conferences and gave many fewer of them than FDR,[65] encouraged "as many interests as possible dependent on government favor,"[66] used his authority to impound and not spend money voted by Congress for policy purposes,[67] made use of the constitutionally mandated pocket veto,[68] tried to extend the concept of executive privilege,[69] and was extremely concerned with leaks regarding foreign policy.[70] All of these behaviors were geared, it was asserted, toward establishing a "plebiscitary presidency" wherein one presidential election every four years would serve as the only check and balance on presidential authority.

These are a disparate hodgepodge of complaints. Leaving aside Nixon's clearly felonious behavior, which surprisingly is not included in the list, we are really left with two major charges: that these presidents tried to pull power into the executive branch and away from Congress, and that they used a sense of emergency to get policies that they wanted.

The problem is that this list describes the behavior of many, if not most, modern presidents—and not only Mr. Bush's. Schlesinger concedes that many of the "constitutional offenses" he lists as part of the imperial presidencies of Nixon and Johnson, such as impoundment of funds, the secrecy of the air war in Cambodia, and continuing the Vietnam War after the Gulf of Tonkin Resolution had been repealed, "were questions that a President might contend—until the supreme court decided otherwise—lay within a range of executive discretion."[71] Further, he says it is "The nature of an activist president to run with the ball until he [is] tackled," and if that doesn't happen "Congress ha[s] primarily itself to blame."[72]

So again the question arises: Is Mr. Bush an imperial president or merely an active one? The balance between executive and legislative power has been a tug of war for over 200 years. The first term of Mr. Bush's presidency has been very active in this regard because of the 9/11 terror attack and its aftermath and Mr. Bush's belief that there has actually been an erosion of presidential power; expect more of the same in a second term.

Schlesinger's charge against Mr. Bush rests on similarly shaky ground. It begins with the allegation, now wholly discredited by Britain's Hutton Commission, that Tony Blair cooked the books on intelligence reports, and alleges the same about Mr. Bush. Yet the evidence to date is that many others, including President Clinton, Congress, France, Britain, and others believed that Saddam Hussein was intent on developing weapons of mass destruction (WMD). The Kay Report confirms this worry was warranted.

But what of the fact that WMDs haven't been found? Schlesinger opines that the failure to find WMDs opens a "credibility gap" for Mr. Bush, presumably similar to President Johnson's during Vietnam. Yet, he says that even if WMDs are found, it doesn't matter because Saddam Hussein didn't use them. Critics seem not to consider relevant any of the UN resolutions demanding Iraq's disarmament or the geopolitical implications in the region of a nuclear-armed Iraq with Saddam Hussein as its leader.

However, it is the doctrine of preemptive or preventive war that Mr. Schlesinger fingers as the primary reason to call Mr. Bush's presidency imperial. He indicts Mr. Bush for wanting a "radical transformation of U.S. strategy." Yet as Gaddis has carefully documented, Bush's policy has a long historical legacy, stretching back to President John Q. Adams, and before.[73] Further, is that not a prudent policy option in a world in which the traditional basis for deterrence, at least with terrorists, has lost much of its value? What do critics suggest is prudent to do in these circumstances? Isn't it possible that the option of preventive war may actually strengthen deterrence and thus make future wars less necessary?[74]

Mr. Bush believes that the nation is under severe threat, and even his critics agree that he is right. The most directly analogous historical circumstances for the Bush presidency are with President Lincoln, who confronted the destruction of the Union through Civil War, and FDR, who had to respond to a surprise attack. Mr. Bush confronts the possibility of catastrophic destruction of another kind. Skeptics might ask: What is the common denominator between a civil war, a world war, and a terrorist attack? The answer is a grievous, possibly irreparable blow to the country's physical, psychological, and political well-being, from which it might have severe difficulty recovering.

In reality, given the similarity of circumstances, Mr. Bush has hardly been "imperial." There are no internment camps for Middle Easterners or Muslims. They have been asked simply to register, as almost all visitors to this country now do. Can the president instruct the immigration service to call in immigrants from selected countries to register with the board? Clearly yes, since this so-called roundup was in fact authorized by Congress.

There has been no suspension of *habeas corpus.* The new powers granted to authorities in the wake of 9/11 are still subject to court oversight as the number of cases before courts of various jurisdictions attest. Can Mr. Bush declare an American citizen an "enemy combatant?" This raises new constitutional questions and the Supreme Court is ready to take up this issue. Far from presiding over an imperial presidency, the system of checks and balances appears to be alive and well.

Mr. Schlesinger raises the specter of a plebiscitary presidency, one in which the president gets elected and then ignores public wishes for the next four years. Yet Brace and Hinckley have demonstrated that, far from being plebiscitary, the modern presidency is repeatedly evaluated by daily referendums on every aspect of presidential behavior in the form of ubiquitous opinion polls.[75] Mr. Bush's presidency has been no exception.

Moreover, the United States still conducts mid-term elections, and the public can (as the 1994 mid-term elections showed Bill Clinton) deliver a powerful and stinging rebuke to a president's policies. Mr. Bush made his presidency the issue in the 2002 mid-term elections and won back control of the Senate.

Although Mr. Schlesinger accuses Mr. Bush of trying to reinstate an "imperial presidency," there is not much evidence, even according to Schlesinger's diverse list of imperial presidential traits. Mr. Bush has a strong cabinet and it does debate the issues. Mr. Bush's cabinet choices, especially in national security, are hardly retiring or shy about their viewpoints. Moreover, there have been epic battles over policy.

He has asked for and received congressional authorization for undertaking the war against terror and against Saddam Hussein. The press is aggressive, as any reading of the repeated questions about WMDs will attest. The courts have not been shy about asserting themselves.

Yes, Mr. Bush doesn't like press conferences and some members of the press. A dislike of press conferences and the assertive, frequently rude and combative questions that are often asked might well lead a president to want to avoid them. Ronald Reagan and Bill Clinton both tried to do that, yet neither is considered particularly "imperial."

Almost every member of the opposition party, and some members of his own party, want more consultation. This is a perennial congressional request of presidents, not Mr. Bush in particular. Yet some members of the opposition have polluted the bipartisan setting of even those committees that review classified terrorism material by making them the venues for political advantage. In short, the complaints about Mr. Bush are little different, even if the opposition decibel level is louder than what most presidents can expect and have experienced.

Critics refuse to recognize that Mr. Bush could have gone in the direction they attribute to him after 9/11, but didn't. He was a model of restraint domestically. He took several occasions to remind Americans that the fight was with terrorists, not Muslims. He publicly condemned the few sporadic outbursts of anger against some Muslims, invited their representatives to the White House, and publicly applauded acts of tolerance by Americans. When you compare that restrained behavior with, say, the long history of racially charged and incendiary rhetoric of Democratic presidential candidate Al Sharpton, the nasty and false accusations that Mr. Bush was AWOL, a deserter from his reserve responsibilities, and worse, Mr. Bush's temperance and sense of proportion come into clearer focus.

Consolidating the Second Transformation: Father and Son

The 9/11 presidency and Mr. Bush's transformation because of it had another, more personal effect. His relationship with his father continued to change and in the end was transformed. He was, of course, as he always would be, his father's son. But 9/11, in fueling George W.'s sense of mission, also fueled the level of vitriol against him. And this in turn brought about a dramatic change of role between father and son—one more step in consolidating George W.'s long-delayed but full arrival into adulthood.

George W. had finally arrived. After a long search and hard work, he had found his place. He would build on that success, running for and winning the presidency against a vice president who should have been a shoo-in. Once there, he would help the country weather the trauma of 9/11 and try to set it in a new direction politically. Yet there is one further set of psychological changes to address here that are at once part of Mr. Bush's growing consolidation of his adulthood and a reflection of his transformation. That is his shifting relationship with his father.

George W. idealized his father, but real maturity requires seeing one's parents as they are, with real virtues and limitations. Looking back on what he learned in working for his father, President Bush said, "I also learned a lot about political capital that I think a lot about. Do you have any political capital going in? The answer is absolutely, and I'm going to spend it all. Because you earn capital by spending it. And the fact that he didn't properly spend capital, much to my chagrin at the time, I think it cost him the presidency."[76]

That's a revealing statement. It attests again to the "watch and see" style that characterizes this president's approach to learning from political experience. And it also speaks to the importance that lessons learned have for Mr. Bush. But it is most revealing as an insight into a changing relationship between the president and his father.

Mr. Bush's relationship with his father changed in another way as well. Consider the following interview between President Bush and Brit Hume on the subject of being in touch with his father and the role reversal it reveals.[77] When Mr. Hume noted that people naturally assume he talks to his father about matters of state, the following exchange occurred:

> BUSH: No, I can understand. First of all, I talk to him really as son to father. I am worried about the fact that he is worried about me. You know you ask a very good question, did I take criticism of him or me easier, and the answer is, I take criticism of me easier.
> (Crosstalk)
> BUSH: Now it's reverse. He reads everything—he listens to everything, and I know he agonizes over every, you know, every tough word. And . . .
> HUME: So you end up calling to comfort him?
> BUSH: I call him to comfort him, really, yeah absolutely. And let him know that, you know, I'm doing good, don't worry about me.[78]

At one level this is a simple and emotionally poignant inside view of a son's changing relationship with a revered father. At another more psychological level, it is a reflection of a son's ability to understand a changed relationship for what it is, and take on a new nurturing role. In this respect, the relationship had begun to come full circle.

CHAPTER 7

PRINCIPLES IN PRACTICE

GEORGE W. BUSH'S
PRESIDENTIAL LEADERSHIP

SHOWING BRITISH REPORTERS AROUND HIS WHITE HOUSE OFFICE, Mr. Bush singled out a picture on his wall titled "A Charge to Keep."[1] It was a picture that he had chosen to hang in his governor's office in Texas, and he had, at the time, sent a memo to all his staff to come in and look at it. It is the title of his campaign autobiography as well.[2] It is quite clear the picture has substantial significance for Mr. Bush.

The president related to his White House guests the religious significance of the painting. It is based on a Methodist hymn, and speaks to the issue "of serving something larger than yourself in life," and the president said it "speaks to his spirituality."[3] Yet the picture itself suggests both another more worldly meaning and a deeper psychological one.

The picture shows three rugged horsemen taking a steep and rough trail at a gallop.[4] One horseman is clearly in the lead with the other two just behind him. They have almost, but not quite, made the crest of the hill, though it is clear that given their effort, they will do so. They are unflagging in their uphill struggle.

In many ways, the picture captures some essential features of Mr. Bush's psychology and his approach to leadership. The quest, or whatever it is that motivates the horsemen, is an uphill battle. It is not an easy grade. The path is strewn with rocks, dead branches, and the detritus of forest decay.

The path is steep and there is risk in not doing it at a more leisurely pace, but the horsemen are having none of that. They are charging up the hill at what seems full speed. There is an urgency to their speed. They must get somewhere important, and the clock is ticking. It is indeed a charge to keep in the double sense of that phrase. There is a rendezvous with purpose and destinies on the other side of that hill, somewhere in their future. And in order to get there they have to keep charging, hard. This can be no charge of half measures.

In his book, Mr. Bush describes the memo he sent to his staff when he was governor. He describes the painting briefly as "horsemen determinedly charging up what appears to be a steep and rough trail," and adds, "This is us." He adds, the picture "speaks of purpose and direction."[5] Yes, volumes.

The horseman in the foreground and leading the charge is a horse-length in front of the others. He clearly is part of the threesome, but not bound by their pace. His eyes look straight ahead. His face is etched with concentration. He is part of the group, but apart from it as well—a parallel to Mr. Bush's character and relationships in real life.

There are three men in the picture and we can't tell if more are following. Perhaps they are the vanguard of a larger group. Perhaps the success of their quest depends on them alone.

One can see much of Mr. Bush's principles of leadership in that picture, and it is one reason why it resonates so deeply for him; perhaps there are other reasons as well. Brit Hume pointed out to the president that the lead rider looked a little like him and asked whether it was an old picture or had been painted with that in mind. Mr. Bush said, "It's a really old picture. And he's determined. And he's on a tough—he's riding a tough trail. You don't know how many horsemen are behind him, you know at least two. . . . It could be 2,000. You just don't know. But you do know it's a pretty rough looking trail, and *there is absolutely no question in your mind he's going to make it.* . . . The painting says two things to me: One, it speaks to my personal faith, but also speaks to the job of the president, which is to capture the spirit of America and call people to service."[6]

It is not a picture you could imagine his father choosing. George W.'s strong identification with the picture reflects his preference for leading rather than governing. The exact reverse was true of his father. A charge to keep is, in the many senses of that phrase, reflective of that fact. The call to service that George W. speaks of alludes to another part of his leadership after 9/11, Mr. Bush as New World prophet.

GEORGE W. BUSH'S PRINCIPLES OF LEADERSHIP

George W. Bush is a theorist of political leadership. Mr. Bush's leadership principles are central to understanding him as president in large part because he has not only thought about leadership, but acts consistently in accord with what he thinks. At a press conference, Mr. Bush was asked about his views of leadership and his response is summarized below:[7]

- The leader cannot do everything and therefore must surround himself with smart capable people;
- A leader must listen, but be decisive enough to make a decision and stick to it;
- In order to lead, you must know what you believe. You have to stand on principle. You have to believe in certain values and defend them at all costs;
- As leader, you must have a vision about where you're going. You must set clear goals and convince people of these goals and constantly lead toward these goals;
- You've got to treat people on your team with respect.

Elsewhere, Mr. Bush has added to these leadership principles as follows:

- A leader should not wait on events. He must try to shape them[8];
- "My job is to stay ahead of the moment. A President can get so bogged down in the moment that you're unable to be the strategic thinker that you're supposed to be, or at least provide strategic thought"[9];
- "[T]he vision thing matters. That's another lesson I learned"[10];
- "[Y]ou earn [political] capital by spending it"[11];
- First thing's first. During the lead-up to the Afghanistan war, some of his advisors pressed for a consideration as well of Iraq; Mr. Bush cut it off with a curt statement, "That's out of the question *at this point.*" Mr. Bush said this despite the fact that he believed that Saddam Hussein was involved somehow in 9/11 and was a growing danger more generally[12];
- "One of my jobs is to be provocative, seriously, to provoke people into— to force decisions, to make sure it's clear in everybody's mind where we're headed"[13];
- "My belief is that the best way to hold this coalition together is to be clear on our objectives, and to be clear that we are determined to achieve them. You hold a coalition together by strong leadership . . ."[14];
- *Corollary to the above: "action—confident action that will yield positive results provides a kind of slipstream into which reluctant nations and leaders can get behind . . ."[15];
- "My job is to lead"[16]; "The most important lesson [of] life in the presidency is to have a clear vision—of where you want to lead, and lead"[17];

- "[O]ne of the jobs of the president is to leave behind a legacy that will enable other presidents to better deal with the threat that we face."[18] Bush is referring here to the recommendations that may come out of the 9/11 commission, and his role in leaving behind new institutional structures and policy understandings for those who follow him.

PRINCIPLES IN PRACTICE

These of course are principles, or theories. Mr. Bush has clearly thought about these matters, a point worth noting given the questions that have been raised about his intelligence, interest, and curiosity. Knowing who you are and what you believe, and sticking to that knowledge, are core elements underlying these principles. They are as well core elements of his psychology. Mr. Bush believes in the efficacy of action, a view that is consistent with his own repeated efforts to make a success of his life over the years. But principles, as useful as they might be as a general guide, are no substitute for a more detailed examination of those principles in practice.

A Focus on Results

The charge up the hill is about getting there, whatever the destination. It is about accomplishing the purpose. In a word, it is about achieving results.

George W.'s emphasis on results is obvious to anyone who has followed what he says or does. "I'm a performance oriented person, I believe in results."[19] He has little patience for long-winded explanations, and less for high-level abstract theorizing. Introducing Secretary of Education Rod Paige at a meeting, he said, "I wanted for the education man, someone that had actually been an educator. We have enough theory in Washington. We wanted somebody that had actually done the job."[20]

Indeed, in almost every policy area, domestic and foreign, Mr. Bush keeps a mental scorecard. Education? Bush has said, "I want this country to be a results-oriented country, starting at the national level. We ought to be focusing on results—particularly when it comes to the education of children."[21]

Speaking of his tax cut initiatives, he has said, "This is a long process and what I look for is the final results."[22] Speaking in support of his faith-based program, Mr. Bush asked his audience to consider what they accomplished: "The argument is, 'Let's focus on the process.' We're saying, 'Let's focus on results.'"[23] Elsewhere, he has bluntly said, "I'm not interested in process. If the process doesn't yield the right results, change the process."[24]

Mr. Bush has carried his scorecard into the arena of foreign policy as well. Of the war against terror Mr. Bush said, "I'm a performance oriented person. I believe in results. And if you want to join the coalition against terror, we'll welcome you in. . . . I have recognized that some countries will do what others won't do. All I ask for is results. If you say you want to join us to cut off the money, show us the money. . . . I appreciate diplomatic talk but I'm more interested in action and results."[25]

What of being a member in good standing of the allied coalition? Here is Mr. Bush on that: "But you asked a very interesting question—do you keep a scorecard? And the answer is I do. I do because I'm an old baseball guy, and I like to keep the score. I like to see who's performing and who's not performing. It's part of being a coalition."[26]

The scorecard, of course, serves several purposes. It lets people know the president is watching and counting. It is therefore a method of accountability, and Mr. Bush has been quite explicit about this.[27] Mr. Bush takes it seriously. When Mr. Bush met with President Ali Abdallah Silih of Yemen, the latter had promised help, but had then placed restrictions on an American operation there. According to Bob Woodward, "this was the kind of divergence of interest that infuriated Bush," since it suggested that "Yemen was really against him."[28] This might be viewed as another example of Mr. Bush's "black or white thinking." Yet it could also be seen in the context of his dislike of leaders, like Yasser Arafat, who say one thing and do another, and Mr. Bush's disinclination to just let such leaders off the hook.

Woodward's observation suggests another function of the scorecard. It is a method to monitor and gauge interpersonal relationships. Mr. Bush, as noted, is a man who does not immediately give his trust, but rather prefers that you earn it. "Observe, then trust" is the president's psychological motto regarding relationships, and the scorecard clearly is a preferred method of making that judgment.

A Pragmatic Presidency?

The frontier culture in the United States gave rise to pragmatic necessity. In a new land, cut off from supporting infrastructure and facing new circumstances, one made do with what one found or perished. Americans of course developed theories where they were needed and useful. However, the basic question remained: Does it work?

George W. Bush is, in many ways, a representative of that tradition. This, I know, is a controversial statement. Isn't Mr. Bush famous for not compromising? Isn't his administration notable for its stubbornness, if not its downright obstinacy? Shouldn't "My way or the highway" be the official motto of the Bush administration? The answers to these questions are: Yes, yes, and yes, if you are looking for a good bumper-sticker slogan.

The administration's reputation stems from its ambitions and its circumstances. Mr. Bush was a man of transformative policy ambitions before 9/11. That attack reframed his ambitions; it did not begin them. It did however lead him to add two regional wars and a worldwide war against terrorism to his list.

Moreover, many of his policy aspirations ran counter to the "mainstream" politics that preceded him. I put the word mainstream in quotes to call attention to the fact that this term reflects a temporary arrangement of policy understandings and principles. It is precisely these understandings that Mr. Bush seeks to change. Mr. Bush's policy ambitions are not incremental. He wants to change the ways in which Americans think about domestic and foreign policy.

Democrats realize this about Mr. Bush and it fuels their resistance, as only the threat of political marginality can. These are very entrenched political interests whose policy views and frameworks have largely prevailed since Lyndon Johnson's massive landslide in 1964. Even Ronald Reagan's two terms didn't really dent Democratic control of Congress and the levers of auxiliary political institutions. It is understandable that having been part of the major political paradigm for 40 years, they have become attached to it.

Mr. Bush has no such attachment to it, of course, and the question for him is how best to overcome and rearrange it. The answer to that question has largely dictated his tactics. So has the fact that that he was elected with a very narrow electoral majority, lost the popular vote, and first had, then lost, then regained a narrow governing majority. Mr. Bush's policy aspirations face strong head winds. Or to use the metaphor of the three horsemen, he has a steep and rough trail. A hard charge is the only way to overcome the obstacles that confront him, including time.

The ten key tactics of the Bush Administration have been listed in an excellent paper by Charles Jones.[29] They are: (1) control the agenda; (2) have your solution to the problem ready; (3) press your advantages to the maximum; (4) don't negotiate with yourself; (5) win where you can and when you can; (6) look for support where you can find it; (7) compromise on what you must and where you can; (8) always close on a good deal; (9) agreements are victories, not defeats; and (10) there is only one commander-in-chief.

This list reflects the actual practices of the administration. It describes a political bargaining process that by its nature is a matter of give-and-take. The fact that the Bush administration seeks to use its advantages, and has been able to do so, speaks to its competence, not its rigidity.

The tactics Jones lists are suffused with flexibility. Reach out, win where and when you can, compromise, look for support, always close on a good deal (even if it isn't all you want), agreements are victories; these are tactics of bargaining, give-and-take. Mr. Bush has, of course, been repeatedly accused of being a shoot-from-the-hip cowboy. Yet contrary to caricature, these are the tactics of a very pragmatic leader.

Of course, like every other administration, this one prefers to take more than it gives. Is Mr. Bush a tough bargainer? Yes. Does his administration "twist arms" to get its way? Yes. Is Mr. Bush a hard charger for his agenda? He certainly is, and given his circumstances and his aspirations, he could hardly be otherwise and still be serious about his purpose.

The question of flexibility comes up in another way when considering the Bush administration's behavior with its agenda. It must deal with deep and sharp ideological divisions in Congress. Party line votes, one measure of both cohesion and partisanship, have appreciably increased. Bipartisanship, which some take as a measure of moderation and flexibility, has become more difficult.

In fact, increased party-line voting and the discipline that underlies it, narrow majorities especially in the Senate, and what amounts to a 60-vote rule in the Senate when the opposition wants to stand fast have made getting any legislation through for presidential signature an accomplishment. This is especially the case given Mr. Bush's avowed purpose to recast the policy debate. How then has he approached this set of political facts?

Here again Jones is helpful.[30] He distinguishes between several types of strategies. These include competitive partisanship, the situation described above; competitive bipartisanship, in which opposition party leaders are invited into the process early on so that they can bring their party along with them; and cross-partisanship, in which particular issues generate support across party lines. Jones also lists true bipartisanship but notes that this has been rare, and mostly confined to the very immediate aftermath of 9/11.

Mr. Bush has made use of all of these different kinds of alliances. Competitive partisanship is the most frequent fate for his proposals. Here, a hard-charging approach coupled with an adroit use of the House-Senate reconciliation committees has delivered major victories. Yet, he has also worked with Democrats Ted Kennedy on the education bill and Max Baucus and John Breaux on the Medicare bill and through this competitive bipartisanship has gained some major victories. The trade negotiation authority Mr. Bush won would be an example of cross-partisanship. In all of his legislative initiatives Mr. Bush has been forced to assemble different "coalitions of the willing." In that respect Bush's leadership in both domestic and international politics have come to mirror each other.

Even general agreement in a policy area does not guarantee a working coalition. Mr. Bush's energy proposal actually drew different supporters and opponents, depending on the specific provisions being discussed. A parallel process can be observed in the war against terrorism and the rebuilding of Iraq, in which countries might agree with the general aims but balk at specific requests.

The critical point here for understanding Mr. Bush's circumstances both at home and abroad is that policy consensus is becoming more and more splintered. The question then is not so much why Mr. Bush has had such difficulty assembling coalitions. It is how he has managed to do so at all.

One way he has prevailed is though intense personal involvement, when needed. When the Patient's Bill of Rights deal, which provided safeguards for patients in managed care programs, was threatened, and a rival Democratic bill looked like it might pass, Mr. Bush sprang into action with a full-court press on the key player, GOP Representative Charles Norwood. At Bush's insistence aides had been meeting with Rep. Norwood for weeks, trying to find common ground. When that groundwork had been laid, they brought Rep. Norwood to the White House for more talks, as a preliminary to seeing Mr. Bush. When the two met, Mr. Bush began by praising Mr. Norwood's long fight for patient's rights, and then abruptly got to the point in a typical Bush way, according to those privy: "So now that I've kissed your [rear end], what do I have to do to get a deal?" Then the real deal-making discussion began. In direct talks that included part schmoozing, part calls for party loyalty, part a direct request by "his president," and lots of give-and-take, Mr. Bush closed the deal.[31]

That same intense involvement can be seen in Mr. Bush's hectic travel schedule on behalf of his tax cut proposals, which did not move public opinion, and his direct involvement in the 2002 mid-term elections, which did. It can also be seen in his active involvement in securing the final votes needed to pass his Medicare bill—making calls at 4 A.M. on his way back from his surprise Iraq trip. These examples, and there are more, suggest two important elements of Mr. Bush's success.

First, he is an adroit politician, perhaps one of the best since Lyndon Johnson. Whereas Johnson was known to beat down his opponents, Mr. Bush uses a wider variety of approaches. The result however, is the same. He is skilled at getting what he wants.

Second, Mr. Bush is far from the lazy and uninvolved oaf depicted in caricatures. During the 2000 presidential campaign, critics pointed to the fact that when Mr. Bush was governor he took long periods out each day to exercise. They failed to mention that the legislature met only 140 days every other year but that the governor was in office all the time. During the campaign, Frank Bruni saw Mr. Bush's gubernatorial schedule and his complaints about the number of events he had to attend, his tiredness, or of being away from home as an indication that George W. had a tendency to coddle himself.[32]

Yet when George Bush was challenged and he lost, as happened when John McCain soundly beat him in New Hampshire, Mr. Bush did not allow himself to fade or falter. On the contrary, he took stock, made necessary changes, and re-doubled his efforts.[33] Part of the effort Mr. Bruni attributes to wounded pride, and perhaps this is so. Mr. Bush, as noted, is very competitive. But part of it is also about the psychology of wanting to make something of himself and not fal-ter again. Here as elsewhere in his life, if Mr. Bush were not to succeed, it would not be for lack of effort.

Bruni also makes clear that by the end of the presidential campaign Mr. Bush had changed. He had outgrown some of the need to let his impish impulses protect him from the seriousness of what he was doing and how important it was to do it well. He still kept the same schedule—up at 5 A.M., in bed by 9:30 P.M., with an exercise break when at all possible.[34] But in matching the pace of his presidency, its many initiatives, meetings, and presidential travels, it seems clear that Mr. Bush has demonstrated repeatedly that he has the energy of his ambitions.

Political dexterity requires psychological flexibility. And in all his domestic negotiations Mr. Bush has been quite flexible on the specific provisions. To give one example, he gave ground on the number of experimental cities in which pri-vate and government Medicare coverage programs would compete.[35] The ad-ministration made a number of other concessions as well.

This flexibility is not about ultimate goals. The Bush administration wants to change policy direction and discourse. As long as policies move in that direc-tion, Mr. Bush is flexible about actual implementation.

Consider the anti-ballistic missile system (ABM). Mr. Bush withdrew from the treaty proscribing the development of such a system. But he did not commit to a par-ticular new system. The administration has invested in a variety of possible defense systems including those that can attack a missile during its critical "launch phase," regional systems, ship-based systems, and territorial systems. The goal, to protect America from its enemies, remains the same, but the means remained flexible.

Mr. Bush's flexibility is evident in the international arena as well. The ad-ministration has changed course repeatedly in its plans for the postwar rebuild-ing of Iraq. Whether the subject is the amount of power for the interim council or which allies will be allowed to bid for reconstruction contracts, an emphasis on results undercuts any tendencies towards inflexibility.

Before the Iraq war, Mr. Bush had warned that those who wouldn't take the risks of ridding Iraq of the Hussein regime would not profit from its rebuilding. He then formulated and announced a policy to do just that.[36] The policy immedi-ately set off loud protests among those excluded countries, among them France, Germany, and Russia.[37] Mr. Bush then used the leverage of this policy to gain concessions on Iraqi debt, saying that even countries that didn't contribute to the war effort might be considered for contracts if they helped in this way with post-war reconstruction or were helpful in wiping out terrorism.[38]

When considering Mr. Bush's hard-charging style, it is well to remember that circumstances as well as psychology play a role. In both the domestic and international arenas, the president's transforming agenda must contend with powerful, entrenched, and hostile interests arrayed against him. That is why a hard charge may be necessary to get you up and over the hill, but a weak one is not likely to make much headway.

Jones says that the administration compromises on what it must and where it can. That last phrase is worth considering. While there are certain similarities between Bush's approach in domestic and foreign policy, there is one profound difference. Bush's presidency and his own sense of purpose were transformed on 9/11 by foreign terrorists, not domestic policy opponents. September 11 underscored John Kennedy's prophetic remark, "Domestic mistakes can only hurt us, but foreign policy can kill us."[39]

"Compromise where you can" suggests there will be policies or arenas where that will not be possible. The Bush administration has been much more insistent on its national security–related policies in the wake of 9/11 than it has on the domestic front. It is hard to find the national security and foreign policy equivalent of compromises on the campaign finance bill, the education bill, the three tax-cut initiatives, the Medicare bill, election reform, welfare reform, pension reform, regulatory reform, cloning, and other legislative issues with which the administration has been involved.

Part of the difference between the domestic and international issues is that in the latter the administration can just say no. And it has done so to several major international treaty initiatives like the Kyoto accords, the ABM agreement, the International Criminal Court, the Biological Weapons Convention, and the revival of the Nuclear Test Ban Treaty defeated by the Senate in 1999. In these matters the administration has been insistent on oversight and enforcement mechanisms. One question the critics must fairly answer is whether, in the wake of 9/11, these objections are not prudent.

Presidential Vision

Vision is important to leaders generally, and transformational leaders like Mr. Bush particularly. It reflects an ability to see beyond the here and now. The Bush White House instituted an Office of Strategic Initiatives, whose purpose is to focus on the long term; but no amount of institutional help can substitute for a leader's capacity to envision the "big picture" and what he would like to accomplish.

Vision, by its nature, must move beyond available information or current circumstances. It represents an act of imagination as well as political audacity. And it reflects, at its best, a blend of pragmatism and creativity. Even grandiose dreams need to be leavened with a dash of realism.

Mr. Bush's father was notoriously inept with the "vision thing," as he called it. That President Bush was more comfortable governing than leading. Yet it is in the act of leadership that vision finds its most appropriate home. George W. Bush is clearly more adept at leading than was his father. But what of the president's vision?

Mr. Bush's critics are convinced he doesn't have one. Anthony Lewis, criticizing Mr. Bush for his failure to ratify the Kyoto Treaty and the Biological Weapons Conventions thinks that, "Underlying Mr. Bush's response on these matters there is a failure of vision. He takes a parochial view, driven by ideology and a narrow sense of where American interests lie."[40]

Thomas Friedman is convinced that "Mr. Bush's greatest weakness is that too many people, at home and abroad, smell that he's not really interested in repairing the world."[41] That pundit piece was written a year *after* Bob Woodward reported the president's "vision clearly indicates an ambitious reordering of the world through preemptive and, if necessary, unilateral action to reduce suffering and bring peace."[42] Or, as the president said of the United States' unique world position, "I will seize the opportunity to achieve big goals. There is nothing bigger than world peace."[43]

In the 2000 presidential campaign, Mr. Bush sounded like a man who was not about to add to American's already large global responsibilities. Yet, as Alan Murray writes, "It's now clear that President Bush, once feared to be an isolationist, has an agenda for remaking the world that rivals those of Harry Truman and Woodrow Wilson in its ambition, scope and idealism. But unlike those two postwar leaders, President Bush has little patience for using multilateral institutions or discussions to achieve his ends."[44]

Still, world peace, however achieved, is a large and amorphous aim. Many possible actions and policies might be argued as contributing to that noble goal. Therefore, one is still left with the question raised by Richard Brookheiser, senior editor of the *National Review* about Mr. Bush: "The unknown quantity is imagination—the imagination to foresee consequences, the imagination to be a wartime President."[45] Mr. Brookheiser does not attempt any answer to these questions. He also provides no hint of what kind of imagination it would take to be a wartime president. This is a question that cannot be resolved in the abstract. One needs to look directly at Mr. Bush's policy for the degree of vision it reflects and I will do so in the next chapter.

George W. Bush:
Amateur National Psychologist

Mr. Bush is well known for following in his father's footsteps when it comes to introspection and "couch questions." Neither likes them. George W. has said of himself, "I don't spend a lot of time thinking about myself, about why I do things."[46] This is not wholly true; George W. can be self-reflective. But it is true enough. It is therefore somewhat surprising and paradoxical to learn that he thinks psychologically about others and especially the American public.

Mr. Bush's comment to Barbara Walters about the human tendency to want to move on is but one of a number of such comments. Mr. Bush remarked to Bob Woodward that "I felt I had the job of making sure the American people understand. They understood the severity of the attack. But I wasn't sure they understood how long it was going to take and what a difficult process this would be." Mr. Bush's repeated comments on rebuilding Iraq, however long it takes, can be seen as a form of public education.[47]

While Mr. Bush might not think much about his own psychology, he clearly has thought a great deal about Americans'. Discussing the period after 9/11 but before the attack on Afghanistan, he said, "I knew at some point in time, the American public was going to say, where is he? What are you doing? Where's your leadership? Where is the United States? You're all powerful, do something."[48] Not only did Mr. Bush believe that the American public wanted action, but a particular kind of action: "The American people want a big bang. I have to convince them that this is a war that will be fought in many steps."[49]

Mr. Bush did believe that Saddam Hussein was somehow connected to 9/11,[50] but he nonetheless took Iraq off the table at first. His reasoning is interesting: "Obviously, there were some who discussed Iraq. That's out of the question at this point. . . . Rumsfeld wanted to make sure the military was active in other regions. *My point was that the degree of difficult had to be relatively small in order to make sure we continued to succeed in the first battle.*[51]

Much like a manager who teams his up-and-coming boxer against opponents who can test, but not beat him, Mr. Bush chose not to begin the war against terror with an attack on both Afghanistan and Iraq. Recall that "first things first" is one of Mr. Bush's leadership principles. It is now clear that there is an understanding of American public psychology underlying them.

What Political Philosophy?

Convictions, even strong ones, are not a governing philosophy. Nor are campaign slogans like "reformer with results," or "compassionate conservatism." As Mr. Bush stands for reelection, he and his party are very much in need of a publicly understandable governing philosophy.[52] Mr. Bush has recently begun to talk about his vision of an "ownership society," but it is unclear if this will do the trick.

His need for an easily articulated vision that captures his policy is critical given that Mr. Bush wishes to transform American domestic policy and politics with a new ongoing governing majority. Mr. Bush is in the paradoxical position of possibly being reelected primarily on the strength of his psychology and leadership. This will further Mr. Bush's short-term fortunes and those of his party, but at the expense of any changes in voter identification with the party that survive his terms in office.

The exact nature of Mr. Bush's dilemma is made clear by what the Republican party used to represent, but doesn't anymore with Mr. Bush. The GOP used to stand for smaller government. That would be accomplished by doing away with whole departments of government, like the Department of Education. Under Mr. Bush, this is clearly not going to happen. The Department of Education is not going to be axed. It has a whole new Bush-generated federal mandate. Nor is government going to get smaller under President Bush. The Defense Department and national security programs are growing and will continue to do so.

The GOP used to say it would reduce government by stopping the expansion of welfare state programs. Under President Reagan, some had the idea that they could starve entitlements with large deficits. Under Mr. Bush, this thinking has clearly changed. He inherited an economic slowdown and then the economy went into recession. A terror attack followed. Yet, that didn't keep him from spending money and passing tax cuts. Mr. Bush was instrumental in passing a new federal entitlement in the form of a major drug benefit for Medicare recipients. It's hard to make the case that the new GOP is against government or spending money. The GOP used to be for limited government, but no more. Mr. Bush will continue to place few limits on government growth, especially in the defense and security sectors. Under President Bush, it appears, America will have as much government as it needs, and that is likely, in some areas, to be a lot.

A look through the range of Mr. Bush's domestic initiatives makes it hard to discern a single theme. This was the import of David Frum's observation about the lack of one big idea. The Bush presidency has policies galore. What it lacks is a framing metaphor.

A closer inspection suggests there are at least four general principles at work in Mr. Bush's domestic vision: *compassion* (faith-based initiatives, drug entitlement, immigration reform); *opportunity* (education reform, Social Security reform); *responsibility* (Social Security ownership/investment, abstinence, civics curriculum, and citizenship); and *effectiveness* (government management reform, regulation reform). Those with a penchant for acronyms could field these as CORE governing principles. Only one of these principles, responsibility, has its roots in traditional Republican principles. The others are more clearly associated with Mr. Bush's emphasis and insistence.

All of them, however, echo Mr. Bush's own psychology and development. They aren't dictated by it, but they are rooted in it. Responsibility—the lack of it and developing it—is a key element in Mr. Bush's development and psychology.

Having overcome his own mixed record of responsibility, it is easy to see how this theme might well resonate with him. Effectiveness, too, has roots in Mr. Bush's psychology and past. After all, it was his long search for effectiveness—read success—that fueled his delayed entry into adulthood.

Compassion too can be traced back to Mr. Bush's earliest encounter with some hard facts of life. Remember that as a six year old he tried to console his mother after his sister's death. It is not too far from that child's effort to the young adult Bush trying to get jobs for all his employees, being moved as governor by his meeting with a black offender in prison, spending hours with the families of 9/11 victims, or championing the aspirations of illegal immigrants in front of Republican audiences hostile to that idea.

Finally, opportunity has deep roots in Mr. Bush's history and his family ethos. Mr. Bush was given many opportunities that he sometimes had difficulty in acknowledging. Yet part of his turn toward a more mature adulthood is a capacity to acknowledge the role of others in his successes. Asked about *his* success in the 2002 mid-term elections, Mr. Bush replied, "Thank you for trying to give it to me, but they deserve the credit. There's case after case of people who have put their reputations on the line, who spent a lot of time away from their homes and their families, shaking a lot of hands and putting their hearts and souls—in both parties."[53] What was now true of him, he could acknowledge about others.

Formulating an understandable set of governing principles is critical for a president who wishes to transform the governing paradigm. The reason is very simple. If you can't name it, you can't sell it.

THE BUSH BULLY PULPIT: MANY VOICES

For many years, both Democratic and Republican presidents have attempted their own version of triangulation. They have "gone public" hoping to influence Congress by doing so. The evidence that this is a successful strategy is sparse.[54] Mr. Bush barnstormed around the country seeking to ignite support for his tax cuts. In the end, however, he failed to arouse public enthusiasm and had to rely on old-fashioned legislative skill.

Still, conventional wisdom dies hard. The bully pulpit, a phrase coined by Teddy Roosevelt, spoke to the power of amplification that the presidency offers its occupant's message. When television became a national media, it helped make the president *the* prime-time political player in American politics. But now in an age of cable television, websites, and bloggers, the president shares the stage with many others. Worse, every president now faces the danger of overexposure. And when the president is off stage, other voices are there around the clock. As Maccaby has observed, "the bully pulpit had been drowned out by bully pundits."[55]

The president no longer commands public attention, he competes for it. Increasingly, it seems, it is a losing battle. Networks no longer routinely carry major presidential addresses or press conferences. When George W. Bush gave a major address in Cincinnati on his reasoning for going to war against Iraq, all three major networks didn't carry it. It wasn't considered news. Still, it is unclear how many people he would have moved had they heard him. Political scientist George Edwards has just completed a major study which found that presidents rarely move public opinion very much and recommends that they spend their time more wisely elsewhere.[56]

The bully pulpit is now more accurately seen as a platform for a political ensemble. Yet, it would be a mistake to completely ignore the power of presidential talk. And for no president would this be more the case than for George W. Bush.

The bully pulpit presupposes one major form of talk: exhortation. Mr. Bush's rhetorical style suggests it is useful to think further about presidential talk. George W.'s talk can be divided into tangled, plain, straight, and blunt.

Tangled Talk

Mr. Bush's well-known battles with the English language stimulate ridicule from some. For his opponents, George W.'s idiosyncratic grammar, syntax, and malapropisms are evidence that he isn't intellectually up to the tasks of the presidency. Oddly, one critic believes that the president's tangled speech reveals a "national disorder."[57]

Mr. Bush is unembarrassed by his lost language battles. He is well aware of these syntactical tendencies, and, borrowing a tactic pioneered by Ronald Reagan, has used humorous self-deprecation to great effect. He has informed listeners, "that more and more of our imports come from overseas." Speaking of the economy, he said "we ought to make the pie higher." Elsewhere, he told an audience, "I understand small business growth, I was one." He is also well known for coining new words: "misunderestimate," "Grecians," and "Hispanically." As Mr. Bush says, "Anyone can give you a coherent sentence, but something like this takes you to an entirely new dimension."[58]

Observers and critics of the president's rhetorical lapses have missed a key psychological point. The lapses help compress the distance between Mr. Bush and his audience. He is, after all, the president. Most members of his audiences can understand a mangled word or phrase, having most likely seen it close-up and first-hand themselves. It is a form of horizontal connection in what is generally a hierarchical relationship.

President Common Guy as Commander-in-Chief

Mr. Bush generally likes people and is able to move toward them. Yet he is not an outstanding wholesale politician. One Bush profiler writes that, "He doesn't have the cheery backslapping style of a conventionally charming politician. He's not a flatterer. He doesn't compulsively throw his arms around strangers and claim to feel their pain or read their books, or deeply appreciate what they have to say. It's the exact opposite of how a politician—in order to succeed—should be."[59]

He is only sporadically charismatic and even then only in limited settings. Charisma is compelling. It is a quality that allows a leader's presence to be palpable through the TV screen or capable of bringing an assembled crowd to its emotional feet. Mr. Bush is not charismatic in this sense.

His magnetism is of a different kind. Bruni notes that "Bush's wattage is more modest and quirkier."[60] Mr. Bush engages people, but in his own idiosyncratic way. He praises one young man for his "articulate remarks" and "appends his high-minded compliments with an unexpected term of endearment, 'Dude.' When an elderly employee at a factory he's visiting pledged her support, Bush enthusiastically responds, 'I'll seal it with a kiss' and does."[61]

This playful, down-to-earth style combines an appealing child with a purposeful adult. The result is a president who comes across as authentic and accessible. Why else would a leader risk cavorting like Mr. Bush does and being viewed as not serious? This is obviously an exceptionally risky style for someone who is criticized as a "lightweight."

The same is true of his embrace of idiosyncratic language, rather than trying to cover his shortcomings. The result is a public impression of a president at ease with himself, but also someone who is human as well as presidential.

This interpersonal style has substantive implications for his leadership. Bush is able to collapse the distance between his elevated status and the lesser altitude of the person beside or in front of him.[62] Bush has, in a sense, continued the democratization of charisma that began with Bill Clinton.

Traditional charisma is hierarchical. It is an integral part of the heroic presidency. That kind of leader stands above and beyond the people who feel compelled by him. With Bill Clinton, charisma started to become horizontal. Clinton had the ability to give each person the impression that he had emotionally entered into their lives and problems. The experience might well be illusory, and it certainly was transitory. Yet, for those who experienced it, it was felt as profoundly intimate and personal. Clinton combined this capacity with a larger-than-life presence fueled by his larger-than-life appetites, for almost every possibility he encountered.

Mr. Bush is not immediately intimate with strangers[63] or, like Clinton, a man who seems larger-than-life because of his appetites. Mr. Bush comes across as warm, funny, and above all sincere. Unlike political leaders with hidden depths to their psychologies that suddenly get publicly revealed, Mr. Bush appears to be hiding very little. He may be paradoxical, "a loving man" with a hard job to do, but the large "what you see is what you get" element in Bush's psychology suggests there are no dense and twisted psychological roots beneath the surface.

Plain Talk

Plain talk keeps words and thoughts on the ground level of politics where most Americans reside. It doesn't seek to showcase the erudition of the speaker or the complexity of his thoughts. Rather its purpose is to convey information in a direct, simple, and understandable way. Some confuse that with a lack of sophistication or brainpower, although it is not necessarily associated with either.

Mr. Bush prefers plain talk both as a tool of self-definition and of political leadership. The words are commonplace, but their expression in the political arena is not. So when asked about his ultimatum to the Taliban government in Afghanistan about turning over Osama bin Laden, he replied "if you cough him up and his people today, we'll reconsider our plans."[64] Asked about the American role, and especially his own, in trying to secure peace in the Middle East, Mr. Bush replied that, "we're going to put a guy on the ground to ride herd on the process," a term he realized was "a little informal in diplomatic terms."[65] Elsewhere, he described the role of Secretary of State Powell's job as being to "clear out [the] underbrush."[66]

Plain talk fits in well with Mr. Bush's psychology and style. Plain talk avoids pretense, which Mr. Bush dislikes. It also helps equalize the distance between the president and others. And it is how Mr. Bush tends to think of things, in direct, straight-ahead ways. It is not a surprising style for a man who is focused on meeting problems head on, is suspicious of abstractions and theories, and, whenever possible, prefers results to ideological purity.

Plain talk is not just about Mr. Bush's stylistic preferences. It is a key building block of the two most important elements in the Bush lexicon of presidential leadership: blunt talk and straight talk. The first reflects an important element in the psychology of Mr. Bush's character integrity, meaning what he says. The second is a reflection of the psychology of his judgment. Both are key ingredients in leadership integrity.

The Importance of "Meaning It"

Meaning what you say could not play a more crucial role in Mr. Bush's psychology or in his leadership. It is central to Mr. Bush's self-definition both as a person and a leader. And it carries with it as well enormous implications for how he conducts his domestic and international responsibilities.

Mr. Bush is quite clear about its centrality to him personally and to his administration. In an interview with an Egyptian reporter, a question arose about mixed messages in his administration regarding efforts toward a Middle East peace. Asked whether Arabs or the people in the region shouldn't really be worrying about voices in the administration opposed to serious efforts by the United States, Bush responded, *"when I say something I mean it. . . . And I think President Mubarak knows that. And I'm going to refresh their memories about the kind of administration I try to run. When I say something we actually go do it. . . .* now I understand it will be tough and difficult, but I believe it can happen."[67]

What does "meaning it" actually mean? "Meaning it" reflects the primacy of the integrity involved in giving one's word. It is a reflection of, and an expectation of, honesty and directness. It is a measure of self and others. It is, in short, a primal calculus for Mr. Bush as a person and a leader.

"Meaning it," psychologically, requires knowing where you stand. This in turn requires clear-eyed views about yourself and your circumstances. It also requires the courage to accept that information and, to the extent possible, act on it.

Yet for a president, knowing where you stand is not enough. Others make up such a large part of political life. It is a matter of great importance that they know where the president stands.

Mr. Bush respects bluntness, even if he doesn't sometimes like its specific content. In the events leading up to the Iraq War, no traditional ally was more publicly hostile to Mr. Bush's plans than France. The same was true after the war as the rebuilding process began to unfold. Yet Mr. Bush said he and Mr. Chirac had a good relationship. How was that possible? Because "There was no question where Jacques Chirac stood, and I made clear—I made it clear where I stood. And that's why I can say we've got good relations, because we're able to be honest with each other."[68] This did not mean that the president would be inviting him out to visit Crawford any time soon.[69]

"Meaning it" is one reflection of seriousness, and a president's seriousness is always being appraised by others. Richard Neustadt pointed out in his classic book *Presidential Power* that the president is surrounded by people trying to gauge his seriousness. The more serious he is, the more serious they have to be about what he says and wants to do.

Neustadt was discussing the president's domestic circumstances. Yet 9/11 has made this president's credibility a cornerstone of prevention and the new deterrence. Mr. Bush is well aware of the fact that "the world watches us. The world examines and tests our will. They want to know whether or not we're people who just talk, or people who are willing to lead."[70]

Knowing a president is serious about what he says has become a critical element in the post-9/11 security environment and Mr. Bush's approach to it. He has frequently commented on the ways in which terrorists and their allies under-estimate American resolve, and is determined to demonstrate the error of their views. The examples of this are legion.

Mr. Bush's willingness to enforce UN resolutions with or without UN support is one obvious example. His determination to stay in Iraq "as long as it takes" to rebuild and transform it is another. His determination to "do what it takes," including incurring continuing casualties, is yet another.

Yet, it is also found in smaller matters. When after 9/11 the United States began prescreening foreign airplane travelers, several countries refused to comply.[71] The United States responded that the passengers of those airlines that didn't comply would have every bag and person subjected to a stringent search, and he followed through on it.[72] Foreign airlines fell into line.

The Nixon administration famously advised journalists to watch what they did, not what they said. Bush invites others to both listen and watch—just as he does.

Loyalty as a Form of "Meaning It"

Mr. Bush makes great use of "meaning it" in his political relationships. Consider the importance he attaches to loyalty. Loyalty is a bond that results from a history of emotional attachment. It is built on affinities—personal, emotional, and professional—that are developed and consolidated in the course of the relationship. Trust and some form of affection or partiality are ordinarily its key ingredients.

Loyalty, from the standpoint of "meaning it," is a mechanism for knowing where you stand with others and letting them know where they stand with you. Demonstrated loyalty allows you to have trust that others are truly considering your best interests, and not theirs. This is especially important in politics, where loyalties are fickle. This was made clear most recently by Al Gore's failure to alert his former vice-presidential partner Joe Lieberman that he was endorsing someone else.[73]

Mr. Bush saw this kind of behavior up close and very personal during his father's failed reelection campaign. Barbara Bush recalls that some in her husband's reelection campaign, including some very senior and well-known advisors, melted away when the going got tough.[74] Small wonder that George W. has said "The definition of friend is someone who is loyal. Loyal means that I'm with you when times are good or times are bad."[75] George W. saw firsthand what misplaced trust and fickle loyalty did to his father, and that was another mistake he was determined not to repeat.

His many friends form a series of concentric circles around Mr. Bush from different periods in his life: Midland, Texas, Andover, Yale, his oil days, and baseball. Those friendships have stood the test of time and of Mr. Bush's style in making them: observe, then trust. Clay Johnson III, who was George W.'s chief of staff as governor and headed his White House transition team said, "He's very sensitive to what people's motivations are. . . . He doesn't want to be used."[76]

Loyalty is not impartial, but neither is it synonymous with agreement. One can be loyal while disagreeing, and agree without being loyal. These matters are often confused in discussions of loyalty's place in George W.'s psychology.

Loyalty can be pledged, but its proof, as Mr. Bush might say, is in one's behavior. In a fickle political culture, Mr. Bush says he prefers advisors "whose primary interest is me."[77] That sounds very self-referential, but it addresses a problem that every president confronts. Every leader needs unvarnished advice, but many advisors are tied to the leader in ways that might compromise giving it.

The major problem for any president here is twofold. The president's political interests may not always coincide with the national interest. Advisors, whose fortunes are tied to the former, may not give adequate weight to the latter. Then, too, there is the problem of the advisor's own ambitions, which may or may not coincide with either the president's or the public's long-term interests.

Mr. Bush addressed this problem in a typically direct way. He made Karl Rove, his campaign advisor, sell his political consulting company. Mr. Bush is now his only client. His selection of Dick Cheney as vice president partially reflects this calculation as well. Mr. Cheney had no ambitions for the presidency, and thus the divergence of interests that became evident in the last two years of the Clinton-Gore administration simply will not arise.

None of this guarantees that Mr. Bush will get good advice, or if he does, make good use of it. However, in Bush decision circles, once a person has demonstrated their loyalty, competence, and judgment, they gain the confidence of the president. And once they have done that, they have the latitude to give frank advice. What the president does with it is addressed in the next chapter.

SECTION V

A TRANSFORMING PRESIDENT
IN PERSPECTIVE

CHAPTER 8

THE POLITICS
OF TRANSFORMATION

GEORGE W. BUSH STANDS POISED TO BECOME the first truly transformational president since FDR. Indeed, if he succeeds in his quest he will have accomplished something FDR never did—transforming America *and* the world. And if he succeeds at that, or even comes close, he will surely be considered a president of the first rank.

Mr. Bush's policy and political ambitions are obviously large and historic undertakings. The odds against his succeeding in either, much less both, are substantial. Yet, make no mistake about it: This is what Mr. Bush wants.

Mr. Bush's role as a transformational leader is, to say the least, paradoxical. He is not by nature, nor did he give much prior evidence of being, a heroic type. As late as the 2000 presidential campaign, he touted himself as a "Reformer with Results." Yes, he had clear views and followed through on them. But that only made him honest, not heroic.

But embedded within many of Mr. Bush's policy remarks and the position papers his campaign issued were some truly transformational ideas. Looking back to the 2000 campaign, almost every policy change that is the basis for Mr. Bush's counter-paradigm to interest-group liberalism was put forward or already tried out in Texas. Testing as the centerpiece for assessing student progress so that no child was left behind, for example, was already on the books in Texas but Mr. Bush actually made use of it.[1] As for dramatic changes in Social Security, allowing individuals to own and invest part of what they pay, Mr. Bush publicly called for that change early in the presidential campaign.[2] Lowering marginal tax rates based on the presumption that government should only tax for its needs, and that these should be carefully considered, was one of Mr. Bush's earliest campaign platforms.[3] The use of tax incentives and voluntary agreements to replace government command and control approaches to cleaning up the environment had also been championed early in the 2000 campaign.[4]

The same is true for Mr. Bush's approach to foreign policy. During the campaign he said he favored a foreign policy of limits. But he also said, "a president must be a clear-eyed realist. There are limits to the smiles and scowls of diplomacy. Armies and missiles are not stopped by stiff notes of condemnation. They are held in check by strength and purpose and the promise of swift punishment."[5]

Yes, he said he wanted to work with our allies, but he also said protecting America must be the first duty of the president, a priority enshrined in his oath of office. He wanted missile defense. Would he sign treaties like the Comprehensive Test Ban Treaty that obligated the United States without enforcement mechanisms for cheaters? No, because:

> It does not stop proliferation, especially to renegade regimes. It is not verifiable. It is not enforceable. And it would stop us from ensuring the safety and reliability of our nation's deterrent, should the need arise. On these crucial matters, it offers only words and false hopes and high intentions—with no guarantees whatever. We can fight the spread of nuclear weapons, but we cannot wish them away with unwise treaties.[6]

About the only transformational policy idea not put forward by then-candidate Bush was his doctrine of preemption, or more accurately prevention. And that policy grew directly out of Bush's stated view of the world that "America has determined enemies, who hate our values and resent our success" and that "The [Soviet] Empire has passed, but evil remains."[7] September 11 provided a dramatic confirmation of Bush's view. Moreover, given that he thought his first and primary responsibility was to "preserve and protect," preventive war or preemption was hardly a radical step.

Mr. Bush's role as a transformational president was somewhat paradoxical. He embraced large transformational ideas, but didn't embrace a heroic leadership stance in calling for them—at least at first. That changed on September 11.

Mr. Bush undertook a heroic task, and took the heroic leadership stance necessary to accomplish it.

A major question however remains: How does he hope to succeed? He came into office by the slimmest of margins. As a result, he could hardly claim a mandate for transformation. Nonetheless, he has begun that process.

Finally, the term "transformation" implies large undertakings. Yet the term itself hardly specifies their nature. What is it about Mr. Bush's domestic policies that are transformational? When the phrase "transforming American domestic politics" is used, does it refer only to policies? Or, is there some further element that is as important? The answer to the latter is yes.

And what, specifically, is it that Mr. Bush seeks to transform in American foreign policy and through it the world? There is no doubt that Bush's foreign policy views and actions are more assertive than those of his predecessor. But if this were all there was to his attempt to transform world politics it would hardly seem to merit the phrase. We must also ask how Bush's aspiration to transform is related to the possibility of realigning the American electorate. Realignment is a term used to describe historic shifts in voter allegiances from one party to another, providing stable governing majorities for decades. Are Mr. Bush's transformations, if successful, likely to result in such historical shifts? The answer to this question is: maybe, but not necessarily.

Political transformation is, in its most essential form, an alteration and shift in the framing, understanding, and associated expectations surrounding policy issues that lead, as a result, to a change in what people think and do about them. It is first and foremost a shift in uderstanding and thinking and, second, a shift in party allegiance. It is quite possible for Mr. Bush to achieve his transformation without turning most Americans into Republicans. Americans could change the way they think about policy, and in the process force the Democratic party to shift as well to remain competitive. There is some evidence that this process is already under way. Gearing up for the 2004 presidential campaign, Democrats said they would not seek to dismantle all of Bush's policy initiatives, for example his emphasis on measuring results in the No Child Left Behind Act. Democratic presidential nominee John Kerry said, "In some places, we have learned lessons"[8]—presumably from Mr. Bush. Still, the more likely result if Mr. Bush is successful is at least a temporary preference of voters for the positions that he and his party stand for. A stable center/right governing majority is possible.

Transformation is as radical and as ordinary as a shift in perspective. It does not require of a person that they change their basic psychology, assume a wholly new identity, or change professions or spouses. It requires them only to look at old things in a new way, understand them differently, and act accordingly.[9]

No paradigm change is possible without new ideas that articulate a clear framing of the alternative. Clearly, championing big new ideas is politically risky for Mr. Bush. He is asking people to replace what they're used to with something yet to be proven. They will only do so if they understand the advantages and risks, and are then willing to take the step. Mr. Bush himself must, of necessity, play a large role in this.

Trading in the old for the untried requires a leap of faith. Leaps require trust to overcome anxiety. If the public doesn't have or loses confidence in Mr. Bush as a leader, his transformations will falter. If he is able to retain their trust, he will have a critical lever by which to help make the transition.

Trust, while essential, is not sufficient. The public will need to be informed, persuaded, and reassured, probably on a continual basis. Sound bites won't do. Nor will terse assertions. Only if he is able to retain public trust and inform public understanding will Mr. Bush be able to accomplish his goal of transformation.

And what exactly are these transformations? They can be easily and directly stated. Domestically, Mr. Bush's new policy initiatives reflect an emphasis on individual choice, personal responsibility, and institutional accountability. Internationally, the president's initiatives reflect a clear-eyed, tough-minded assessment of national interest coupled with a Wilsonian desire to do good. What distinguishes both sets of initiatives is that they reflect large ideas, involve considerable risk for Mr. Bush personally and politically, and are aimed at changing the way Americans think and understand their world. These transformations, especially in the international sphere, are also going to require Americans to change how they understand themselves.

A VISION IN PRACTICE

Visions have an ethereal quality. They are imagined futures. They give voice to ambition's eventual destination, not its means. Policy ideas, on the other hand, can be conceptualized and made concrete. It is at the intersection of these two vectors that many of the president's proposals for transformation lie.

One important aspect of any evaluation of the Bush policy oeuvre is the sheer number of policy initiatives. In chapter 3, I listed 17 substantial policy initiatives that included at least 6 major ones. And these were only for Mr. Bush's first-year agenda.

In truth, when the final numbers for the president's first-term policies are tallied, it is safe to say Mr. Bush will prove to have been an exceptionally active policy president. This is somewhat of an anomaly for a Republican. But that is not the only way that President Bush is different.

Domestic Policy Visions in Practice

What stands out about Mr. Bush's policies is their departure from traditional approaches to solving public problems. This can be seen in policy matters large and small. Consider his faith-based initiative to help religious organizations provide social services. This is a bold expansion of the traditional idea of government help to those in need and a new kind of public-private partnership. Yet its implications go beyond that. In Florida, Governor Jeb Bush recently dedicated the country's first voluntary faith-based prisons, in which faith ministries will be a part of the rehabilitation process.[10] Traditional approaches to keeping criminals from becoming repeat offenders have not succeeded. Could faith help?

Or consider the president's three tax cuts. Critics have focused on who gets what while Bush's allies have focused on the salutary effects of the cuts on the country's economy. Arguably more important, however, is another neglected dimension to Bush's tax policies. They have modified Keynesian economic assumptions as practiced by generations of Democratic presidents and congressmen. They had acted on the assumption that stimulus meant government spending; Mr. Bush acted on a contrary assumption, that you could stimulate the economy more directly by giving money back to the public in the form of tax relief.

This view was consistent with the president's overall domestic policy paradigm of returning choice and control to individuals, along with the responsibility to use that choice wisely. Interestingly, Bush's tax cut policy provides another example for how his new policy views have already started to shift the lines of debate. Gearing up for the 2004 presidential election, the Democratic party has adapted the president's tax cut paradigm, but has differed with him on the amount of tax relief and the specific ways it would be distributed.

The president's new approach to policy was not only to be found in the visible policy initiatives that caught public and media attention, but in the smaller ones that got little attention. Consider the president's management agenda.[11] Unlike the Clinton initiative on "reinventing government," the administration's proposal title is less grand, but its contents are no less ambitious. It wants to "reform" and "rethink" government.[12] The Bush proposal lays out the administration's strategy for measuring, for the first time, the performance of every cabinet department and executive branch agency in five management categories—personnel, competitive sourcing, financial management, e-government, and program effectiveness.[13] In keeping with the president's preference for results (and immediate ones at that) the introduction to the documents says "that it reflects the administration's commitment to achieve immediate, concrete and measurable results in the short term."[14] Future funding for each agency will be linked to performance.

The president's emphasis on results is clearly manifest in his approach to education. Talking about results is not transformational. Insisting on them is.

Or consider the administration's approach to government rules and regulations. It is a not a media-catching topic, but its impact reaches into every corner of American life. Mr. Bush issued an executive order that required agencies "to systematically seek outside opinions when evaluating scientific findings or disagreements, a process called peer review."[15] The new procedures would mandate the use of independent peer-review cost-benefit and cost-effectiveness analyses in all agencies that develop government regulations.

Critics worried that, "Although such independent appraisals are widely respected in science, critics said the process could quickly get murky when applied to such issues as global warming, pesticide use and ergonomic safety, in which the risks and benefits of regulations would be complex, expensive and politically charged."[16] Why science could not handle complexity, or why, when billions of possibly misspent dollars might be saved by independent analysis, peer review should be avoided was not made clear.

As for worries about politics intruding on policy decisions, this seems either naïve or disingenuous. At least in the case of major environmental regulation, however, this did not happen. A September 2003 major study by the Office of Management and Budget (OMB) of tough environmental regulations imposed on industry "concludes that environmental regulations are well worth the costs they impose on industry and consumers, resulting in significant public health improvements and other benefits to society. . . . It has pleasantly surprised some environmentalists who doubted the Bush administration would champion the benefits of government regulations. . . . But an industry official said the report may have greatly understated the costs associated with environmental regulations."[17]

Finally, any appraisal of the new directions in the Bush administration approach to policy issues must include its emphasis on market mechanisms to supplement, and in some cases replace, the traditional emphasis on regulation by government rules and advocacy group lawsuits. Some of that conceptual approach is found in the cost-benefit and cost-effectiveness analysis of the OMB regulation initiative discussed above. Some of it is to be found in the administration's "Clear Skies" program that allows for the accumulation and trading of "pollution credits." This is the same mechanism used by the Kyoto Convention on climate control. These programs show that what was once novel and startling is no longer so.

With that in mind, consider a proposal the administration has discussed regarding some animals on the endangered species list. The idea is to allow the limited hunting, or capturing for use as pets, of a small number of such animals. On first glace, this approach seems scandalous and certainly paradoxical. A fee would be paid to countries that would then be used to safeguard those species.[18] It is a startling proposal in the United States, but it is already a policy in Western European countries. It may prove to be a poor proposal or perhaps a useful one. What is very clear is that it is an example of the administration's capacity to think outside the conventional box of domestic policy analysis.

Foreign Policy Visions in Practice

Without doubt, it is the Bush foreign policy that has become the most visible exemplar of policy transformation. Not surprisingly, it is also the most controversial. The charges are many. Mr. Bush ignores "traditional" allies. It is a unilateralist "my way or the highway" administration. Mr. Bush has abandoned the web of international commitments that have been forged over the last three decades and thus increased international insecurity and America's.

These complaints become focused on the war against Saddam Hussein. However, they are by no means limited to it. Among the other criticisms are that the administration refused to sign the Kyoto agreement, the biological weapons convention, and the International Criminal Court agreements, and that it abrogated the ABM treaty. Critics omit the fact that the first two treaties were signed by the Clinton administration, but not submitted to the Senate as constitutionally required, or that the Senate voted 95–0 against signing the Kyoto accords. There were good reasons for both decisions.

The Kyoto accords exempted developing countries from polution standards while imposing substantial economic costs on developed ones. In addition, while scientists concluded that some portion of global warming was related to "human activity," it was unclear exactly what portion that was, or the exact mechanisms by which it happened. Barring more information about these critical matters it was hard to gauge how much of the treaty was scientifically based and how much politically driven environmental philosophy.

The convention against biological weapons committed the signatories to abstain from developing such weapons and to allow facilities where such weapons could be made, including pharmaceutical companies, to be opened to inspection. The convention, however, contained no enforcement mechanisms. The U.S. position was that without compliance mechanisms, the convention did not deter cheaters, stop proliferation, or enhance verification. The European Union and United Nations position was that, "Though flawed . . . the protocol reflected compromises that most of the treaty's 143 members could accept and hence was the best way of strengthening the treaty."[19] The Bush administration felt, with some justification, that a treaty that did not provide any real protections against cheaters, gave only the illusion of progress, and was therefore dangerous.

A third issue that arose between the United States and some of its allies concerned the creation of an International Criminal Court (ICC) to try human rights crimes. The Clinton administration signed this document, but did not submit it to the Senate for ratification. Mr. Bush unsigned the protocol.

The chief concern of the United States was that its leaders and soldiers would be subjected to politically motivated indictments. This was not a fantastic fear. A Belgian court claimed universal international jurisdiction on all human rights crimes, and in short order war crimes suits were filled against President Bush, Colin Powell, Dick Cheney, General Tommy Franks, and others. Belgium modified the law to prevent such political uses, but the experience stuck. Trying such crimes is not only a legal, but also a political process. Indeed, the selection of judges for the ICC has already taken a turn toward the political, with formulas being put forward to guarantee a particular number of gender and geographical seats.[20]

International court advocates defended their criticism of Mr. Bush by pointing out that, "under the treaty, national courts take precedence, so *if* governments *conscientiously prosecute war crimes* by their own citizens, the international court would not have jurisdiction to take over those cases."[21] The obvious problem with such a reform is that it leaves unclear just who will decide if governments are conscientiously prosecuting war crimes by their own citizens. There are many people, some of whom might well be a party to making those decisions, who believe that a war undertaken without explicit UN approval is illegitimate. Waging such a war could be considered a crime. And the protocol contains no immunity for heads of state. There are a number of other issues surrounding the functioning of such a court, enough certainly to give pause to facile condemnations of the administration's position.

One former Clinton official who supports the court wrote that the United States should sign the treaty and then "should use its leverage as signatory and as leader of the campaign against terrorism to secure agreements that prevent the surrender of Americans to the court, while still supporting the treaty's basic purpose."[22] Why the United States should negotiate not handing over Americans to the court while signing a document that mandates it is unclear. That official further writes that if the United States doesn't sign it, "The court's leadership might see little point in favorably considering the interests and concerns of a country opposed to its very existence." However, this point simply reinforces critic's concerns that the court's or a country's "interests" and not only legalities will be part of that court's adjudication processes.

Finally, there is the ABM treaty signed in 1972 during the Cold War as a way to ensure mutual assured destruction. If neither the United States nor the Soviet Union could build a missile to destroy the other sides', neither would launch an attack against the other for fear of retaliation and annihilation. The exact role this treaty played in the fact that there was no nuclear exchange between the two countries is difficult to specify, but it is certainly conceivable that it helped stability.

With the demise of the Soviet Union and the end of the Cold War, its continuing purpose became unclear. New threats came from so-called rogue nations and from strategic competitors (as Mr. Bush referred to China) that were developing missile technology that put parts of the United States and many of our allies in range. In a speech at the Citadel three months after 9/11, Mr. Bush signaled his intention to withdraw from the treaty, and six months later did. The reaction from Russia was muted.

Each of these four decisions has set the United States against some of its traditional allies and members of the "international community." Each of them has set the interests of the United States, as this administration understands them, against business as usual in that community. And each of them has generated considerable criticism of the president and his administration.

Some of the reasons for the allies' and the world community's displeasure are easily understood within the confines of traditional international relations theory. For example, Bob Jervis points out that it is entirely consistent both with international relations theory and past practice for nations, even allies, to try and constrain the power of "hegemons," in this case the United States.[23] Even a democratic, non–empire building country whose power and reach are unrivaled stimulates worry and concern. And, of course, not every country believes in America's benign intentions.

Clearly, American leaders (including President Bush) are more certain of their good intentions than others are. Americans are surprised when others don't share our view. We might call this the *good intentions gap,* but it is not the only, or even the most important, one.

The United States is the primary world power and chief target of catastrophic terrorism. The president takes an oath of office to "preserve and protect" the country, and in the wake of 9/11 the seriousness of this responsibility has come into sharp and unavoidable focus. On the other hand, other countries, including some of America's traditional allies and certainly its competitors and enemies, have a different view. They are neither powerful enough to have the United States' worldwide responsibilities nor central enough to the terrorist vision to require framing their actions through the lens of these core facts.

NATIONAL SECURITY QUESTIONS FOR CRITICS

Critics disparage the Bush administration, but hardly ever offer answers to novel questions that the Bush administration must address on a daily basis. The questions carry with them the most profound implications for American national security. While critics understandably focus on the setbacks and difficulties that accompany any policy decision, they act as if they don't have to answer the more basic dilemmas Bush faces. Here are several:

- *How much trust should be put into the capacity to deter terrorists intent on inflicting catastrophic harm to the United States?* Deterrence was the cornerstone of American national security during the Cold War. It was based on an emotionally difficult but easy to understand premise. Nuclear war became "unthinkable" because assured retaliation would guarantee that the aggressor would be vaporized as well. Ever-unfolding and roughly symmetrical advances in both offense and defense assured that no offending country could escape the nuclear gallows. Their cities, population, country, and culture were held hostage.

Mr. Bush has been roundly criticized for his cowboy politics, most particularly his willingness to entertain, and in the case of Iraq, follow through on his doctrine of preventive war. Yet as already noted even strong critics agree that "The Bush administration is right to see the trinity of terrorists, tyrants, and technologies of mass destruction as the *principle* threat to American security."[24]Another Bush administrations critic calls the fact that "small bands of terrorists—perhaps aided by outlaw states—may soon acquire highly destructive nuclear, chemical and biological weapons that can inflict catastrophic destruction . . . *[a] grim new reality*."[25] What then is a president to do?

Catastrophic terrorism has unraveled the link between behavior and consequences that formed the cornerstone of deterrence. Afghanistan was the exception, a country that allowed its government to provide a public home for those that struck us on 9/11. It no longer exists as it was. But we cannot always count on such brazen stupidity. Paradoxically, the American response to 9/11, the toppling of the Taliban, Saddam Hussein, and the war against terror, have weakened our enemies but also driven them further underground. There, they are even less directly susceptible to the logic and psychology of deterrence.

Terrorists have no country to lose, no economy to worry about, and no love of life that exceeds their hatred and determination to inflict mortal harm on their enemies, primarily the United States. Given such circumstances, what policies are open to the United States for self-protection? UN resolutions against the use of WMDs? The word of countries like Iraq under Saddam Hussein that say they have no further interest in WMDs?

Critics overlook one salutatory consequence of the American wars in Afghanistan and Iraq. They may have lessened the need for preemptive war in the future. Deterrence depends on both capacity and will. A country needs to have the power to make war, if necessary, but it also needs to have the will to do so. Terrorists and their allies watch and carefully calculate their enemy's resolve. In the past, after Vietnam, Lebanon, Somalia, the first bombing of the

World Trade Center, and the bombing of U.S. embassies in Africa and of the U.S.S. *Cole,* they didn't have a high regard for ours.

Mr. Bush's response to 9/11 in both Afghanistan and Iraq added new information about American resolve to the terrorists' calculations, and more importantly the states that might want to help them. Libya decided to change course and Syria must be thinking hard. States with the infrastructure to help terrorists and inclined to do so now risk a strong military response from the United States. That is deterring.

- *If traditional allies do, as international relations theory and past practice suggest, try to limit the reach and "hegemony" of countries in a position that the United States now occupies, how much of the security of the United States are you willing to leave in their hands?* A number of international relations specialists have pointed to the fact that the United States is *the* preeminent world power and that carries with it consequences. As one put it, "Whether or not the United States views itself as an empire, for many foreigners it increasingly looks, walks and talks like one."[26] These specialists are agreed that, historically, no matter how benign the intentions of the preeminent country the result is the same. Other countries try to limit, evade, and if possible nullify that power. Fair enough. But what then should the United States do?

It can't cede its power to others. It can't unilaterally diminish it without jeopardizing its security. It can't ignore the threats that it confronts. Just what would critics have the Bush administration do?

Their answer is uniformly the same. In one form or another it consists of the advice to be more "user friendly" to our allies and to build "a more stable world order" based on strengthening international institutions and the "international community."[27] The problem with this advice is that in reality, the United States already does much of what its critics ask, but the basic problem of its national security remains nonetheless.

Critics talk as if the choice is between the wonderful old days of American internationalism and support for the international community and the bad new days of unilateralism. The truth about American self-interest is that it has always been a prominent feature of our foreign policy since the founding of the republic.[28] And America's alliances over the years have also been used to help secure its interests.

The choice is not between American unilateralism and American support for the international community. In the real world the United States must, and does, do both. Critics focus on the few occasions when the president has felt America's most basic and vital interests—its survival and security from catastrophic attack—have been at stake and pretended that all the Bush administration's actions follow that assumption. They have not.

The Bush administration is often criticized for ignoring "traditional American allies." Those countries obviously are France, Germany, and Belgium. They, along with Russia, the Arab states, and others were most strongly opposed to the war against Saddam Hussein. Yet the truth is that the administration works every day with its allies, even those who disapproved of the Iraq War, on security matters of mutual concern and much else. France and the United States, allies with the most contentious relationship since Mao Tse-Tung and Leonid Brezhnev, agreed and acted jointly in getting Jean-Bertrand Aristide to step down as president of Haiti. They have also worked together and do so every day to interdict clandestine arms shipments and WMD components.

Nor is American international cooperation limited to its security concerns. President Bush has championed free trade agreements, has dramatically increased American foreign aid, and has proposed a sweeping vision of democracy worldwide, with real follow-up steps taken and accomplished in the new Afghanistan and Iraqi (interim) constitutions. Critics could argue that these steps benefit the United States. But if that's true, are the only "good" policies those that damage us?

- *How much faith are you asking this country to have in the efficacy of the international community?* Strengthening international institutions has a nice ring to it. By all means let's try to do so—although once you look at specifics the magnitude of the task looms large.

Critics urged that the United States turn Iraq over to the UN, but would that be prudent and sensible? They were unable to act coherently, strongly, and consistently against Saddam Hussein for decades. The United Nations has never fought an insurgency and has neither the manpower or skill to do so. What other countries would fight in place of the United States? France? Russia? Germany? Belgium? Most likely it would be the United States that would continue to shoulder the military burden, but now that burden has a political purpose: democracy and freedom in Iraq. Should the future of Iraq be in the hands of countries that opposed the war? Would putting the Security Council or General Assembly in charge really be a realistic and productive option?

While thinking about that question, consider the United Nation's oil-for-food program. When it was operating it employed 10 international agencies, 900 international staffers, and 3,000 Iraqi nationals inside Iraq. The United Nation's involvement put it in the position of overseeing $15 billion a year, 5 times its core budget. Between 1996 and 2003 that figure totaled more than $100 billion, of which the United Nations collected a 2.2 percent commission fee for administration.[29] This put the United Nations in the position of profiting from Saddam Hussein's continuation in power, with all that entailed. Moreover, it is now a documented fact that Saddam Hussein skimmed billions from this program for his own personal use, which meant keeping himself in power. It was, as the *New York Times* reported, "an open secret."[30]

My point here is not that the United Nations isn't a worthy organization; it is. Nor is my point that it is uniformly inept or complicit. Rather, the truth is that the United Nations is an organization that has struggled to do good in the world with a membership of self-interested nation-states, a number of whose governments govern at home in direct contradiction of stated UN ideals, and act the same way internationally.

By all means the United Nations should be reformed, but that will take decades, if it happens.[31] A recent UN monitoring committee complained "that 108 nations have failed to file required reports on their actions in the war against terrorism, such as freezing assets and reporting the names of suspected terrorists."[32] What should the United States do in the meantime?

• *How much risk are you asking this country to shoulder if your views prove to be wrong? Who will pay the price of any errors?* We are now at the heart of the matter. These are not theoretical questions. They are direct and profound questions of life and death. Most importantly, those with national responsibilities, chiefly Mr. Bush, must answer them.

Bush critics find much to worry about in America's changed relationships with some of its allies. They detail the advantages of having allies, and there are many. Yet they don't raise or answer the question of what the president and his advisors should do when they think that the interests of the United States and its allies diverge on matters central to American national security. When a distinguished scholar worries that "The United States may be the latest in a long line of countries that is unable to place sensible limits on its fears and aspirations,"[33] one must ask: What is sensible and who determines that?

"The Bush Doctrine" is a lightning rod for criticism. Two of Mr. Bush's chief critics make the point that his approach to foreign policy is revolutionary, and "potentially even radical."[34] They don't mean those terms as a compliment. These critics put themselves in the curious position of characterizing the president's approach to foreign policy as radical because it relies on a theory, realism, that has been at the center of academic understandings of how nations behave since it was introduced in systematic form by Hans Morgenthau in 1948.

192 \ In His Father's Shadow

They accuse Mr. Bush of operating under the assumption that the world is a dangerous place.[35] The rise of catastrophic terrorism and the events of 9/11 would suggest that it is. They criticize him because his policy emphasizes that self-interested states are the primary actors in international politics. Aren't they? They criticize his view that power is a chief resource in international politics. Isn't it? They criticize Bush's view that multilateral agreements and institutions are neither essential nor necessarily conducive to American interests. Given the verification and enforcement issues with many international treaties already noted, is this view unreasonable?

Academics and pundits provide theories and explanations, but they are not charged with real-world responsibilities and there are few consequences if they are wrong. Some act as if they have full knowledge. Others spin theories about what *might* be happening, how things *could* turn out, and what they prefer. Theirs is a world where doubts and risk were banished by the magic of their confidence in their own (most often post-hoc) assessments.

Clearly, there is not only a divergence of viewpoints, but also a *responsibility gap* between the president and his critics. Theorists and pundits have the luxury, and it is one, to offer advice without responsibility. Regretfully, real presidents must often decide *now,* not after the fact, on the basis of limited and ambiguous evidence, competing claims and theories, no crystal ball, and the gravest consequences if they are wrong.

ARE BUSH'S TRANSFORMATION AMBITIONS POSSIBLE?

Mr. Bush wants to transform the dominant policy paradigms in both domestic and international politics. We are forced to ask if that is possible. And if it is, how can it be done? To answer these questions we need to look more closely at recent American history, policy, and psychology.

We might summarize the state of American politics prior to September 11, 2001, as follows. Beginning with the initiation of Lyndon Johnson's "Great Society" programs, the dominant paradigm in American domestic politics was interest-group liberalism. That paradigm was developed and consolidated by a number of advocacy groups and institutions that now call themselves "progressive," allied with government bureaucracies at the local, state, and national level. They portrayed their efforts as remedial, addressing the imbalances they saw in American political life. Yet in the process they attempted to reshape the fundamental premises on which the country operated.

America, they argued, had to be more democratic, more inclusive, and more sensitive to the concerns of those groups that felt marginalized. Since those who had benefited from previous economic, cultural, and political arrangements could not be counted on to surrender their privileges voluntarily, there must be government-enforced mandates to ensure that they did. In every area of public life, government must use the full force of its power to ensure that their views of a fairer and more democratic America were enforced.

Exactly what does it mean to be the dominant paradigm? The dominant paradigm of interest-group liberalism was firmly entrenched in the Democratic party and its allies. It was entrenched as well in the major universities and the education establishment more generally. It permeated the media and many major foundations. And it was the primary paradigm in many major governmental bureaucracies and throughout state and local governments in almost every region but the South.

Race, gender, and cultural issues of many kinds became the lens through which most American domestic policies were framed. This attempt to reform, or as critics understood it, transform, traditional American cultural practices and institutions led to a surge of opposition. Over the next 30 years, cultural and political warriors and their political allies fought each other to increasingly poisonous stalemates.

For three decades America experienced a cultural form of civil war. Institutions that both reflected and reinforced America's social, economic, and cultural foundations become embroiled in harsh conflicts about their premises, fairness, and suitability. Not surprisingly, these conflicts spilled over into American politics and its associated institutions.

Congress, too, was increasingly divided along partisan lines. Safe districts decreased party competition and ensured election. In these circumstances, the purest partisans were able to gain and keep offices and, as a result, bipartisanship failed. Having refined the techniques to make it politically effective, interest groups became adept at first stimulating, then mobilizing, outrage.

The larger number of Americans whose views did not reflect either of the warring sides seemed to be in a political twilight zone. They did not fully accept the arguments of either warring side, but had no alternative position to embrace. The dominant paradigm of interest-group liberalism still prevailed, but its assumptions and consequences were increasing called into question. Alternative policy views were developing and with them the structural vehicles to disseminate them. However, this alternative paradigm had yet to congeal into a coherent package. Nor did it yet have a clear and determined voice to spearhead its acceptance. The one clear voice that might command such attention was the president's, but that institution too was caught up in the paradigm clash.

Presidents and the Failed Search for Ascendancy:
A Brief History

The presidency could not and did not escape the conflict roiling American culture and politics. Not only was it increasingly hard to gain and keep the office, it also became increasingly difficult to govern. In three successive presidential elections, 1992, 1996, and 2000, successful candidates were not elected with a majority of the votes cast. Third-party candidates in these years offered a vehicle for voter dissatisfaction and many voters decided to take a test drive. Even when they managed to get elected by more than a plurality, presidents and the presidency generally didn't fare well. The sixties saw the assassinations of John F. Kennedy in 1963 and his brother Robert in 1968, and was punctuated by repeated racial violence. Lyndon Johnson won a landslide victory in 1964, enacted a large number of government programs collectively called the "Great Society," and fought an increasingly difficult war in Vietnam.

President Johnson chose not to run for reelection in 1968 because of activists' outcry over the Vietnam War and public uneasiness. Richard Nixon won a landslide reelection in 1972 but was forced from office by his felonious behavior. Gerald Ford succeeded to the presidency, but couldn't survive his pardon of Richard Nixon. Jimmy Carter became president in 1976 by promising an honest administration, a promise that he honored. Yet he was less adept at leadership and was voted out of office after one term. Ronald Reagan in 1980 and 1984 became the first two-term president to finish out his terms since Dwight D. Eisenhower almost three decades before.

George H. W. Bush followed President Reagan into office in 1988. Mr. Bush's strong and successful decision to resist Saddam Hussein's invasion of Kuwait brought him to the pinnacle of public popularity. However, for reasons that are still unclear, Mr. Bush did not use any of the prodigious amounts of political capital he had earned and his presidency gradually leaked away in the face of economic difficulties and public malaise. He was not reelected in 1992.

Americans, beset by economic, political, and cultural uncertainties, turned to Bill Clinton, who promised to avoid the pitfalls of the left and right and govern smartly and from the political center as a "New Democrat." However, immediately upon his election, Mr. Clinton declared himself the heir not only of the votes he got, but those of rival Ross Perot, and said that an overwhelming majority of Americans had voted for change. That may have been so, but it is an open question whether the change they wanted is the change they got. With a decidedly left-of-center Democratic Congress as his partner, the president temporarily lost track of his promise to govern as a "New Democrat" and increasingly began to look to many like an old one.

The result was a cataclysmic repudiation of the president and his party in the 1994 congressional, state, and local elections. A decade after the end of Ronald Reagan's first term, Republicans gained control of both houses of Congress for the first time since the early years of the Eisenhower administration.[36] In the House they won 52 seats.[37] In the Senate, they added eight additional seats. At the state level the GOP picked up 12 governorships,[38] 15 state legislatures,[39] and made gains on the local level as well.[40]

Then came the 2000 presidential election, one of the closest and most controversial in American history. Mr. Bush won, but barely, and in the eyes of about a quarter of the population, almost all Democrats, unfairly. The GOP, while still controlling the House, lost seats. In the Senate the GOP had nominal control, but only by virtue of Vice President Cheney's tie-breaking vote, only when the GOP could gain straight party-line adherence on one policy matter or another. Small wonder that many wondered whether any president could effectively govern in such circumstances.

Mr. Bush chose to govern as if he had a mandate. In truth, he was gambling that he could build one. Yet, as noted, he was on increasingly shaky ground. This was especially true after Senator Jeffords bolted the GOP and caucused with the Democrats in the Senate, giving them control. The result was more divided government, but more importantly, a structural barrier to the president's domestic agenda. That was where matters stood on September 11, 2001.

Presidential Leadership in a Divided Society

Divided societies pose particular problems for the exercise of presidential leadership. Major initiatives are likely to bring firestorms of criticism and hyper-agitated complaints from advocacy groups and their allies. These are then skillfully amplified in news accounts, talk show debates, nightly news reporting, and various forms of political theater like the public mobilization of injured parties for public consumption. Campaigns of mischaracterization, selective information, and outright distortion complicate any presidential attempt to challenge the existing paradigm.

Consider the successful reform of existing welfare policy in 1996. Conservatives had argued for decades that welfare policy did not reward work and encouraged government dependency. When, after many years, circumstances allowed for it to be reconsidered, dire predictions were raised. Millions of children would be left homeless to live on the streets. Poverty rates would dramatically rise, and so on. None of them came true. Yet the fight to get these changes was truly difficult. Two separate bills were sent to President Clinton and he vetoed both before signing a third version shortly before his reelection campaign began. Wags said the law should have been renamed the Clinton Reelection Welfare bill.

Presidents have tried different strategies to navigate these stormy political waters. Richard Nixon tried to blur the lines of his ideology and policy beliefs. He was a Republican, but rejected discussions of whether he was "conservative" or "liberal." He saw himself as "pragmatic" rather than ideological and his policies tended to follow from that. Mr. Nixon was a conservative anticommunist for the most part. But he was also prepared to engage in strategic negotiations with his adversaries when possible. For example, Mr. Nixon's anticommunist views did not keep him from forging a new relationship with China.

In domestic policy, one could observe the same blending of ideological strands. Nixon was "tough on crime," in both rhetoric and policy. Was Mr. Nixon as a conservative Republican a mortal foe of the liberal welfare programs? No; indeed, he attempted to reform and improve several of these programs. In answer to the question of whether Mr. Nixon was a moderate, liberal, or conservative, one would have to answer in truth, "it depends on the issue."

Jimmy Carter tried the same thing in his 1976 and 1980 campaigns, only once successfully. Mr. Carter, a southern Democrat, ran on a personal platform in which supporting a "strong defense" and being "tough on criminals" played prominent roles. Was Mr. Carter a traditional democratic liberal? No, not really, but he was not exactly a "conservative," either. In some respects he was liberal, but in others, conservative. Mr. Carter, like Mr. Nixon before him, campaigned and governed as a pragmatist, not an ideologue.

In the presidential election of 1988 the same trends were observable for both candidates. George H. W. Bush, the Republican candidate, so blended and moderated his views on many policy issues that numerous analysts asked, "Who is George Bush?" Mr. Bush's rival for the presidency, Michael Dukakis, completely disavowed any political ideology, liberal or conservative, Democratic or Republican. His campaign slogan was that the election was "about competence, not ideology."

In the 1992 presidential campaign, Bill Clinton promised a candidate who reflected a "new Democratic party," presumably one that was unlike its predecessor. His policy positions, expressed in general terms, continued the trend of blending positions. Thus candidate Clinton was for "a strong America," but also promised to drastically reduce the military budget. He was a supporter of social welfare programs, but promised to "end welfare as we know it" during his presidency, and so on. The "New Democrat" was one who blended, if he did not transcend, liberal and conservative ideologies.

In reality, Clinton was a strong supporter of the dominant liberal interest-group paradigm, and did all he could while in office to save it.[41] Yet, in order to do so, in a divided society, he had to develop a strategy. The strategy he chose was to mask his support of the dominant paradigm and maintain a public façade of evenhandedness, symbolically captured by the term "triangulation."

Triangulation was a presidential leadership strategy that presented the president as having borrowed elements of both the right and the left to develop some form of center policy amalgam. So, Mr. Clinton famously declared "The era of big government is over" in a State of the Union address. Yet in that same address he listed numerous new government programs. He promised to make abortion "safe, legal, and rare." Yet in practice he would authorize no policy change dealing with the last of these three. On the divisive issue of affirmative action, he promised to "mend it, not end it." In fact he did very little concrete about the former and everything to ensure the latter.

Mr. Clinton was intentionally deceptive about his intentions.[42] However, the dilemma he faced as president of a country that was deeply divided along the lines already noted, and whose divisions were amplified by structural developments, was real enough. How was it possible in these circumstances for a president to lead, much less to govern?

REALIGNMENT OR TRANSFORMATION?

Given the decades-long and increasingly harsh stalemate in American politics, political pundits and analysts have been like anxious sailors at sea too long, searching the horizon for signs of a new political landfall. That new political terra firma was realignment. Not surprisingly, every possible political upheaval was scanned for evidence that it had finally arrived.

The Search for Realignment

Academics and pundits have long searched for evidence of that fabled political state, realignment.[43] Did Ronald Reagan's election and reelection herald its arrival? It turned out that it didn't. Ronald Reagan's election and landslide reelection showed that many Americans were sympathetic to right-center charges that government had become too big, divisive arguments about America's basic institutions and frameworks had gone too far, and criticisms about American power and its use abroad were overwrought. Mr. Reagan was a personable right-center candidate, yet he lacked three elements to bring about a long-term fundamental shift in the dominant paradigm.

While Mr. Reagan had clear basic principles—less government, less taxes, a more muscular foreign policy—his alternative vision couldn't overcome interest-group liberalism's structural advantages. He certainly had policies that ran counter to the dominant paradigm both domestically (for example, firing the air traffic controllers who illegally went out on strike) and in foreign affairs (his missile defense initiative), but his administration too was better at acting on principles than explaining them. It is the latter that fuels transformation.

Mr. Reagan also did not commit his administration to take on the dominant paradigm in its many policy and governmental manifestations. Mr. Reagan did not lack courage or conviction, but he was not a combative man. Even if he had been, it is questionable whether he would have made much progress. His party did not control Congress or much of the bureaucracy. Moreover, right-center advocacy institutions and think tanks were largely in the early stages of their development.

Last, there was no major domestic or international event that could lend its weight to a public reassessment of the dominant paradigm. In the absence of some paradigm-shaking event such as the economic depression of the 1930s or 9/11, it was hard for people to see that their conventional assumptions might need reevaluation. For all these reasons, the Reagan presidency was a step on the road to a possible paradigm shift, but not the beginning of the shift itself.

What of the GOP midterm election landslide in 1994? It was clearly a Republican electoral landslide. However, its meaning was another matter. Was 1994 a classic realignment election? Or, was it just one more indication that the country's traditional governing alignments were breaking apart? Was it only a repudiation of the Clinton administration, or did it represent a turning away from government itself? Twenty-five years before, Theodore Lowi had confidently predicted the end of the welfare state.[44] Was this election a confirmation of that assertion?

Those questions were soon answered. Republicans, flush with victory and confidence, declared that realignment was at hand, liberalism a historical relic, and a Republican in the White House just a matter of the passage of time. However, borrowing a well-worn page from Mr. Clinton's political career, Republicans, in some ways understandably, began to confuse the opportunity given to them to create a mandate with already having been given one. Americans may have wanted less government in some areas, but apparently they were not prepared to have the government shut down. And, as a result of Republican miscalculations and President Clinton and his party's extremely adroit political use of them, an almost fatally weakened presidency was revived.

In the ongoing realignment watch, the most recent candidate was the 2002 mid-term elections. Defying precedent, and taking another risk to expand his political capital, Mr. Bush put his popularity on the line and won big: 21 out of the 23 House members and 12 of the 16 Senate candidates Bush campaigned for won their races. The GOP regained control of the Senate and increased its majority in the House. Only three other times in the past century has a president's party gained seats in the House in an off-year election, and not since the Civil War had the president's party won back a Senate majority in a midterm contest. Bush's tremendous and successful effort at self-help made him the first Republican president since Dwight Eisenhower to have outright majorities in the House and Senate with which to lead and govern.

The 2002 mid-term elections were a substantial victory for Mr. Bush and his party to be sure, but were they a harbinger of realignment? If you measure transformation by realignment, and realignment by FDR standards, the answer is clearly maybe.

Mechanisms of Realignment

On their face, America's divisions would indicate that Mr. Bush has to conquer the public opinion equivalent of Mt. Everest if his quest for transformation is to be realized. Actually, a closer look at the actual data suggests Mr. Bush's climb may be somewhat less daunting, and he may well have established a base camp already.

Part of the confusion lies with the misuse of the words "divided" and "polarized" as if they are interchangeable. Journalists and others who should know better continue to confound them. Andrew Kohut, director of the Pew Center poll, was quoted as saying that the spirit of national unity following 9/11 "has dissolved amid rising polarization and anger," and "It is still the 50–50 nation."[45] Divided? Yes. Polarized? Do the two halves of America have diametrically different visions? Does one side see them as 100 percent one way, and the other 100 percent the other? No; but that's what a polarized country would mean. What he means is that highly partisan Democrats and highly partisan Republicans see things very differently, but there are an awful lot of Americans who are neither.

The same confusion pops up in an E. J. Dionne article entitled "One Nation Deeply Divided," in which the author asserts that a recent survey's "overall findings pointed to an evenly divided and politically polarized country."[46] The study didn't find that *Americans* were becoming more deeply divided, but rather that the most avid partisans of the two major political parties are. Likewise, it is not *the country* that is deeply and evenly divided, but the political parties. A quick look at the data on party identifications shows why.

According to the Pew data,[47] 27 percent of its sample identify themselves as Republicans, 29 percent as Democrats, 36 percent as independents, and 8 percent as other. This means that whatever polarization and division exists is confined to a little over half the adults in the country. It does not apply to about 44 percent of those surveyed. It is the whole sample that is more accurately characterized as "the nation" or "Americans." The Pew report focuses only on a subset of those categories, the two major political party memberships.

On many policy issues that most distinguish Democrats from Republicans, the views of independents can be found somewhere between the two major parties. How close independents are to either party depends on the issue. There are also important differences within parties on the basis of ideology.

The Pew Poll finds that religion is increasingly tied to political matters.[48] Yet, while 52 percent of liberal Democrats affirm the importance of prayer, believe in Judgment Day, and have strong beliefs in God, 80 percent of conservative or moderate Democrats hold such beliefs. Indeed, conservative or moderate Democrats are closer in religious views to conservative Republicans, 81 percent of whom are more religious, than their fellow Democrats. The same is true of conservative Republicans, 81 percent of whom are religious, who are closer to conservative Democrats, 80 percent of whom are religious, than to moderate or liberal Republicans, 72 percent of whom are religious.

The country, to repeat, is divided, not polarized. And what looks at first glance like a country divided down the middle turns out on closer inspection to be something else. Strongly partisan Democrats differ from their moderate and conservative counterparts in the same party, and the same is true of Republicans.

Interestingly, the Pew data contains some other good news for George W.'s attempt to transform domestic politics. Of the total sample, 18 percent identify as conservative Republicans, while only 10 percent of Democrats are self-described liberals. Additionally, 19 percent of Democrats self-identify as being moderate or conservative, while only 9 percent of Republicans self-identify as being moderate or liberal. What this means is that more Democrats are available to be drawn toward a GOP orbit than visa versa. This is roughly analogous to the position of conservative Democrats in Congress, who sometimes, depending on the policy issue, are more comfortable voting with the GOP than with their own party. And there are other important favorable realignment trends as well.

One of the most important is the rise of parity between those who identified themselves as Republicans or Democrats. According to the Pew results, "the September 11 terrorist attacks marked a major turning point. GOP Party identification rose to 30%, while the Democrat Party identification fell to 31%."[49]

To gain some perspective on these numbers recall that in 1977, more than half the public (51 percent) identified themselves as Democrats, and only 21 percent as Republicans. As late as 1997 and 1998 Democrats maintained a 5 percent advantage (33 percent to 28 percent).[50] Moreover, the overall parity has distributional implications: "Republicans now have an edge among registered voters in the states that have been voting their way over the past three election cycles—so-called Red States—and *have achieved parity with Democrats in swing states.*"[51]

Realignment does not necessarily require switching the party allegiance of a majority of voters. It requires only that a party be able to develop enough solid electoral and state victories to ensure governing majorities. The Pew data suggest it is possible.

Mr. Bush will, of course, make every effort to win over new converts to his views. But there is another route to change and that is the movement of generations. Younger age groups are continually entering the political arena and replacing older groups whose generational members have died. The Depression era generation looks very different on many policy issues than those who grew up knowing only prosperity. Those who came of political age during the sixties had very different experiences than those whose first remembered president is Ronald Reagan.

Contrary to what you would expect, if you believe youth to be generally liberal, George W. does very well among the young. Harvard's annual Institute of Policy survey of undergraduates taken in October 2003 shows that 61 percent of the sample has a favorable view of President Bush. A comparable national survey taken at the same time showed a public rating of 53 percent.[52] Six months earlier, his ratings had been exactly the same.

What accounts for Mr. Bush's somewhat surprising campus popularity? Two other survey questions suggest an answer. When asked whether the terrorist attacks of 9/11 affected how they thought about politics and national issues, 82 percent said yes.[53] Asked which presidential characteristics were most important in a president, students overwhelming chose strong leadership qualities (55 percent), a quality that far surpassed being in policy agreement with the president (34 percent).

Realignment and the Political Center

Conventional wisdom says that Americans prefer their presidents to govern from the political center. That fabled Archimedean point is the Holy Grail of American politics where north, south, east, and west, men and women, urban and suburban, left and right, and race and ethnicity are found in harmonious political balance. It is the fulfillment of the modern alchemist's dream of transmutation— of views into votes, and political conflicts into public consensus. Yet, it appears increasingly difficult to discern, much less to lead from, the political center in contemporary American politics.

Where, exactly, is the political center? That term is often used as if it has an obvious and singular meaning, but neither is true. In reality, that term is the political equivalent of Akira Kurosawa's classic movie *Rashomon*. There seem to be as many views of what constitutes the political center as there are political observers and pundits. There is the "vital center,"[54] the "moral majority,"[55] Nixon's "silent majority," and the new "American majority."[56] Depending on your views the political center is economically conservative, socially progressive,[57] or wholly "progressive,"[58] or the "radical middle,"[59] the "sensible center,"[60] or both.[61]

All of these terms describe different political centers, leaving unanswered the most important question: How do you get there? Is the political center the sum of political extremes, divided in half? Is it reached by small incremental policies on divisive issues or are bold historic compromises a better model?

Recall from the first chapter that, in a divided society such as now exists in the United States, there are essentially four ways for presidents to occupy the political center: *split-the-difference trench warfare; segmented coalitions; blending ideologies;* and *shifting the political center of gravity.* The last has been George W.'s choice as he has tried to move the center of gravity of the political culture from moderate left-of-center to moderate right-of-center, and in the process transform the premises and frames of policy debates. This is the most dramatic, high-risk, and difficult policy ambition that a president can undertake.

FDR's Realignment: A Misleading Model?

The focus of realignment can be misplaced, and I want to argue here that it is. The model of FDR's presidential landslide is not the only way in which realignments can take place. What if the focus on the substantial changes in voters' party allegiance has obscured an equally, perhaps more important process, that of the transformation of policy debate? I want to argue here that it has.

Realignment, in the classic formulation, involves the wholesale switching of political party allegiance and the coming together of a new stable collation that provides a new national governing majority. The only modern example of this is the FDR election in 1932 at the height of the Depression, in which Democrats gained the presidency and swept both houses of Congress. In the process, the Democratic party won the allegiance of white southerners, Catholics, and organized labor. In the 1936 presidential election, Roosevelt further cemented his collation with the addition of African Americans and Jews. That coalition held at the presidential level until 1968, when disaffected southerners began their migration out of the Democratic party by voting for George Wallace.

There are a number of elements that are central to the FDR realignment model and critical for a consideration of George W. Bush's chances to repeat history. Most accounts of the FDR model stress the wholesale change and consolidation of voters' allegiances. From the standpoint of the political horseraces and scorecards this is understandable. Yet it obscures a key element of the realignment, the fact that at its core was a national trauma, a president whose optimistic outlook offered hope, and a change in policy direction and assumptions that have continued with us to this day.

So, it is important to ask *why* voters changed their allegiance. The change in the dominant policy was key. That fundamental change can be directly stated. It was a change in perspective and expectation from a laissez-faire economic policy in which government was essentially a bystander to a central role for government in providing economic stability and growth.

That shift in framing was not revolutionary, but it was profound. All of the key American public institutions remained intact. But instead of having nowhere to look, the people recast their gaze and expectations to the government for economic answers, not to business or the market. They expected solutions that worked, or at least that were tried. Above all, they expected government action.

This was a new policy paradigm and in its basic form it is still with us today. The New Deal coalition may have broken apart, but its policy paradigm has remained intact. This suggests an important lesson: *The two are not synonymous.*

It is also critical to note the role that FDR played. He rejected a laissez-faire approach and in doing so rejected what was then the dominant "mainstream" thinking. *His* shift in thinking preceded and stimulated the public's shift in thinking. The changes from that shift in perspective have cascaded across almost every corner of America in the decades since, but it is important to keep in mind that they began with a shift in perspective in the mind of one person and his advisors. It was their judgment that broke with convention and set in motion that frame of understanding, expectation, and presidential behavior that is today's mainstream and now thoroughly conventional orthodoxy.

FDR's paradigm shift involved economics and politics, not culture. President Roosevelt had nothing to say about what it meant to be an American, whether a commitment to this country and its institutions were worthwhile, or whether one's identity as an American ought to be replaced by ethnic or racial identities. All of these things were not a matter of real debate, as they are now. Thus, any discussion of changing the dominant paradigm today must take into account that the divisions to be breached are cultural and political rather than economic and political as they were for FDR.

Finally, there is the matter of the president's psychology. There is FDR's optimism, willingness to take risks, his capacity not to be deterred by failure, and above all his determination to find something that would work. Few scholars credit FDR's alphabet programs with ending the Depression. They do credit World War II. Yet his administration's programs did help, and they did result in a shift and realignment of perspective that is with us today. These programs were driven by his psychology.

These character traits find their echo in Mr. Bush's psychology and mission. He has been seized by a fierce and steely determination that began before 9/11 and was crystallized by it. This was added on top of an already legendary ability to focus and a willingness to engage and fight on behalf of his beliefs. If Mr. Bush succeeds in his transformation, he will owe it as much to his psychology as to his policies.

THE NATURE OF POLITICAL TRANSFORMATION

In future years, if George W. Bush is even partially successful in what he has undertaken, historians and political scientists will be debating just what to call what he did. Indeed, that process is already beginning, although Mr. Bush has only established the possibility of success, not accomplished it.

His critics shout that Mr. Bush's decisions or choices are "out of the mainstream." The assumption of such a phrase is that the "mainstream" is inviolate, not dynamic, and Mr. Bush's critics are its sole arbiters. This is, of course, nonsense. The "mainstream," whatever that term might mean at any particular time, is always changing. As FDR's transformation makes clear, at one time mainstream thinking supported many political and cultural ideas that are no longer followed or even acceptable.

It is the content of what is considered mainstream that George W. Bush wishes to change. So of course his ideas will not be synonymous with "accepted" or "conventional" policy views. Isn't this one meaning of the term *transformational?*

Another term, which is already gathering momentum as a political description of what Mr. Bush is attempting to accomplish, is "revolutionary,"[62] or its evil twin, "radical." The word "revolution" conjures up masses marching through the streets with the former nobility in their oxcarts on their way to the guillotine. It summons up historic institutions and practices swept away, an abrupt and radical reversal of existing practices often accompanied by sweeping emotional and material dislocations, the substitution of groups formally in power with wholly new ones, and a radical new direction in policies and programs. We used to reserve such terms for the overthrow of governments and ways of life, not the substitution of one president and his advisors for another, with the institutions and bureaucracies remaining intact.

Nothing that Mr. Bush is attempting to do is "radical" or "revolutionary" in any normal understanding of those words. He is not attempting to do away with capitalism or democracy, the two cornerstones of American society. But Mr. Bush's leadership and policies are a departure from business as usual. But any president who wished to transform the policy paradigms he found could hardly do otherwise.

One major difference between a revolutionary and a transformer is pragmatism. Mr. Bush's deep emotional commitment to results and what works are psychologically inconsistent with being a revolutionary. Mr. Bush did not seek to dismantle any government agencies. He did not try to dismantle the welfare state. What he wants are new and better ways to achieve American policy goals. That cast of mind and psychology cannot seriously be called revolutionary.

Mr. Bush touted himself during the campaign as a "reformer with results."[63] Reform accepts most of a given institution or set of practices and seeks to improve them. Skowronek calls this the "politics of articulation," and presidents who fit in this category are "orthodox innovators."[64] Yet surely transformation is more than reform.

Political transformation is an alteration and shift in the framing, understanding, and associated expectations surrounding an issue that leads, as a result, to a change in what people think and do about it. In psychoanalytic work, a shift of perspective brought about by therapeutic analysis and insight can seem profound. However, this work often involves issues of the most intense, intimate, and important part of a person's life. But in the United States, political transformations of the kind being discussed here, of reframing policy understandings, do not carry such profound emotional weight for most people.

It is not that politics or policies are unimportant. They are. However, for most Americans politics is far from their daily or central concerns, and not central to their personal identities.

This might make the task both easier and harder for Bush. His transformation tasks will be made easier because what he wants to do is not so central to how people view themselves. It is perfectly possible to believe, for example, that you should be able to invest part of your Social Security taxes yourself, without having to change your identity. On the other hand, because such policy details are not central to most people, Mr. Bush will have to overcome the inertia that comes with that fact. Of course, either possibility is moot if Mr. Bush does not win reelection.

The Tools of Transformation

Transformation doesn't happen because a president wills, wants, or works for it. Nor does it happen because large historical circumstances dictate its occurrence. It happens because a particular kind of president is faced with a specific set of circumstances and knows enough, has ambition enough, and has skill enough to take advantage of them.

What circumstances give rise to paradigm change? One necessity is the depletion or exhaustion of the old dominant paradigm. It must have failed to provide answers to new questions, failed to answer old ones, or both. Interest-group liberalism and its most recent permutation, identity politics, have been in that position for at least two decades.

When the old paradigm fades or fails, it will continue so long as no alternative is available, and even when one is, it does not simply disappear. After decades in power, the liberal paradigm has institutional and group support at every level of politics. It has drawn the support of the important law firms, lobbyists, trade associations, publicists, news organs, educational institutions, federal bureaucracies, and think tanks. The power of a paradigm is not confined to Congress or the presidency.

FDR's New Deal realignment bequeathed the model of catastrophic transformation. George W. Bush's possible success may give us another. It is the slow, step-by-step accumulation of the machinery of power. In his party's case, first in Congress in 1974, then in the Senate in 2003, and with the presidency in between in 2000, and perhaps 2004. It is measured in the rise to parity of important law firms, pundits, news organizations, foundations, and think tanks dedicated to putting forward a new center-right paradigm. And it is measured by interest groups such as the American Association of Retired Persons that have been closely associated with the Democratic party but are now willing to do business with the GOP, in this case on the issue of Medicare reform.[65]

A second basic transforming element is an event that leads the public to see the need, or at least be open to, a change in how they think and understand public affairs. The economic depression of the 1930s forced people to see that boom-or-bust capitalism needed to be changed. Likewise, 9/11 played an important role in the public's readiness to entertain President Bush's views, especially on national security matters.

It is useful to compare the transformational effects of the Depression that ran from 1929 roughly through 1940 that President Roosevelt inherited and the 9/11 terrorist attack that transformed Mr. Bush's presidency and Mr. Bush. The Depression was national, affecting all parts of the country in a direct and concrete way. It affected people's livelihood on a national scale and in doing so had direct effects on families, communities, and ultimately on support of the organization of the country's economic and political system. Its effects were nationwide, direct, and profound.

The 9/11 terrorist attack was more limited in its direct material effects. We did not lose the equivalent of our Pacific fleet. But Americans did lose 3,000 lives, sustained billions in economic damage, and received a profound psychological shock. Just as the Depression called into question assumptions about capitalism as usual, so, too, did 9/11 shock the foundations of American's assumptions about their security.

Before 9/11 most Americans took their safety for granted, and there seemed every reason to do so. We had immense military and economic power. We had powerful investigative agencies both abroad (the CIA) and at home (the FBI). We had a range of allies with whom we shared common purpose. There seemed to be a robust international community that developed treaty after treaty to rid the world of those things most to be feared. Yet all of those comforts proved to be insubstantial on 9/11.

We now know, thanks to the testimony and work of the 9/11 commission, that the terrorist threat had been gathering momentum for over a decade. An escalating series of attacks made it clear to a very few in the U.S. government that Arab and Muslim radicals had declared war on the United States. Those major attacks included: the Marine barracks in Lebanon in 1983; the hijacking of the

Achille Lauro in 1985; the rise of Al Qaeda and the bombing of the World Trade Center in 1993; the attacks on American installations in Saudi Arabia in 1995 and 1996; the two East Africa embassy bombings of 1998; and the attack on the U.S.S. *Cole* on October 12, 2000. President Clinton's response to all those acts that took place on his watch from 1992 to 2000 was minimal. As Condoleezza Rice told the 9/11 commission, "The terrorists were at war with us, but we were not yet at war with them."[66]

The profound psychological shock to American assumptions of safety and security was not only to be found in the fact that America had been hit, and hit very hard. It was also to be found in the additional fact that all those relationships and institutions that we had assumed would protect us didn't. The reasons varied, but not the result. The FBI came out of a culture of fighting crime and had a difficult time adding prevention to its tools against terrorists. The CIA said it was given ambiguous signals by the Clinton White House about just how far it could go in killing Osama bin Laden and members of his group. The CIA was aware that terrorist operatives were setting up operations in the United States, but there was a legal wall, mistaken it turns out, that kept the FBI and CIA from sharing important information. President Bush realized the threat that Al Qaeda represented and had shaped a plan to move aggressively against it on many fronts. But that plan came too late to stop 9/11. Not only did our security institutions fail to stop the attack, neither allies nor international institutions helped avert the blow.

Institutions, allies, and the international community might be very helpful in the future. But the defense of the American community had to start elsewhere, with Americans and their understandings and purpose. The world had to be looked at anew, with clear eyes. Business as usual in national security affairs could now be seen as a death warrant for the United States. A new security paradigm was needed at home and abroad, one that emphasized offense and prevention. One that looked for allies everywhere, but did not delegate America's ultimate security to them.

The new paradigm needed a focal point, an exemplar, a person who could easily embody both the message and the virtues embedded in the new paradigm. That person now is obviously President Bush. One task of the president in pushing the new paradigm forward is to flesh out campaign slogans like "compassionate conservatism."

Another is to demonstrate through his commitment and resolve that the change is worth making, and he will not falter in trying to do so. Polls show that the public consistently gives Mr. Bush high marks for strong leadership—in one of many such findings, an *L.A. Times* poll taken between November 15 and 18, 2003, found that 61 percent of the public saw him as a strong leader.[67] That included 62 percent of self-described political moderates and 64 percent of independent voters.

Conservatives (74 percent) and Republicans (83 percent) rated him a strong leader. Only liberals (42 percent) and Democrats (39 percent) disagreed.[68]

A later *Washington Post*/ABC News Poll, reported on April 19, 2004, found that 64 percent found him a strong leader.[69] That figure included 91 percent of Republicans and 65 percent of independents, and, surprisingly, 35 percent of Democrats. The reason why came from another question asked about the president: Does he stick with his positions? Seventy-nine percent said he did and that figure included 93 percent of Republicans, 79 percent of independents, and a striking 66 percent of Democrats. When asked whether the president was honest and trustworthy, 55 percent said yes. That figure includes 87 percent of Republicans, 54 percent of independents, and, as expected, only 27 percent of Democrats.

It is not only his strength as a leader that is a resource for Mr. Bush's transformation efforts, but the fact that people generally like and trust him. That same *L.A. Times* poll[70] found that 40 percent liked the president and his policies; 6 percent liked his policies and disliked him; 28 percent liked him and disliked his policies; and 20 percent disliked him and his policies. Almost three-quarters liked the president or his policies.

In a Pew poll taken in February 2001, 67 percent thought he was warm and friendly. When that same question was asked again in 2003, that figure had risen to 70 percent.[71] Further details provided some surprises. For example, in the *L.A. Times* poll a net of 40 percent liked the president and his policies. However, that included a figure of 19 percent for liberals and 18 percent of Democrats. For moderates that figure was 35 percent and for independents 38 percent. Again, the nation is divided, but not polarized.

Asked whether the president was "honest and trustworthy," 56 percent of the sample said yes.[72] This number surprisingly included 31 percent of political liberals and 36 percent of Democrats, his worst critics. A majority of moderates (52 percent) and independents (59 percent) thought so too. And of course, conservatives (76 percent) and Republicans (85 percent) thought so in high numbers. In the Pew poll taken in 2001, 60 percent of the respondents thought he was trustworthy. In September 2003, that figure had risen slightly to 62 percent.[73]

These poll numbers and Mr. Bush's situation are almost the reverse of his predecessors'. In April 1998 at the height of the Clinton impeachment controversy, polls found that 65 percent of those asked said they approved of the way President Clinton was handling the presidency, yet only 35 percent thought him honest and trustworthy, and only 29 percent felt he had high personal moral and ethical standards.[74] Interestingly, during the same period that the public saw Mr. Clinton as having low moral standards and being dishonest and untrustworthy, they also saw him as being a strong leader (62 percent). Mr. Bush is seen as being both strong and honest. Yet, his ratings on policy specifics are not as favorable. It is one of the most central questions of the Bush presidency—whether being honest and strong will be enough to buy time for him to make a successful policy pitch for transformation.

Public trust is a particularly important resource of leadership capital.[75] This is especially so when the president is asking the public to let go of its older ways of understanding and accept the new way he champions. Mr. Bush's psychology is not only a major resource to him as a president, but also as a transformational president.

That is what the opposition assaults on Mr. Bush's credibility with regard to WMDs in Iraq, the budget deficits, and allegations that he was AWOL from his reserve responsibilities are meant to undermine. If the opposition is successful in making these changes take hold among the American public, they will deprive Mr. Bush of one of his chief tools for accomplishing transformation. In that event his reelection and efforts at transformation are likely to falter and fail.

Yet, while a president's psychology and the public view of it are important, the president must demonstrate by his decisions and actions that he is not operating under the rubric of business as usual. If he does, he lends support to the paradigm he seeks to replace. Mr. Bush has been quite consistent and public in disregarding business as usual. At the contentious United Nations Conference Against Racism, Racial Discrimination, Xenophobia and Related Intolerance, virulently anti-Semitic and anti-western rhetoric dominated the planning conferences preceding the general conference itself. In response, the United States sent a low-level delegation, and it walked out of the conference when participants failed to moderate their rhetoric or their chief demands. A reworded draft document "was reluctantly accepted by European diplomats, who described the draft as 'fairly moderate' compared with other texts that have assailed what their authors call 'the racist practices of Zionism.'"[76] This was the same mindset that allowed European diplomats to accept a biological weapons treaty without enforcement mechanisms. Mr. Bush refused to accept the best of the worst as a reasonable position.

Mr. Bush's refusal to conduct business as usual has annoyed some of his conservative allies as well. Alan Murray, writing in the *Wall Street Journal,* criticized the president for denying France, Germany, and Russia the chance to compete for the big core contracts in rebuilding Iraq. His advice was to do the same thing, but essentially hide it: "There was little chance that French, German or Russian companies would ever be able to navigate the government's cumbersome procurement procedures. And even if they did, *the Pentagon could easily figure out a reason to deny the contract, without generating the publicity of a blanket ban.*"[77] Mr. Bush, however, preferred directness to hypocrisy.

Mr. Bush's paradigm of assertive defense in national security matters and market choice and personal autonomy in domestic matters is being given the equivalent of a political audition. The transformations for Mr. Bush, unlike those of President Roosevelt, are unlikely to happen quickly or dramatically. Rather they will, if successful, more likely unfold over time.

It will take people some time to get used to the new way of seeing and doing things. People do not give up their habits, how they think, or how they act quickly or easily. They will no doubt have anxieties regarding the transition, which adherents of the old paradigm will do their best to stimulate.

Mr. Bush has his work cut out for him. A May 2003 *Wall Street Journal* poll found that, in answer to the question of whether Mr. Bush had the right policies on domestic issues for the times, 44 percent thought he did, 32 percent thought he didn't, and 25 percent weren't sure. Those figures had improved slightly from a January 2003 poll in which 33 percent thought he did, 37 percent thought he didn't, and 29 percent weren't sure.[78] These figures suggest the scope of the challenge Mr. Bush faces in transforming the dominant paradigm to one more congenial to his vision.

In foreign policy, difficult months in Iraq with mounting causalities have led Americans to question involvement there and President Bush's handling of it. In April 2004, 46 percent of respondents said the United States had done the right thing in becoming involved in Iraq, down from 58 percent the month before. Asked whether it was a mistake to have become involved in Iraq in the first place, 48 percent said yes and 46 percent said no. Asked whether the United States should stay in Iraq as long as it takes to ensure Iraq is a stable democracy or leave as soon as possible, 46 percent supported staying, and 46 percent support leaving as soon as possible even if Iraq is not fully stable.[79]

Americans were clearly worried about events in Iraq and this in turn has eroded support for what the president was trying to accomplish there. These figures suggest that public support for the president's strong stance in dealing with regimes like Iraq will be difficult to maintain. Here, too, Mr. Bush's attempt to change the way Americans look at the world, and what they are prepared to do about it, faces an ongoing and uphill struggle.

The Hidden Dimension of Transformation: American Psychology

FDR's transformation of the dominant paradigm from economic laissez-faire to government stewardship involved more than a change in perspective. It had psychological implications. When you change people's understandings, you change their expectations, and when you do that, you change their psychology.

After FDR, government became a direct and major player in the American economy, but in doing so, it also became a major player in America's national psychology. Americans no longer looked wholly inward for the answers to their economic circumstances. Nor did they look out horizontally to their local communities for relief and answers. They looked upward toward Washington and the president. As a result, both became central figures in America's public psychology.[80]

The transformation that President Bush seeks in both domestic and foreign affairs will require adjustments to some patterns and long-standing trends of American psychology. Some of them will be difficult to make. Taking more personal responsibility for your own circumstances puts additional weight on people to make informed and better judgments. Giving primacy to American security interests may require citizens to feel more comfortable in going it alone and enduring difficult times abroad as in Iraq. Neither will be easy.

Transforming Domestic Psychology

Domestically, many of Mr. Bush's initiatives involve giving individuals more freedom and choice. His tax cut rhetoric has repeatedly underscored that the money returned is the citizen's, not the government's. While this policy reflects many economic and political considerations, it also is consistent with other Bush initiatives to devolve decision power from government to individuals.

The same theme can be found in education. The president's support of vouchers reflects many policy objectives, but it tries to give parents a choice and a means to exercise it. The same can be said of aspects of the No Child Left Behind initiative that allows parents in failing schools that don't improve to go elsewhere or get help. A similar theme can be found in the administration's plans for Social Security reform that will allow future participants to invest and personally own a portion of the money they pay into the program.

It is also possible to see the administration's position on abortion through this lens. In focusing on abstinence, the administration is, in essence, picking up on Mr. Clinton's unkept promise to make abortion safe, legal, and rare. The Bush administration has tried to refocus the issue further back in the decision process. In asking young people to think about delaying sexual exploration and gratification until they are in the context of a committed long-term relationship, Mr. Bush is doing several things. The policy reflects a statement about values, the importance of commitment and marriage, and so on.

Yet he is also placing the responsibility for making a difficult decision directly on the shoulders of the individuals facing the choice. The same could be said of the education initiatives and his Social Security reform plan. Of course it's the government that is providing the tools in education or Social Security reform. Yet the change in perspective embedded in these efforts is the effort to provide the tools for individual choice in place of government's choosing. In this domestic initiative package Mr. Bush is attempting to move the locus of control, decision-making and responsibility, away from government and back toward individuals. This is wholly consistent with the strong elements of freedom, responsibility, and self-reliance that have been part of the American cultural and psychological tradition since this country was first settled.

Transforming American Psychology
Toward the World

George W. Bush is trying to engineer another change in American psychology as well. Mr. Bush is not a man who shies away from making judgments, some of them quite strong. He "loathes" the leader of North Korea because he enslaves and starves his people. Those who attacked the United States are "evil." There are countries, named, that form the "axis of evil." These are blunt words, but they are also strong judgments.

Americans, on the other hand, have become increasing reluctant to make judgments of any kind about others, except perhaps, paradoxically, their political leaders. Daniel Yankelovich, the noted pollster, wrote two decades ago that "Traditional concepts of right and wrong have been replaced by norms of 'harmful' or 'harmless.' If one's actions are not seen as penalizing others, even if they are 'wrong' from the perspective of traditional morality, they no longer meet much opposition."[81]

This live-and-let-live approach to personal values and convictions has led to a new ethic that can be summed up by what has become almost an eleventh commandment for many Americans, "Thou shall not judge." The "non-judgmentalism of middle class Americans," in matters of religion, family, and other personal values, emerges as the major finding of Wolfe's in-depth interviews with mainly suburban clusters of Americans across the country.[82] He attributes it to an emphasis on pragmatism rather than values in making tough personal decisions, a reluctance to second guess the tough choices of other people, and ambivalence or confusion as the "default" moral position.

Mr. Bush's thinking clearly entails judgments of good and evil that he is not afraid to make. Yet, he leads a country that has, in past decades, turned from making such judgments and has been applauded in many institutional quarters for doing so. Clearly there is a mismatch here between the president's psychology and the public's. It is not the only one.

Mr. Bush is a man, as noted, who can stand apart. It is a trait that has been as evident in his capacity to resist pressures to scale back or abandon his domestic initiatives as it has in his foreign policy convictions. Indeed, at one point in the discussions leading up to the attack on Iraq, Secretary Powell said that every country would back the use of force against Afghanistan, but that expanding the war to other terror groups or countries could cause some of them to back out. Mr. Bush replied he didn't want other countries setting terms or conditions on that war and went on, "At some point we may be the only ones left. That's OK with me."[83] It is unclear that it would be equally OK with a number of Americans.

Mr. Bush was also ready to and did stand apart from others on a number of matters including the ABM treaty, the Kyoto agreement, the Biological Weapons convention, and the International Criminal Court, to name several. This made Americans distinctly uneasy. Wasn't the United States the champion of international law? Had this country not been one of the chief moving forces behind the establishment of the United Nations? Worse, America, it was said repeatedly, had ignored the warnings and advice of its 'traditional" European allies on the war and all of these treaties.

If non-judgmentalism was the key judgment frame for domestic politics, having friends and support from other countries was its international counterpart. Mr. Bush might think it all right to go against the advice of allies and the "international community," but Americans are reluctant, at best, to do so. There were many reasons for this.

Americans are a friendly, outgoing people in general. They also like to get along with others and dislike arguments. David Riesman's famous analysis of Americans as "other directed"—that is, looking to others to provide cues and approval—has not been diminished in an age in which Americans prefer ambiguity and relativity to difficult judgments.[84]

Mr. Bush went to the United Nations to seek its agreement in disarming Saddam Hussein, in large part because it was necessary to show that he was making the effort. Americans demanded it. To cite just one of a number of such polls, a January 2003 *Newsweek* poll showed that support for the war if major allies and the United Nations supported it was 83 percent; with allies but not the United Nations, 47 percent approved; and with neither major allies or the United Nations that approval dropped to 34 percent.[85]

Mr. Bush did obtain unanimous UN agreement demanding that Saddam Hussein disarm and provide documentation of doing so or suffer the consequences. Yet when Bush went back to get the United Nations to act on its resolution, he failed in part because France promised to veto any such measure and another of our "traditional allies" (Germany) followed France's lead.

Then there was an unusual development for Americans. They began to show their displeasure with the United Nations. A March 10, 2003, CBS poll found that 63 percent approved of taking action against Saddam Hussein, and 53 percent approved even if the United Nations did not approve of it. In that same poll, 58 percent of the public thought the United Nations was doing a poor job regarding Iraq.[86] By August 2003, a Gallup Poll found that 60 percent of Americans thought the United Nations was not doing a good job dealing with the problems it faced.[87] An ABC/*Washington Post* poll taken March 17, 2003, found that 75 percent disapproved of the way the United Nations was handling the situation with Iraq. A Fox News survey taken April 9, 2003, found that 79 percent thought the failure to enforce its own resolutions had hurt the United Nations.

That displeasure was also seen in ratings of our "traditional allies" that opposed the war. A Harris Poll looks each year at America's allies and opponents. It found that

> Many of the 25 countries included in the list have not changed their ratings or positions substantially since last year. The biggest changes that have taken place clearly reflect world events, particularly the Iraq war. France, which was most outspoken in its opposition to the Iraq war, has slipped all the way from eighth place to nineteenth place this year. Germany, which was almost as strong in its criticism, has fallen from sixth to fourteenth place.[88]

Still, the ABC/*Washington Post* poll found 70 percent wanted the United States to continue its relationship with the United Nations. And a PIPA poll taken April 18–22, 2003, found that the United States should not feel freer to use force without U.N. authorization in the future. The operative word to describe these conflicted views is "ambivalence."

Mr. Bush sees the world as a place where American freedom of action must be preserved, with allies if possible, without them if necessary. Americans on the other hand find understandable comfort in the support of others. Reconciling these two views, if possible, will be no small accomplishment.

A Sea Change? Public Support of Preemption

The implications of the 9/11 attacks are not easily summarized. Some things rose, like church attendance, and then returned to normal. The same was true of the temporary bipartisanship that briefly characterized American political life. Yet other things did change, apparently for the long term.

Americans became more patriotic.[89] More Americans expressed love, support, and appreciation for their country. In that respect they came closer to the president's unusually outspoken feelings on the subject.

The president and the country have become aligned on this important matter. They and he are also willing to take tough measures to protect it. The president's doctrine of striking at enemies, even if they have not attacked the United States, is both novel and controversial. For a country that wants to be liked in the international community, support for such a policy represents an important development.

There is some evidence it is taking place.[90] In September 2002, a CBS/*New York Times* poll asked whether the United States should be able to attack any country it thinks might attack the United States, and 41 percent said yes. In an April 2003 poll that number had risen to 47 percent. Asked in 2002 whether the United States should be able to attack groups and countries "if we have evidence that they are preparing to commit terrorist acts," 67 percent said yes. Asked by Pew in June of 2002 if "attacking potential enemies first if we think they are going to attack us would be effective," 63 percent thought it would be. In June of 2002, Gallup/CNN/*USA Today* proposed a series of hypothetical circumstances and asked if an attack by the United States would be justified. Those circumstances were: the country was aiding terrorists who were making plans to attack the United States (87 percent); the country was an enemy and developing chemical/biological weapons (81 percent); the country was an enemy and developing nuclear weapons (75 percent).

In an April 2003 NBC/*Wall Street Journal* poll the following question was asked: "The United States' decision to go to war against Iraq represents a change of military policy from one in which we respond to military actions by hostile countries to one in which we initiate hostilities when there is a threat of hostility. Do you agree or disagree with this new military policy?" Whereas 63 percent agreed in April of 2003, 55 percent agreed when the same question was asked in July 2002.

Finally, a Pew poll conducted April 8 to 9, 2003, asked the following question: "Do you think that using military force to remove dictators of countries that may threaten the United States but have not attacked us is usually the right thing to do, sometimes the right thing to do, or rarely the right thing to do?" Fifteen percent thought it usually right, 51 percent thought it sometimes right, and 20 percent thought it was rarely right.

Support for preventive military action has limits. In August 2002 a CBS poll asked whether the United States had the right to weaken or overthrow governments it believed posed a threat to the United States; 57 percent said yes. However, when the wording was changed to "unfriendly to the U.S," rather than "a threat," 55 percent said no.

Overall, the results point to a change in public psychology regarding national security matters. Americans are hesitant but willing to be more critical of allies and international communities that fail them in time of need. And they are more likely to support action to defend themselves even if it means not waiting until they are attacked. These changes can be traced to 9/11. Mr. Bush seems on his way to at least one of his proposed transformations.

MR. BUSH'S PERSONAL TRANSFORMATION
AS A TEMPLATE

Mr. Bush's efforts to transform American psychology specifically and domestic politics more generally are doubtlessly aided by his own experiences along these lines. The two transformations that Mr. Bush seeks are, counting his own transformation at late mid-life and his transformation after 9/11, his third and fourth such efforts. His own personal transformation at mid-life has provided both the model and the success on which to base these new presidential efforts.

Mr. Bush transformed himself from a person with more of a past than a future to a skilled player at the highest levels of politics. And he transformed his presidency from one struggling for small amounts of political traction to a major historical administration, perhaps of the first rank. Surely, such a person would not think it excessive or grandiose to attempt to change the domestic politics of this country or reorient America's stance toward the world. The question is whether he can avoid the pitfalls of his success.

Over his career, many have offered their views on Mr. Bush—his psychology, development, policies, and prospects. In the final chapter I will take my turn at this enterprise. Mr. Bush has made a remarkable life journey, and it needs summing up. He has in the process of transforming himself and his administration reached a point where he has the chance to both transform the country and the world. It is both a pinnacle of opportunity and a precipice.

THE DILEMMAS OF A TRANSFORMING PRESIDENT

EVERY FOUR YEARS AMERICANS BET ON THEIR FUTURE. They hope to select a president who will put their interests before his own. They hope he will understand the world as it is and act accordingly. They hope to select a president with the maturity, judgment, and insight to navigate through perilous times and unforeseen circumstances.

They want to feel safe at home and, if not admired, at least understood abroad. They want to feel secure economically and live in a culture that values their autonomy, freedom, and values. And they want a president who is strong enough to lead and sensitive enough to care. The question they face in November 2004 is whether George W. Bush is that man.

It is not an easy question to answer. To do so requires knowledge of the man, of course—who he is and how he came to be that way. It requires a balance sheet of his strengths and weaknesses. And it requires some evaluation of whether the policies he stands for are adequate to the circumstances the country faces.

The George W. Bush presidency is framed by a remarkable confluence of four transformations. The first is a personal transformation that began in mid-adulthood and has been picking up psychological momentum at surprising speed ever since. The second, directly attributable to the 9/11 terrorist attack, hastened that momentum and sealed its psychological consolidation. That pivotal event also helped fuel the change in focus that reconfigured the Bush presidency toward foreign policy and pushed his new approach into the political equivalent of overdrive. And finally, but not insignificantly, Mr. Bush, remembering his father's fate, and having his own strong views on domestic policy, has forged ahead on that, the fourth transformation, as well.

Mr. Bush may, or may not win a second term. But win or lose he has clearly been personally transformed and established strong presidential markers. His life history can be seen as a narrative of struggle and redemption. It can be viewed as a story of overcoming repeated false starts and persevering until he found the right path. It is a story of having at last found the footing of success, and leveraging it to unanticipated and undreamed-of heights.

His presidency now stands on the threshold of a remarkable series of transformations. His reelection will not magically erase the partisan divisions that permeate the country any more than his defeat will. America is divided and will remain so for the foreseeable future. However, gaining a second term will consolidate his perspectives in both domestic and foreign policy. It will ensure that he has four more years in which to publicly audition his new center-right paradigm, extend it into new areas, and consolidate what he has already done. That alone will ensure its impact for years, and more likely many years after he leaves office.

This is a profound change for someone who had to flash his photo identification card on the stump to point out in irritation that he was not his father. Few would confuse the two today. It is, psychologically and politically, a quintessential American success story. Yet, there is no guarantee of a happy ending. Mr. Bush faces formidable challenges. Some of them are, paradoxically, a consequence of his success.

The challenges to Mr. Bush have almost as much to do with his own psychology and leadership style as they do with the monumental transformations he hopes to accomplish. Mr. Bush has leveraged these traits well, but they are not without their limits. It is as yet unclear whether Mr. Bush appreciates what they are, and if he does, whether he will be able to do anything much about them. Hard charging is central to Mr. Bush's leadership style and psychology, and is very appropriate to getting up a steep hill. Yet once the summit has been gained it may be necessary to reconsider the pace. Mr. Bush's leadership style asks a great deal of people. It is an open question as to how many are up to the task.

Mr. Bush also has to contend with the fervent efforts of his critics to derail his ambitions. They are formidable because they are fighting with the tenacity and ferocity of those whose cherished paradigms stand in danger of eclipse. In Mr. Kerry they have found a candidate whom they hope will breathe new life into their old paradigm.

A SURPRISING AND SUCCESSFUL ODYSSEY, AT LONG LAST

Mr. Bush's personal and professional success is now a clearly established matter of public record. For a man whose claims to achievement were considered by critics to be unearned, or at best, ambiguous, this by itself is a satisfying, confidence-consolidating experience. His accomplishments were built on perseverance when repeated opportunities didn't work, until he finally forged a good fit between his talents and his life purpose.

The path by which Mr. Bush came to occupy the White House has been called an "unlikely odyssey."[1] And in some ways it is. If, as Freud said, the child is father to the man, then this President Bush, it must be said, is a very surprising adult.

He grew up in a large, wealthy, loving, competitive, and accomplished family. Yet he had no obvious or traditional excellence on which to build, and so struggled to find his own place and identity. These matters were made more difficult by having a famous and accomplished father whom he idealized and a tart-tongued mother who loved but didn't spare him.

His family name was both a blessing and curse. That name helped open doors, but also perennially raised questions in others' minds about how much his accomplishments were his own and how much he owed to his family's name and relationships. It is likely that Mr. Bush himself had trouble sorting out the real contributions of both.

He had the capacity for accomplishment, but for many years did not see much in the way of results. He was a hard worker, a good friend, a fast wit, but also somewhat wild and undisciplined. Much of what he did starting in elementary school and extending through college he did well enough, but just that.

That began to change when he joined the Air National Guard and mastered becoming a jet pilot. Still, this did not lead anywhere directly. The same could be said, at first, of his Harvard MBA, a program he secretly applied to in order to test the impact of his own efforts. Marriage and family life marked a major turn toward maturity for Mr. Bush. Yet his years in the Texas oil fields, despite hard work, produced frustration not success, and a corresponding effort to ease or erase those feelings with alcohol.

On reaching his early forties, Mr. Bush abruptly traded his Wild Turkey for cold turkey. He was aided by his wife, a close family friend (the Rev. Billy Graham), and his newfound personal faith. But most of all he was aided by his own determination, sheer force of will, and strong desire to succeed, to make his mark and forge his place.

The oil business where he hoped to stake his claim was buffeted by an industry downturn. And he never found that saving "liberator," as he called it, an oilwell strike that would have in one gusher recouped his fortune, psychological and economic. Approaching mid-life, he had reached another dead end. When the oil business really got tough, George W. looked for a way to preserve his stake for another day. He found help. It was not the first time, nor the last time, his initiative would prove to be a salvation.

George W. had a reprieve, but not a real place. That came, in what was clearly becoming a psychological pattern, from his own initiative and self-help. Mr. Bush helped put together the Texas Rangers deal. In doing so, he helped engineer a place for himself, and the rest, as they say, is history.

His rise from struggling business owner (Arbusto, Spectrum 7) to employee (Harkin Oil) to part-owner and front manager of the Texas Rangers baseball team, and from there to two-term Texas governor and then president, can only be described as meteoric. In those 14 years, Mr. Bush more than caught up with the curve of his life's ambitions. In doing so he established what had for almost his whole life eluded him—a central place that he had earned with his own skills and hard work, and an increasing recognition from those paying attention that there is a lot more to Mr. Bush than meets the eye. Some pundits and critics are still taking in that fact.

As one might expect, the experience of having realized his life's ambition to find a secure and valued foothold in adulthood brought about some changes in Mr. Bush's psychology. Early on Mr. Bush had developed the personal confidence that comes with having been accepted for *who* you are. What he lacked until later life was the confidence that comes from applying yourself, successfully, in *what* you do.

Those two sources of confidence, personal and occupational, finally came together for Mr. Bush in his late forties, first as managing partner of the Texas Rangers baseball team and then as a two-term governor of Texas. For the first time, at mid-life, Mr. Bush had consolidated the basis of adulthood. He had married a warm, supportive, intelligent, and emotionally grounded woman and started to raise a family. He had also finally reached success in his two arenas of lifelong interest, business and politics. If, as Freud said, a well-realized and successful life rested on the twin pillars of love and work, Mr. Bush had finally arrived.

One reflection of this change was his relationship with his father. George W. grew up idealizing his father. It is easy to see why. His father was ambitious and successful. But he was also something more that was crucial. He was warm, nurturing, and absent. That is a powerful emotional mix.

Young George followed in his father's footsteps out of love, respect, and identification with his father's ambitions and interests. His father however, proved to be a hard act to follow. In such cases, it is possible for idealization to take several turns.

The son having never measured up can simply quit trying. The result is a lifelong feeling of inadequacy. Sometimes resentment can creep in as a son views his own disappointments as the fault of his father.

Another possible outcome is for the son to simply make his peace with his father's greater success and find his own life niche, most often away from the fields in which a comparison would be too obvious and painful. Neither of these is the path that George W. chose. With that dogged determination that has been the hallmark of his psychology since early adulthood, he pressed on.

When at last he found success, he also found the confidence that comes with making a satisfying place in the world for yourself. As he did so, his relationship with his father changed as well. George W. had worked with his father and seen him close up. He wanted to follow in his father's footsteps by pursuing a political career. He helped his father win the presidency and he saw his father lose it. The psychological question was: which would triumph, idealization or the lens of clear-eyed thinking? Clear-eyed thinking won, even to the point of being very critical of his father's decision to leave Iraq in 1991 prematurely.[2] The lessons he learned about politics, the presidency, and leadership by watching his father succeed and then fade made an indelible impression. And he carried that understanding into the White House.

CHARACTER IN THE WHITE HOUSE

Looking back on Mr. Bush's life, it's clear that his struggles to establish himself, and how he overcame them, had implications for how he acted once he did. It is not surprising that he reached inside himself for the psychological template of his personal success to apply to the presidency. Remember that Mr. Bush is a man who watches carefully and draws lessons. Having done so with his beloved father, it is unlikely he would fail to do so for himself.

Although his father was president, there is no evidence that his son hungered for that position, even when he ran for it. His ambitions were more modest and personal—to find a successful place in the world. He was drawn to politics to be sure, but he was not purposefully trained for it at an early age as was, say, Al Gore. That is one reason why Mr. Bush, unlike Mr. Gore, while having a very competitive psychology, doesn't have a cutthroat one.[3]

His rather late presidential ambition—he indicated even while running that winning or losing didn't define who he was—influenced his conduct in the White House. The presidency was not the Mt. Everest of his life's dream, a mountain he had been assiduously climbing for decades. It wasn't treated as a family birthright or a personal necessity to make up for a father's failed ambitions. It was, like many other accomplishments in Mr. Bush's life, a matter of one thing leading to another.

One result of this is that while Mr. Bush respects the office, enjoys what he can do with it, and relishes making decisions, his identity isn't dependent on it. Nor is the fact that he is or isn't critically popular important to him personally. Mr. Bush receives his sense of personal validation elsewhere.

Validation simply refers to the importance of having other people acknowledge you for the things that you, yourself, find important. If you value intelligence
before beauty, it will not help if someone tells you that you are handsome. "Meaning it" and acting accordingly is George W. Bush's source of self-validation.

That is why almost all of his major decisions in office have shown that he's
much more interested in doing what he thinks is right than what he needs to do for
reelection. Yes, he is a skilled politician; political considerations are not wholly absent from his thinking, as his imposition of temporary steel tariffs demonstrates.
He is competitive and prefers to win, and yes, he would like a second term. But on
the big items such as Afghanistan, Iraq, tax cuts, the ABM missile development,
forceful interdiction of black-market items useful for WMDs, Middle East peace
and the encouragement of democracy, encouraging energy development and a
worker/immigration program, and others, he has stood his ground.

In some cases, like the war with Iraq, he has risked his reelection. At other
times, like his call for Middle East democracy, he has taken on a difficult and
long-term project with little immediate prospect of gain, and every prospect of
difficulty and loss. Agree with him or not, he is a man who has repeatedly put his
own view of the country's self-interest before his own political interests.

Thoughtful Americans making a judgment about Mr. Bush, and who aren't
already wholly for or against him, will have a great deal to consider. For example, his critics portray him as a simpleton. Yet Mr. Bush is far from a simple
man. He is very smart, but not in the usual way. He's not learned in the traditional academic sense, but he's got a large capacity to see the essence of important things. He's got little patience for ethereal discussions, but does have a mind
that hones in like a laser on results. He has strong views, but can be extremely
flexible. He can stand apart from people and be obstinate and tough, but also
publicly tear up when he discusses the losses of 9/11 or when he talks about his
love for this country, or spends countless hours consoling grieving families after
the raw emotional experience of the destruction of the World Trade Center.

He will do hard things he believes to be right. But they will be controversial.
Mr. Bush asks a great deal of those who support him. He is guiding the country
through unprecedented dangers. His plans to meet them require the public to
have focus, courage, determination, and resilience, not surprisingly the same
traits that propelled him into the presidency. Not everyone is up to it.

Some people admire a leader who speaks his mind. Others are scared by it.
Mr. Bush persists in doing it.

Some find comfort in the company of allies, an international version of
safety in numbers. Mr. Bush, however, has made clear that when it comes to a
tradeoff between protecting America and getting along with allies, he will always choose the first. Understandably, the wish of some Americans is to do both.
But is that always possible?

Mr. Bush asks Americans a great deal domestically as well. His transformation of domestic policies asks Americans to entertain new ideas. This is easy in the abstract. However, the reality is that people become attached to their habits. People are anxious about giving up what they know for what they don't. And the opposition can be counted on to stimulate fears of change.

And then there is the issue of ideology. Mr. Bush is a different kind of Republican. He is not afraid to spend government money. He does not want to abolish the Department of Education, but strengthen it. And he is open-minded and supportive of illegal immigrants, but also supports a constitutional amendment against gay marriage. But he is a Republican and a conservative one at that.

He is insistent on returning responsibility back to individuals. Not everybody wants it. He wants to give individuals more choice. Not everybody is comfortable exercising it. Open-minded voters looking for easy answers here will not find them.

TO BE OR NOT TO BE HEROIC

Voters not willing to be guided by caricatures will have to resolve their own ambivalence about another key issue in 2004: whether they prefer heroic or reflective leadership. In the past there were two presidencies, one focused on domestic concerns and the other on foreign affairs. Since presidents were always more constrained domestically, the argument went, they would be tempted to turn toward foreign policy for accomplishments.[4]

Mr. Bush's experiences with Afghanistan and Iraq suggest that, while a president can institute decisive action abroad, there is no free ride. Presidential prerogatives abroad have become like the bipartisan trench warfare in Congress where each and every decision, and the decisions that flow from those decisions, becomes an occasion for recriminations, debate, and second-guessing. It takes a lot of fortitude and conviction to withstand the constant, orchestrated onslaught.

In the past, the American public may have given presidents real latitude in foreign policy. But that was based on a consensus that no longer exists. The presidencies of Truman, Eisenhower, Kennedy, and the first part of the Johnson administration were all predicated on the bipartisan assumptions of a bipolar Cold War. That consensus began to shatter as a result of the Vietnam War and it has never been reconstituted.

Public expectations changed as a result. During the Cold War, the public, at first reluctantly but ultimately more solidly, came to understand and support the necessity of giving the president leeway in that fight. The successful end of the Cold War, however, provided a reason for Americans to do what they have always historically preferred, to turn inward toward domestic issues.

By the time of the Gulf War in 1991, George H. W. Bush could not count on either a congressional bipartisan foreign consensus or much leeway from the public. Mr. Bush got more support from the United Nations for undoing Iraq's invasion of Kuwait than he got from Congress. And after a spectacular victory, Mr. Bush could not even gain a second term, because he had failed in people's minds to sufficiently address their concerns about the domestic economy.

Domestic policy and security is now one aspect of American national security worldwide. For Mr. Bush, and for future presidents, the line between national and domestic security has blurred and merged. After 9/11, the two presidencies have become one.

Americans still want a good economy, an excellent education, and a world-class health system, to name a few things on their list. And they still expect the president to help deliver those things. They therefore want a president who is accessible and who listens to them.

At the same time, they want a president who is strong and will protect them. They want a president who will stand up to their enemies, and if necessary their allies. They want a president who, when it comes to American security, will not take no for an answer. They want a president who will endure any hardship and persevere on their behalf.

In short, they want two different presidents. September 11 and its implications shattered the old two-presidencies theory, but has given birth to a new one. The two presidencies, one for domestic policy and the other for foreign policy, are ever-more distinguished by the requirements for successful leadership. Foreign policy leadership in a world in which there is no consensual agreement that can operate to frame specific issues requires of the president decisiveness, clearly articulated purpose, and determination. In foreign policy, Americans want *heroic leadership*. Paradoxically, given the deep divisions and partisan trench warfare that now permeates national legislative politics, a certain degree of tough heroic presidential leadership is necessary there, too. Yet, what Americans accept and even desire in their president for the grave issues of war, peace, and national security, they are uneasy about in domestic politics.

One reason for this is the continuing allure of bipartisanship. Americans continue to wonder why the two major parties can't just get along. But the reality is they don't, and Americans are reluctant to draw the difficult conclusion that a president who wants to get anything done legislatively in these circumstances will have to be tough and persistent, if not necessarily heroic.

The other factor at work here is the public's desire for a domestic president who is accessible and *reflective*. The public may want a presidential lion in foreign policy, but it continues to want a political version of the famous painting "The Peaceable Kingdom"—where lions and lambs coexist—domestically. Therefore, domestically, a president must emphasize compromise and common purpose. In domestic policy Americans want *reflective* leadership.

The new *dual presidency* is not so much a function of constitutional mandates, but of leadership psychology. It is not so much a matter of spheres of presidential activity as it is of a president's stylistic flexibility. And it is not so much a consequence of constraint as it is of the public psychology that follows from public expectations. And it remains for the president, who is after all one person—psychologically—with his singular set of ambitions, skills, ideals, and ways of carrying through relationships with all those in his personal and political world, to bridge that divide. Nowhere is this bifurcation of leadership responsibilities more clearly evident than in the presidency of George W. Bush.[5]

This new bifurcated heroic/reflective presidency presents a dilemma for Mr. Bush's opponent, John Kerry. Mr. Bush said he was a loving man with a tough job to do. Mr. Kerry has given little public evidence for the first, and is unproven in his capacity to do the second. Of course few non-incumbents can hope to match the experience of a sitting president running for reelection. And it is easy to say what you would do in every instance when you don't actually have to. But Mr. Kerry's record of accomplishment in the Senate starting in 1982 is thin. In a paradoxical turnaround for Mr. Bush, his can-do psychology and record may well be contrasted with "what's he done?" questions for Mr. Kerry.

Mr. Kerry presents a heroic demeanor and his service record matches it. But one question that faces Mr. Kerry is whether he has strong convictions and the courage of them. A *New York Times* analysis noted, "Throughout his campaign, Mr. Kerry has shown a knack for espousing both sides of divisive issues."[6]

He served honorably in the Vietnam War, then turned against that war, which was certainly his right. Yet, in speaking against the war he made a number of serious and, it turned out, inaccurate charges, some of which he has recently retreated from. He very publicly threw away what he said were his medals in protest, but it turned out he kept the ones that really mattered to him.

His record in the Senate on important issues has been diverse. He voted for the Iraq War, but then immediately backpedaled and voted against money to rebuild Iraq. He voted for the Bush tax cuts, but then condemned them, and so on. Tough talk is no substitute for real political courage and a record of having taken principled stands and having stuck with them.

When he was running against Senator John Edwards, the contrast between Edwards' sunny disposition and Kerry's was marked. The *New York Times,* clearly hoping for a match between the two, touted one of Senator Edwards' "great virtues as a candidate is his ability to connect with people, the warmth of his message, and his talent as an orator."[7] Mr. Kerry, on the other hand, is frequently described as aloof.[8] He often comes across as harsh when he talks about President Bush, and his speaking style can lean to the didactic and meandering.

These are matters of personal psychology and style, of course, and have little to do directly with a candidate's judgment. They do, however, have something to do with presidential leadership. Being aloof is different than being able to stand apart. And tough talk is not the same as making and standing by hard decisions.

Yet both Mr. Kerry and Mr. Bush are caught in the same dilemma. The public wants a heroic president who will protect them and a reflective one they can relate to, preferably on a one-to-one level. Mr. Bush comes from a wealthy background but he is more at home with his feet on the table, as his mother will attest, than he is in a tux. Mr. Kerry also comes from a privileged background, and because he seems aloof, appears to embody it.

Mr. Bush's dilemma is that he has established himself as a heroic leader in foreign policy, needs to be one to make any progress on his domestic ambitions, but faces a public who would prefer a reflective bipartisan domestic president. The problem for Mr. Kerry is that he must spend much of the campaign proving that he can be as heroic as the president. But all he will have to work with is talk. He will at the same time have to showcase his sensitivity and common touch. Doing both at the same time will be hard.

THE CONSEQUENCES OF A SECOND TERM

When a president runs for reelection, voters have a lot to consider. They can look back over his record and make a judgment about him as a person and leader and from that they can gain a sense of what a second term might be like, if given. How such a term might actually play out of course depends on circumstances, many of them unforeseen. Given that fact, it is probably best when making judgments about the man to look back, carefully, at his core psychology and style. In Mr. Bush's case, given the forcefulness of his psychology and the directness with which he responded to the circumstances that faced his presidency, these matters seem rather clear. Mr. Bush is and will remain a forceful president. Yet there is much more to Mr. Bush and his presidency than being forceful.

The balance of Mr. Bush's psychology was well captured by his own self-assessment after 9/11—"I'm a loving man but I've got a job to do." Mr. Bush has the capacity to be nurturing, like his father, but also to be tough-minded like his mother. Or, to put it another way, he is both reflective and heroic.

Since 9/11, Americans have seen a great deal of the heroic, tough-minded president, and modest amounts of the more nurturing, reflective one. This balance seems unlikely to dramatically change in a second term, because the threat of catastrophic terrorism will still be with us for the foreseeable future. Mr. Bush is likely to remain a no-nonsense foreign policy president.

Yet Mr. Bush also wishes to transform domestic policy. He will try to revamp Social Security. He will fight to put more market mechanisms into environmental policy. He will continue to emphasize individual choice and responsibility in a variety of policy areas (citizenship, sex education, individual savings accounts, school choice). He will stress opportunity in the form of tax relief and a more open immigration policy. And he will continue to increase the overall size of government, while changing the size of its various parts. He will expect results from all these programs.

In the process of doing this he will change, though not transform, his party. The GOP will become more center-right than conservative. As a result, it will become more competitive nationally, one important step in the transformation of the domestic policy paradigm.

Some Second-Term Advice

I don't know Mr. Bush personally. However, having spent four years immersed in the details of his life and leadership, I feel that I have come to understand some things about him. Mr. Bush has not solicited my advice about a possible second term. Nonetheless, I would like to offer some based on what I'm sure is his and every citizen's hope for a productive second term, if it is offered.

One of the psychological paradoxes of any presidency is found in the irony of its success. In Mr. Bush's case, these ironies are to be found in his clear-eyed insight and good judgment about the nature and implications of 9/11. And it is also to be found in the very traits of character that have brought him success.

His response to 9/11 is a classic illustration of reaching a fitting conclusion about a novel set of circumstances, the essence of good judgment. Mr. Bush certainly merits America's appreciation. The striking words, "We're at war," succinctly and aptly summarized a variety of key understandings—about the nature of the attack, the people who did it, and America's new circumstances. It is hard to think of a similar singular flash of such profound insight by a modern president.

That insight and the emotions that accompanied it—of anger, regret, and loss—added purpose and a meaning to his presidency that transcended ordinary presidential ambition. The primary mission of his presidency was now to protect America, and much has followed from that key development.

As several administration officials, including Mr. Bush, have made clear, the decision to invade Iraq was made in large part because 9/11 changed the way they understood the risks to the United States. Saddam Hussein and Iraq looked different after 9/11. In testimony before the Senate Armed Services committee, Secretary Rumsfeld said, "The coalition did not act in Iraq because we had discovered dramatic new evidence of Iraq's pursuit of weapons of mass murder. We acted because we saw the existing evidence in a new light, through the prism of our experience on September 11th."[9] This change of perspective is understandable and arguably prudent.

Yet also here is the danger that Mr. Bush, having been correct in assessing the severity of the danger confronting the United States, will tend to forget that this lens only fits one large problem, not every problem. The danger is not that because the United States invaded one country it will invade every country that represents a risk. That is literally an absurd worry. The administration's approach of talking with North Korea illustrates that Mr. Bush does not make decisions by automatic pilot.

The danger is that in focusing on this one enormous and central problem, and all the policy questions it raises, it will become the administration's dominant decision paradigm in foreign policy. Many foreign policy areas can, of course, be viewed through the lens of national security. The question is whether that lens doesn't obscure elements of the problem that deserve their own independent scrutiny from other perspectives. Overgeneralizing a good insight will be a particular second-term danger in large part because the insight was so powerful and fitting.

This will be hard for Mr. Bush to correct by himself. September 11 is indelibly etched in his experience and psychology. Those who advise him will need to be aware of this danger and help him where necessary. Congress can also play a constructive part in his process, but not if members are more interested in partisan posturing than in improving our prospects. The press, too, can play a role if they are willing to ask questions designed to elicit this kind of information and understanding, rather than trying to trap the president in an inconsistency or assuming deceit or incompetence.

Taking care with framing the issues that face the president and giving each their just understanding is not the only paradoxical issue a second Bush term would have to address. Another is the fact that every good presidential trait has its limits. Jimmy Carter had great attention to detail, a helpful trait in a presidency in which problems and information can be overwhelming, but that focus got in the way of clearly seeing the larger picture. Bill Clinton has an incredibly facile and churning mind, yet as president he had trouble reaching a conclusion.

Mr. Bush has demonstrated many admirable and useful traits for a president. He is generally direct, not much interested in pomp, and much more concerned with results than rhetoric. He has proven himself to be determined, able to stand apart from and consider the many demands that are placed on him, and able and willing to take positions that are difficult and controversial.

He has also demonstrated that he is a compassionate and caring man, much in the tradition of his father. Yet given the war on terror and, more specifically, the difficult days and weeks of the Iraqi post-war effort, this side of his psychology has been eclipsed by the strength of his determination. He needs to remember that his success as president will rest on both his *heroic* and *reflective* sides. The public is, understandably, losing sight of the latter. In a March 10–14, 2004, *Washington Post* poll, 49 percent of the respondents thought that Mr. Bush had governed as a compassionate conservative. In February 2003, that number had been 64 percent.[10] In part, Mr. Bush is responding to the focus of the press and public concern, but Americans want compassion as well as strength. Mr. Bush is fortunate in that both are elements of his psychology and he doesn't have to manufacture either one. But he must not forget that successful leadership in this divided society requires both parts of his psychology, not one.

Stubborn?

Mr. Bush has demonstrated that he is a strong person and president. Yet, an important question that arises in considering Mr. Bush for a possible second term is this: Given the president's determination and persistence raises the issue of where, exactly, is the dividing line between conviction and stubbornness? Stubbornness, by itself, is not necessarily or inherently, detrimental. Persistence in the face of adversity represents a critical trait in persevering in pursuit of important national goals. However, a president's persistence can shade off into a stubborn refusal to recognize that some goals, even necessary ones, can't always be obtained even if you are willing to pay a high price.

The reality of politics is that there is always a gap between the clarion calls of presidential rhetoric and the more difficult facts of presidential decisions at ground level. John F. Kennedy famously said in his 1961 inaugural address, "Let every nation know, whether it wishes us well or ill, that we shall pay any price, bear any burden, meet any hardship, support any friend, oppose any foe to assure the survival and the success of liberty."[11] Yet, just three months later the president thought it prudent not to provide airpower support to an invasion of Cuba that he had approved. Mr. Bush, like other presidents, has not been exempted from this gap. The distance between calling North Korea a part of the "evil empire" and Mr. Bush's prudent approach in dealing with the dangerous and mercurial Kim Jong Il is one of several such reflections of this fact.

Still, Mr. Bush has acknowledged of himself, "I can be pretty stubborn."[12] The question that arises then about his stubbornness is whether he sticks to his convictions long past the time when they are prudent or feasible to implement. Critics have called Mr. Bush's focus on Iraq and his commitment to his policies to develop post-war democracy and stability there "stubborn."[13]

His recent decision to turn to the United Nations to help with the transition from U.S. occupation to Iraqi sovereignty and authority has fueled the stubbornness charge. It is argued that Mr. Bush is doing reluctantly and as a last resort what he should have done much earlier—turn responsibility for Iraq over to the United Nations. In this view, only his stubbornness kept him from doing the "right thing" to begin with.

The war in Iraq and its aftermath is one of the most critical undertakings of the Bush presidency. It is an extraordinarily high-stakes investment on the president's part, personally. He was and remains determined to succeed. Such situations are historically tailor made, psychologically, for some presidents to dig in their heels in an all-or-nothing effort, as Woodrow Wilson did with his League of Nations[14] and Lyndon Johnson did with Vietnam.[15]

Yet, in fact, a review of the record shows that the president has shown repeated flexibility through the twists and turns of the Iraqi occupation. A *New York Times* review of his actions over the period of the occupation found:

> an increased willingness to reverse or alter elements of its occupation tactics, and a new hesitation to engage in military confrontations that could inflame the Iraqis even if they involve scrapping or rewriting plans that the White House or the head of the American occupation in Iraq, L. Paul Bremer III, announced months ago. The new tactics include ceding substantial power to the United Nations to pull together a transitional government; easing the ban on Baath Party members in the new government; and reopening the question of whether the United States should have disbanded the Iraqi Army.[16]

There had been other earlier indications of flexibility as well, for example, the early replacement of General Jay Garner with Paul Bremer.

As to turning the political part of the transition process over to the United Nations, this indeed did represent a change, but not as much as it was presented as being. The administration had tried several formulas for accomplishing that goal, and proved able to change formulas each time their ideas seemed to run into a dead end. The enlisting of the United Nations was one more attempt to find a successful formula, hardly an indication of rigidity. Indeed, the fact that the administration turned to the UN for this part of the post-war process in no way invalidates the decision not to simply turn over the total responsibility for post-war Iraq to them.

Had the United States turned over the rebuilding and security to the United Nations would they have been competent for those twin tasks? The United Nations would still face determined insurgents using terror as a weapon, and it is not organized to fight guerilla wars. Whose troops would fight? The Security Council is still made up of countries with very different agendas for Iraq, not all of them favorable to U.S. national security concerns. Should the United States defer to them? In fact, in asking the United Nations to take on one aspect of the transition, Mr. Bush was repeating an invitation he made some time ago in inviting the UN to be involved in overseeing the election process when he had been asked to define more clearly what he meant by the "vital" UN role. Mr. Bush has always said he would take help that was consistent with America's national security from whoever offered it, whatever its limits, and presumably that included from the United Nations.

Overall, in the circumstances that have most stimulated and tempted presidential stubbornness and rigidity, Mr. Bush has proved himself *not* to be a prisoner of a rigid determination to do things only in one set way. On the contrary, stubbornness and a determined focus on achieving results are, for the most part, psychologically incompatible. Mr. Bush may be stubborn but he is, paradoxically, flexible.

Reconsidering Success?

Paradoxically, in order to consolidate his political and policy successes to date, Mr. Bush is going to have to reconsider, at least to some degree, the very traits that brought him to where he stands. Whether he can do that remains to be seen. Consider one of Mr. Bush's most useful leadership traits—his preference for plain talk. He doesn't talk in ever-expanding paragraphs where the original meaning is hard to keep track of, as Bill Clinton did. He doesn't talk in shorthand phrases as Bob Dole did, leaving his followers to surmise what lay beyond his terse elliptical comments. Mr. Bush speaks plainly and directly, but not always informatively.

You can see the tension when Mr. Bush delivers a statement that he expects carries its own self-evident weight, but doesn't. He looks straight at the questioner, expectation etched in his face, awaiting the response he anticipates should come, but it doesn't. The reason for this is that what is so self-evident to Mr. Bush is not always self-evident to others. Assertion is not the same as persuasion.

This is not, it should be underscored, a matter of simply talking more. After his April 14, 2004, news conference, Peggy Noonan observed of the president: "Mr. Bush has turned garrulous. He has taken to speaking at great length in venues of his choosing, and more and more he chooses. . . . When I mentioned to a friend that I'd never heard of Mr. Bush speaking so long, the friend, who sees him often, said the president had recently spoken for more than an hour at a lunch, to the startlement of listeners who wound up furtively checking their watches. Another Washington denizen shared a similar story."[17] The point here is that it is the quality of the explanations that matter, not the length of the talks.

This distinction is especially important for Mr. Bush to keep in mind given that he wishes to transform the public's understanding and acceptance of new policy options. The public will need more than talking points or political epigrams designed to highlight a point. It will need explanations of what's different and why it's better on a regular basis. It will take time for these understandings to sink in (if they do), and Mr. Bush will have to be ready to commit himself with the same level of determination for explanation as he does now for exclamation.

Finally, there is the matter of Mr. Bush's admirable focus on results. In politics, talk is often cheap and actions speak louder than words. Actions consistent with words, as has been Mr. Bush's style overall, are more valuable still.

But it is likely that if Mr. Bush has a second term he will again confront the frustrations that lie in wait for presidents with strong personalities, deep beliefs in the importance and legitimacy of what they are doing, and confidence that they are doing the right thing. The office of the president might correctly be described as a reservoir of vast resources to accomplish national purposes. But it can equally correctly be described as the epicenter of resistance to any president's plans, especially one whose success would result in the marginalization of the opposition. His opponents, domestically and internationally, will continue to oppose him at every turn, hoping to move the goal posts and run out the clock on his presidency.

The temptations to act in response will be strong. The pressure to do so from his own partisans will be enormous. Mr. Bush might well feel, given term limits, that he has little to lose, while acutely feeling the days of his presidency and his chances to consolidate his domestic legacy slipping away.

Yes, Mr. Bush resisted the pressure and internal impulse to strike hard too quickly after 9/11. But part of the reason for that delay was the desire to make sure that retribution, when it came, was an unmistakably powerful beginning to a long and difficult war. These inhibitions won't work for domestic policy in a second term stymied by the opposition. If he gets it, his second term is likely to be another difficult, long slog without much prospect of a quick and satisfying capstone, like defeating the Taliban.

So Mr. Bush will have to depend on his own well-developed sense of focus and clear-eyed thinking. The wish to get even with those who harm or stymie what you care about is always a temptation for activist presidents. And Mr. Bush is not afraid of taking on his enemies. Nonetheless, he should think twice, at least, about any suggestion or impulse to respond in a way commensurate with the tactics of some of his opponents.

The president has expressed regret that he has not succeeded in changing the tone in Washington. It was probably too much to hope for given his transformational agenda and the Washington culture of partisan trench warfare. Yet Mr. Bush has succeeded in one sense. He has held his tongue and his options in the face of often extreme and ugly provocation. In doing so he has demonstrated that it is possible to be both tough and restrained. It is a balance worth keeping and a model worth maintaining.

Second Term Policy—Foreign Affairs

The shape of a second Bush term in foreign policy is possible to trace in broad outlines, understanding that no one can truly anticipate the future. In foreign policy, the chief focus of the administration will continue to be on terrorism, rogue states, and weapons of mass destruction. The administration will continue to act in concert with its many allies, and this includes even troublesome allies like France, as in Haiti,[18] and with many others (including Germany) in tracking down one of the world's chief terrorists.[19]

Interestingly, it's possible that the Bush administration's preventive war–making days are behind it. There is no obvious candidate against whom to apply this doctrine without prohibitive costs, although limited preventative strikes are certainly a possibility. Realistically, Iran and North Korea can probably rest easy, although, given the Bush Doctrine, they won't.

One reason that Mr. Bush's days of major war may be behind him is that he has already demonstrated that he is not afraid to use the military, not afraid to suffer casualties, and not afraid to take on and stick with big tasks like rebuilding Iraq. Having demonstrated will, courage, persistence, and resilience, he is less likely to have to prove the point again. But of course, if he does have to, he will. Another limit is that difficult struggles are emotionally tiring, and it is unclear if Americans are ready for another Iraq soon.

It is likely that the Bush Doctrine itself will be refined. During the Cold War the failure to distinguish between "massive retaliation" and "limited war" complicated the search for effective responses to the Soviet threat.[20] The same is likely to happen with the Bush Doctrine. That doctrine is likely to evolve into an array of powerful responses, some of which will entail military actions and others of which will entail an updated version of containment coupled with coercive diplomacy and economic incentives.

Among the most pressing general issues for Mr. Bush internationally is what he plans to do with the fact of American hegemony. He is right to believe that, generally, in strength there is security, but strength alone isn't enough, as 9/11 demonstrated. Mr. Bush is often urged to be more accommodating to others and to be responsive to the world community. This is both good advice and a trap.

Mr. Bush believes, correctly in my view, that American national security must be his primary obligation, and if in pursuing that he differs with the interests of others, so be it. Yet world opinion matters, and as ill-informed, envious, or just downright hostile as it may be, Mr. Bush and this country must still address it. But here the Bush administration faces a real dilemma.

The world opinion wants many things from the United States, much of it contradictory. They want America to stop interfering with other countries, even when those countries are dangerous. They want vastly expanded foreign aid, without the United States asking much about how it will be spent and by whom. They want the United States to adhere to every treaty thought up by the United Nations to strengthen the international community, without asking how much of a risk it is for the United States. And they want the United States to support democracy, but refrain from interfering in countries where we are trying to promote it.

Perhaps it is possible for the Bush administration to figure out a way to square all these circles, but I doubt it. But respond it must to the growing mismatch between how America sees itself and how it is seen. One way would be to distinguish between primary and secondary interests. An administration can be more flexible with the second than the first. Another possible approach comes from what enlightened coaches do when their team is obviously going to win the game; they don't run up the score. Being the biggest and the best, say in basketball, doesn't mean you have to win every game by 104–35 scores. Indeed, you would be wise if you didn't. The Bush administration is serious about its responsibilities but it doesn't have to win as much as possible in every circumstance.

Perhaps his best chance to square the circle is in Iraq. That rebuilding project, elevated by an effort to develop democracy in a brutalized country in a difficult region, is one of the most ambitious tasks the United States has ever undertaken. It's certainly comparable in terms of ambition and vision to the rebuilding of Western Europe and the development of democracy in Germany and Japan. A stable, democratic Muslim Arab state in the heart of the Middle East would itself be transforming, and a demonstration that some circles can with grit and determination be squared.

Second Term Policies—Domestic

Every president seeking reelection does so at least in part on the basis of his unfinished business, and in Mr. Bush's case this makes more sense than it ordinarily would. Mr. Bush is man with a heaping plate full of second-term presidential aspirations. He wants to replace America's reigning liberal domestic paradigm with one as-yet unnamed, characterized by the virtues of compassion, opportunity, responsibility, and effectiveness. He will be trying to do all of this in a domestic context in which his opponents will try almost anything to resist, delay, or defeat him. And, while the president's allies are generally united, they are not on every issue, as the president's recent immigration proposal makes clear.

Mr. Bush has really only put his vision of domestic policy before the American public in discrete and sometimes unrelated ways. He is for more choice, but hasn't used that as a systematic frame to promote his vision. He is for people taking more responsibility for the choices they make, but he hasn't pushed that view very hard, perhaps because many Americans are more interested in what they will get than the responsibilities that come along with it. He will have to speak to this issue more directly, though not too stridently.

Mr. Bush's specific second-term domestic agenda already has several large items on it. He wants to make his tax cuts permanent, and he wants to pass an energy bill. There is now on the table as well a constitutional ban on gay marriage, continuing environmental issues on clear air and global warming, lagging initiatives on faith-based social services and vouchers, and continuing agitation over drug benefits and reforming Medicare.

Two very large second-term domestic agenda items are reforming and revamping Social Security and the very large issue of immigration. The first of these entails a sea change in Social Security by allowing workers the option of investing part of their Social Security fund themselves. That will be a large and, most likely, a successful fight.

The same cannot be said about the president's immigration proposals. They entail setting up procedures to allow workers who come here illegally to do so legally for a limited time if they have work. There are some attractive features in what Mr. Bush proposes. It is certainly compassionate and recognizes that people who come here want to better their circumstances and those of their families. It matches workers with work, for those who take part in the program. Yet Mr. Bush has not yet addressed what will happen to those who bypass it.

Mr. Bush wants to make the United States a more welcoming society to immigrants and in this he is surely right. He offers more opportunity, yet he has been silent about immigrants' responsibilities. Of course Americans have a right to expect immigrants to abide by our laws. But must they learn English? Of course we want to honor immigrants' heritage. But does this mean we should encourage them to retain their allegiance to their "home" countries by voting there or advocating here on their behalf?

The United States admits between 800,000 and 950,000 immigrants per year, legally. The United States does very little to integrate these immigrants into its social, cultural, and political frameworks. Many became "assimilated," but in a segmented, partial, and sometimes shallow way. There are also somewhere between 8 and 11 million illegal immigrants already in this country, with about 350,000 more entering illegally each year. For many reasons this illegal flow must be stopped.

The question of American national identity and our attachments to our country given our diversity is one, if not *the,* most important domestic national question facing this country.[21] The issue is not confined to immigrants. Americans, too, know very little about their history and government. Mr. Bush has made new initiatives in the areas of American civics. Yet few people have ever heard of them. Mr. Bush has rarely discussed them; he should. Indeed, all of his efforts for domestic transformation will ring hollow even should he succeed if he does not also succeed in helping us to reunite as Americans.

MR. BUSH'S LEGACY:
WIN OR LOSE

It is, of course, possible that Mr. Bush will not win a second term. How would that affect Mr. Bush personally? What effect would it have on his legacy?

To understand the impact of such a loss, you have to understand a key paradox about Mr. Bush's psychology that is rarely discussed. He is a very competitive man, having been nurtured in a competitive family. He competes hard and to win. Yet, he is at the same time a man surprisingly able to place himself and his circumstances in perspective and find some inner peace and serenity in doing so. This is a side of Bush's psychology that is not often on public display. We have seen Bush the fighter, Bush the heroic prophet rallying Americans against the evil that was done to them and steeling them for the long haul, but we have rarely seen Bush the accepting.

When Mr. Bush was asked whether the tensions of the presidency kept him in knots, he replied, "Well, there are some things I can't control and some things that I can influence, and I'm able to distinguish between the two."[22] The reporter, Frank Bruni, thought this sounded like an aphorism that might "be embroidered, framed and hung above a fireplace . . . a platitude, a cluster of easy words to run out the clock."[23] Later, after watching Mr. Bush in the aftermath of 9/11, Bruni wrote of seeing "something true and meaningful in his description of his outlook on the presidency and on life, an explanation for his ability to ride out storms that might lay waste to someone with a less keen sense of destiny and a less ready acceptance of fate."[24]

Bruni attributes Bush's capacity for serenity to his faith. So does Mr. Bush. In his autobiography, he writes, "Faith frees me. Frees me to put the problems of the moment in proper perspective."[25] Mr. Bush used the same explanation, faith, to explain his turn from drinking.

Perhaps; but there is a prior and more powerful explanation for Bush's capacity for detachment and acceptance of what one can't control—his sister's death when George W. was six. Recall his words about the experience, "Minutes before I had had a little sister, and now I didn't. Forty-six years later, those moments remain the starkest memory of my childhood, a sharp pain in the midst of an otherwise happy blur."[26] Or, "You think your life is so good and everything is perfect; then something like this happens and nothing is the same."[27] George W. received an early and sharp lesson in the limits of control, and it stayed with him "forty-six years later" as "a sharp pain." It was a profound lifelong lesson.

Mr. Bush himself, in an earlier interview about the effect on him of his sister's death, realized the source of his capacity for detached serenity. Asked about that sad event, he said, "I am somewhat fatalistic in this sense. Take this potential run for the presidency. I feel like saying, God's will be done. That if I win, I say that, I told people, I mean, if I win, I know what to do. If I don't win, so be it. So be it. And I feel that way. I do. I feel liberated in that sense. . . ."[28]

Loss is never pleasant, especially for a competitive man who believes in himself and what he is doing. Bush often presented himself while campaigning as being beyond caring deeply whether he won or lost. "I don't fear success or failure," he told one reporter.[29] He would be all right, having tried, if the people selected Al Gore. His redoubling of his efforts after losing the New Hampshire primary to John McCain, however, belied this assertion. The more he invested, the more he cared, and he has invested a lot in his presidency.

Mrs. Bush summed up a fact of emotional life about possibly losing the presidency in two recent interviews. In the first, she was asked if she's thought about the fact that she might have to move, and replied that she knew they were "running for an office that had a limit, you know, it was a four-year term, or if you're re-elected, an eight-year term . . . we knew would only be temporary, however long it was."[30] Asked if she looked forward to returning to Crawford, she said yes, then, alluding to the possibility that her husband could possibly not be reelected, said, "After you've been in office it will be much more disappointing than had you lost that first one."[31]

Presidents react differently to the loss of office. Not surprisingly, their response reflects their psychology. Richard Nixon resigned the presidency and spent the rest of his life trying to rehabilitate his reputation. President Ford, who retired after filling in for departed President Nixon, is spending his retirement years playing golf and speaking. Jimmy Carter continued his efforts to do good and be recognized for it. Bill Clinton publicly lamented that he couldn't run for a third term and was reluctant to board the plane carrying him back to Little Rock. He has spent his post-president years, as he spent his presidency, ensuring that he stays in the limelight.

What of George W.? Will he stay active in politics whether he leaves office this year or four years hence? One answer to this question is: Mr. Bush is after all truly a homebody. Whenever he leaves the presidency, Crawford will be seeing a lot of him.

Given George W.'s lifelong battles against his father's shadow, losing the election would have a particular power and irony over and above the obvious disappointment that any one-term president would feel. Mr. Bush has spent a lifetime measuring up to and being measured by his father's accomplishments.

If both became one-term presidents, one can easily anticipate the rivers of ink that will belabor this parallel. All of these will most likely be able to be summarized by the easy, but inaccurate, aphorism: like father, like son. Of course the two men and their circumstances are in no relevant way alike.

The senior Mr. Bush preferred governing. The younger Mr. Bush prefers to lead. His father disliked conflict; George W. doesn't avoid it. His father developed no committed policy philosophy; his son did. George W. spent his political capital. His father saved it. George W. tried to transform what he found objectionable; his father found little that he couldn't work with.

Indeed, the most relevant difference between them is related to this last fact. The senior President Bush lost office because he did too little. If his son loses in November 2004, it will primarily be because he tried to do too much.

Lost opportunity is the sibling of regret. If Mr. Bush loses, he will not be able to continue or consolidate the transformation of a decaying paradigm. Interest-group liberalism will have gained time, but still will be on political life-support. The reasons for its decay will remain. It will either change or eventually wither.

While Mr. Bush may well regret that he won't be able to continue his domestic transformation, I think this will wind up mattering less than what he has accomplished internationally. After all, his mission became to protect America, and toward that end he has taken irreversible steps. All of the many steps taken after 9/11—tightening border-check systems, airlines identification systems, cargo inspections, rapid deployment interdiction teams to stop WMDs, a new ABM system, a modernized army, a Homeland Security Agency, and many more—were all accomplished on George W.'s watch. It is a legacy that no serious president dedicated to protecting the American people will dismantle.

Recall that validation is being recognized for what is important to you. Mr. Bush's mission after 9/11 was protecting this country, and he can feel confident that he did much that is important and will be lasting in that regard. That validation is a large offset to disappointment.

Out from Beneath his Father's Shadow?

Of course, it is equally likely that Mr. Bush will win a second term. The economy is on the mend. Mr. Bush is still given high marks for strong leadership and his fight against terrorism. Moreover, the record of the Democratic party nominee John Kerry, presents many opportunities for Mr. Bush to make his case.

If he wins, the personal issues that we have discussed above will play out differently. He will have an opportunity to further develop and consolidate his transformation of domestic and international politics. He will have, then, at the end of his second term been given eight full years to audition his new right-center policy paradigm. More people are likely to feel comfortable with it. As a result, the decaying paradigm of interest-group liberalism will further wither and slowly fade into history.

Mr. Bush will take a victory in November as a partial vindication of his leadership approach. He will feel, legitimately, that it is possible to take tough, even unpopular positions, see them through, and still get the overall support of the public. He will no doubt feel energized, as will his administration.

Mr. Bush is not a man who likes to rest on his laurels. A second Bush term, as already noted, would be just as active politically and just as full of policy initiatives as the first. Yet unless Mr. Bush gains enough Senate seats to prevent the opposition from making him reach 60 votes on every major issue, he will still have many domestic fights on his hands. It will not be a quiet four years.

There is one way in which a second Bush term is likely to be different than the first and that is with our "traditional allies." Several of them have endured Mr. Bush's foreign policies rather than support them. However, Mr. Bush has now demonstrated beyond question that he is serious about what he says and no nation can afford to ignore that. I think it possible that the larger fights that come with having and acting on new ideas will dissipate somewhat, if only because other leaders have become used to and realize they have to accommodate somewhat to his style. It won't quite be the "era of good feeling," but it will be less contentious.

There is another more psychological and personal aspect for George W. regarding his reelection, should it happen. The shadow that has followed George W. throughout his life has been his father's. Comparisons remain natural. Yet three-and-a-half years into his first term, several observations are clear. George W. is a better and more enthusiastic campaigner than his father was. He is certainly less politically naïve. It is hard to imagine George W. promising not to raise taxes and then doing so. It is harder still to think that if, like his father, Mr. Bush thought it necessary to do so for the public interest, he would have taken strong steps to protect himself politically, as his father did not.

George W. is repeatedly bold in his leadership and policy initiatives. His father was only occasionally so. George W. feels quite at home with the demands and stresses of leadership. His father, as noted, preferred to govern.

If President Bush wins a second term he will, obviously, achieve a measure of presidential success that eluded his father. Indeed, by that measure alone he will have accomplished something so many of his modern presidential counterparts failed to do. And with that achievement comes a historic opportunity to further carry out his twin transformations in domestic and foreign policy.

In truth, having won the presidency and demonstrated his own unique brand of leadership and courage in response to 9/11, Mr. Bush has already clearly and decisively stepped out from behind his father's shadow. Yet, in doing so, he has stepped into the light of history's judgment. That history had been gathering for a decade and reached its turning point for the United States on September 11. It is ironic that Mr. Bush, having stepped out from behind one shadow, has been immediately confronted with another.

Obviously, George W. Bush is a controversial president. Yet his central insight into the circumstances facing this country is one we will be living with for many years to come. Like Bush or not, reelect him or not, we would be very foolish indeed not to take his insights seriously.

Mr. Bush's efforts to transform American domestic politics will be one pillar of his eventual reputation. That effort, to the degree it succeeds, will no doubt raise his historical standing. Yet that alone will not be sufficient to cement it.

It is on his effectiveness in moving the United States and its allies out of this second more lethal shadow of catastrophic terrorism and the threats of rogue and failed states that Mr. Bush will ultimately be judged. If he can forge a series of policies and alliances that substantially reduce those risks, his will be considered one of the most successful and important presidencies of the twentieth century. If, in addition, he can succeed in changing the underlying premises of America's domestic and international policy practices, he will be an outstanding candidate for being seen historically, and appropriately, as a president of the first rank.

NOTES

NOTES TO THE INTRODUCTION

1. Those with deeper interests in the theoretical, methodological, and epistemological issues involved in analyzing leaders psychologically should consult Renshon 1998b.
2. Wildavsky 1966; Shull 1991.

NOTES TO CHAPTER 1

1. Neustadt 1991, 127.
2. Schlessinger 2003; see also 1989.
3. Balz 2003b; see also Thomma 2003.
4. Quoted in Benedetto 2003.
5. Quoted in Balz 2003b.
6. Senator Robert Byrd, quoted in Cooper 2003.
7. Dick Gephart, quoted in Nagourney 2003.
8. Traub 2003.
9. Greeley 2003.
10. Krugman 2003.
11. Scheer 2003.
12. Lind 2003, 168.
13. Bill Moyers, quoted in Brooks 2003b.
14. Crowley 2003.
15. *New Republic* September 29, 2003 issue.
16. Chait 2003b; see also Chait 2003a.
17. See "Mother's Day Banned at Manhattan School," NY1 News May 12, 2001 (www.ny1.com/ny/NewsBeats).
18. Teachout 2001, 242.
19. Ibid., 24; see also Himmelfarb 1999, 2001.
20. Himmelfarb 1999.
21. Barone (2001) put it thus: "the two Americas apparent in the 48 percent to 48 percent 2000 election are two nations of different faiths. One is observant, tradition-minded, moralistic. The other is unobservant, liberation-minded, relativistic."
22. Barone 2001.
23. Barone and Cohen 2003, 1.
24. Fineman and Lipper 2003.
25. Harwood 2003.
26. Quoted in Bruni 2000f.

27. Quoted in Simon 2003.
28. Columnist Richard Cohen said George W. "may be the dullest president since Calvin Collidge. . . . He wades into groups of Democrats, patting them on the back, bestowing pet nicknames on them and proving . . . that he is impossible to dislike." (2001, A19).
29. Hunt 2003; emphasis mine.
30. A *Washington Post*/ABC poll taken February 6–9, 2003 found that the president had a 63 percent approval rating. Yet beneath those overall figures, there were stark partisan differences. Ninety-one percent of Republicans approved of the president, while only 46 percent of Democrats approved. A later *Washington Post* poll taken August 7–11, 2003 found the president's overall approval rating at 59 percent. This and other *Washington Post* polls can be found on line at: www.washingtonpost.com/wp-srv/politics/polls/vault. That same *Washington Post* poll (Balz and Deane 2003) found that "In other areas, the two parties are mirror opposites of one another, with 80 percent of Democrats disapproving of Bush's handling of the economy and 77 percent of Republicans approving. On the federal budget, 76 percent of Democrats disapprove of Bush's handling of the issue, while 71 percent of Republicans approve."
31. Baltz and Deane 2003. The same dramatic partisan divide was evidenced in views of the war itself. The Pew Center (2003, 22) found in late April 2003 that 93 percent of Republicans and 59 percent of Democrats thought going to war was the right decision. In August 2003, 90 percent of Republicans still thought so, but only 45 percent of Democrats did.
32. Wayne et al. (2003, 329) presented estimates from a number of 1998 Gallup Polls that found that 36 percent of the public identified themselves as Democrats, 30 percent as Republicans, and 34 percent as independents. More recent polls (Pew 2003) found that 27 percent of its respondents considered themselves Republicans, but only 14 percent considered themselves strongly so identified. That same poll found that 31 percent considered themselves Democrats, but only 15 percent considered themselves strongly identified with that party.
33. Hunt 2003, 12.
34. In the July 2003 WSJ/NBC poll, respondents were asked on a scale of ranging from 0 (never) to 10 (definitely) whether they would vote to re-elect the president. Thirty percent said "never" (0), and 32 percent said "definitely" (10). So, roughly less than one-third of the each party's strong partisans would not vote for the other party's candidate. Is this polarized or normal?
35. The poll figures for specific questions can be found by following the links embedded in the story at: www.washingtonpost.com/wp-dyn/articles/A50026–2003Nov1.html (November 3, 2003). All figures in the paragraph that follows are drawn from those links.
36. The poll can be found at: www.nytimes.com/2003/10/03/national/03POLL (October 3, 2003).
37. Data on the public's view of Mr. Bush's personal characteristics in the first two years of office can be found in Edwards (2004).
38. Renshon 2001a, b.
39. Mitchel 2001.
40. See for example, the remarks of Senator Joseph Lieberman (2003).
41. Dreazen 2000; Associated Press 2000.

42. Another way to look at the election is this: Mr. Bush won 30 states, Mr. Gore 20. Mr. Gore won 676 counties across the United States, while Mr. Bush won 2,436 counties. In terms of the population of the counties won, those that went to Mr. Gore contained 127 million, those that went to Mr. Bush, 143 million. Among counties that increased population from 1990 to 1999, Mr. Gore's counties increased 5 percent and Mr. Bush's increased 14 percent. Each candidate's strength was geographically concentrated, giving rise to the famous red-and-blue map and the metaphors that evolved from it.
43. Stout 2000.
44. Quoted in Apple 2000.
45. Quoted in Eilprin 2001; see also Balz 2001.
46. Beschloss 2000.
47. Pooley 2000.
48. Quoted in Smith and Walch 2001.
49. Quoted in Doyle 1999, 97.
50. Milkis and Nelson 2003, 316.
51. Quoted in Doyle 1999.
52. Gelerntner 2003.
53. Quoted in Doyle 1999, 97.
54. Babington 2001.
55. In a memo to Secretary of State John Foster Dulles (quoted in J. Renshon, chapter 7; emphasis added), Eisenhower comments on what he should do to "educate our people":

    We should patiently point out that any group of people, such as the men in the Kremlin, who are aware of the great destructiveness of these weapons . . . must be fairly assumed to be contemplating their aggressive use. It would follow that our own preparation could no longer be geared to a policy that attempts only to avert disaster during the early "surprise" stages of a war, and so gain time for full mobilization. Rather, we would have to be ready, on an instantaneous basis, to inflict greater loss upon the enemy than he could reasonably hope to inflict upon us. This would be a deterrent—but if the contest to maintain this relative position should have to continue indefinitely, the cost would either drive us to war-or into some form of dictatorial government. In such circumstances, we would be forced to consider whether or not our duty to future generations did not require us to *initiate* war at the most propitious moment that we could designate.
56. This category includes: Alterman and Green 2004; Abraham 2000; Begala 2000, 2002; Bonifaz 2003; Caldicott 2002; Corn 2003; Dean 2004; Dowd 2004; Dubose, Reid, and Cannon 2002; Frank 2004; Guilfoile 2001; Hatfield 2002; Huberman 2004; Ivins and Dubose 2003; Lind 2003; Miller 2002; Moore and Slater 2003; Moore 2004; Waldman 2004; Weisberg 2001; Wilson 2004.
57. Among these are: Podhoretz 2004; Kessler 2004; Rosenberg 2003; and Sammon 2002; 2004.
58. Among them are: Bruni 2002; Frum 2003; Minutaglio 1999; Mitchell 2000; Woodward 2002, 2004. The author is indebted to the excellent reporting contained in these books. More recent academic books—Greenstein (2003a,b), Rockman (2003), Gregg and Rozell (2003), and Schier (2004)—have examined specific aspects of the Bush presidency but have attempted no overarching analysis of it.

NOTES TO CHAPTER 2

1. Minutaglio 1999, 173.
2. Colloff 1999.
3. Bush 2001k, 785.
4. Bush 1999a, 60.
5. Quoted in Reinhold 1986, 14.
6. Minutaglio 1999, 201.
7. Frum 2003, 283.
8. Quoted in Minutaglio 1999, 158.
9. George H. W. Bush's political resume is a long one: chairman of the Republican Party, Harris County, Texas, 1962; U.S. Senate candidate, 1964 (lost); congressional candidate, 1966 (won); reelected to Congress, 1968; candidate for the U.S. Senate, 1970 (lost); ambassador to the United Nations, 1970; Republican National Committee chairman, 1972; ambassador to China, 1974; director of the CIA, 1976; presidential candidate, 1980 (lost); vice president, 1980–1988; and, finally, president of the United States, 1988–1992.
10. Quoted in Minutaglio 1999, 101.
11. Bush 1999a, 50–51.
12. Ibid., 167; emphasis mine.
13. Bush 2001u, 1300.
14. Minutaglio 1999, 5, 14, 214, 306.
15. Bush 1999a, 42.
16. Bruni 2002, 181.
17. Quoted in Walsh 2000.
18. Allen 2001b.
19. Parmet 2001, 293–94.
20. Woodward (2002, 22) says that in their years in the House Rumsfeld had found Bush Sr.: "to be a lightweight who was more interested in friendships and public relations and public opinion polls than substantive policy."
21. Bush 1999a, 181.
22. Ibid., 182.
23. Quoted in Mitchell 2000, 256.
24. When he was asked which was worse, his own loss to Bill Clinton or his son's suspended state as the Florida recount played out, he replied that "now was a hell of a lot worse" (quoted in Bruni 2002, 205). The reporter adds, "His haggard expression and empty gaze backed up his words."
25. Quoted in Kilian 2002, 52.
26. There were smaller, more intimate parallels as well (Mitchell 2000, 97). Long before he married Laura Welch, George W. was engaged to Cathy Wolfson. She was a Smith College student as George W.'s mother had been. George W. was twenty years old at the time of the engagement, the same age as his father had been when he married Barbara. George W. and his fiancée made the decision to get engaged at Christmastime, the same time of year that his parents had wed. And their plan was to spend senior year in New Haven, where George W. was at Yale, just as his parents had done.
27. Parmet 2001, 37, 65.
28. Bruni 2002, 134–35.
29. Parmet 2001, 40, 41, 66.

30. The quotes in this paragraph are all drawn from Minutaglio (1999).
31. Ibid., 13.
32. Ibid., 180.
33. Ibid., 188.
34. Ibid., 7.
35. Ibid., 153.
36. Ibid., 276.
37. Bruni 2002, 216.
38. Bush 1999a, 183.
39. Radcliffe 1989, 67.
40. Kilian 2002, 99.
41. Quoted in Kilian 2002, 50.
42. Barbara Bush quoted in Lardner and Romano 1999a, A1.
43. Quoted in Lardner and Romano 1999a.
44. Bruni 2002, 142.
45. Bush 1999a, 26; see also Mitchell 2000, 296.
46. Romano and Lardner 1999, A1.
47. Beshear 1989; see also Minutaglio 1999, 243; Mitchell 2000, 252.
48. Quoted in Kilian 2002, 52.
49. Bush 1999a, 14.
50. Quoted in Lardner and Romano 1999a.
51. Ibid.
52. Bush 1999a, 15.
53. Quoted in Lardner and Romano 1999a, A1; see also B. Bush 1994, 45.
54. Colloff 1999.
55. The title of the part of newspaper series on George W. that deals with this tragedy was "Tragedy Created Mother-Son Bond."
56. B. Bush 1994, 47.
57. Ibid.
58. Kilian 2002, 41.
59. Bruni 2002, 65–66.
60. Bush 2001e, 374.
61. Romano and Lardner 1999c; Heclo 2003, 36; Mitchell 1999, 36.
62. Minutaglio 1999, 13–14; emphasis mine.
63. Bush 1999a, 51–54.
64. Ibid., 53.
65. Ibid., 54.
66. Ibid., 52.
67. Quoted in Stevenson 2004.
68. Mitchell 2000, 170.
69. Quoted in Romano and Lardner 1999b.
70. After his father lost his reelection campaign to Bill Clinton, George W. began to train hard for the Houston-Tenneco marathon, every day, rain or shine.
71. Wischnia and Carrozza 2003; emphasis mine.
72. Ibid.
73. Quoted in Lardner and Romano 1999b.
74. A more detailed examination of Mr. Bush's time at Harvard can be found elsewhere. Solomon 2000; Minutaglio 1999, 31, 145–63.
75. Hollandsworth 1999.

76. Quoted in Minutaglio 1999, 148.
77. Bush 1999a, 3; Berka 1999.
78. Quoted in Gerhart 2004, 49.
79. Quoted in Anderson 2002, picture caption 27.
80. Roberts 1999.
81. Bush 1999a, 80–81.
82. Walters 2001; see also Woodward 2003, 171.
83. Quoted in Mitchell 2000, 163.
84. Bruni 2002, 179.
85. Ibid., 3.
86. George W.'s experience includes the following: worked on his father's unsuccessful campaign for the Senate, 1964 (George W. is 18); worked on his father's successful campaign for Congress, 1966 (George W. is 20); worked on his father's
successful reelection campaign for Congress, 1968 (George W. is 22); worked on
his father's unsuccessful campaign for U.S. Senate, 1970 (George W. is 24); considered run for Texas State Legislature, 1971 (George W. is 25); toured Texas in
1976 for Gerald Ford's presidential campaign (George W. is 30); attended GOP
candidate school, 1976; worked for GOP candidate Edward J. Gurney in Florida,
1977 (George W. is 31); ran for congressional seat, 1978 (George W. is 32);
worked on his father's 1980 presidential race (W. is 34); worked on the U.S. Senate race in Alabama of Winston Blout, 1981 (W is 35); worked on his father's
1984 reelection campaign (W. is 39); campaigned for his Yale friend Victor Ashe
running for U.S. senator in Tennessee, 1984; served as senior advisor to his father's successful presidential campaign, 1987–88 (W. is 41); considers, but decided against, run for Texas governorship in 1989 (W. is 42); served as campaign
advisor (not in Washington) to father's unsuccessful presidential reelection campaign, 1992 (W. is 45); runs for, and wins office, as Texas governor, 1994 (W. is
47); re-elected Texas governor, 1998 (W. is 51); runs for, and wins, the presidency,
1999–2000 (W. is 53).
87. Minutaglio 1999, 75.
88. Ibid., 140–41.
89. Helco 2003, 37.
90. Minutaglio 1999, 190.
91. Mitchell 2000, 179–81; Romano and Lardner 1999b.
92. Quoted in Neal 2000a.
93. Bruni 2002, 108.
94. Kristoff 2000b; Mitchell 2000, 1050.
95. Mitchell 2000, 205.
96. Bush 1999a, 135.
97. Ibid.
98. Ibid., 133–37
99. George W. stopped smoking the same way he stopped drinking. First, he told his
wife he was going to do so. Then he quit cold.
100. Mitchell 2000, 204; Minutaglio 1999, 210.
101. Minutaglio 1999, 171.
102. Bruni 2002, 179. In one interview, Laura Bush did admit that she had confronted
her husband with a stark choice regarding his drinking, but then quickly downplayed it.

MS. ROBERTS: It sounds like you've both been there. He's been quoted as say-
ing that you said, "It's either me or Jim Beam."
LAURA BUSH: Well, that was a joke. Of course I didn't really say that.
BARBARA BUSH: You didn't? [Laughter.]

Roberts 1999; see also Anderson 2003, 146, for a somewhat fanciful version of
this event.

103. Mitchell 2000, 203; Romano and Lardner 1999a; Anderson 2003, 146.
104. Romano and Lardner 1999a.
105. Bush 1999a, 136.
106. Mitchell 2000, 206, 248, 262.
107. Bill Keller (2003) has argued that "the essential fact about Mr. Bush is that God
was his 12-step program. At the age of 40, Mr. Bush beat a drinking problem by
surrendering to a powerful religious experience, reinforced by Bible study with
friends. This kind of born-again epiphany is common in much of America—the
red-state version of psychotherapy—and it creates the kind of faith that is not
beset by doubt because the believer knows his life got better in the bargain." This
is only half right. While George W. found faith, in addition to his faith in a personal God, he also found faith in himself and in his own inner strength.
108. Quoted in Romano and Lardner 1999a.
109. Levinson 1978.
110. Minutaglio 1999, 80, 84–97.
111. Cited in Romano and Lardner 1999a.
112. Minutaglio 1999, 239–40; Mitchell 2000, 239–44.
113. Romano and Lardner 1999a.
114. On the debate, see Mitchell 2000, 248–49.
115. Bush 1999a, 198.
116. Patoski 1999.
117. Quoted in Patoski 1999.
118. Quoted in Minutaglio 1999, 235–36.
119. Ibid., 241; see also Mitchell 2000, 253.
120. Quoted in Pooley 1999.
121. Minutaglio 1999, 242.
122. Ibid., 270.
123. Ibid., 274.
124. Quoted in Romano and Lardner 1999c, A1.
125. Quoted in Romano and Lardner 1999c, A1; emphasis mine.

NOTES TO CHAPTER 3

1. Jones 1994, 1.
2. Renshon 1998b.
3. Kohut 1971; 1977.
4. CNN interview 1999.
5. Dewar 2003; Mollison 2003.
6. Quoted in Minutaglio 1999, 85.
7. Seib 2002, A24.
8. Minutaglio 1999, 277–79; Mitchell 2000, 304–5.

9. Adam Clymer (2001) wrote, "During both of Mr. Bush's terms as governor, the issues he pushed were the same ones he embraced during his campaigns, much as his
speech to the Congress tonight echoed his presidential campaign themes of education reform, big tax cuts and support for so-called faith-based charitable organizations. In Texas, his strategy of hewing to a few issues allowed him to receive credit
for legislative accomplishments like education spending, tort reform and lower
property taxes, and by not becoming embroiled in too many legislative fights."

10. Clymer 2001.

11. Broder 2001b, A24.

12. Milbank 2001.

13. Broder 2001c, B07.

14. Cooper 2001.

15. To these he might have added an unexpected and controversial initiative to "regu-
larize" the status of millions of illegal immigrants in this country (Schmitt 2001); a
major plan for a "new federalism" (Allen and Balz 2001); a new civics and history
education initiative (Bush 2002u, 1516); a new initiative to provide housing for the
disabled (Allen 2001a); a new plan to enforce and refine gun control; a "New Freedom Initiative" to help the disabled (Hunt 2001b); and a review of a host of regulatory rules in areas including ergonomics (Dewar and Skyrzycki 2001), medical
records privacy (Pear 2001a), and a number of areas in environmental enforcement
including air pollution (Pianin and Mintz 2001), land usage and control (Jehl
2001), and the reform of the Endangered Species Act (Seelye 2001a).

16. *Washington Post* columnist Joe Klein (2003) characterized the president's agenda
"as a joke. . . . There is no program—except for the never-ending quest for unwarranted (and unwanted, if the polls are right) tax cuts and a quietly corrosive effort
to undermine existing government rules and regulations."

17. Balz and Neal 2000.

18. Bruni 2000d.

19. Quoted in the Associated Press 1999.

20. Kristof 2000c.

21. Bruni 2000d.

22. Carelson 1999, 104.

23. Stevens 2001, 125.

24. A list of Mr. Bush's policies or orders that have angered parts of his conservative
base would include the following: (1) The president's support of a large expansion
of government, something that traditionally has been anathema to conservatives
(Goldberg 2003; Broder 2003); (2) Support for increased government spending,
not all of it by any means earmarked for defense. In one two-month stretch after effectively wrapping up the GOP nomination in March 2000, Bush rolled out $60
billion worth of social and education proposals (Neal 2003). According to one
budget analyst using figures from the Office of Management and Budget, spending
under Mr. Bush showed an average rate of spending growth in constant dollars of
4.7 percent. Under former president Clinton, it averaged 1.5 percent; under Bush's
father the average was 1.9 percent; under Reagan 2.6 percent; under Carter 4.2 percent; under Nixon 3 percent; and 5.1 percent under Kennedy and Johnson; (3) He
has pushed a major extension of Medicare and a large new drug payment entitlement program, leading one senior GOP member of Congress, Jeff Flake (R-AZ), to
complain, "we've abandoned our principles" (Eilperin 2003); (4) Mr. Bush announced rules easing the introduction of generic-brand drugs. Large pharmaceuti-

cal companies had strongly opposed this initiative (Stevenson 2003) and sued the Bush administration to overturn his decision (Luck 2001). The United States also did not pursue trade sanctions again poor countries that violated international patent agreements regarding AIDS medicine (McNeil 2001); (5) President Bush urged Congress to fight AIDS internationally with a $15-billion plan that advocates condom use and in effect permits money to go to groups that promote abortion, making clear that his credentials as a "compassionate conservative" were of greater concern in this instance than fear of aggravating part of his conservative base; (Bumiller 2003a); (6) Mr. Bush supported a ban on assault weapons, a position that put him at odds with the National Rifle Association (NRA), which had strongly supported him (Lichtblau 2003b); (7) In addition to providing more funding to the United Nations, President Bush decided against withholding dues in retaliation for America's ouster from a seat on the Human Rights Commission (Sipress and Eilperin 2001); (8) Mr. Bush proposed a $560 million dollar allocation for nationwide volunteer programs which incurred the wrath of then-House Majority Leader Dick Armey and other congressional conservatives (Sammon and Boyer 2002); (8) Despite "a fierce lobbying effort by conservative Republicans and some coal, oil and industry groups, which are urging Mr. Bush to abandon his campaign stance and any mention of carbon dioxide," Mr. Bush pledged cuts in emissions from older coal-burning power plants (Revkin 2001); (9) He imposed "Over the fierce objections of the long-haul trucking industry and Republican lawmakers, including Speaker J. Dennis Hastert . . . hefty new penalties for the makers of diesel engines that do not reduce their emission pollutants by October" (Seelye 2002); (10) He angered his conservative allies by choosing moderates over conservatives in a number of GOP primaries nationwide (Allen 2002); (11) The Bush Justice Department filed suits against Florida and three other states for violation of the Voting Rights Act in failing to provide sufficient English-language assistance to minorities, among other failings (Kulish and Spors 2002); (12) The Bush administration intervened "on the side of workers and environmentalists" in a four-year-old lawsuit over alleged environmental abuses at a Kentucky factory that once produced enriched uranium for the U.S. nuclear arsenal (Warrick 2003); (13) Complaints by conservatives that the president has placed politics before principle in not taking a stand against affirmative action (Eastland 2003); (14) Conservatives complained about the president's support of a Medicare bill that lacked the essential market mechanisms that they thought critical (Goldstein 2003 A08). This led to a revolt by conservative congressmen and their allies like the *Wall Street Journal* (Editorial 2003); (15) Mr. Bush disappointed members of the "isolationist" wing of the Republican party by making it very clear the United States must be internationalist in perspective; (16) In an unprecedented opinion piece, entitled "The Bush Betrayal," the libertarian president of the CATO Institute said that the president had abandoned his principles in supporting new entitlements and larger government (Boaz 2003 B07; Bandow 2003; see also Milbank 2003); (17) Mr. Bush warned Taiwan against holding a referendum and unambiguously asserting its "One China" policy. This provoked a furious reaction from conservative critics of Beijing, who had strongly supported Bush's invasion of Iraq and his vow to further a "world democratic movement" (Milbank and Kessler 2003).

25. Lambro 2002.
26. Kristof 2000c At one point, an attorney for Pat Robertson, founder of the Christian Coalition, contacted Bush's General Counsel Al Gonzales, to ask about

clemency for Tucker. After a front-page *New York Times* article described the intense political pressure Bush was under and appeared to suggest that he might bow to this pressure, Bush told a concerned Al Gonzales: "Don't worry, Al. . . . We'll do the right thing when the time comes" (Bush 1999a, 146).

27. Kristof 2000b, A23.
28. Mitchell 2000, 46–72.
29. Minutaglio 1999, 95; Mitchell 2000, 86–113.
30. Powell 1999.
31. Bush 2001w, 1308.
32. Bruni 2002, 24–25.
33. Bush 2001c, 346.
34. B. Bush 1994, 414.
35. Bruni 2002, 4.
36. Ibid., 26.
37. Ibid., 19.
38. Ibid., 20.
39. Ibid.
40. The documentary, entitled "Travels with George," was shown on HBO (*Washington Post* 2002, C01). The dialogue reported is my transcription of the relevant portion from the film.
41. Woodward 2001, 71–72.
42. Minutaglio 1999, 207; emphasis mine.
43. Mitchell 2000, 203; Bush 1999a, 64.
44. Maraniss 1995, 388.
45. Quoted in Maraniss 1995, 389.
46. Bush 2002g, 572.
47. Ibid.
48. Bush 2001r, 1147; emphasis mine.
49. Carlson 1999, 108. Bush later said he had been misquoted. Yet it is consistent with Mr. Bush's tendency for sharp, sometimes sarcastic tartness and his dislike of celebrity campaigns.
50. Hamburger and Hitt 2003.
51. Stolberg 2003.
52. Milbank and VandeHei 2003.
53. Ibid.
54. Neustadt 1990, 89–89.
55. Horney 1930.
56. Renshon 1998, chapter 10.
57. Lewis 2001.
58. Bush 200ln, 947; see also Bush 2002j, 868; Bush 2003n, 1278.
59. Bush 2001t, 1216.
60. Bush 2002h, 689.
61. Martin 2003.
62. Bush 2003n, 1278; emphasis added.
63. Elsewhere Putin said, "We have many points of coincidence of our views on many issues. *And it is precisely these things that enable me to call President Bush my friend,* not only personally—because personally, I do like him a lot, but as my counterpart and the President of a friendly nation." (Quoted in Bush 2003f, 708; emphasis mine).

64. George 1980, 22, 93–94; Janis 1972; T' Hart 1990.
65. Hallow 1999.
66. Krauthammer 2004.
67. Asked about turning points in the war and working with allies, Donald Rumsfeld said "Another key turning point was the decision that *we would not have a single coalition* but rather we would use floating coalitions or multiple coalitions and recognize that because this would be long, because it would be difficult, and because different countries have different circumstances, different perspectives and different problems, that we needed their help on a basis that they were comfortable giving it to us and we should not, ought not, and do not expect everyone to do everything. And that's fine. So if someone wants to help in this way but not that, that's fair enough. The critical element of that is that that way *the mission determines the coalition.* The opposite of that would be if the coalition determined the mission. Once you allow the coalition to determine the mission, whatever you do gets watered down and inhibited so narrowly that you can't really accomplish, you run the risk of not being able to accomplish those things that you really must accomplish. That was an important decision it seems to me." (Interview 2001; italics mine). I would like to thank Tom Ricks, the senior *Washington Post* reporter who directed me to this interview. *Washington Post,* "Text: Interview with Donald Rumsfeld," December 10 2001 (www.washingtonpost.com/wpsrv/nation/specials/attacked/transcripts/rumsfeldinterview_121001.html, December 20, 2001).
68. A partial list can be found in the *Wall Street Journal* editorial "The New Multilateralism" (January 8, 2004).

NOTES TO CHAPTER 4

1. Associated Press 2002; De Young 2002.
2. Bush 2002t, 1532.
3. Hook 2003.
4. These include Miguel Estrada, Priscilla Owen, William Prior, Carolyn Kuhn, and Henry Saad.
5. Lewis 2003.
6. Editorial 2003.
7. Other examples include Mr. Bush's three tax cuts (Barnes 2003) and his decision to put gaining control of the Senate front and center in the 2004 midterm elections at a time that he was preparing the public for a possible war with Iraq, and others (Milbank 2002).
8. An exception appears to be Mr. Bush penchant for candies (Mansfield 2003, 173; Milbank 2003, A26).
9. Mitchell 2000, 307.
10. Quoted in Kurtz 2003.
11. Seelye 2003.
12. *New York Times* 2002.
13. CBS 2003.
14. Crowley 2003.
15. Apple 2002.
16. Quoted in Apple 2002.
17. Bush 2003j, 1038.
18. Mitchell 2000, 151.

19. Quoted in Woodward 2002, 158.
20. Bush 2001g, 561; Sanger 2001.
21. Bush 2001h, 577.
22. Quoted in Woodward 2002, 27.
23. Hume, 2002.
24. Bush 2001v, 1303.
25. Bush quoted in Noonan 2003b, 130.
26. Quoted in Woodward 2002, 168.
27. On November 17, he literally yelled at Secretary Powell, "barking orders" (Woodward 2002, 98). He demanded the secretary immediately issue an ultimatum to the Taliban to turn over Osama bin Laden, or else.
28. Woodward 2002, 145.
29. Ibid., 144–45.
30. Ibid., 62.
31. Ibid., 144.
32. Ibid., 1450.
33. Quoted in Woodward 2002, 145.
34. Woodward 2002, 74.
35. Ibid., 158.
36. Ibid., 152.
37. Ibid., 153.
38. Ibid., 917.
39. Milbank 2001.
40. Quoted in Allen 2001.
41. Neustadt 1990, 130.
42. Allen 2002, A01.
43. Allen 2001a, A02.
44. Broder and Goldstein 2003.
45. Hult (2003, 56, n. 12), in her study of policymaking in the Bush White House, mentions two major ones: the "strategy group" that meets twice a week to generate ideas and the Office of Strategic Initiatives, charged with developing longer-term ideas.
46. This analysis of Mr. Clinton draws on Renshon (1998).
47. Drew 1994, 83.
48. Quoted in Page 1993, 70.
49. Bruce Lindsey, senior presidential aide, quoted in Drew (1994, 134–35; emphasis mine).
50. Drew 1994, 340; Ifil 1993, A28.
51. Woodward 2002, 137.
52. *New York Times* 2001.
53. Quoted in Davis, Hitt, and Murray 2003.
54. Another example of timing is the senior's drug discount card that is part of the newly passed Medicare Bill. It will be distributed in the early fall of 2004, just as the presidential election gets under way (Lambro 2003).
55. Pew 2004.
56. Stevens 2001, 102, 127. Others agree. A *Washington Post* headline on Mr. Bush's stance as he faced criticism on his Iraq policy was titled: "Problems Abound, but Bush Stays Confident" (Balz 2003a, A01).
57. Bruni 2002, 44.

58. Bruni 2002, 46.
59. Keen, Welch, and Stone 2003.
60. Daalder and Lindsay 2003a, 136.
61. Fineman 2003; see also Gergen 2003.
62. Neal and Romano 2000, A01.
63. Rich 2001.
64. Dowd 2003.
65. Quoted in Kornblut 2003.
66. *New York Observer,* 2004.
67. Quoted in Parmett 2001, 23.
68. Bush 1999a, 167
69. Bruni 2002, 140.
70. Mitchell (2000; 206, 248, 262) says that before his real successes, George W. "never seemed to acknowledge adequately the roll of the carpetlayers in his life."
71. Mitchell 2000; Minutaglio 1999.
72. Bush 2002w, 1999.
73. Quoted in Woodward 2002, 100.
74. Clinton 2001; see also Krauthammer 2001.
75. Allen 2003a, A06.
76. Bruni 2002, 226.
77. Broder 2001c, B07.
78. Quoted in Woodward 2000, 120.
79. Bush 2003o, 1401.
80. Bush 2001t, 1217.
81. Bush 2001w, 1307–8.
82. Bruni 2002, 203, emphasis in original.
83. Bush interview, *Washington Post*, 1999; emphasis mine.
84. Milbank 2002, A15. He later confirmed it at a town meeting in Orlando: "I was quoted in the press the other day as saying I haven't regretted one thing I've decided. And that's the truth. Every decision I made I stand by. And I'm proud of the decisions I've made" (Bush 2001bb, 1754).
85. Walters 2003.
86. Woodward 2002, 257.
87. Quoted in Woodward 2002, 259; see also Keen 2003.
88. Woodward 2002, 259. Woodward notes that Colin Powell told him that he (Powell) "had counted seven editorials calling for his resignation or implying that he should quit" because he was being disloyal to the president's positions, a criticism he said was not true (Woodward 2002, 345). Secretary Powell obviously is paying close attention to what he being said about him and is upset by it.
89. Ibid., 258.
90. Ibid., 259.
91. Ibid., 262.
92. Quoted in Isaacson 2000; see also *Meet the Press,* November 21, 2000.
93. Minutaglio 1999, 48.
94. Ibid., 56–58.
95. Quoted in Minutaglio 1999, 62.
96. Mitchell 2000, 61.
97. The section that follows draws on Mitchell 2000, 314–26 and Minutaglio 1999, 301–7.

98. Mitchell 2000, 318.
99. Ibid., 326.
100. Ibid., 325.
101. Ibid., 215.
102. Stevens 2001, 89–92.
103. Bruni 2002, 184–85; see also Stevens 2001, 177.
104. Stevens 2001, 194–95.

NOTES TO CHAPTER 5

1. Bush 2001bb, 1753.
2. Ibid.
3. Ibid., emphasis mine.
4. Bush 2002a, 17; emphasis mine.
5. Quoted in Balz and Woodward 2002, A01.
6. Quoted in AEI transcript, 2001.
7. Psychologically, good judgment reflects a set of composite skills. Among them are the ability to:
   1. See the framing decision for the crucial choice point that it represents;
   2. Understand the essential elements of a problem and their significance, and place it within an appropriate judgment framework;
   3. Consider and reflect on the range of issues and values raised by the situation in order to adequately deal with the various interests (political, social, and psychological) involved;
   4. Consider and reflect on information which is frequently limited and often discordant;
   5. Make use of, but not be subservient to, feeling or impulse, including the anxiety generated by uncertainty and high risk;
   6. Place these considerations in a framework of understanding that adequately assesses the basic nature of the problem and points to a range of responses that preserve, and even perhaps advance, the values and interests at risk to develop a fitting solution;
   7. Draw on the understanding of the past and present (point 1) to consider how alternative choices will shape the future (the extrapolation of implications).

   Interested readers are referred elsewhere (Renshon 1998, chapter 8) for a more technical discussion of the elements and their relationship to character psychology and presidential leadership.
8. Renshon 1998b, chapter 8.
9. Daalder and Lindsay 2003a, 135.
10. Bush 2002a, 17.
11. Quoted in Woodward 2002, 137; see also, 145, 168.
12. Bush 2001e, 374.
13. Mitchell 2000, 289; emphasis added.
14. Quoted in Harris and Balz 2001. In an interview with the *New York Times,* Bush said, "Incumbents have to project into the future, offer a fresh vision. My father didn't do it." Quoted in Mitchell 2000, 255.
15. Bush 2001y, 1368; emphasis mine.
16. Quoted in Sciolino 2001.
17. Myre 2002.

18. Bush 2002g, 572; see also Bush 2002b, 195.
19. Bush 2003d, 677.
20. Quoted in the *Washington Post,* 2002, C1.
21. Bush 1999a, 115.
22. Quoted in Shapiro 1999; emphasis mine.
23. Bush 2003h, 719.
24. Woodward 2004, 66.
25. Berke 2000; Merida 2000.
26. Suskind 2004; Milbank 2004.
27. VonDrehle 2003, A01.
28. Schneider 2003.
29. Slevin 2003, A01.
30. Woodward 2002, 343.
31. Ibid., 80.
32. Ibid.
33. Ibid., 344.
34. Bush 2002w, 2002.
35. Ibid., 2006–2007.
36. Powell 2003.
37. Jervis 2003, 383.
38. Bush 2002w, 2002.
39. Jervis 2003, 373.
40. Lefkowitz 2003.
41. Powell 2001.
42. Berke 2000.
43. Bush 2003h, 721.
44. Quoted in Berke 2000.
45. Editorial 2004.
46. Quoted in Shesgreen 2003; emphasis mine.
47. *New York Times* editorial, 2004.
48. Broder 2004, B07.
49. Gardner quoted in Merida 2000; see also Gardner 1993.
50. Bush 2003h, 721.
51. Bush quoted in Smith and Walsh 2001.
52. Bush quoted in Hume 2003.
53. Quoted in Woodward 2002, 106; emphasis mine.
54. Quoted in Woodward, 2002, 307.
55. Quoted in Woodward 2002, 235.
56. Quoted in Woodward 2002, 235.
57. Quoted in Woodward 2002, 244.
58. Quoted in Woodward 2004, 140; see also Woodward 2004,11.
59. Chandrasekaran and Slevin 2003.
60. Graham 2003.
61. Brinkley 2003.
62. Berke 2000.
63. Bruni and Schmitt 1999, A30.
64. Mitchell 2000, 333.
65. Sanger and Myers 2001.
66. Quoted in McGeary 2001.

67. Quoted in Woodward 2002, 134.
68. Quoted in Woodward 2002, 164.
69. Quoted in Woodward 2002 164.
70. Quoted in Woodward 2002, 218.
71. Woodward 2002, 195; emphasis mine.
72. Woodward 2004, 384.
73. Ibid., 249.
74. Balz and Neal 2000.
75. Sanger 2001; Hoagland 2002.
76. Quoted in Woodward, 2002, 130.
77. Quoted in Woodward 2002, 131.
78. Quoted in Licthblau 2004.
79. Friedman 2003b.
80. Woodward 2002, 79.
81. Bush 2003b, 438; emphasis mine.
82. Weisman 2003.
83. Sawyer 2003.
84. In previous testimony before the 9/11 commission, National Security Adviser Condoleezza Rice had fleshed out the context of that quote, pointing out that Bush was comparing his feeling before the September 11th attacks with how he felt afterward. Mr. Bush repeated this understanding in response to the question, whereupon Ms. Bumiller, clearly not satisfied, asked him the same question about taking personal responsibility again.
85. Transcript, President's News Conference, p. A12.
86. Woodward 2002, 95–96.
87. Ibid., 261–62.
88. Friedman 2003b.
89. Friedman 2003b.
90. Woodward 2002, 344–46; emphasis mine.
91. Ibid., 163; emphasis mine.
92. Bush 1999a, 97.
93. Cummings 2001.
94. Quoted in Berke 2003, 323.
95. Bush 1999a, 97; see also Berke 2003, 321.
96. Mr. Bush established a system so that five aides—National Security Advisor Rice, former Communications Director Karen Hughes, Political Aide Karl Rove, Chief of Staff Andrew H. Card, Jr., and Press Secretary (at the time of the interview) Ari Fleischer—could see him on the spur of the moment (Woodward 2002, A01).
97. In domestic policy, Josh B. Bolton (Office of Management and Budget), Micheal Levitt, (Environmental Protection Agency), Tommy Thompson (Health, Education and Welfare), Rod Paige (Education), Elaine Chow (Labor), John Ashcroft (Justice), Don Evans (Commerce), and Gail Norton (Interior) are solidly in that center-right range of views. In foreign policy, Donald Rumsfeld (Defense) and Colin Powell (State) also represent that same range of balance. Vice President Dick Cheney is a key advisor to the president on both domestic and foreign matters and leans towards the conservative right-of-center.
98. Gigot 2001; Broder 2001.
99. Dowd 2002.
100. Quoted in Smith and Walsh 2001; emphasis mine.

101. Bruni 2002, 245.
102. Woodward 2002, 176–83.
103. Transcript: Colin Powell 2002, emphasis mine.
104. Quoted in Shapiro 1999.
105. Transcript: *Meet the Press* 2001; emphasis mine.
106. Dowd 2000, 2001.
107. Cohen 2003b, A23.
108. Moore and Slater 2003.
109. Dubose, Reid, and Cannon 2003.
110. Quoted in Smith and Walsh 2001.
111. Bush 2001s, 1206.
112. Woodward 2002, 38.
113. Ibid., 49.
114. Ibid., 30.
115. Quoted in Woodward 2002, 145–46.
116. Bush 2002w, 2006; emphasis mine.
117. Chait 1999, 26–29.
118. Bruni 2000, 55.
119. Mitchell 2000.
120. Greenstein 1994.
121. Bush 2003e, 689.
122. Bush 2002p, 1193.
123. Quoted in Kristoff and Bruni, 2000.
124. Mitchell 2000, 316.
125. Woodward 2004, 102; 249, respectively.
126. Merida 2000.
127. Diehl 2004, A23.
128. Goldberg 2004.
129. Shapiro 2003.
130. All quotes from the president's news conference in this section can be found in transcript, president's news conference, *New York Times,* April 14, 2004, A12-A13.
131. Fassihi, Farnaz, Gred Jaffe, Yaroslav Trofimov, Carla Anne Robbins, and Yochi J. Dreazen 2004, A1.
132. Shanker 2004, A1.
133. Vick 2004, A12.
134. Kay quoted in Schweid, 2003.
135. Transcript, president's news conference, p. A13.
136. Kay quoted in transcript, "NewsHour interview with David Kay," 2004.
137. Quoted in Kurtz 2004.
138. Quoted in Ollove 2004.

NOTES TO CHAPTER 6

1. Harwood and Cummings, 2001.
2. Brody 2001, 2003.
3. Brody writes (2001, 25; see also Jacobson 2003) that in the first seven weeks of his presidency between 70 percent and 75 percent of those expressing views rated Mr. Bush positively. Yet, "Over the next ten weeks, from early March to mid-May, the

level of 'relative approval' dropped eight-plus percentage points. The polls for the remainder of May and for the last three weeks of June showed further five to seven point erosion in his level of relative support. President Bush finished his first five months in office 17 percentage points of relative support below where he started. . . ."

4. Jones 2003, 175–76.
5. Frum 2003, 272.
6. Ibid., 274.
7. Barone 2004,
8. Carter, Deutch, and Zelikow 1998.
9. Beschloss 2001; Seib 2001; Editorial, 2001, A26; Broder 2001a, A31; Fineman 2001.
10. Berke 2001, Dec. 9; see also VandeHei, 2001. Mr. Bush's natural buoyancy returned by degrees in the post-9/11 period.
11. Fineman 2001; Howard Rosenberg, a reporter for the *Los Angeles Times* quoted in Harper 2001; Hunt 2001a.
12. Editorial 2001, A24.
13. Milbank 2001, A25.
14. Sanger and Bumiller 2001; Sanger and Van Natta 2001.
15. Fineman and Lipper 2002. Laura Bush said, "Well, I guess what I've noticed the most is the characteristics that I already knew he had." (quoted in Hume 2002). Karl Rove said, " I for one don't buy this theory that September 11th somehow changed George W. Bush . . . great events do not transform presidents" (American Enterprise Institute transcript, 3).
16. Bush 2001dd, 1830. Later the president clarified 9/11's impact when he said, "I don't think a single event can change anyone's basic values" (2002, 1194). Of course, the fact that his basic values have not changed does not mean other important elements of his psychology, including the understandings that frame his leadership and judgment, haven't.
17. Bush 2001w, 1307.
18. Bush 2003f, 1635; emphasis added.
19. Wildavsky 1966.
20. Bumiller 2002 A1.
21. "What an honor it is to walk into the Oval Office. . . . It's a honor that—it's hard for me to describe how—what an honor it is" (Bush, 2001n, 947). Or: "It's an unbelievable honor to represent the great people of this country, the greatest country on the face of the Earth . . ." (Bush 2001b, 321; see also Bush 2002n, 1046). One could cite many, many more such sentiments. While many presidents might feel it, Mr. Bush says it, often. Bruni referred to it as a "profound personalized patriotism that courses through much of what he did" (2002, 229).
22. How long would we be after them?, the president was asked. "As long as it takes," he replied (Bush 2001x, 1320). Asked the same question again, he replied, "The definition is, whatever it takes."
23. Bush 2003i, 959.
24. Woodward 2002, 39.
25. Ibid., 224.
26. Bush 2003a, 143–44; emphasis mine. See also Bush 2003m, 1265.
27. Quoted in Woodward 2002, 39; emphasis mine.
28. Senator Charles Schumer reported that the president told him that after 9/11 his life's work would never be the same, and that "he is staking his whole presidency

on this—that the mark of whether he's successful is in wiping out terrorism" (quoted in Bruni 2002, 248).

29. Quoted in Bruni 2002, 256.
30. Walters interview 2001.
31. Bush quoted in Goodstein 2000.
32. Sawyer interview, 2003.
33. Quoted in Pfaff 2000
34. Brokaw interview 2003.
35. Quoted in Bruni 2002, 247; emphasis mine.
36. Quoted in Bruni 2002, 107, 109.
37. Burns 1978, 1.
38. Freud 1920.
39. Brooks 2003, A19.
40. Bush 2003o, 1398.
41. Bush 2001p, 1049.
42. Bush 2002b, 194.
43. At a town hall meeting, Mr. Bush had the following exchange; asked abut the role of government in helping people, Mr. Bush said, "Look, the government can never guarantee success in the private sector. That's not what happens in a system based on free enterprise. We can help people but there are no guarantees about business" (Bush 2001bb, 1747).
44. Recall Bush's speech to the United Nations in which he appealed to their pride (and vanity) as an organization founded on the hope that its "deliberations would be more than talk" and its resolutions "more than wishes." He reminded the United Nations that Iraq's conduct was a threat to its authority and, by implication, to its legitimacy and continued relevance. In short, he asked the United Nations to act as seriously as it wished to be taken.
45. Woodward 2002, 244.
46. Bush 2002g, 575.
47. Editorial 2001, A24
48. Quoted in Babington and Milbank 2001.
49. Milbank and Kessler 2003.
50. Bush 2002j, 870, 871.
51. Walters 2001.
52. Woodward 2002, 117; see also 107, 329.
53. Quoted in Woodward 2002, 340.
54. The same is true of Iran, also a charter member of the "axis of evil." Yet no discernible steps have been taken against that country other than to get the United Nations to declare it out of compliance with its nuclear program treaty obligations.
55. Brownstein 2001.
56. Quoted in Tyler 2002.
57. Schlesinger 2003.
58. Schlesinger 1973, 182–84.
59. Ibid., 185–87.
60. Ibid., 187–88.
61. Ibid., 189.
62. Ibid., 220.
63. Ibid., 216, 220.
64. Ibid., 221.
65. Ibid., 227.

66. Ibid., 233.
67. Ibid., 235–39.
68. Ibid., 242–43.
69. Ibid., 246–47.
70. Ibid., 256–57.
71. Ibid., 379.
72. Ibid., 378–79, 202.
73. Gaddis 2004.
74. I am indebted to Jonathan Renshon for this observation.
75. Brace and Hinckley 1992.
76. Smith and Walsh 2001. Elsewhere, George W. noted, "Dad never spent the capital he earned from the success of Desert Storm. . . . I learned you must spend political capital when you earn it, or it withers and dies" (Bush, 1999a, 185–86).
77. Barbara Bush confirmed these conversations (Bumiller 2003c, A18).
78. Hume 2003.

NOTES TO CHAPTER 7

1. Bush 2003p, 1602; see also Bush 2003q, 1632.
2. Bush 1999a, 44–45.
3. Bush 2003p, 1602.
4. The picture is reproduced on the back jacket of the autobiography.
5. Bush 1999a, back book jacket.
6. Hume 2000; emphasis mine.
7. Bush 2002m, 917.
8. Bush 2001a, 271.
9. Woodward 2002, 136.
10. Ibid., 341.
11. Smith and Walsh 2001.
12. Woodward 2002, 137; emphasis mine.
13. Ibid., 144.
14. Ibid., 281.
15. Ibid., 341.
16. Bush 2001a, 271.
17. Bush 2003q, 1632. This principle might appear redundant since leadership is about leading, but Bush's emphasis here is on the principle is on *doing it*— a specific commitment to action, not a set of abstract understandings.
18. Bush news conference transcript, A13.
19. Bush 2001cc, 1816.
20. Bush 2003k, 1212.
21. Bush 2001i, 601.
22. Bush 2001f, 414.
23. Bush 2001l, 789.
24. Carlson 1999, 108.
25. Bush 2001aa 1459.
26. Bush 2001cc, 1817.
27. Woodward 2002, 111.
28. Ibid., 327.
29. Jones 2003, 193–94.
30. Ibid., 182–83.

31. Milbank and Eilperin 2001, A09. This is a much sanitized reprise of a similar and legendary interchange between Democratic Lt. Governor Bob Bullock and Mr. Bush. When Mr. Bush first took office, Texas was dominated by democrats, and the most dominating democrat was Mr. Bullock, a tough, savvy chain-smoking, hard-drinking politico who gave no quarter to his enemies and little to his friends to get what he wanted done in the legislature. Bush went out of his way to establish a relation with the Lt. governor, whom many saw as the most powerful man in the state. The two worked together on legislation and this was the origin of Mr. Bush's bipartisan credentials. Yet, one morning in 1997 at a meeting Bullock told Bush he planned to support a bill that Bush opposed. "I'm sorry governor," he said, "but I'm going to have to fu*k you on this one." Upon hearing this, Bush got up in front of all the assembled staff, grabbed Bullock by the shoulders, pulled him forward and kissed him, saying "if you're going to fu*k me, you'll have to kiss me first." Bush's irreverent, but pointed, spontaneity cemented their very productive political collaboration. See Carlson 1999, 104.

32. Bruni 2002, 67–68; Bruni 2000b, A23. Mr. Bush told reporters that he didn't sleep well away from home, one reason for his constant state of tiredness.

33. Bruni 2002, 81–82.

34. Ibid., 261–62.

35. Goldstein 2003.

36. Jehl 2003.

37. Arvedlund 2003.

38. Quoted in Bruni 2002, 248.

39. Quoted in Adler 1997.

40. Lewis 2001b, A27.

41. Friedman 2003a, A14.

42. Woodward 2002, 341.

43. Quoted in Woodward 2002, 281.

44. Murray 2003.

45. Brookheiser 2003.

46. Bush 2003h, 721.

47. Woodward 2002, 94. So too, Mr. Bush told Mr. Woodward that his provocative "dead or alive" statement regarding Osama bin Laden was "to let the public know where he was headed" (2002, 100). The day he used that phrase, he was about to sign an executive order lifting the ban on killing or capturing such persons worldwide.

48. Woodward 2002, 168. Mr. Bush understood enough about American public psychology to realize that public impatience was an issue. He told Bob Woodward that he told his advisors, "Look, don't get pressured into making irrational decisions. And don't worry about my second guessing what you do. Make the best decision you can and I'll protect our team as best as I can by explaining to the public that this is going to take a long time" (2002, 113).

49. Quoted in Woodward 2002, 49.

50. Woodward 2002, 99.

51. Quoted in Woodward 2002, 137; emphasis mine.

52. Brooks 2003, A19.

53. Bush 2002v, 1999.

54. Edwards 2004.

55. Maccaby 2000.

56. Edwards 2003.

57. Woodward 2004, 202; Bruni 2002, 34.

58. All of the questions in this paragraph are taken from Bush (2001j, 673).
59. Carlson 1999, 106.
60. Bruni 2002, 33–34.
61. Ibid., 34.
62. Ibid.
63. One reporter assigned to profile of Bush reported the following arms-length encounter (Carlson 1999, 106): "When he meets someone, Bush stands two paces back and stares. His eyes get beady. He doesn't seem eager or smile right away. When he talks it's sometimes in grunts and usually out of the side of his mouth. The effect is somewhat between the prelude to a bar fight—What'd you say?—and the way a close friend looks at you before telling you a secret, at once intimate and faintly menacing. It's weirdly compelling."
64. Bush 2001aa, 1459.
65. Bush 2003h, 725–26.
66. Quoted in Hunt 2003.
67. Bush 2003d, 677.
68. Bush 2003g, 710.
69. Bush 2003c, 477.
70. Bush 2002e, 451.
71. Pear 2001a.
72. Pear 2001c.
73. Cadwell and Wyatt, 2003.
74. B. Bush 2003, 7–8.
75. Quoted in Romano 2000a, A01.
76. Quoted in Romano 2000b, A37. Speaking of their friends, Laura Bush said, "They weren't our friends because his dad was the vice president. They were already our friends, we'd known them all of our lives. And I think there's a lot of security really in having that sort of history" (Quoted in Romano 2000a, A01).
77. Quoted in Romano 2000b, A37.

NOTES TO CHAPTER 8

1. Cooper 1999.
2. Balz 2000b, A01.
3. Pianin and Neal 1999.
4. Bruni 2000e, A18; Scarlett 2000.
5. This quote and those in the next two paragraphs are drawn from Bush (1999b).
6. Ibid.
7. Ibid.
8. Quoted in VandeHei 2004.
9. I don't use the term transformation here as Jim Burns did in characterizing a leader who "recognizes and exploits an existing need in his followers," and in doing so "may convert them to moral agents" (1978, 4).
10. Farrington 2003.
11. OMB Management Agenda 2002.
12. Ibid., 5.
13. Ibid.; see also Norton 2002.
14. Ibid., 6.
15. Vedantam 2003a, A01; Revkin 2003; OMB 2003.

16. Vedantam 2003a, A01.
17. Pianin 2003, A01.
18. Vedantam 2003b, A01.
19. Miller 2001.
20. Bravin 2002.
21. Preston 2002.
22. Scheffer 2002.
23. Jervis 2003, 384–86.
24. Daalder and Lindsay 2003a, 135; emphasis mine.
25. Ikenberry 2003, 50.
26. Simes 2003, 93; see also Mallaby, 2003; Ikenberry 2003.
27. Ikenberry 2003, 60.
28. Mead 2001; Gaddis 2004.
29. These figures are drawn from Rossett (2002, 2004).
30. Sachs 2004.
31. Bravin and Stecklow 2003.
32. Pisik 2003.
33. Jervis 2003, 366.
34. Daalder and Lindsay 2003b, 13, 40.
35. Ibid., 41–45, 188–200.
36. Berke 1994, A1.
37. Wilcox 1995, 1.
38. Verhovek 1994, A1.
39. Wilcox 1995, 1. Before the election that Democrats controlled 64 chambers, the Republicans 31 (3 were tied). After the election the figures were 49 and 46 respectively (again, with 3 tied). For the first time since Reconstruction, the number of Republican State Legislators (3,391) approached the number of their Democratic counterparts (3,847).
40. In North Carolina, for example, Republican county officials increased their numbers by 56 to 217 seats from 161. Of that state's 100 counties, Republicans became the majority in 42 local governments, up from the 27 they had controlled before the election (Smothers 1995, A16).
41. Renshon 1998a.
42. I have documented the specifics of these observations elsewhere (Renshon 1998a) and refer the interested reader there.
43. Mayhew 2002.
44. Lowi 1969.
45. Quoted in Brownstein 2003.
46. Dionne 2003, A31.
47. Pew 2003c, 90.
48. Pew 2002, 73.
49. Pew 2003c, 10.
50. Ibid., 17–18.
51. Ibid., 18; emphasis mine.
52. IOP 2003, 13.
53. Ibid., 17.
54. Schlesinger 1968, 1998; see also Schlesinger 1978.
55. Robertson 1993.
56. Greenberg 1998.

57. Tsongas 1995.
58. Greenberg and Skocpol 1997.
59. Klein 1995.
60. Darman 1995.
61. Judis 1995.
62. Daalder and Lindsay 2003b, 2.
63. Neal 2000b, A11.
64. Skowronek 1993, 41.
65. Blankley 2003.
66. Rice, testimony before the 9/11 commission, April 8, 2004.
67. *Los Angeles Times* 2003, 20.
68. Ibid. 2003, 3.
69. Figures in this paragraph are drawn from the *Washington Post*/ABC poll at:http://www.washingtonpost.com/wp-srv/politics/polls/vault/stories/trend041804.html (April 19, 2004).
70. *Los Angeles Times* 2003, 12.
71. Pew 2003, 12.
72. *Los Angles Times* 2003, 20.
73. Pew 2003, 12.
74. *The Washington Post,* April 5, 1998; see also Renshon 2002a, 2002b. Unless otherwise cited, all data drawn from *The Washington Post* polling results on the Clinton scandals can be found at: http://www.washingtonpost.com/wpsrv/politics/polls/vault/.
75. Renshon 2000.
76. Quoted in Swarns 2001.
77. Murray 2003; italics mine.
78. Hart and Teeter 2003, 9.
79. See Stevenson and Elder 2004. The complete survey can be found at: http://www.nytimes.com/2004/04/29/politics/29POLL.html.
80. Studies of the political development of children dating back to the 1960s confirm that the president is the object of first political attachment for children as young as six (cf. Hess and Easton 1960).
81. Yankelovich 1981, 88.
82. Wolfe 1998.
83. Quoted in Woodward 2002, 81.
84. Riesman 1950.
85. Bowman 2003b, 28.
86. CBS poll 2003.
87. This figure and those that follow in this paragraph are drawn from Bowman (2003b).
88. Taylor 2003.
89. Bowman 2003a.
90. The figures in the following three paragraphs are found in Bowman (2003b, 94–95). Readers should keep in mind that question wording influences results.

CHAPTER 9

1. Bruni 2002.
2. The exact George W. Bush quote is: "What I'm telling you is that freedom will prevail, so long as the United States and allies don't give the people of Iraq mixed

signals, so long as we don't cower in the face of suiciders, or do what many Iraqis still suspect might happen, and that is *to cut and run early, like happened in '91"* (Sammon 2004, 324).

3. Bruni (2000a) covered both men and wrote, "Vice President Al Gore comes off as one of the most ardent, ambitious aspirants to the Oval Office in quite some time, a man who would crawl across broken glass to get there. Mr. Bush comes off as a man who wants it, but not at any price, and sometimes not as much as he wants to wake up in his own bed at the Governor's Mansion in Austin, Tex., wander downstairs to make a pot of coffee, let out the pets and fetch the newspaper."

4. 1966; Shull 1991.

5. George Will (2001; see also Kahn 2001) notes another element of Mr. Bush's bifurcated leadership, "During the current war, Americans are told that it is patriotic to crank up consumption—to go to a mall, a movie and anywhere on a plane. This is the peculiar context in which the president is attempting bifurcated leadership. He must keep the country focused on war far away and involving, so far, few Americans in combat, but the country must also regain its jaunty equilibrium, meaning its money-spending ways."

6. Halbfinger 2004.

7. Editorial 2004, A22.

8. Beatty 2004.

9. Quoted in Dinan 2003.

10. *Washington Post* poll, "Bush as a Compassionate Conservative," March 20, 2004. http://www.washingtonpost.com/wp-srv/politics/polls/vault/stories/data031404.html.

11. Kennedy 1961.

12. Bush quoted in *New York Times* Interview, 2000.

13. Balz 2004.

14. George and George 1956.

15. Burke and Greenstein 1989.

16. Stevenson and Sanger 2004.

17. Noonan, Peggy. "Unhappy Warriors," *Wall Street Journal on Line,* April 15, 2004.

18. Sciolino 2004.

19. Van Natta, Jr. 2004.

20. J. Renshon 2004.

21. I take up the question of American national identity in a forthcoming book (Renshon 2005, in press).

22. Quoted in Bruni 2002, 222–23.

23. Bruni 2002, 233.

24. Ibid., 233.

25. Bush 1999a, 6.

26. Ibid., 14.

27. Quoted in Lardner and Romano 1999a, A1.

28. Bush 1999a, 15.

29. Benac 2000.

30. *New York Times,* Interview with Laura Bush, February 6, 2004.

31. Quoted in Lipper 2004.

BIBLIOGRAPHY

Abraham, Rick. *The Dirty Truth: The Oil and Chemical Dependency of George W. Bush.* Tex.: Mainstream Publishing Company, 2000.

Adler, Bill. *The Quotable Kennedys.* New York: Avon, 1997.

Allen, Mike. "Bush Names Iraqi Administrator." *Washington Post,* May 7, 2003b, A23.

———. "Bush Vetoes 'Hail to the Chief,' Preferring the Hum of Humility." *Washington Post,* February 4, 2003a, A06.

———. "Bush Faces Sustained Dissension on the Right 'A Sense of Disappointment Is Spreading." *Washington Post,* April 22, 2002, A01.

———. "Post Interview with President Bush." *Washington Post,* March 10, 2001b, A6.

———. "Kennedy Joins Bush in Unveiling Aid for Disabled." *Washington Post,* February 2, 2001a, A02.

———. "Democrats Stroke Hollywood at Dinner." *Washington Post,* September 20, 2000, A19.

Allen, Mike, and Dan Balz. "Bush Unveils 'New Federalism.'" *Washington Post,* February 27, 2001, A10.

Alterman, Eric, and Mark Green. *The Book on Bush: How George W. (Mis)leads America.* New York: Viking, 2004.

Alvarez Lizette. "Bush Faces New Dispute over Payment of U.N. Dues." *New York Times,* August 17, 2001, A9.

American Enterprise Institute (AEI)," A Discussion with Karl Rove," December 11, 2001. (http://www.aei.org., accessed December 15, 2001).

Anderson, Christopher. *George and Laura: Portrait of An American Marriage.* New York: William Morrow, 2002.

Apple, R. W., Jr. "Bush Presidency Seems to Gain Legitimacy." *New York Times,* September 16, 2001, A6.

———. "Recipe for a Stalemate." *New York Times,* November 9, 2000, A1.

Arvedlund, Erin E. "Allies Angered at Exclusion from Bidding." *New York Times,* December 11, 2003, A18.

Associated Press. "Bush Calls on U.N. to Show Backbone." September 14, 2002.

———. "U.S. Rejects Draft Enforcement Plan for 1972 Ban on Biological Weapons." *Wall Street Journal,* July 26, 2001, A1.

———. "Report: Gore Won Popular Vote by 539, 987." *Washington Post,* December 21, 2000, A09.

———. "Gore Offers Teacher Standards Plan." May 5, 2000.

———. "Bush again Lobs Criticism at His Own Party." October 6, 1999.

Babington, Charles. "Bush Moving in 'Landslide' Fashion." *Washington Post,* May 16, 2001.

Babington, Charles, and Dana Milbank. "Bush Advisers Try to Limit Damage, No Change in Policy Toward Taiwan." *Washington Post,* April 27, 2001, A19.

Balz, Dan. "Kerry Says Bush Stubbornness Hurts Troops." *Washington Post,* April 15, 2004, A02.

———. "Democrats Criticize President on Economy, Security." *Washington Post,* May 18, 2003b, A04.

———. "Problems Abound, but Bush Stays Confident." *Washington Post,* March 18, 2003a, A01.

———. "President's Words Belie His Tactics, Democrats Charge." *Washington Post,* March 4, 2001, A01.

———." Bush Maps His Changes for Social Security." *Washington Post,* May 16, 2000b, A01

———. "Race Still Too Close to Call." *Washington Post,* November 7, 2000a, A17.

Balz, Dan, and Claudia Deane. "Public Opinion on Bush Stabilizes." *Washington Post,* August 13, 2003, A01.

Balz, Dan, and Terry M. Neal. "Questions, Clues and Contradiction." *Washington Post,* October 22, 2000, A01.

Balz, Dan, and Bob Woodward. "10 Days in September: Inside the War Cabinet America's Chaotic Road to War Bush's Global Strategy Began to Take Shape in First Frantic Hours after attacks." *Washington Post,* January 27, 2002, A01.

Bandow, Doug. "Righteous Anger: The Conservative Case against George W. Bush." *The American Conservative,* December 1, 2003.

Barnes, Fred. "Taxing Issues." *Weekly Standard,* January 8, 2003.

Barone, Michael. "Bush's Reelection Campaign." *U.S. News and World Report,* February 25, 2004, 1710–16.

———. "The 49% Nation." *National Journal,* 33:23, June 8, 2001, 1710–16.

Beatty, Jack. "The Real, Real Deal." *The Atlantic Monthly* online, January 26, 2004, http://www.theatlantic.com (accessed March 5, 2004).

Begala, Paul. *It's Still the Economy Stupid: George W. Bush, America's CEO.* New York: Simon & Schuster Adult Publishing Group, 2002.

———. *Is our Children Learning: The Case against George W. Bush.* New York: Simon and Schuster, 2000.

Benac, Nancy. "George W. Bush: 'I Don't Fear Failure . . . or Success.'" *Associated Press,* July 14, 2000.

Benedetto, Richard. "Democrats Keep 'Misunderestimating' Bush." *USA Today,* April 21, 2003.

Berke, John. "The Bush 200 Transition: The Historical Context." In *The White House World,* ed. Martha Joynt Kumar and Terry Sullivan, 318–325. College Station, Tex: Texas A&M Press, 2003.

Berke, Richard L. "Jokes Remain, but Bush Shows Signs of War's Burden." *New York Times,* December 9, 2001, B7.

———. "Gore Dots the I's that Bush Leaves to Others." *New York Times,* June 9, 2000, A1.

Beschloss, Michael. "Bush Faces the Greatest Test." *New York Times,* September 17, 2001, A15.

———. "The End of the Imperial Presidency." *New York Times,* December 18, 2000, A27.

Beshear, Tom. "Motherly Advice." *Courier-Journal* (Louisville, Ky.), April 29, 1989, 2A.

Blankley, Tony. "Power in Washington Is Shifting." *Washington Times,* November 23, 2003, A15.

Boaz, David. "The Bush Betrayal." *Washington Post,* November 30, 2003, B07.

Bonifaz, John. *Warrior-King: George W. Bush and the Looming Irrelevancy of our Courts, Congress, and Constitution.* New York: Context Books, 2003.

Bowman, Karlyn H. "America after 9/11: Public Opinion on The War on Terrorism, the War with Iraq, and America's Place in the World." Washington, D.C.: American Enterprise Institute, 26 December 2003b. (www.aei.org., accessed December 30, 2003).

———. "Polls on Patriotism." Washington, D.C.: American Enterprise Institute, April 28, 2003a. (www.aei.org.) (accessed December 30, 2003).

Brace, Paul, and Barbara Hinckley. *Follow the Leader.* New York: Basic Books, 1992.

Bravin, Jess. "War-Crimes Court Faces Key Test in Naming Judges." *Wall Street Journal,* September 6, 2002.

Bravin, Jess, and Steve Stecklow. "U.N. Tackles a Changing Globe with Routines that Rarely Do: Decades-Old Deals Rooted In Geography Live On; Old Agenda Items Do too." *Wall Street Journal,* December 16, 2003, A1.

Brinkley, Joel. "Meeting of Iraqi Leaders Gives Life to U.S. Plan on Power Shift." *New York Times,* November 28, 2003, A1.

Broder, David S. "Incurious Bush." *Washington Post,* April 11, 2004, B07.

———. "So, now Bigger Is Better?" *Washington Post,* January 12, 2003, B01.

———. "A New Reality for George W. Bush." *Washington Post,* September 13, 2001e, A31.

———. "Now Comes the Hard Part." *Washington Post,* September 2, 2001d, B07.

———. "The Reticent President." *Washington Post,* April 22, 2001c, B07.

———. "Mr. Bush's Agenda." *Washington Post,* February 28, 2001b, A24.

———. "Not His Father's Cabinet." *Washington Post,* January 7, 2001a, B07.

Broder, David S., and Dan Balz. "Nation again Split on Bush." *Washington Post,* November 2, 2003, A01.

Brody, Richard A. "The American People and George W. Bush: Two Years of Rally Volatility and Grinding Erosion." In *The Bush Presidency: An Early Assessment,* ed. Fred I. Greenstein. Baltimore, Md.: Johns Hopkins Press, 2003.

———. "Is the Honeymoon over?" *PRG Report* 24: 1(2001), 23–28.

Brooks, David. "A Fetish for Candor." *New York Times,* December 13, 2003c, A19.

———. "Democrats Go Off the Cliff." *Weekly Standard,* June 30, 2003b.

———. "Running on Reform." *New York Times,* January 3, 2003a, A15.

Brookshiser, Richard. "The Mind of George W. Bush." *The Atlantic Monthly,* April 2003, 55–69.

Brownstein, Ronald. "Survey Finds Americans Are Increasingly Divided," *Los Angeles Times,* November 6, 2003, A20.

———. "Bush's Success Partly Lies in Measured Response." *Los Angeles Times,* December 10, 2001, A5.

Bruni, Frank. *Ambling Into History: The Unlikely Odyssey of George W. Bush.* New York: HarperCollins, 2002.

———. "Bush Stakes Claim as Unifier." *New York Times,* November 6, 2000f.

———. Bush Plans to Ease Rules for Use of Polluted Land." *New York Times,* April 4, 2000e, A18.

———. "Bush Signaling Readiness to Go His Own Way as an Unconventional Republican." *New York Times,* April 3, 2000d.

———. "A Borrowed Pitch Achieves the Desired Result for Bush." *New York Times,* February 20, 2000c.

———. "Campaign Notebook: A Wistful Bush Reflects on Hearth and Home." *New York Times,* January 28, 2000b, A23.

————. "The Front Runner: Weary Bush Reflects on Long Hard Quest." *New York Times,* January 26, 2000a.

Bruni, Frank, and Eric Schmitt. "Bush Rehearsing for World Stage." *New York Times,* November 19, 1999, A30.

Bumiller, Elisabeth. "Out of the White House, But Still in the Loop." *New York Times,* October 27, 2003c, A18.

————. "The President Goes Off Duty, with a Vengeance." *New York Times,* May 12, 2003b, A20.

————. "Bush Pushes AIDS Plan Criticized by Some Conservatives." *New York Times,* April 30, 2003a, A22.

————. "What the Public Sees May Not Be What it Gets." *New York Times,* December 16, 2002b, A20.

————. "For Most-Favored Term, a Presidential Workout." *New York Times,* March 18, 2002a, A1.

Burka, Paul. "The W. Nobody Knows: What He's Like in Real Life." *Texas Monthly,* June 1, 1999, 114–15, 135–37.

Burke, John P., and Fred I. Greenstein. *How Presidents Test Reality: Decisions on Vietnam 1954 & 1965.* New York: Russell Sage, 1989.

Burns, James MacGregor. *Leadership.* New York: Harper & Row, 1978.

Bush, Barbara. *Reflections: Life after the White House.* New York: Scribner's, 2003.

————. *A Memoir.* New York: Scribner's, 1994.

Bush, George W. 2003q. "Interview with Trevor Kavanagh of the Sun" (November 17, 2003), *Weekly Compilation of Presidential Documents* (November 24), 39: 47, 1632–39.

————. 2003p. "Interview with British Journalists" (November 14, 2003), *Weekly Compilation of Presidential Documents* (November 17), 39: 46, 1601–10.

————. 2003o. "Interview with Asian Print Journalists" (October 16, 2003), *Weekly Compilation of Presidential Documents* (October 20), 39: 42, 1393–1402.

————. 2003n. "The President's News Conference with President Vladimir Putin of Russia at Camp David Maryland" (September 27, 2003), *Weekly Compilation of Presidential Documents,* (October 6), 39: 40, 1274–79.

————. 2003m. "Remark Following a Meeting with Congressional Conferees on Medicare Modernization and an Exchange with Reporters" (September 25, 2003), *Weekly Compilation of Presidential Documents* (September 29), 39: 39, 1253–71.

————. 2003l. "Address to the United Nations General Assembly" (September 23, 2003), *Weekly Compilation of Presidential Documents* (September 29), 39: 39, 1256–60.

————. 2003k. "Remarks at the Power Center in Houston, Texas" (September 12, 2003), *Weekly Compilation of Presidential Documents* (September 22), 39: 38, 1211–16.

————. 2003j. "Remarks Following a Meeting with the Secretary of Defense Donald H. Rumsfeld and an Exchange with Reporters in Crawford, Texas" (August 8, 2003), *Weekly Compilation of Presidential Documents* (August 11), 39: 32, 1035–39.

————. 2003i. "Remarks in Philadelphia, Pennsylvania" (July 24, 2003), *Weekly Compilation of Presidential Documents* (July 28), 39: 30, 958–63.

————. 2003h. "Interview with Members of the White House Press Pool" (June 4, 2003), *Weekly Compilation of Presidential Documents* (June 9), 39: 23, 717–26.

————. 2003g. "Remarks Prior to Discussions with President Jacques Chirac and an Exchange with Reporters in Evian-les-Bains, France" (June 2, 2003), *Weekly Compilation of Presidential Documents* (June 9), 39: 23, 709–10.

————. 2003f. "The President's News Conference with President Vladimir Putin of Russia in St. Petersburg, Russia" (June 1, 2003), *Weekly Compilation of Presidential Documents* (June 9), 39:23, 704–708.

———. 2003e. "Interview with Print Journalists" (May 29, 2003), *Weekly Compilation of Presidential Documents* (2 June), 39: 22, 680–91.

———. 2003d. "Interview with Nile TV of Egypt" (May 29, 2003), *Weekly Compilation of Presidential Documents* (2 June), 39: 22, 676–77.

———. 2003c. "Interview with Tom Brokaw of NBC News" (April 24, 2003), *Weekly Compilation of Presidential Documents* (April 28), 39: 17, 472–84.

———. 2003b. "Remarks on Arrival from Camp David and an Exchange with Reporters" (April 13, 2003), *Weekly Compilation of Presidential Documents* (April 21), 39: 16, 437–39.

———. 2003a. "The President's News Conference with Prime Minister Tony Blair of the United Kingdom" (January 31, 2003), *Weekly Compilation of Presidential Documents* (February 3), 39: 5, 141–44.

———. 2002w. "The President's News Conference" (November 7, 2002), *Weekly Compilation of Presidential Documents* (November 11), 38: 45, 1998–2008.

———. 2002v. "Remarks Following Discussions with Prime Minister Ariel Sharon of Israel and an Exchange with Reporters" (October 16, 2002), *Weekly Compilation of Presidential Documents* (October 21), 38: 43, 1779–81.

———. 2002u. "Remarks Announcing the Teaching American History and Civics Education Initiatives" (September 17, 2002), *Weekly Compilation of Presidential Documents* (September 23), 38: 38, 1516–63.

———. 2002t. "Address to the United Nations General Assembly" (September, 12, 2002), *Weekly Compilation of Presidential Documents* (September 16), 38: 37, 1529–33.

———. 2002s. "Remarks Prior to a Meeting with Senate Minority Leader Trent Lott and an Exchange with Reporters" (September 4, 2002), *Weekly Compilation of Presidential Documents"* (September 10), 37: 36, 1264–66.

———. 2002r. "Remarks Following a Meeting with the Secretary of Defense and an Exchange with Reporters in Crawford, Texas" (August 21, 2002), *Weekly Compilation of Presidential Documents* (August 26), 38: 34, 1390–94.

———. 2002q. "Remarks at the Small Investors and Retirement Security Session of the President's Economic forum in Waco" (August 13, 2002), *Weekly Compilation of Presidential Documents* (August 19), 38: 33, 1337–38.

———. 2002p. "Interview with Polish Journalists" (July 12, 2002), *Weekly Compilation of Presidential Documents* (July 22), 38: 29, 1190–97.

———. 2002o. "Remarks on the Middle East" (June 24, 2002), *Weekly Compilation of Presidential Documents* (July 1), 38: 26, 1088–91.

———. 2002n. "Remarks to the United Brotherhood of Carpenters and Joiners of America Legislative Conference" (June 19, 2002), *Weekly Compilation of Presidential Documents* (June 24), 38: 25, 1042–46.

———. 2002m. "Remarks and a Question-and-Answer Session with Students at St. Petersburg State University in St. Petersburg" (May 25, 2002), *Weekly Compilation of Presidential Documents* (June 3), 38: 22, 913–18.

———. 2002l. "Interview with Claus Kleber of ARD German Television" (May 21, 2002), *Weekly Compilation of Presidential Documents* (May 27), 38: 21, 858–60.

———. 2002k. "Interview with Giulio Borrelli of RAI Italian Television" (May 21, 2002), *Weekly Compilation of Presidential Documents* (May 27), 38: 21, 860–62.

———. 2002j. "Interview with European Journalists" (May 21, 2002), *Weekly Compilation of Presidential Documents* (May 27), 38: 21, 866–73.

———. 2002i. "Remarks on the Situation in the Middle East and an Exchange with Reporters in Crawford, Texas" (April 28, 2002), *Weekly Compilation of Presidential Documents* (May 6), 38: 18, 699–701.

———. 2002h. "Remarks following Discussions with Crown Prince Abdullah of Saudi Arabia and an Exchange with Reporters" (April 25, 2002), *Weekly Compilation of Presidential Documents* (April 29), 38: 17, 688–90.

———. 2002g. "Interview with the United Kingdom's ITV Television Network" (April 4, 2002), *Weekly Compilation of Presidential Documents,* (April 15), 38: 15, 571–76.

———. 2002f. "Remarks on the Situation in the Middle East" (April 4, 2002), *Weekly Compilation of Presidential Documents* (April 8), 38: 14, 560–63.

———. 2000e. "Remarks at the Summit on Women Entrepreneurship in the 21st Century" (March 19, 2002), *Weekly Compilation of Presidential Documents* (March 25), 38: 12, 446–52.

———. 2002d. "Remarks at a State of Utah Olympic Reception" (February 8, 2002), *Weekly Compilation of Presidential Documents* (February 18), 38: 7, 207–9.

———. 2002c. "Remarks on Transmitting Proposed Tax Cut Plan to the Congress" (February 8, 2002), *Weekly Compilation of Presidential Documents* (February 11), 37: 6, 271–73.

———. 2002b. "Remarks Following Discussions with Prime Minister Ariel Sharon of Israel and an Exchange with Reporters" (February 7, 2001), *Weekly Compilation of Presidential Documents* (February 11), 38: 6, 194–97.

———. 2002a. "Remarks at a Town Meeting in Ontario, California" (January 15, 2002), *Weekly Compilation of Presidential Documents* (January 14), 38: 2, 11–19.

———. 2001dd. "Remarks Welcoming General Tommy R. Franks and an Exchange with Reporters in Crawford, Texas" (December 28, 2001), *Weekly Compilation of Presidential Documents* (December 31), 37: 52, 1828–34.

———. 2001cc. "Remarks on the New Oval Office Carpet and an Exchange with Reporters" (December 21, 2001), *Weekly Compilation of Presidential Documents* (December 24), 37:51, 1813–1817.

———. 2001bb. "Remarks at a Townhall Meeting in Orlando" (December 4, 2001), *Weekly Compilation of Presidential Documents* (December 10), 37: 49, 1743–54.

———. 2001aa. "The President's News Conference" (October 11, 2001), *Weekly Compilation of Presidential Documents* (October 15), 37: 41, 1454–62.

———. 2001z. "Remarks on United States Financial Sanctions against foreign Terrorists and Their Supporters and an Exchange with Reporters" (September 24, 2001), *Weekly Compilation of Presidential Documents* (October 1), 37: 39, 1364–68.

———. 2001y. "Remarks on the United States Financial Sanctions against Foreign Terrorists and Their Supporters and an Exchange with Reporters" (September 24, 2001), *Weekly Compilation of Presidential Documents* (October 1), 37: 39, 1364–68.

———. 2001x. "Remarks in a Meeting with the National Security Team and an Exchange with Reporters at Camp David, Maryland" (September 21, 2001), *Weekly Compilation of Presidential Documents* (September 24), 37: 38, 1319–21.

———. 2001w. "Remarks in a Telephone Conversation with New York City Mayor Rudolph Giuliani and New York Governor George Pataki and an Exchange with Reporters" (September 11, 2001), *Weekly Compilation of Presidential Documents* (September 17), 37: 37, 1304–8.

———. 2001v. "Remarks While Touring Damage at the Pentagon in Arlington, Virginia" (September 12, 2001), *Weekly Compilation of Presidential Documents* (September 24), 37: 37, 1302–3.

———. 2001u. "Remarks on the Terrorist attack on New York City's World Trade Center in Sarasota, Florida" (September 11, 2001), *Weekly Compilation of Presidential Documents* (September 17), 37: 37, 1300.

———. 2001t. "The President's News Conference in Crawford, Texas" (August 24, 2001), *Weekly Compilation of Presidential Documents* (August 27), 37: 34, 1209–18.

———. 2001s. "Remarks and a Question-and-Answer Session with Students at Crawford Elementary School and an Exchange with Reporters" (August 23, 2001), *Weekly Compilation of Presidential Documents* (August 27), 37: 34, 1202–9.

———. 2001r. "Exchange with Reporters Following the 'World Leaders Build' in Waco, Texas" (August 8, 2001), *Weekly Compilation of Presidential Documents* (August 13), 37: 32, 1146–47.

———. 2001q. "Remarks Prior to Discussion with President Jacques Chirac of France in Genoa, Italy" (July 21, 2001), *Weekly Compilation of Presidential Documents* (July 30), 37: 9, 1078.

———. 2001p. "Remarks at the World Bank" (July 17, 2001), *Weekly Compilation of Presidential Documents* (July 23), 37: 29, 1048–51.

———. 2001o. "Remarks on Accepting a Bust of Winston Churchill and an Exchange with Reporters" (July 16, 2001), *Weekly Compilation of Presidential Documents* (July 23), 37: 29, 1045–51.

———. 2001n. "Remarks to the Business Roundtable" (June 20, 2001), *Weekly Compilation of Presidential Documents* (June 25), 37: 25, 946–50.

———. 2001m. "The President's News Conference with President Jose Maria Aznar of Spain in Madrid, Spain" (June 12, 2001), *Weekly Compilation of Presidential Documents* (June 18), 37: 24, 880–88.

———. 2001l. "Remarks to Leaders of Hispanic Faith-Based Organization" (May 22, 2001), *Weekly Compilation of Presidential Documents* (May 28), 37: 1, 788–90.

———. 2001k. "Commencement Address at Yale University in New Haven, Connecticut" (May 21, 2001), *Weekly Compilation of Presidential Documents* (May 28), 37: 21, 784–85.

———. 2001j. "Remarks at a Celebration of Reading in Houston, Texas" (April 26, 2001), *Weekly Compilation of Presidential Documents* (April 30), 37: 17, 672–74.

———. 2001i. "Remarks at Concord Middle School in Concord, North Carolina" (April 11, 2001), *Weekly Compilation of Presidential Documents* (April 16), 37: 15, 587–602.

———. 2001h. "Remarks and a Question-And-Answer Session at the American Society of Newspapers Editors Convention" (April 5, 2001), *Weekly Compilation of Presidential Documents* (April 9), 37: 14, 574–78.

———. 2001g. "Remarks Following Discussions with President Hosni Murbarak of Egypt and an Exchange with Reporters" (April 2, 2001), *Weekly Compilation of Presidential Documents* (April 9), 37: 14, 561–63.

———. 2001f. "Remarks Prior to a Meeting with Treasury Secretary Paul H. O'Neill and an Exchange with Reporters" (March 7, 2001), *Weekly Compilation of Presidential Documents* (March 12), 37: 10, 413–515.

———. 2001e. "Question and Answer Session at Lakewood Elementary School in North Little Rock, Arkansas" (March 1, 2001), *Weekly Compilation of Presidential Documents* (March 5), 37: 9, 373–74.

———. 2001d. "Exchange with Reporter during a Tour of Control Concepts Corporation in Beaver, Pennsylvania" (February 28, 2001), *Weekly Compilation of Presidential Documents* (March 5), 37: 9, 357–58.

———. 2001c. "Remarks Prior to a Cabinet Meeting and an Exchange with Reporters" (February 26, 2001), *Weekly Compilation of Presidential Documents* (March 5), 37: 9, 345–47.

————. 2001b. "Remarks at a Tax Family Reunion in St. Louis" (February 20, 2001), *Weekly Compilation of Presidential Documents* (February 26), 37: 8, 320–21.

————. 2001a. "Remarks on Transmitting Proposed Tax Cut Plan to Congress" (February 8, 2001), *Weekly Compilation of Presidential Documents* (February 12), 37: 6, 271–73.

————. *A Charge to Keep*. New York: William Morrow, 1999a.

————. "Text of George W. Bush's Foreign Policy Speech at the Ronald Reagan Presidential Library." *Washington Post,* November 19, 1999b.

————. Interview. "Governor George W. Bush: In his own words: I remember the sadness." *Washington Post,* July 26, 1999: A11

Caldicott, Helen. *The New Nuclear Danger: George W. Bush's Military-Industrial Complex.* New York: The New Press, 2002.

Cardwell, Diane, and Edward Wyatt. "Call by Gore Does Little to Soothe Lieberman." *New York Times,* December 10, 2003, A22.

Carlson, Tucker. "Devil May Care." *Talk,* September 1999: 103–110.

Carter, Ashton B., John Deutch, and Philip Zelikow. "Catastrophic Terror: Tracking the New Danger." *Foreign Affairs,* November/December (1998), 80–94.

CBS Poll, "Losing Patience with the U.N." March 10, 2003. (www.cbsnews.com/stories/2003/03/10/opinion/polls, accessed March 11, 2003).

Chait, Jonathan. "The Case for Bush Hatred." *The New Republic,* September 29, 2003b, 20–24.

————. "Blinded by Bush-Hatred." *Washington Post,* May 8, 2003a, A31.

————. "Race to the Bottom." *The New Republic,* December 10, 1999, 26–29.

Chandrasekaran, Rajiv, and Peter Slevin. "Bush Shakes Up Iraq Administration." *Washington Post,* May 11, 2003, A01.

Clinton, William J. "Transcript: former President Clinton's Farewell." *Washington Post,* January 20, 2001, W2.

Clymer. Adam. "A Short Shopping List." *New York Times,* February 28, 2001, A1.

CNN Interview. "First in the Nation: George W. Bush." February 3, 1999.

Cohen, Richard. "Master of Fiction." *Washington Post,* October 28, 2003b, A23.

————. "Bush the Believer." *Washington Post,* July 22, 2003a, A17.

————. "Yawngate." *Washington Post,* February 22, 2001, A19.

Colloff, Pamela. "The Son Rises." *Texas Monthly,* June 1, 1999, 105–6, 140–42.

Connolly, Ceci. "Politicians Court Hispanic Vote Census Data Show Latino Population Increased 35% in the '90s." *Washington Post,* September 16, 1999, A12.

Cooper, Helen. "New Trade Representative Faces an Old Obstacle: Fast-Track Fight." *Wall Street Journal,* April 6, 2001, A16.

Cooper, Kenneth J. "Standardized Exam Faces Test in Texas Trial Gauges Discriminatory Effect." *Washington Post,* September 22, 1999, A19.

Cooper, Matthew. "Lionized in Winter." *Time Magazine,* May 29, 2003.

Corn, David. *The Lies of George W. Bush: Mastering the Politics of Deception.* New York: Crown Publishing Group, 2003.

Crowley, Michele. "Graham's Retreat." *The New Republic,* September 10, 2003.

Cummings, Jeanne. "Bush White House May Have Too Many Chief of Staff Types." *Wall Street Journal,* January 9, 2001, A24.

Daalder, Ivo H., and James M. Lindsay. "Bush's Foreign Policy Revolution." In *The George W. Bush Presidency: An Early Appraisal,* ed. Fred I. Greenstein, 100–37. Baltimore, Md.: Johns Hopkins University Press, 2003a.

————. *America Unbound: The Bush Revolution in Foreign Policy.* Washington, D.C.: Brookings Institution, 2003b.

Darman, Richard. *Who's in Control? Polar Politics and the Sensible Center.* New York: Simon and Shuster. 1995.

Davis, Bob, Greg Hitt, and Shailagh Murray. "Bush Leaned on Legislators To Score Win on Tax Cuts." *Wall Street Journal,* May 23, 2003.

Dean, John. *Worse Than Watergate: The Secret Presidency of George W. Bush.* Boston: Little Brown, 2004.

Dewar, Helen. "Congress Wraps Up Mixed-Bag Session." *Washington Post,* November 28, 2003, A12.

Dewar, Helen, and Cindy Skyrzycki. "Workplace Health Initiative Rejected." *Washington Post,* March 7, 2001, A01.

Diehl, Jackson. "Dubious Threat, Expensive Defense." *Washington Times,* April 26, 2004, A23.

Dinan, Stephen. "9/11 Spurred War, Rumsfeld Says." *Washington Times,* July 10, 2003, A01.

Dionne, Jr., E. J. "One Nation Deeply Divided." *Washington Post,* November 7, 2003, A31.

DeYoung, Karen. "Bush's Speech Brings U.S., U.N. Closer on Iraq." *Washington Post,* September 15, 2002, A23.

Dowd, Maureen. "Disco Dick Cheney." *New York Times,* December 11, 2002, A35.

———. "How Green Is their Valley?" *New York Times,* May 2, 2001, A19.

———. "A Babysitter for Junior." *New York Times,* July 26, 2000, A23.

Doyle, William. *Inside the Oval Office: The White House Tapes from FDR to Clinton.* New York: Kodansha International, 1999.

Dreazen, Yochi J. "Voter Turnout Remains Low, Despite Ad Barrage, Close Race." *Wall Street Journal,* November 9, 2000.

Drew, Elizabeth. *On the Edge.* New York: Simon and Schuster, 1994.

Dubose, Lou, Jan Reid, and Carl M. Cannon. *Boy Genius: Karl Rove, The Brains Behind the Remarkable Political Triumph of George W. Bush.* Boulder, Colo.: Perseus Publishing, 2002.

Eastland, Terry. "Punting on Principle." *Weekly Standard,* January 20, 2003.

Editorial. "The Price of Incuriosity." *New York Times,* April 15, 2004, A24.

Editorial. "Smug President Has Painted U.S. into a Corner." *New York Observer,* April 14, 2004, p. 1.

Editorial. "The Eight Month Election." *New York Times,* March 3, 2004, A22.

Editorial. "The New Multilateralism." *Wall Street Journal,* January 8, 2004, A22.

Editorial. "Fueling the Fight." *Washington Post,* October 30, 2003, A22.

Editorial. "The Presidential Bubble." *New York Times,* September 25, 2003, A26.

Editorial. "Mr. Bush's New Gravitas." *New York Times,* October 12, 2001, A21.

Editorial. "Demands of Leadership." *New York Times,* September 13, 2001, A26.

Editorial. "Foreign Policy Missteps." *Washington Post,* May 4, 2001, A24.

Editorial. "Reviving the Test Ban Treaty." *New York Times,* January 9, 2001, A18.

Edwards, George C. III. *On Deaf Ears: The Limits of the Bully Pulpit.* New Haven, Conn.: Yale University Press, 2003.

———. "George W. Bush's Strategic Presidency." In George C. Edwards III and Philip Davies, eds. *New Challenges for the American Presidency.* pp. 23–48. New York: Longman, 2004.

Eilperin, Juliet. "Medicare Bill has House Conservatives Grumbling." *Washington Post,* July 15, 2003, A04.

———. "Hill Democrats Ready to Resist GOP Push." *Washington Post,* January 3, 2001, A01.

Enrich, David. "Impeaching Bush." *National Review,* March 6, 2003.

Farrington, Brendan. "791 Inmates, 26 Religions in 'Faith-Based' Fla. Prison." *Washington Post,* December 25, 2003, A02.

Fassihi, Farnaz, Greg Jaffe, Yaroslav Trofimov, Carla Anne Robbins, and Yochi J. Dreazen. "Early U.S. Decisions on Iraq Now Haunt American Efforts." *Wall Street Journal,* April 19, 2004, A1.

Fineman, Howard. "A Big Win for Bush." *Newsweek,* April 10, 2003.

———. "End of Innocence: Can Bush Lead America through this Nightmare?" *Newsweek,* September 11, 2001.

Fineman, Howard, and Tamara Lipper. "Same as He Ever Was." *Newsweek,* September 9, 2002.

———. "What Me Worry? Reelection Plan for a Newly Vulnerable President." *Newsweek,* October 6, 2003, 26–34.

Fox News. "Raw Data: Text of Bush Interview." September 22, 2003. (www.foxnews.com, accessed September 23, 2003).

Frank, Justin. *Bush on the Couch.* New York: Regan Books, 2004.

Freud, Sigmund. "Group Psychology and the Analysis of the Ego (1920)." In *Standard Edition of the Complete Psychological Works of Sigmund Freud,* vol. 18. London: Hogarth Press, 1974.

Friedman, Thomas L. "On Listening." *New York Times,* October 16, 2003b, A29.

———. "Repairing the World." *New York Times,* March 16, 2003a, Sec. 4, A14.

Frum, David. *The Right Man.* New York: Random House, 2003.

Gaddis, John Lewis. *Surprise, Security, and the American Experience.* Cambridge, Mass: Harvard University Press, 2004.

Gardner, Howard. *Intelligence Reframed: Multiple Intelligences for the 21st Century.* New York: Basic Books, 2000.

———. *Frames of Mind: The Theory of Multiple Intelligences.* New York: Basic Books, 1993.

Gelerntner, David. "GWB & JFK." *Weekly Standard,* February 3, 2003, 29–33.

George, Alexander L. *Presidential Decision Making in foreign Policy: The Effective Use of Information and Advice.* Boulder, Colo.: Westview Press, 1980.

George, Alexander L. and Juliette L. George. *Woodrow Wilson and Colonel House: A Personality Study.* New York: Dover, 1956.

Gergen, David. "A Sense of Proportion." *U.S. News and World Report,* May 5, 2003, 70.

Gerhart, Ann. *The Perfect Wife.* New York: Simon and Schuster, 2004.

Gigot, Paul. "Bush's Cabinet Has Mortgages—and Agendas." *Wall Street Journal,* January 5, 2001, A10.

Goldberg, Jonah. "Clarke 4 Bush-Cheney 2004." *National Review* online, April 7, 2004.

———. "Bush becomes 'big government conservative.'" *Washington Times,* July 18, 2003.

Goldstein, Amy. "For GOP Leaders, Battles and Bruises Produce Medicare Bill." *Washington Post,* November 30, 2003, A08.

Goodstein, Laurie. "Matters of Faith: Bush Uses Religion as a Personal and Political Guide." *New York Times,* October 22, 2000, A21.

Graham, Bradley. "Pentagon Considers Creating Postwar Peacekeeping Forces." *Washington Post,* November 24, 2003, A16.

Greeley, Andrew. "Big Lie on Iraq Comes Full Circle." *Chicago Sun Times,* September 19, 2003.

Greenberg, Stanley B. *Middle Class Dreams: The Politics and Power of the New American Majority.* Revised and updated edition. New Haven: Yale University Press, 1998.

Greenberg Stanley B., and Theda Skocpol, eds. *The New Majority: Toward a Popular Progressive Politics.* New Haven: Yale University Press, 1997.

Greenstein, Fred I. *The Presidential Difference.* New York, Free Press, 2003b.

———, ed. *The George W. Bush Presidency.* Baltimore, Md.: Johns Hopkins University Press, 2003a.

———. *The Hidden Hand Presidency: Eisenhower as Leader.* Baltimore, Md.: Johns Hopkins University Press, 1994.

Gregg, Gary L., and Mark J. Rozell, eds. *Considering the Bush Presidency.* New York, N.Y.: Oxford, 2003.

Guilfoile, Ken. *My First Presidentiary: A Scrapbook by George W. Bush.* New York: Crown Publishing Group, 2001.

Halbfinger, David M. "Kerry's Shifts: Nuanced Ideas or Flip Flops." *New York Times,* March 6, 2004, A1.

Hallow, Ralph Z. "Interview with Governor George W. Bush." *Washington Times,* September 20, 1999.

Hamberger, Tom, and Greg Hitt. "Bush Hardball Leaves Bruises." *Wall Street Journal,* December 5, 2003, A4.

Harris, John F., and Dan Balz. "Conflicting Image of Bush Emerges, Bush Makes Political Investments, but Will They Make Him?" *Washington Post,* April 29, 2001, A01.

Hart, Peter, and Robert Teeter. "Study #6035." *Wall Street Journal,* May 1–3, 2004.

Harwood, John, and Jeanne Cummings. "Bush's Approval Rating Slips to 50%, a Five Year Presidential Low." *Wall Street Journal,* June 20, 2001, A18.

Hatfield, James. *Fortunate Son: George W. Bush and the Making of an American President.* New York: Soft Skull Press, 2002.

Helco, Hugh. "The Political Ethos of George W. Bush." In *The George W. Bush Presidency: An Early Assessment,* ed. Fred I. Greenstein. 17–50. Baltimore, Md.: Johns Hopkins University Press, 2003.

Hess, Robert D., and David Easton. "The Child's changing Image of the President." *Public Opinion Quarterly* 24 (1960): 632–44.

Himmelfarb, Gertrude. *One Nation, Two Cultures?* New York: Knopf, 1999.

———. "Two Nations or Two Cultures." *Commentary,* January 2001, 29–30.

Hoagland, Jim. "Nuclear Preemption." *Washington Post,* March 17, 2002, B09.

Hockstader, Lee. "Israel Sets Out Charges Arafat Supported Terror Israeli Report Alleges Arafat Supported Terrorism." *Washington Post,* May 6, 2002, A01.

Hollandsworth, Skip. "Younger. Wilder?" *Texas Monthly,* June 1, 1999, 108–11, 143.

Hook, Janet. "Bush, Democrats Come Out Slugging at Opening Bell." *Los Angeles Times,* January 13, 2003, A13.

Horney, Karen. *The Neurotic Personality of our Times.* New York: Norton, 1937.

Huberman, Jack. *The Bush-Hater's Handbook.* New York: Nation Books, 2004.

Hughes, Karen. *Ten Minutes from Normal.* New York: Viking, 2004.

Hume, Brit. "Raw Data: Text of Bush Interview." *Fox News,* September 22, 2003.

———. "Brit Hume Goes One-on-One with First Lady Laura Bush." *Fox News,* September 9, 2002.

Hult, Karen M. "The Bush White House in Comparative Perspective." In *The Bush Presidency: An Early Assessment,* ed. Fred I. Greenstein. 51–76. Baltimore, Md.: Johns Hopkins Press, 2003.

Hunt, Al. "Another Polarizing President." *Wall Street Journal,* July 31, 2003, A17.

Hunt, Albert R. "An Army of Opposition to Disability Rights." *Wall Street Journal,* March 15, 2001b, A19.

———. "All Hat and No Cattle." *Wall Street Journal,* March 1, 2001a, A23.

Hunt, Terence. "Bush Trusts Instincts." *Las Vegas Sun,* June 5, 2003.

Ifil, Gwen. "56 Long Days of Coordinated Persuasion." *New York Times,* November 19, 1993, A28.

Ikenberry, G. John. "America's Imperial Ambition." *Foreign Affairs,* September/October 81: 5, 2002, 44–60.

Institute of Politics. 2003. "Undergraduate Survey," Harvard University, October 3–12. (www.iop.harvard.edu, accessed October 23, 2003).

Isaacson, Walter, and Jim Kelly. "Interview with George W. Bush." *Time,* August 7, 2000, 86–89.

Ivins, Molly, and Lou Dubose. *Shrub: The Short but Happy Political Life of George W. Bush.* New York: Knopf Publishing Group, 2000.

———. *Bushwhacked: Life in George W. Bush's America.* New York: Random House, 2003.

Jacobs, Lawrence R., and Robert Y. Shapiro. *Politicians Don't Pander: Political Manipulation and the Loss of Democratic Responsiveness.* Chicago: University of Chicago Press, 2000.

Jacobson, Gary. "President Bush and the American Electorate." In *The George W. Bush Presidency: An Early Assessment,* Fred I. Greenstein, ed. 197–227. Baltimore, Md.: Johns Hopkins University Press, 2003.

Janis, Irving. *Victims of Groupthink.* Boston: Houghton Mifflin, 1972.

Jehl, Douglas. "Pentagon Bars Three Nations from Iraq Bidding." *New York Times,* December 10, 2003, A1.

———. "White House Considering Plan to Void Clinton Rule on Forests." *New York Times,* May 2, 2001, A16.

Jervis, Robert. "Understanding the Bush Doctrine." *Political Science Quarterly,* 118: 3, 365–388.

Jones, Charles O. *The Presidency in a Separated System.* Washington, D.C.: The Brookings Institution, 1994.

———. "Capitalizing on Position in a Perfect Tie." In *The George W. Bush Presidency: An Early Assessment,* Fred I. Greenstein, ed. (173–96). Baltimore, Md.: Johns Hopkins University Press, 2003.

Judis, John. "Off Center." *The New Republic,* October 16, 1995.

Kahn, Joseph. "The Nation: Trying to Fight Two Wars at Once." *New York Times,* October 7, 2001, Sec. 4, p. 3.

Keen, Judy. "Strain of Iraq War Showing on Bush, Those Who Know Him Say." *USA Today,* January 4, 2003, A01.

Keen, Judy, William M. Welch, and Andrea Stone. "Tension with Republicans Ties Up Bush's Legislation." *USA Today,* May 12, 2003, A01.

Keller, Bill. "God and George W. Bush." *New York Times,* May 17, 2003, A17.

Kennedy, John F. Inaugural Address, Washington D.C., January 20, 1961. Available at http://www.jfklibrary.org/j012061.htm.

Kettl, Donald. *Team Bush: Leadership Lessons from the Bush White House.* New York: McGraw Hill, 2003.

Kessler, Glenn. "Cutting Arafat Loose, but Not by Name," *Washington Post,* June 29, 2002.

Kessler, Ronald. *A Matter of Character: Inside the White House of George W. Bush.* 2004.

Kilian, Pamela. *Barbara Bush: Matriarch of a Dynasty.* New York: St. Martins, 2002.

Klein, Joe. "How to Make the Victory Stick." *Time,* April 21, 2003.

———. "Stalking the Radical Middle." *Newsweek,* September 25, 1995, 32–37.

Kohut, Heinz. *The Restoration of the Self.* New York: International Universities Press, 1977.

———. *The Analysis of the Self.* New York: International Universities Press, 1971.

Kornblut, Anne E. "Defining George W. Bush." *Boston Globe,* May 4, 2003.

Krauthammer, Charles. "A Farewell to Allies." *Time,* January 5, 2004.

———. "A Tale of Two Presidents." *Washington Post,* January 26, 2001, A23.

Kristof, Nicholas D. "The Decision: for Bush His Toughest Call Was the Choice to Run at All." *New York Times,* October 29, 2000c, A1.

———. "How Bush Came to Tame His Inner Scamp." *New York Times,* July 29, 2000b, A23.

———. "Political Memo: Rival Makes Bush Better Campaigner." *New York Times,* March 3, 2000a, A15.

Kristof, Nicholas D. and Frank Bruni. "Man in the News: A Confident Son of Politics, George W. Bush, Is Making an Uncommon Rise." *New York Times,* August 3, 2000, A1.

Krugman, Paul. "George Q. Queeg." *New York Times,* March 14, 2003, A29.

Kulish, Nicholas, and Kelly K. Spors. "U.S. Voting-Rights Suit to Focus on Language Issues, Voting Lists." *Wall Street Journal,* May 23, 2002.

Kurtz, Howard. "Media Notes: Bush Admits No Mistakes." *Washington Post* online, April 14, 2004.

———. "Some Understand Covert Journey; Others Fear Bad Precedent." *Washington Post,* November 28, 2003, A44.

Lambro, Donald. "Bush Decisions Rankle Conservatives." *Washington Times,* March 27, 2002, A1.

———. "Master Electoral Move . . . or Big Miss." *Washington Times,* December 1, 2003, A19.

Lardner, George Jr., and Lois Romano. "At Height of Vietnam, Bush Picks Guard." *Washington Post,* July 28, 1999b, A1.

———. "Tragedy Created a Bush-Son Bond." *Washington Post,* July 26, 1999a, A1.

Lefkowitz, Jay. " The Facts on Stem Cells." *Washington Post,* October 30, 2003, A23.

Levinson, Daniel J. *The Seasons of a Man's Life.* New York: Knopf, 1979.

Lewis, Anthony. "The Vision Thing." *New York Times,* July 28, 2001b, A27.

———. "The Two George W. Bushes." *New York Times,* April 14, 2001a, A13.

Lewis, Neil A. "Bush Selects Two for Bench, Adding Fuel to Senate Fire." *Washington Post,* July 26, 2003, A11.

Lichtblau, Eric. "Irking N.R.A., Bush Supports Ban on Assault Weapons." *New York Times,* May 8, 2003, A1.

———. "British Cancel another Flight Bound for U.S." *New York Times,* January 3, 2004a, A1.

Lieberman, Joe. "Interview." *Face the Nation,* CBS, August 31, 2003.

Lipper, Tamara. "First Lady: 'We're Not Relaxed.'" *Newsweek,* February 16, 2004.

Lind, Michael. *Made in Texas: George W. Bush and the Southern Takeover of American Politics.* New York: Basic Books, 2003.

Los Angeles Times. "Poll #491." November 20, 2003.

Lizza, Ryan. "Campaign Journal: Stuck." *The New Republic,* March 15, 2004.

Luck, Sarah. "Two Pharmacy Groups File Suit Opposing Bush's Drug Discount." *Wall Street Journal,* July 28, 2001.

Mallaby, Sebastian. "The Reluctant Imperialist: Terrorism, Failed States and the Case for American Empire." *Foreign Affairs,* March/April 2000, 81: 2, 2–7.

———. "The Bullied Pulpit: A Weak Chief Executive Makes Worse foreign Policy." *Foreign Affairs,* January/February 2000.

Mansfield, Harvey C., Jr. *Taming the Prince: The Ambivalence of Modern Executive Power.* New York: Free Press, 1989.

Mansfield, Stephen. *The Faith of George W. Bush.* New York: Tarcher/Penguin, 2003.

Maraniss, David. *First in His Class: A Biography of Bill Clinton.* New York: Simon and Schuster, 1995.

Martin, David A. "Immigration Policy and the Homeland Security Act Reorganization." *Migration Policy Institute,* no.1, April 2003.

Mayhew, David R. *Electoral Realignments: A Critique of an American Genre.* New Haven, Conn.: Yale University Press, 2002.

McGeary, Johanna. "How the White House Engineered a Soft Landing: A Carefully Engineered Game Plan Helped Bush Bring the U.S. Flight Crew Home." *Time,* April 16, 2001, 2–8.

McGrory, Mary. "Caught in the Switch." *Washington Post,* February 27, 2000, B01.

McNeil, Donald G. "U.S. at Odds with Europe over Rules on World Drug Pricing." *New York Times,* July 2001 20, A8.

Mead, Walter Russell. *Special Providence: American Foreign Policy and How It Changed the World.* New York: Knopf, 2001.

Meet the Press. "Interview with Governor George W. Bush." *NBC,* November 21, 2000.

Merida, Kevin. "George W. Bush: Is He or Isn't He Smart Enough?" *Washington Post,* January 19, 2000, C1.

Meyerson, Harold. "The Most Dangerous President Ever." *The American Prospect,* 14:5, 2003.

Milbank, Dana. "White House Fires Back at O'Neill on Iraq." *Washington Post,* January 13, 2004, A01.

———. "Conservatives Criticize Bush on Spending." *Washington Post,* December 6, 2003, A01.

———. "To Johnson-Thune, Add Bush-Daschle." *Washington Post,* November 1, 2002b, A22.

———. "A Doctrine of Presidential Infallibility." *Washington Post,* January 8, 2002a, A15.

———. "White House Staff Switches Gears Response to attacks Is Now Focus of almost All Presidential Aides." *Washington Post,* September 17, 2001, A25.

Milbank, Dana, and Glenn Kessler. "President Warns Taiwan on Independence." *Washington Post,* December 10, 2003, A01.

Milbank, Dana, and Juliet Eilperin. "On Patients' Rights Deal, Bush Scored with a Full-Court Press." *Washington Post,* August 3, 2001, A09.

Milbank, Dana, and Jim VandeHei. "Bush's Strong Arm Can Club Allies too." *Washington Post,* March 21, 2003, A06.

Milkis, Sidney M., and Michael Nelson. *The American Presidency: Origins and Development 1776–2002.* 4th ed. Washington, D.C.: CQ Press, 2003.

Miller, Judith. "U.S. Explores other Options on Preventing Germ Warfare." *New York Times,* July 25, 2001, A4.

Miller, Mark Crispin. *The Bush Dyslexicon: Observations on a National Disorder.* New York: W. W. Norton & Co., 2002.

Minutaglio, Bill. *First Son: George W. Bush and the Bush Family Dynasty.* New York: Times Books, 1999.

Mitchell, Allison. "Official at Last: Bush Defeats Gore." *New York Times,* January 7, 2001.

———. "McCain Is Latest Victim of Pop Quiz." *New York Times,* December 20, 1999, A33.

Mitchell, Elizabeth. *Revenge of the Bush Dynasty.* New York: Hyperion, 2000.

Mollison, Andrew. "Flurry of Bills Awaits President." *Washington Times,* November 27, 2003.

Moore, James, and Wayne Slater. *Bush's Brain: How Karl Rove Made George W. Bush Presidential.* New York: John Wiley and Sons, 2003.

Moore, James. *Bush's War for Reelection: Iraq, The White House and the People.* New York: John Wiley and Sons, 2004.

Morgenthau, Hans J. *Politics Among Nations: The Struggle for Power and Peace.* New York: Alfred A. Knopf Press, 1948.

Murray, Alan. "Bush Must Show that U.S. Is Defined by More than Might." *Wall Street Journal,* December 16, 2003b, A4.

———. "Bush Agenda Seeks to Remake World without Much Help or Discussion." *Wall Street Journal,* June 3, 2003a, A4.

Myre, Greg. "Captain Links Cargo of Weapons to Fatah." *Associated Press,* January 8, 2003.

Nagourney, Adam, with Jodi Wilgoren. "In First Encounter, Democrats Hit Bush over Jobs and Iraq." *New York Times,* September 5, 2003, A1.

Neal, Terry M. "Bush's Tax Cut: Back to the Future?" *Washington Post,* January 9, 2003.

———. "Bush Energized by S.C. Victory." *Washington Post,* February 20, 2000b, A11.

———. "Bush to Recovering Addicts: 'I Understand.'" *Washington Post,* January 22, 2000a, A07.

Neal, Terry M., and Thomas B. Edsall. "Bush Tries to Grab Tag of 'Reformer.'" *Washington Post,* February 8, 2000, A12.

Neal, Terry M., and Ceci Connolly. "Hollywood Draws Cash for fore, Ire in GOP." *Washington Post,* September 14, 2000, A01.

New York Times. "First Lady Fiercely Loyal and Quietly Effective: Excerpts of an Interview with Laura Bush." February 7, 2004, 1A1.

———. "Text of Senator Hillary Clinton's Speech to Congress." May 17, 2002.

———. "Campaign Roundup." May 10, 2001.

———. "Interview with George W. Bush." May 16, 2000.

Nightline. "The Clinton Years: Interview with Leon Panetta." ABC.com, December 27, 2000.

Noah, Timothy. "Dubya: Smart? Or Dumb." *Slate,* March 13, 2003.

Noonan, Peggy. "Unhappy Warriors." *Wall Street Journal* online, April 15, 2004.

———. "Be Proud of What We Stand for: Interview with the President and Mrs. Bush." *Ladies Home Journal,* October 2003b, pp. 118–20, 124, 127, 130, 134.

———. "Human, but Not to a Fault." *Wall Street Journal,* January 6, 2003a.

Norton, Rob. "Every Budget Tells a Story, and This Is No Exception." *Washington Post,* March 10, 2002, B01.

Ollove, Michael. "Being president means never having to say you're sorry." *Baltimore Sun* online, April 18, 2004.

OMB. 2003. "Informing Regulatory Decisions: 2003 Report to Congress on the Costs and Benefits of Federal Regulations and Unfunded Mandates on State, Local, and Tribal Entities." Executive Office of the President: Washington, D.C. (http://www.whitehouse.gov/omb, accessed January 1, 2004).

OMB. 2002. "The President's Management Agenda." Executive Office of the President: Washington, D.C. (http://www.whitehouse.gov/omb, accessed January 1, 2004).

Parmet, Herbert S. *George Bush: The Life of a Lone Star Yankee.* New Brunswick, N.J.: Transaction Press, 2001.

Patoski, Joe Nick. "Team Player." *Texas Monthly,* June 1, 1999.

Pear, Robert. "Airline Security: U. S. Pressures Foreign Airlines over Manifests." *New York Times,* November 27, 2001c, A1.

————. "Foreign Cooperation: Egypt and Saudi Arabia Won't Supply List of Passengers Flying to U.S." *New York Times,* October 18, 2001b, B9.

————. "White House Plans to Revise New Medical Privacy Rules." *New York Times,* April 8, 2001a, A22.

Pelly, Scott. "Part III: Bush on Bin Laden." *CBS News,* September 11, 2002.

Perlez, Jane. "How Powell Decided to Shun Racism Conference." *New York Times,* September 5, 2001, A8.

Pew Research Center for the People and the Press, 2003c. "The 2004 Political Landscape: Even Divided and Increasingly Polarized." The Pew Center for the People and the Press, November 5. (www.people-press.org, accessed November 15, 2003).

Pew Research Center for the People and the Press, 2003b. "Bush Reelection Margin Narrows to 45%–43%: Once again, Voters Say: It's the Economy." September 25, 2003. (http://people-press.org, accessed October 23, 2003).

Pew Research Center for the People and the Press, 2003a. "Democrats Frustrated with Party even as Candidates Gain Visibility." Washington, D.C., August 7, 2003.

Pew Research Center for the People and the Press, 2004. "Iraqi Prison Scandal Hits Home, but Most Reject Troop Pull Out." Washington, D.C. May 12, 2004.

Pfaff, William. "Religious Litmus Test Emerges." *Los Angeles Times,* January 4, 2000.

Pianin, Eric. "Study Finds Net Gain from Pollution Rules." *Washington Post,* September 27, 2003, A01.

Painin, Eric, and John Mintz. "EPA Seeks to Narrow Pollution Initiative Utilities, Fight Clinton Rules On Coal-Fired Power Plants." *Washington Post,* August 8, 2001, A01.

Pianin Eric, and Terry M. Neal. "Bush to Offer $483 Billion Tax-Cut Plan Working Poor, Middle Class Would Get Much of Relief." *Washington Post,* December 1, 1999, A01.

Pisik, Betsy. "108 Nations Decline to Pursue Terrorists." *Washington Times,* December 2, 2003, A01.

Podhoretz, John. *Bush Country: How Dubya Became a Great President While Driving Liberals Insane.* New York: St. Martin's Press, 2004.

Pooley, Eric. "Can Bush Bring Us Together?" *Time,* December 17, 2000, 66–74.

Pooley, Eric, with S.C. Gwynne. "George W. Bush Profile." *Time,* 1999, 153:24.

Powell, Colin. "Text: U.S. Secretary of State Colin Powell Addresses the U.N. Security Council, February 5, 2003" (www.whitehouse.gov).

Powell, Michael. "EPA Orders Record PCB Cleanup GE to Foot $480 Million Bill to Dredge Upper Hudson River." *Washington Post,* August 2, 2001, A05.

Preston, Julia. "U.S. Rift with Allies on World Court Widen." *New York Times,* September 10, 2002, A6.

Radcliffe, Donnie. *Simply Barbara Bush.* New York: Warner Books, 1989.

Reinhold, Robert. "In Troubled Oil Business, It Matters Little if Your Name Is Bush." *New York Times,* April 30, 1986, A14.

Renshon, Jonathan. "The Psychological Motivations for Preventive War." Unpublished honor's thesis, Wesleyan University, 2004.

Renshon, Stanley A. *The 50% American: National Identity in a Dangerous Age.* Washington, D.C.: Georgetown University Press, 2005 (in press).

———. "Assessing the Character and Performance of Presidential Candidates: Some Observations on Theory and Method." In Jerrold M. Post, M.D. (ed.), *The Psychological Assessment of Political Leaders: Theories, Methods, and Applications.* Ann Arbor, Mich.: University of Michigan Press, 2003.

———. "The Comparative Psychoanalytic Study of Political Leaders: John McCain and the Limits of Trait Psychology." In Ofer Feldman and Linda O. Valenty (eds.), *Political Leadership for the New Century: Lessons from the Study of Personality and Behavior among American Leaders.* Westport, CT: Greenwood, 2002d.

———. *America's Second Civil War.* New Brunswick, N.J.: Transaction, 2002c.

———. "The Public's Response to the Clinton Scandals, Part I: Inconsistent Theories, Contradictory Evidence." *Presidential Studies Quarterly,* 32: 1, 2002b: 169–84.

———. "The Public's Response to the Clinton Scandals, Part II: Diverse Explanations, Clearer Consequences." *Presidential Studies Quarterly,* 32: 2, 2002a: 412–28.

———. "Political Leadership as Social Capital: Governing in a Fragmenting Culture." *Political Psychology* 21, no. 1 (2000): 199–226.

———. *High Hopes: The Clinton Presidency and the Politics of Ambition.* New York: Routledge, 1998a.

———. *The Psychological Assessment of Presidential Candidates.* New York: Routledge, 1998b.

Revkin, Andrew C. "White House Proposes Reviews for Studies on New Regulations." *New York Times,* August 29, 2003, A12.

———. "Despite Opposition in Party, Bush to Seek Emissions Cuts." *New York Times,* March 10, 2001, A1.

Rice, Condoleezza. "Testimony before the 9–11 Commission." April 8, 2004. Available at www.9–11commission.gov.

Riesman, David, with N. Glazer and R. Denny. *The Lonely Crowd: A Study of the Changing American Character.* New Haven, Conn.: Yale University Press, 1950.

Roberts, Cokie. "Bush Mother & Wife Interview." *ABC This Week,* December 19, 1999. (http://www.abcnews.go.com/onair/thisweek/transcripts, accessed 12/20/99).

Robertson, Pat. *The Turning Tide.* World Books, 1993.

Rockman, Bert, ed. *The George W. Bush Presidency: First Appraisals.* New York: Chatam House, 2003.

Romano, Lois. "For Transition, Bush again Turns to 'Mr. Inside.'" *Washington Post,* November 29, 2000b, A37.

———. "Understanding Bush: Fiercely Loyal Inner Circle." *Washington Post,* July 26, 2000a, A01.

Romano, Lois, and George Lardner, Jr. "Bush's Move Up to the Majors." *Washington Post,* July 31, 1999c, A1.

———. "Young Bush, a Political Natural, Revs Up." *Washington Post,* July 29, 1999b, A1.

———. "Bush's Life-Changing Year." *Washington Post,* July 25, 1999a, A1.

Rosenberg, Jeffrey. *George W. Bush: An Heroic First Year.* Pleasantville, N.Y.: Reader's Digest, 2003.

Rossett, Claudia. " A New Job for Kay." *Wall Street Journal,* February 25, 2004.

———. "Kofi Annanderson," *Wall Street Journal,* September 25, 2002.

Sack, Kevin. "Democrats Raise Money, Republicans Raise Hay." *New York Times,* September 15, 2001b, A30.

————. "Gore Takes Tough Stand on Violent Entertainment." *New York Times,* September 11, 2001a, A1.

Sachs, Susan. "Hussein's Regime Skimmed Billions from Aid Programs." *New York Times,* February 29, 2004, A1.

Safire, William. *Before the Fall.* New York: Doubleday, 1974.

Sammon, Bill. *Fighting Back: The War on Terrorism from Inside the White House.* Washington, D.C.: Regnery, 2002.

————. *Misunderestimated: The President Battles Terrorism, John Kerry, and the Bush Haters.* Washington, D.C.: Regan Books, 2004.

Sammon, Bill, and Dave Boyer. "Armey Rips Bush Volunteer Proposals." *Washington Times,* February 6, 2002.

Sanger, David. "Citing 'New Day' in U.S.-Russia Relations, Bush Pledges Warhead Cuts." *New York Times,* November 13, 2001, A1.

Sanger, David E., and Elisabeth Bumiller. "The President: In One Month, a Presidency Transformed." *New York Times,* October 1, 2001, A1.

Sanger, David E., and Don Van Natta. "Four Days that Transformed a President, a Presidency and a Nation, for all Time." *New York Times,* September 16, 2001, A1.

Sanger, David E., and Steven Lee Myers. "How Bush Had to Calm Hawks in Devising a Response to China." *New York Times,* April 13, 2001, A1.

Sawyer, Diane. "Transcript: Interviews with President Bush." *ABC News,* December 16, 2003.

Scarlett, Lynn. "Bush's Friendlier Path to Clean Air." *New York Times,* May 9, 2000, A25.

Scheer, Robert. "When Bombs Fall, U.S. Will Join Ranks of War Criminals." *Los Angeles Times,* March 11, 2003.

Scheffer, David J. "A Treaty Bush Shouldn't 'Unsign.'" *New York Times,* April 6, 2002.

Schier, Steven E., ed. *High Risk and Big Ambition: The Presidency of George W. Bush.* Pittsburgh, PA: University of Pittsburgh Press, 2004.

Schlesinger, Arthur, Jr. "The Imperial Presidency Redux." *Washington Post,* June 28, 2003, A25.

————. "The Vital Center: 50 Years Later." *Society* 35, May/June, no. 4 (1998): 52–56.

————. *The Imperial Presidency.* Boston: Houghton Mifflin, 1973.

————. *The Vital Center: The Politics of Freedom.* New York: Da Capo Press, 1968 [1949].

Schmitt, Eric. "Bush Aides Weigh Legalizing Status of Mexicans in U.S." *New York Times,* July 15, 2001, A1.

Schnieder, William. "Bush Lets It All Ride on His War." *Los Angeles Times,* March 23, 2003, M2.

Schweizer, Peter, and Rochelle Schweizer. *The Bushes: Portrait of a Dynasty.* New York: Doubleday, 2004.

Schweid, Barry. "Kay: Bush Should Admit Error on Iraq WMD." *Associated Press,* February 13, 2003.

Sciolino, Elaine. "U.S. Jewish Leaders Call President Blunt in Assailing Arafat." *New York Times,* December 14, 2003, A1.

Seelye, Katharine Q. "Clarke Lays Responsibility for 9/11 at Bush's Feet." *New York Times,* October 29, 2003, A14.

————. "Administration Approves Stiff Penalties for Diesel Engine Emissions, Angering Industry." *New York Times,* August 22, 2002, A11.

————. "Ending Logjam, U.S. Reaches Accord on Endangered Species." *New York Times,* August 30, 2001, A1.

————. "Before a Hollywood Crowd, Democrats Lower the Volume." *New York Times,* September 20, 2000, A1.

Seib, Gerald F. "Don't Expect the Bush Focus to Blur Much." *Wall Street Journal,* January 23, 2002, A24.

Shanker, Thom. "Hussein's Agents are behind Attacks in Iraq, Pentagon Finds." *New York Times,* April 29, 2004, A1.

Shapiro, Walter. "There Must Be a Plot to Bring Back the Conspiracy Theory." *USA Today,* December 18, 2003.

————. "Apt Student Bush Making the Grade." *USA Today,* November 11, 1999, A08.

Shesgreen, Deirdre. "Gephardt Courts Democrats in South Carolina, Offers Harsh Criticism of Bush." *St. Louis Post Dispatch,* January 11, 2003.

Shull, Steve (ed). *The Two Presidencies.* Chicago: Nelson Hall, 1991.

Simes, Dimitri K. "America's Imperial Dilemma." *Foreign Affairs,* November/December 2003, 82: 6, 91–102.

Simon, Roger. "The Doctor Is in Your Face." *U.S. News and World Report,* August 11, 2003, 12–17.

Simple, Kirk. "U.N. Report Says Lack of Resolve Hinders Terror Effort." *New York Times,* December 1, 2003, A10.

Sipress, Alan, and Juliet Eilperin. "Congress Urged Not to withhold U.N. Dues in Retaliation." *Washington Post,* May 10, 2001, A14.

Skowronek, Stephen. *The Politics Presidents Make: Leadership from John Adams to George Bush.* Cambridge, Mass.: Harvard University Press, 1993.

Slavin, Peter. "U.S. Promises Democracy in Middle East." *Washington Post,* August 8, 2003, A01.

Smith, Evan. "George, Washington." *Texas Monthly,* June 1, 1999, p. 111.

————. "What His First Stint there Taught Him about Loyalty." *Texas Monthly,* June 1, 1999, p. 111.

Smith, Stephen G., and Kenneth T. Walsh. "A Conversation with Bush." *U.S. News & World Report,* January 28, 2001.

Smothers, Ronald. "G.O.P. Gains in South Spread to Local Level." *New York Times,* April 7, 1995, A16.

Solomon, John. "Bush, Harvard Business School and the Makings of a President." *New York Times,* June 18, 2000, Sec. 3, 17.

Stevens, Stuart. *The Big Enchilada: Campaign Adventures with the Cockeyed Optimists from Texas Who Won the Biggest Prize in Politics.* New York, Free Press, 2001.

Stevenson, Richard W. "Bush Announces an Easing of Rules on Generic Drugs." *New York Times,* June 13, 2003, A28.

Stevenson, Richard W., and David E. Sanger. "for Bush, Same Goal in Iraq, New Tactics." *New York Times,* May 2, 2004, A13.

Stevenson, Richard W., and Janet Elder. "Support for War Is Down Sharply, Poll Concludes." *New York Times,* April 29, 2004, A1.

Stolberg, Sheryl Gay. "Instead of Dialogue, Bush Gives Senators Bottom Line." *New York Times,* October 18, 2003, A6.

Stout, David. "The Electors Vote, and the Surprises are Few." *New York Times,* December 19, 2000, A31.

Suskind, Ron. *The Price of Loyalty: George W. Bush, the White House, and the Education of Paul O'Neill.* New York: Simon and Schuster, 2004.

Swarns, Rachel L. "Conferees Fail to Resolve their Disputes at Race Talks." *New York Times,* September 7, 2001, A5.

Taylor, Humphrey. "Britain, Canada, Australia, Israel and Mexico Top the List of Countries Seen as our Closet Allies." Harris Poll #52, September 10, 2003. (http://vr.harrispollonline.com) (accessed December 29, 2003).

Teachout, Terry. "Republican Nation, Democratic Nation?" *Commentary,* January 2001, 23–29.

T' Hart, Paul. *Groupthink in Government.* Amsterdam: Swets and Zeitlinger, 1990.

Tomma, Steven. "Dean's Anger at Bush, Democrats Puts Him Ahead of the Pack for Now." *Knight Ridder Newspapers,* July 31, 2003.

Transcript. The President's News Conference: Iraq and Terrorism. *New York Times,* April 14, 2004, A12-A13.

Transcript. "NewsHour interview with David Kay." *PBS* online, January 29, 2004 (http://www.pbs.org/newshour/bb/middle_east/jan-june04/kay_01–29.html).

Transcript. Colin Powell on Fox News. *Fox News,* September 9, 2002.

Transcript. *Meet the Press:* Joe Lieberman, *NBC News,* April 29, 2001.

Traub, James. "Weimar Whiners." *New York Times Magazine,* June 1, 2003, Sec. b, p. 11.

Tsongas. Paul E. *Journey of Purpose: Reflections on the Presidency, Multiculturalism, and Third Parties.* New Haven: Yale University Press, 1995.

Tyler, Patrick E. "With Time Running Out, Bush Shifted Middle East Strategy." *New York Times,* June 30, 2002, A12.

Van Natta, Don, Jr. "How Tiny Swiss Cellphone Chips Helped Track Global Terror Web," *New York Times,* March 4, 2004, A1.

VandeHei, Jim. "President Adopts a More Serious Tone As Response to attacks Molds His Term." *Wall Street Journal,* September 27, 2001.

———. "Democrats Will Try a Hybrid of Old, New Policies." *Washington Post,* February 15, 2004, A01.

Vedantam, Shankar. "U.S. May Expand Access to Endangered Species." *Washington Post,* October 11, 2003b, A01.

———. "Bush Would Add Review Lawyer for Rules." *Washington Post,* August 30, 2003a, A01.

Verhovek, Sam Howe. "Republican Tide Brings New Look to Legislatures." *New York Times,* November 12, 1994, A1.

Vick, Karl. "U.S. Official Acknowledges Mistakes in Iraq." *Washington Post,* April 24, 2004, A12.

VonDrehle, David. "Bush Bets Future on Iraq." *Washington Post,* March 16, 2003, A01.

Waldman, Paul. *Fraud: The Strategy Behind the Bush Lies and Why the Media Didn't Tell You.* Naperville, Ill.: Sourcebook, Inc., 2004.

Walsh, Edward. "Bush Addresses Silent Influences." *Washington Post,* October 25, 2000, A18.

Walters, Barbara. "Interview with President George W. Bush and First Lady Barbara Bush." *ABC News Special,* December 7, 2001.

Warrick, Joby. "Administration Sides with Workers in Uranium Factory Suit." *Washington Post,* May 31, 2003, A02.

Washington Post. "Curious 'George.'" October 1, 2002, C01.

Washington Post. "Text: Interview with Donald Rumsfeld." December 10, 2001. (http://www.washingtonpost.com/wpsrv/nation/specials/attacked/transcripts, accessed December 20, 2001).

Washington Post. "I Made Mistakes: Interview with George W. Bush." July 25, 1999, A20.

Wayne, Stephen J., G.Calvin MacKenzie, David M. O'Brien, and Richard L. Cole. *The Politics of American Government.* New York: St. Martin's, 2003.

Weisberg, Jacob. *George W. Bushisms: The Slate Book of the Accidental Wit and Wisdom of our 43rd President.* New York: Simon and Schuster, 2001.

Weisman, Jonathan. "Tariffs Help Lift U.S. Steel Industry, Trade Panel Reports." *Washington Post,* September 21, 2003b, A12.

———. "Iraq Chaos No Surprise, but too Few Troops to Quell It." *Washington Post,* April 14, 2003a, A28.

Wildavsky, Aaron. "The Two Presidencies." *Trans-Action,* 4 (1966): 5–15.

Wilcox. Clyde. *The Latest American Revolution: The 1994 Elections and their Implications for Governance.* New York: St. Martin's Press, 1995.

Will, George F. "Needed: A Confidence Infusion." *Washington Post,* November 18, 2001, B07.

Wilson, Joseph. *The Politics of Truth: Inside the Lies that Led to War and Betrayed My Wife's CIA Identity.* New York: Carroll & Graf, 2004.

Wischnia, Bob, and Paul Carrozza. "20 Questions for President George W. Bush: A Running Conversation." *Runner's World* online. http://www.runnersworld.com/footnotes/gwbush. 2003, accessed August 23, 2003).

Wolfe, Alan. *One Nation after All.* Chicago: University of Chicago Press, 1998.

Woodward, Bob. *Plan of attack.* New York: Simon and Schuster, 2004.

———. *Bush at War.* New York: Simon and Schuster, 2003.

———. "A Course of Confident Action." *Washington Post,* November 19, 2003, A01.

Wright, Robin, and Dana Milbank. "Bush Defends Barring Foes of War from Iraq Business." *Washington Post,* December 12, 2003, A01.

Yankelovich, Daniel. *New Rules: Searching for Self-Fulfillment in a World Turned Upside Down.* New York: Random House, 1981.

INDEX